David J. Decker, MA

Stopping the Violence
A Group Model to Change Men's Abusive Attitudes and Behaviors

Pre-publication
REVIEW

Stopping the Violence
A Group Model to Change Men's Abusive Attitudes and Behaviors

Stopping the Violence
A Group Model to Change Men's Abusive Attitudes and Behaviors

David J. Decker, MA

HMTP

The Haworth Maltreatment and Trauma Press
An Imprint of The Haworth Press, Inc.
New York • London • Oxford

Published by

The Haworth Maltreatment and Trauma Press, Inc., an imprint of The Haworth Press, Inc., 10 Alice Street, Binghamton, NY 13904-1580

Cover design by Jennifer M. Gaska.

Library of Congress Cataloging-in-Publication Data

Decker, David J.
   Stopping the violence : a group model to change men's abusive attitudes and behaviors / David J. Decker.
      p.   cm.
   Includes bibliographical references and index.
   ISBN 0-7890-0169-1 (hc. : alk. paper).—ISBN 0-7890-0891-6 (pbk. : alk. paper).
   1. Abusive men—Rehabilitation—Handbooks, manuals, etc. 2. Violence—Psychological aspects—Handbooks, manuals, etc. 3. Family violence—Prevention—Handbooks, manuals, etc. 4. Abusive men—Counseling of—Handbooks, manuals, etc. 5. Behavior therapy—Handbooks, manuals, etc. I. Title.
RC569.5.V55D43 1999
616.85′822′0081—DC21   98-51556
                                                                                                              CIP

To my father, David Garrison Decker,
who taught me that we, as men, really do have the ability to change;

my partner, Jane Carlstrom,
who has been my lover, my friend,
and my supporter in our life together;

and

the men with whom I have worked
who have made the choice to stop violence and abuse in their lives.

*   *   *

"There is not one among us in whom a devil does not dwell.
At some time, on some point, that devil masters each of us.
It is not having been in the dark house but having left that counts."

Theodore Roosevelt

ABOUT THE AUTHOR

David J. Decker, MA, is a licensed psychologist in private practice at Birchwood Centers, Inc., an outpatient mental health clinic in Minneapolis, Minnesota. Providing general mental health and domestic abuse services for individuals, couples, and families, his areas of expertise include stress management, anger regulation, domestic abuse, depression, anxiety, and shame and family of origin issues. Prior to Birchwood, Mr. Decker worked for ten years at a community mental health center in Minneapolis, where he directed a domestic abuse program and developed the treatment model discussed in his book. Other positions in his twenty-seven-year career in the mental health field include serving as director of a residential chemical dependency program for adolescents and as director of a residential facility for adults with serious and persistent mental illness.

In addition to his clinical work, Mr. Decker frequently presents training sessions, seminars, and workshops to professionals and community groups on assertiveness, shame and empowerment, anger regulation, conflict resolution, sexual harassment, men's issues, and domestic abuse. He also has assisted agencies in implementing their own anger management and domestic abuse programs, has made frequent media appearances on issues related to anger and domestic violence, and has served as an organizational development consultant to the nonprofit and for-profit sector.

CONTENTS

CHAPTER III: THE INDIVIDUAL MEMBER TASKS

CHAPTER IV: THE EDUCATIONAL UNITS

Acknowledgments

Many of the ideas contained in these materials have been an integral part of domestic abuse treatment in Minnesota and the United States for a number of years and some of the initial work on aspects of this model was done while I was employed at the Domestic Abuse Project (DAP) in Minneapolis, Minnesota, from 1984 to 1986.

I worked with closed-ended and time-limited groups at both the Domestic Abuse Project, and initially, at Pyramid Counseling Center, a community mental health clinic where I was employed for ten and a half years. During this time, it became apparent to me that an open-ended and ongoing group model was significantly more effective in addressing and meeting abusive clients' needs. This model is also helpful in reducing the stress on therapists that is often associated with providing domestic abuse treatment. Open-ended and ongoing group work had been used in a variety of other types of therapies for years, including chemical dependency treatment and in mental health settings. From 1986 to 1987, I developed this model and the materials involved with it (although they have been revised on several occasions since that time) after consulting with a number of agencies in the Twin Cities area. This group model was implemented at Pyramid in May 1988 and continues to function in my private practice at Birchwood Centers, Inc., in Eden Prairie, Minnesota.

A special and heartfelt thanks to my good friends and mentors, Joanne Kittel, LICSW, the former clinical director at DAP, Jeanie Seeley-Smith, Executive Director at Perspectives Family Center in St. Louis Park, Minnesota, and Nancy Kampa, a colleague at Birchwood Centers in Eden Prairie, Minnesota, whose ongoing support, ideas, and encouragement have been absolutely critical in the development of this model, in the writing of this manual, and in maintaining my mental health during that process.

I wish to acknowledge the friendship of H. Stephen Pranschke, LICSW, the former clinical director at Pyramid, who wholeheartedly and unselfishly encouraged and supported me in my clinical practice and in the exploration and development of this domestic abuse group model.

I also want to thank those on the domestic abuse team at Pyramid Counseling Center over the years. They included Laura Helling-Christy, Carol Meyer, Greg Meyer, Ruth Olson, Dan Bannister, John Andreozzi, Paul Olson, Tim

Balke, and David Lueck. Their ideas, hard work, and encouragement have been instrumental in developing this package as it exists today and in making the domestic abuse model as effective as it has been. No matter what the model, it is the people doing the work who really make a difference. Many dedicated and knowledgeable people across this country are actively working to end the violence.

In addition, I gratefully acknowledge ideas and suggestions from other colleagues at the Domestic Abuse Project, namely Roger Gruyznski, Dora Schumacher, Jim Brink, and Gunnar Bankovics, and from practitioners in the community who were willing to share their ideas with me in 1986, including Mike McGrane at the Wilder Domestic Abuse Program, Don Jaehne at Human Services, Inc., George Ellis at Project Pathfinder, Tom Cytron-Hysom at the Center for Domestic Abuse, Jan Frederickson at West Suburban Counseling Center, Sandy Parnell and Mike Schock at Minneapolis Family and Children's Service, and the many others who have been willing to converse with me over the years about domestic abuse treatment. This dialogue and the ideas that have been generated are important. There is no one right way to address the issue of domestic abuse. "One size fits all" approaches will not work to stop violence in the home or anywhere else.

I want to thank Bob Geffner, Senior Editor at The Haworth Press, Inc., for his original interest in this program and manual and for his many helpful and insightful suggestions through several revisions of the manuscript.

Finally, I want to thank my brother, Art Decker, and my good friends, Vic Sandler and Mike Obsatz, for their support, caring, and willingness to be with me through my life's journey. They continually help me understand more about what it means to be the kind of man I want to be.

INTRODUCTION

Overview of the Program

Domestic abuse is an epidemic in this country. It is estimated that 2 to 4 million American women are battered each year by their husbands or intimate partners. Often, the violence becomes lethal, as is demonstrated by FBI data revealing that 1,400 to 1,500 women are murdered by their male partners each year. The costs of domestic abuse are staggering, creating emotional, physical, and financial consequences for the battered women, their children who witness or experience abuse themselves, the batterers, and society as a whole.

The issue of domestic abuse cries out for solutions. The goal in writing and disseminating this treatment manual, *Stopping the Violence: A Group Model to Change Men's Abusive Attitudes and Behaviors,* is to offer pragmatic step-by-step strategies that will guide us in the right direction. These strategies take a profeminist approach, acknowledging also the importance of identifying the presence of, and intervening in, other mental health and chemical use issues that may be contributing to the occurrence of domestic abuse.

Domestic abuse has generally been regarded by feminist groups and by managed care as a social problem. And it certainly is. However, this is only part of the total picture. Many batterers have underlying mental health issues that are integral to who they have been and how they have functioned for years. The devastating effect of violence and abuse on children who experience and witness domestic abuse today (Jaffe, Wolfe, and Wilson, 1990) is frequently noted. In addition, the author's clinical experience and the research about risk markers for domestic abuse (Hotaling and Sugarman, 1986; Straus, 1980) show that many batterers were also observers or targets of abuse in their own families of origin. They, too, have been left with emotional scars from long ago.

Thus, the other part of this picture of domestic abuse involves depression, anxiety, chemical use/abuse issues, and the additional emotional concerns that must be adequately addressed to stop abuse and violence and to replace such behavior with prosocial attitudes.

HAVING A DOMESTIC ABUSE
PROGRAM PHILOSOPHY

A critical part of developing and maintaining a domestic abuse program for men involves being clear about your philosophy regarding the issue of domestic abuse. This section highlights important philosophical considerations related to this model.

In this model's view, violence is an unacceptable conflict resolution and problem-solving strategy in human relationships. Although violence may be perpetrated by anyone and is unacceptable no matter which partner commits the violent act, it is this model's assessment that the gender of the perpetrator is critical in determining the meaning and ongoing impact of abusive behavior. In the vast majority of violent situations in heterosexual intimate relationships, it is men rather than women who are more likely and more able to direct systematic and persistent physical force against their partners to dominate and control. Even when men are the targets of physical abuse, they are generally not as likely to experience the fear, intimidation, humiliation, or severity of injury that female victims report. Due to differences in hormone composition, genetic makeup, size, musculature, and acculturation, men are generally significantly more likely to be able to impose their will through the use of physical force than are their female partners.

When even one act of physical or sexual abuse has occurred in a relationship, subsequent emotional or verbal abuse, threats of violence, and other controlling behaviors have the potential to take on increased and additional impact. As a result, emotional and verbal abuse become much more demeaning, detrimental, threatening, and psychologically controlling for the female victim.

It is this model's assessment that, in the vast majority of situations, a man who is violent is making a clear choice to strike out in a particular way at a particular time, although he may be unaware of this decision-making process prior to treatment. This striking out is a means to control his partner or the situation, to get revenge, to relieve the stress he is experiencing, to avoid intimacy, or to assuage his feelings of shame, low self-esteem, and powerlessness. Most batterers are not mentally ill, nor do they suffer from a generalized lack of impulse control (Ganley, 1981). This is pointedly demonstrated by their ability to control their violent outbursts in other situations outside the family when they are angry. This model's view is that the man is responsible for the violence he perpetrates and that the primary tasks for him in treatment are to:

- learn to control himself and eliminate his use of physical force, threats, and intimidation when he is feeling explosively angry;
- acknowledge and work toward changing other controlling attitudes and behaviors underlying his abusive behavior;
- learn stress management techniques to more effectively cope with his life stress (including both relationship and outside stressors);
- open himself to experiencing emotions in addition to anger and to learn to share them honestly and respectfully with his partner and others as a means to increase his ability to experience intimacy and to broaden his emotional support system;
- accept responsibility for physical, sexual, verbal, and emotional abuse that he has perpetrated in the past and to better understand its current impact on his partner and children;
- begin to understand how abuse he experienced or observed in his family of origin relates to his current abusive patterns;
- recognize how his shame and feelings of powerlessness relate to his violent and abusive acting out; and
- work at raising his self-esteem and increasing his compassion and empathy for his partner, his children, and others.

An important goal of this program is to help the man become aware of all his controlling attitudes and behaviors that form the foundation and underpinning for his violence. This is the only way to begin to promote significant and long-lasting change that will contribute to a marked decrease in emotional and verbal abuse and other more covert controlling and manipulative behaviors. This model's view is that the preferred treatment modality for men who abuse is group therapy that provides both educational and process components. A group setting is advantageous because it allows men to become more accountable for their current and past abuse, diminish the shame they feel about their behavior, self-observe and notice negative cognitions and emotional arousal, learn to interact and communicate more effectively with others, begin to take emotional risks, and start to trust and use other men for emotional support (Rose, 1977; Yalom, 1975). This group model involves cognitive, behavioral, and affective components.

This model's view is that individual therapy is much less effective in promoting long-lasting, attitudinal change in batterers, but may be undertaken if a man is not court-ordered to treatment, hopefully as a means of moving him toward eventual group participation. Individual therapy can still provide some basic tools that some men may be able to put into practice. If violence and threats recur during individual therapy, the man needs to discontinue that therapy and enter the group program. If he is unwilling to do this, he is referred elsewhere for treatment.

Currently, some couples and family therapy practice approaches do directly address violence and may be appropriate for those couples who meet certain criteria (Geffner and Mantooth, 1995; Neidig and Friedman, 1984). Couples and family therapy that do not address the violence directly are contraindicated because abuse might occur as a result of marital conflict in the sessions. If a man has not yet learned alternative ways to cope with his anger escalation and his desire to control, the woman's safety becomes a paramount concern and should not be compromised. Ongoing couples or family therapy to address relationship issues is not appropriate until a high degree of certainty exists that the man will not respond to his partner in a violent fashion, even if he becomes angry as a result of what she says or does inside or outside therapy.

However, both couples and family therapy, if the threat of violence is significantly diminished, are considered to be a vital part of the recovery process, particularly if the couple and the family are planning to remain together. These types of treatment, however, in this model's view, generally should occur later in the recovery process, not at the beginning of treatment. A basic assumption that this model makes regarding ongoing couples therapy—once the violence has stopped and its effects have been addressed and overcome—involves a belief that both partners have a responsibility in building and maintaining a healthy relationship.

This model does not view a woman in a battering relationship as responsible for her partner's violence. It is not believed that she provokes or causes his violence nor that she wants or deserves to be physically abused. Women stay in battering relationships for a variety of reasons, including fear, lack of alternatives and resources, family and societal pressures, economic and emotional dependence, the love they feel for their partners when they are not abusive, a strongly socialized sense of responsibility for the well-being of the relationship, and, for some, the culturally ingrained belief that they, as women, are not allowed or able to make healthy choices for themselves. It is this model's belief that women who are involved in abusive relationships can also benefit greatly from their own therapy process, although this may not be necessary. The primary tasks for a woman in therapy are to:

- increase her ability to protect herself and her children (if she has any);
- become aware of legal options and community resources available to her;
- begin a healing process related to overcoming the effects of the violence and abuse;
- learn more effective stress management and interpersonal skills;
- more fully understand and intervene in cultural messages about who she is as a woman; and
- work at reestablishing and/or raising her self-esteem.

The preferred treatment modality for women is also group therapy due to the power of the group in diminishing shame, learning new tools, and gaining insight and support from other women. However, individual therapy is also appropriate and can be very valuable in and of itself as a means to help a woman understand the dynamics of abuse, tap into community resources, strengthen herself, and move toward making positive and healthy decisions in her life. As noted previously, couples and family therapy that do not address the violence directly are contraindicated initially due to concerns about the woman's (or her children's) safety, but they are considered crucial if she plans to remain with the man who has been violent with her. Effective group programs for women also involve cognitive, behavioral, and affective components.

This model in general views battering and abuse as learned behaviors, and, as such, they can be "unlearned" and replaced with healthier and more productive ways of interacting. Most batterers have either witnessed or experienced controlling attitudes and emotional, verbal, and physical abuse in their families of origin and have come to believe that violence and abuse are acceptable ways of resolving conflict. This is especially true when a man believes that he is not likely to be physically hurt himself because he is more powerful than his partner and his children.

Thus, it is this model's assessment that male-to-female battering is the result of an unequal power relationship between men and women, as well as a consequence of social messages that promote violence in our culture. This power differential and the cultural roots of battering need to be addressed in the treatment process. Violence itself is not caused by a poor marital relationship, job frustration, financial worries, sexual dysfunction, parenting problems, or the like, although these factors may indeed be present and may contribute to a man's decision to be violent.

This model views domestic abuse as a primary therapy issue. The potential for violence and the enormous shame associated with domestic abuse demand that it be addressed directly, especially if resolutions to marital or other individual mental health issues are ever to be found. It should not be presumed that a man's mental health issues, such as depression or anxiety, are the cause of his battering behavior. However, this may be part of what needs to be addressed (e.g., through the use of antidepressant medication) if the man is to benefit as fully as possible from a domestic abuse treatment program.

Likewise, the use of alcohol or other drugs should not be presumed to be the cause of battering, despite the high correlation between the two (Tolman and Bennett, 1990). The issues relating to chemical abuse must be addressed separately and prior to a man's involving himself with, and benefiting from, a domestic abuse program. In some cases, even after a man is sober, his violence and abuse may intensify because his emotional crutch (i.e., the chemical) has been removed and other more effective coping strategies have not yet replaced it. Chemical dependency treatment and sobriety are no assurance that controlling and abusive attitudes and behaviors will not continue. Mental health issues, chemical use, and domestic violence are separate and freestanding issues, and they all need to be addressed.

Children are often the overlooked and ignored victims of domestic violence, even though they frequently witness or experience the abuse that occurs in the home. It is estimated that annually, between 3.3 million (Carlson, 1984) and 10 million (Straus, 1991) children in this country are at risk of witnessing domestic abuse. Children who grow up in violent homes live a terrifying reality and are always affected by the abuse around them. Research indicates that children can be strongly affected emotionally, physically, behaviorally, and socially by the violence and are often left feeling confused, frightened, angry, depressed, and shameful about what has oc-curred (Burman and Allen-Meares, 1994; Fantuzzo et al., 1991; Westra and Martin, 1981; Jaffe et al., 1986).

This model's view is that it is important for children to be therapeutically assessed to determine if and how they have been impacted and that it is vital for them to receive ongoing education, therapy, and support, if appropriate. This is particularly true if the children themselves are involved with acting-out behaviors at home or in school or are having strong emotional reactions that are otherwise unexplainable. It is also this model's recommendation that at some point, children have the opportunity to discuss their thoughts and feelings about the violence and the chaos in the household directly with their parents, if it is determined safe for them to do so.

IMPORTANT CHANGE ELEMENTS IN THIS MODEL

What are the critical elements in the change process for a batterer? The model being presented in this manual identifies the following elements as important to address:

- A man needs to have some level of honesty regarding his past control, abuse, and violence; some acknowledgement that he has a problem with abusive and controlling attitudes and behaviors; and some level of motivation that indicates he is willing to address the abuse and con-trol issues directly (Pagelow, 1984; Edleson and Tolman, 1992).

- An extensive initial assessment should begin the process of looking directly at the abusive behavior; it should also clearly identify and start to intervene in other mental health and chemical abuse issues that may interfere with the treatment and education necessary for real and long-lasting change to occur (Edleson and Tolman, 1992).
- A man needs to develop a clear understanding of:
  1. what abuse and battering are, in all of their forms (Edleson and Tolman, 1992; Pence and Paymar, 1993);
  2. how the desire to assume power and control over others serves as the foundation for abusive behavior (Ganley, 1981; Schecter, 1982; Pence and Paymar, 1993);
  3. the very real power differential related to physical size and strength that exists between men and women, which becomes especially problematic if threats or physical violence are part of a relationship (Straus, 1978; Adler, 1981; Pagelow, 1984; Dutton, 1988); and
  4. the current and potential consequences that exist for him as a result of his controlling and abusive attitudes and behaviors (Cautela, 1967; Edleson and Tolman, 1992).
- A man must come to realize the true impact of abuse on those against whom it is directed and develop empathy and compassion for those he has victimized (Carr, 1981; Edleson and Tolman, 1992; Stosny, 1995).
- A man needs to develop a willingness to take clear and unequivocal responsibility for his past and current violence and abuse and for his current thoughts, feelings, and actions (Ganley, 1981; Edleson and Tolman, 1992).
- A man needs to understand how traditional male socialization, cultural dynamics, and the messages that arise from these create beliefs about male entitlement and male privilege that contribute to unrealistic and sexist expectations of women and to abuse and violence in intimate relationships (Dobash and Dobash, 1979; Gelles, 1980). This includes beginning to see clearly the payoffs and rewards that previous violence, with partners and others, has brought him (Adams, 1989; Edleson and Tolman, 1992).
- A man must understand how he has learned controlling and abusive attitudes and behaviors from his family-of-origin dynamics and childhood experiences (Bandura, 1973; Rosenbaum and O'Leary, 1981b; Stark and Flitcraft, 1987) and how this learning has contributed to feelings of shame, negativity, victimization, and powerlessness. Such feelings decrease his self-esteem and his compassion for himself and others, interfere with his effective life functioning, and lead to devastat-

ing emotional consequences for him and to his victimization of others in the present (Kaufman, 1980; Ganley, 1981; Miller, 1981, 1983; Stosny, 1995; Dutton, 1995, Real, 1997).

- The program should provide clearly delineated structure and expectations that can be adapted to individual men's needs, abilities, and levels of motivation (Ganley, 1981; Edleson and Tolman, 1992).
- The program should encourage clear accountability regarding acknowledgement of current abusive and controlling attitudes and behaviors and regarding the accomplishment of expected tasks and assignments in the group (Ganley, 1981; Edleson and Tolman, 1992).
- The program should provide an ongoing treatment group format that can encourage:
  1. learning, from being a part of other men's experiences, sharing, and task accomplishment (Yalom, 1975; Rose, 1977);
  2. development of a positive peer culture that can foster confrontation of controlling and abusive attitudes and behaviors (Ganley, 1981; Gondolf, 1984); and
  3. support, empathy, and emotional connection with other group members that can decrease a man's shame, isolation, and over-dependence on his female partner and increase his self-esteem and his ability to feel empathy and compassion for himself and others (Yalom, 1975; Gondolf, 1985).
- The program should focus on education and skill building (Ganley, 1981; Neidig and Friedman, 1984; Rosenbaum and Maiuro, 1989; Edleson and Tolman, 1992; Geffner and Mantooth, 1995) that can assist a man in:
  1. learning to self-monitor the internal and external cues related to violent and abusive behavior to interrupt his pattern of escalation and to help him realize that he is continually making choices and is not out of control at any point (Ellis, 1970; Novaco, 1975; Martin, 1985; Gondolf and Russell, 1986; Edleson and Tolman, 1992);
  2. becoming more aware of and changing his negative, vindictive, and despairing cognitions that contribute to his becoming controlling and abusive (Ganley, 1981; Adams, 1989) and to his remaining shame based, depressed, and anxious (Ellis, 1977; Meichenbaum, 1977); and
  3. developing and using other practical tools on a daily basis in the areas of emotional awareness, anger regulation, stress management, assertiveness, communication, and conflict resolution (Neidig and Friedman, 1984; Edleson and Tolman, 1992; Stosny, 1995; Mathews, 1995).

- The program should involve sufficient time spent in the group process for a man to identify and start to question and change the controlling and entitled attitudes and beliefs that fuel his abusive behavior (Edleson and Tolman, 1992).
- The program should encourage the development of a strong and positive male identity that leads to a sense of self-esteem, personal empowerment, and being in control of himself rather than seeking to control, dominate, and victimize his partner, his children, and others (Kaufman, 1983; Real, 1997).

This manual addresses all these elements and contains everything necessary for the assessment and treatment process from the time an abusive man comes through the door for therapy until the time he completes the batterers' treatment group. It focuses not only on ending the physical violence but also on addressing the emotional and verbal abuse, the intimidation, and the controlling attitudes that underlie domestic abuse.

Many counselors, mental health workers, and therapists will come into contact and work with the issue of domestic abuse during the course of their professional careers. Often practitioners are unaware that they are, in fact, seeing this issue and its disturbing ramifications in their offices on a regular basis. Others may be aware that abuse is occurring but do not know how to respond. This manual can be helpful in understanding more about, and responding directly to, the issue of domestic abuse and can be used by beginning as well as experienced practitioners. In addition, it forms a concrete and practical basis for an effective batterers' group in a domestic abuse program, an outpatient mental health agency, or any other clinical setting.

THE TREATMENT MODEL

The treatment group is ongoing and structured and, as such, can be adapted to a client's individual needs. Specific expectations are set for clients in terms of both the time spent in the program and the tasks they have to write out and present to complete the process. The tasks will be discussed in detail in Chapter III. Because of the group's ongoing nature, it is particularly well suited to small or medium-sized agencies and to rural areas where it is often difficult to continually form and maintain closed-ended and time-limited groups.

This treatment model was developed in 1986; it began operating at an outpatient community mental health center in Minneapolis, Minnesota, in 1987. Since then, it has undergone a number of revisions to reach its present form.

The treatment model is profeminist, behavioral, and cognitive in its orientation. The goal in developing the model, as previously mentioned, was to incorporate feminist principles of male power and control, the historical and cultural contexts in which battering occurs, and the need for batterer accountability while effectively identifying and addressing the individual's mental health and chemical use issues, which are often catalysts of abusive behavior. Depression, anxiety, and other comorbid emotional concerns, as well as alcohol and drug use, may be contributing to the occurrence of domestic abuse (Maiuro et al., 1988; Rosenbaum and Maiuro, 1989). Also important is recognizing the batterers' victimization in his own family of origin and the impact this has had on his sense of shame, low self-esteem, and wholehearted assumption of patriarchal and disrespectful attitudes toward his partner and women in general.

The profeminist and mental health models should not be mutually exclusive (Rosenbaum and Maiuro, 1989). Accountability can coexist with these models and still address intrapersonal and interpersonal issues for the individual men. Contrary to models that believe a holistic approach means colluding with or pampering the batterer, this approach is respectful to both men and women and supports strongly the absolute right of women, children, and men to be safe and free from emotional, verbal, sexual, and physical abuse in their lives.

Mental health issues, simply because they are present, do not have to be used as an excuse for abusive or controlling behavior. They are not allowed to be used this way in the model presented in this manual. Statements such as "I did it because I was depressed (I was drunk; I grew up in an abusive family)" are directly confronted as the rationalizations that they are.

However, batterers still need to be respected and treated as human beings who are multifaceted in their strengths as well as their weaknesses. A hallmark of this program is treating clients in a respectful, nonshaming, and nonpunitive manner (Rosenbaum and Maiuro, 1989; Edleson and Tolman, 1992). A critical part of working with abusive clients is modeling attitudes and behaviors, in interactions with them, that are believed to be important for them to incorporate into their relationships with their partners, their children, and others.

The majority of batterers' groups are male oriented, as has been the experience of this author. Therefore, the language used in this manual refers to men. However, women can also be abusive and, at times, batterers, sometimes with their partners, but more frequently with their children (Chesney-Lind, 1997; Hamberger, 1997). It is the author's belief that much of what is discussed in this program manual is applicable to a woman who fits the profile of a batterer in her relationship with her partner or in those with her children. In fact, many of the handouts in this model are currently being used in anger management classes offered for women at a large managed care organization in the Minneapolis-St. Paul area.

WHAT HAPPENS IN THE INTAKE

Men come to this program from a variety of sources. Some are ordered to treatment by the courts. Generally, over the years, this has been a little more than half the group participants. Some are "ordered" by their partners, in the sense that their partners have told them to get help or risk losing the relationship. No one, in the program's history, has come simply because he recognized that a domestic abuse problem existed. Some sort of external pressure has always been the driving motivation.

Many domestic abuse programs have relatively brief assessments, often consisting of no more than one or two hours (or sessions). The intake for this program, on the other hand, generally requires four to six individual sessions (and longer, if necessary).

This longer intake serves two functions. First, it is an opportunity to do a thorough chemical use and mental health screening and assessment. Second, it offers the chance to immediately begin presenting educational material and homework related to abuse and control. This helps to better assess whether the man will actually follow through with addressing his abuse and control issues, which the group, in an even more comprehensive way, will ask him to do.

In essence, with a lengthier intake, a clearer picture emerges about a man's overall level of motivation to address the issues that have brought him to the domestic abuse program. This is helpful in eliminating, relatively early in the process, those men who proclaim loudly that "She's the one with the problem" or "The only reason I'm here is because the court told me to come." It is important to be clear with men that being court-ordered to treatment will not get them into the program if they categorically deny problems related to anger, abuse, and control.

This model views it as counterproductive to put a man into a domestic abuse group when he has little or no interest in being there (Edleson and Tolman, 1992). Often there is significant pressure from a variety of sources to "do something" with this man. However, placing him in the group, whether he has any motivation or not, tells him that he will be able to control the treatment process in much the same way that he has controlled his partner and children in the past. The man needs to comply at least verbally, by admitting that he has a problem related to control and abuse. Otherwise, ongoing and destructive power struggles are likely to occur in the group.

A member's negative attitude and behavior will also tend to detract from the experience of other men who may have some motivation and might otherwise benefit more from the process. One or two acting-out participants can significantly damage the group atmosphere and make the therapist's job even more difficult and stressful.

With a longer assessment, a man generally ends up better prepared and more open to the group process because of the time spent gaining an understanding of some basic concepts related to control and abuse. Another important aspect of this longer intake process is that the man has the opportunity to spend more time effectively connecting with a therapist. This helps the man to feel more comfortable in the group when he arrives and helps the facilitator to have a clearer picture of the man's abuse and control issues. For this reason, it is especially important to place men in a group with an intake therapist who also is a facilitator.

WHAT HAPPENS IN THE GROUP

Once a man has completed the intake, he begins the group. The group is ongoing, so men enter and leave on their own schedule and there are always men who are working on different tasks in the program. Each two-hour group generally proceeds as follows:

1. The group opens with a ten- to fifteen-minute *check-in,* during which members:
   - state their names;
   - talk about how they are feeling at that moment;
   - review their past week, noting
     a. escalations and use of time-outs and other de-escalation strategies,
     b. positive accomplishments,
     c. whether they made their required phone call and completed the expected exercise, and
     d. whether they have followed contracts they have with the group (e.g., a Sobriety Contract or a No-Suicide Contract); and
   - ask to "take time" during the group session to present tasks that they are ready to share or to address other issues that have arisen during the course of the week.
2. The next twenty minutes are spent discussing *educational units* that address a variety of topics relevant to the treatment process, including such subjects as anger regulation, stress management, communication, conflict resolution, assertiveness, parenting, and shame and empowerment.
3. The next section of the group, which takes up most of the actual group time, involves members *taking time to present their completed individual tasks.*

4. The final five to ten minutes are devoted to a *check out*, during which members discuss:
   • how they are feeling about that day's group and their reactions to what has happened in the group and
   • significant plans, activities, or potential escalations during the upcoming week.

SIZE OF THE GROUP

Group size should involve anywhere from five to ten members. With fewer than five members, the interaction among the members and the learning they can get from one another often decrease. In groups of more than ten members, men have difficulty getting consistent time to present their individual tasks and they may lose their focus on why they are in the program or become frustrated and resentful about the lack of time to complete their assigned work.

Anytime the group includes eight or more members, time becomes a critical issue. Men are generally given twenty minutes to present their tasks and five minutes for feedback from other members and the therapist(s). This is also the amount of time given for personal issues they may wish to address in group. Men should be encouraged to stay within this time limit by remaining focused and being complete and clear about what they are presenting and what they would like from other members. Other group members can help by "watching the time" and holding the man who takes too much time accountable.

This assists in developing group cohesion and an attitude of responsibility for one another. It also helps teach communication, assertiveness, and conflict resolution skills in a real-life situation. Many groups have also come up with systems of their own for keeping track of who gets time and when they get it. Having members taking responsibility for one another and themselves in this manner is a far better way to promote individual member learning than having group leaders monitor and make decisions about time issues.

WHAT THE PROGRAM ADDRESSES

Individual Member Tasks

This program for batterers addresses three primary areas. The first major area of the program is individual member tasks. The objectives of the tasks, a narrative description of what they are and what to expect from members doing them, and the tasks themselves appear in Chapter III. These tasks are done in sequence, from the point the man enters the group, in the order that they appear in Chapter III.

The tasks must be written out completely prior to group and then actually presented in group. Men cannot present more than one task in any particular group session, and several of the tasks (e.g., the Escalation Prevention Plan, the Abuse Inventory, and the Family of Origin and Childhood tasks) generally require several sessions to complete. The tasks cannot be completed in fewer than twenty weeks, since men's minimum involvement with the group is for this length of time. This has rarely become an issue because other men also need time to present their own individual tasks (see "Length of the Program" later in this section for more information).

Since this is an ongoing group, the men in each session often are working on different tasks. This adds to the learning process because senior members can review tasks they have already completed when newer members present their tasks and newer members have the chance to think about the issues related to later tasks when senior members are presenting theirs.

Providing structure for group members is a critical part of an effective program (Edleson and Tolman, 1992). Batterers frequently are people who look for shortcuts and are resistant to give of themselves in their relationships with partners, children, and others. The structure provided by the tasks gives them specific expectations to fulfill and translates to an enhancement of their ability to give and follow through with responsibilities in other relationships. Men cannot complete the group until they have presented all of the expected tasks.

Another important issue addressed by the tasks is that they give men the opportunity to practice listening to input from others on a regular basis. This is another significant problem area that abusive men tend to have: the unwillingness to truly hear and accept feedback from others. Part of the emphasis of the program, in the assessment and in the group, is asking men to listen to the feedback without reacting, becoming defensive, or "shutting down." Men are told early in the process that they are not expected to immediately accept the feedback as the gospel or to even agree with it.

It is clearly communicated, however, that they need to listen to feedback and take time to think about it, after which they may apply it to themselves and use it in their day-to-day lives or discard it. This listening process is viewed as absolutely critical to their learning in the program. If they immediately react in a defensive manner (as they often do with their partners and others), it is very unlikely that they will even think about the ideas or suggestions that are being presented to them.

Thus, men in this program literally force themselves to listen to feedback, even when they are feeling uncomfortable, tense, or agitated. This serves as excellent practice for doing the same thing with their partners or others outside the group. It also serves as an important tool for decreasing the frequency of power struggles in the group. Power struggles still occur, but they are less likely to become the major focus of group time. In addition, men always have the option of taking a time-out in group if they are escalating to the point of becoming explosive. It is expected, however, that the member will then return to group and talk about his feelings in much the same manner as he is encouraged to do with his partner.

Education and Skill Building

The second area that the program addresses is education and skill building. The educational topics, including all handouts and a narrative description that discusses how the therapist can use them, are addressed in Chapter IV.

Because this is an ongoing group, the educational topics are presented in a cyclical fashion. Thus, a man may start the group and enter the cycle of educational presentations at any point in the process. This means that some men, if they finish in twenty sessions, may not get through all the educational units. It also means that men who remain in the group longer than thirty to thirty-five sessions may hear the same educational presentations on two occasions. When the latter has happened, men often state that they gain new insights from the material or, in some cases, report that they feel as if they are hearing it for the first time because of their experiences in the group since they last heard it. The tasks and educational units do not correspond in any way and are two distinct and separate parts of the treatment process.

Education is a critical element of this program, but education alone (as is practiced in many weekend or short-term programs) is not enough for most men who come to treatment as a result of their long-standing patterns of controlling and abusive behavior.

Batterers frequently are men who have limited understanding of some very basic interpersonal skills, particularly when applying them to their relationships with intimates. Often, they have few ways to conceptualize their internal experiences and their interactions with others. They also tend to lack empathy and compassion and often report being unaware of the ongoing impact of their words and actions on their partners and children. The educational sections offer them basic skills training in topics such as stress management, anger regulation, assertiveness, communication, and conflict resolution. Education also provides the opportunity to focus on the power and control tactics and the effects of their abuse in a way that tends to trigger less defensiveness.

As previously noted, education is integrated within the treatment group sessions and is generally held for twenty minutes each group after check-in. Educational handouts and specific suggestions about ways to present the educational material are included in Chapter IV. When the therapist presents educational topics, an important aspect is to relate the subject matter to the major purpose of the group—addressing violence, abuse, and control. At least one or two men will personalize the educational topic being discussed and relate it to something that has happened during the week or to one of the individual member tasks on which they are working. This tie-in helps to integrate the educational material, in a powerful and immediate way, with their personal lives.

Length of the Program

The last area to be addressed by this program is the idea that men need to receive treatment for a certain amount of time to truly begin to address the attitudes that fuel their violent, abusive, and controlling behavior. Many of the participants hold deeply embedded notions of male entitlement. They view intimidation, control, abuse, and violence as reasonable tools for addressing differences and resolving conflicts, especially with those close to them. These attitudes are not easily acknowledged and changed. For that reason, weekend or short-term programs for batterers may be less helpful and may, in fact, exacerbate their potential to be abusive.

Men are expected to make the minimum commitment of twenty weeks of group sessions to complete the program. Most men take thirty to forty sessions to finish the program. Occasionally, men have completed the group in twenty sessions; the longest time a man has been in group is sixty weeks. The actual time spent in the program depends, in large part, on how responsible the member is in writing out and taking time to present the expected individual tasks, as all of these must be presented to complete the group.

HOW THIS MANUAL IS SET UP

This manual has been written for those who are actually working with batterers. Throughout the manual, the terms therapist, leader, and facilitator are used interchangeably to refer to those persons conducting the intake and directing the group. The manual itself is divided into several sections. It includes all materials and handouts that men receive in the intake process and the domestic abuse group itself and comprehensive instructions, in step-by-step fashion, of how these materials are actually used. Client handouts are marked (HO) at the bottom of each page.

A client workbook also is available from the publisher and can be purchased separately. It includes all the intake materials, client tasks, and educational handouts that are described and discussed in this manual and offers clients everything they will need to participate in the domestic abuse group treatment program.

The following is a summary outline of the contents of this manual:

- Chapter I discusses issues related to working with batterers and issues related to group leadership.
- Chapter II discusses the intake process and includes all materials that are used in the initial four to six individual assessment sessions.
- Chapter III discusses each of the twelve tasks that individual group members need to write out and take turns presenting in the latter part of each two-hour group session. Also included in this chapter is the entire domestic abuse group member booklet, which consists of the domestic abuse group description; information about group goals, rules, and expectations; a discussion about how to participate in the group treatment setting; the individual member tasks; and a client reading list for those members who are looking for more information about the topics covered in the group.
- Chapter IV provides a narrative description of the twelve educational units that the therapist presents and all the accompanying handouts that are used in the first part of the two-hour group session.
- Finally, a list of references is included for clinicians who wish to learn more about the program's theoretical underpinnings, the issue of domestic abuse, and effective interventions for batterers.

The materials in this manual offer a comprehensive treatment model to address men's violence, verbal and emotional abuse, controlling attitudes and behaviors, and entitlement beliefs. In addition, the educational topics discuss concepts that are commonly addressed in the mental health field and may be added to or changed depending on a particular therapist's background, experience, and style.

This manual offers some ideas, exercises, and materials that can be helpful in working with, or designing a program for, men who batter. The issue of domestic abuse often appears overwhelming, and our society seems to be at a critical point. The need for dialogue and solutions is paramount. This manual is intended to be one more piece to the puzzle of how to end the violence and abuse occurring in American families today. We cannot afford to continue in the direction we appear to be heading. The violence has to stop.

CHAPTER I:
GROUP LEADERSHIP

WORKING WITH ABUSIVE MEN

Abusive men can be difficult clients. They frequently tend to be demanding, self-absorbed, self-centered, blaming, defensive, argumentative, hostile, intimidating, and controlling, although they may, at times, appear to be compliant and passive. They are often experts at finding a therapist's vulnerabilities and insecurities and using them against the therapist. They are often unhappy about being in treatment and are generally externally motivated, whether they are court-ordered or not.

Abusive men do not usually come into therapy to address their abusive and controlling attitudes and behaviors. They often come to therapy for other reasons, such as depression or "communication problems." However, even if they identify their abuse as a problem, almost always some sort of coercion is at work. The most obvious form of coercion is involvement with the legal system and a court order to seek treatment. The less obvious form is pressure from a partner to change, generally because she is threatening to leave or get a divorce or has already left. Therapists need to invest an enormous amount of emotional and physical energy to engage batterers in addressing the real issues that need to be confronted.

Directly addressing batterers' psychological defenses is a critical part of working with them. Abusive men offer a variety of defenses to avoid taking responsibility for themselves, both in the intake process and throughout the group. The following are some of the most common defenses a therapist is likely to confront, with specific examples that indicate their presence.

Denying: Completely Refusing to Acknowledge That a Problem Exists or That He Is Responsible for the Problem

- I didn't do it.
- I never touched her.
- I don't remember the incidents./It was so long ago.
- I was out of control./I was just just seeing red./I didn't know what I was doing.
- I was drunk./I was high.
- I was in a blackout.
- I was in a "dry-drunk" blackout.
- I'm sober now so my anger isn't a problem for me anymore.
- I don't get angry anymore.

- Our real problem is that we just can't communicate.
- I don't have an anger and abuse problem.
- I'm not abusive.
- I'm not controlling.

Blaming: An Attitude of Focusing on His Partner, Her Behavior, and Her "Problems" or on Any Other External Circumstances

- She knows how to push my buttons.
- She provoked me.
- She started it.
- She's always "ragging" on me.
- She's the one who should be in an abuse group. (i.e., "She's a lot more violent than I am.)
- She hit me first.
- She's a drunk.
- I wouldn't have slapped her if she hadn't flipped me off.
- She acts crazy/out of control.
- She's always flirting with other guys.
- It was just a bad time in our marriage.
- My father had just died.
- I was putting in too many hours at work when it happened.
- I was drinking too much at the time.

Minimizing: Making the Problem Less Than It Really Is

- I only hit her once.
- I didn't really hurt her./She bruises easily.
- It's not that big a deal.
- I'm not nearly as bad as my dad was.
- This is nothing compared to what my friends do to their wives.
- I didn't hit her very hard.
- She's a big/strong woman. (i.e., "She can take it.")
- I "kind of" pushed her.
- I just gave her a "little" shove.
- She "fell down" after I pushed her.
- She exaggerates.
- The police just overreacted.
- It didn't really happen that way.

Fighting for Control: Bullying, Intimidating, or Attempting to Divert the Therapist from Addressing the Domestic Abuse Issues

- What would you have done in my situation?
- You would have reacted the same way I did.
- Are you married?
- Do you have kids?
- You probably go home and get abusive with your wife.
- I'd only be willing to attend twelve weeks of group.
- I have to be out of town for business once a month. Is that OK?
- What I do isn't really abuse (i.e., shouldn't be defined as abuse by the therapist).
- I'm not willing to go into a group.
- I'm not willing to tell anyone else about my problems.
- I'm not willing to listen to other peoples' problems.
- I want couple therapy. That's what we really need.
- Interrupting, talking over you, being unwilling to listen.
- Arguing, becoming defensive.
- Trying to "stare you down."

For men court-ordered to treatment, close contact with their probation officer is a must. Probation officers can provide arrest reports, information from Orders for Protection and from the presentence investigations (if any were done), and specific details about the court order to treatment. All of this can add important data that may directly contradict the man's denial and minimization concerning his domestic abuse and chemical use issues. If a client continues to deny a problem, several strategies can be helpful. At times, the probation officer has actually attended an intake session to confront the client. At other times, the man has been sent back to court to argue that he is not angry and abusive and should not have to attend domestic abuse treatment.

Contacting a man's partner can also be useful in addressing his defensiveness. His partner is called during the intake to get her perspective about the history of abuse, control, and chemical use in the relationship. This information can be used to confront denial and minimization directly in the intake, as well as throughout the group, if she feels safe enough to be that involved with the program. In any case, her input is helpful, even if it cannot be used, because it offers a clear picture of whether the man is being honest and actually putting into practice the tools he is being taught.

Court-ordered or not, it is important to appeal to a man's self-interest. Because of an abusive man's self-centeredness and self-absorption, this is a more pragmatic strategy initially than trying to get him to empathize with his victims. However, eventually, he needs to experience a sense of compassion for himself and others if he is to effectively intervene in all of his controlling and abusive behaviors (Stosny, 1995). Research has demonstrated that hostility, cynicism, and aggressive behavior have damaging physical consequences (Williams and Williams, 1993). This initial strategy involves assisting him in focusing on himself and the parts of his behavior that he sees as self-destructive and counterproductive to his life goals and priorities.

An important part of this process is helping the man to begin clearly identifying the past, present, and possible future consequences if he continues to be abusive, including legal, relationship, financial, and family-related consequences. Most men do not want to spend time in jail, lose their partner, or end up with less time with their children. Most men do not want to see their children continue the legacy of abuse and shame in their own adult lives. Appealing to self-interest helps point out how his abusiveness affects him personally and how it interferes with obtaining what he says he wants. It is also helpful to talk about how his abusive and controlling attitudes may have affected past relationships and how they will continue to affect future relationships if he is unwilling to change them.

GROUP LEADERSHIP: EDUCATION, TRAINING, AND EXPERIENCE

The therapists plays two major roles in the group. The first is as a facilitator of each man's individual progress in the group, as members write out and present the tasks that are outlined in Chapter III. This means asking relevant questions to expand on client statements, empathizing with a man's emotional pain when appropriate, and confronting subtle and overt attitudes and behaviors that underlie his abuse and control. The second role is as a teacher, in presenting the educational materials that are discussed in Chapter IV. Therapists need to be familiar with the various topics and able to present them clearly during the allotted education time in each group.

A strong academic background and other experiences can be helpful in effectively implementing this model, although no absolute prerequisites exist for becoming a group leader. A variety of work, volunteer, and life experiences can be a part of becoming an effective facilitator of this program. Still, several forms of learning and experience can be useful.

A master's or doctorate in psychology, social work, counseling, or other related field and a license to practice in the specific field of training can aid the group leader in developing competency in:

- mental health assessment and diagnosis,
- the individual and group therapy process,
- the development of a personal model of how human beings change and grow, and
- the base of knowledge that forms the core of the educational topics section of this program.

Most therapists who have worked with this model have had a master's or a doctorate degree, and this level of academic preparation to help develop clinical skills is recommended due to the therapeutic approach of this model. In addition, skill building for clients is an important part of the change process, and this academic background can also be helpful in presenting the educational topics in this program. However, academic training and licensure are not, in and of themselves, enough. If therapists do not have a clear understanding of domestic abuse and possess the personal characteristics noted in the following section, they are unlikely to be effective with this population.

Knowledge of issues surrounding domestic abuse is critical. This experience should involve workshops, training, and readings in the area of domestic abuse and ideally should include actual domestic abuse group facilitation. An important part of working with this program, or with any domestic abuse program, is developing and being able to clearly articulate a personal philosophy regarding domestic abuse and its treatment.

Experience with court-ordered clients is useful because many domestic abuse clients will be mandated to treatment by the legal system. It is also helpful to have worked with clients who have personality disorders because many domestic abuse clients exhibit, in varying degrees, personality disorder traits.

Finally, even if the therapist has little direct experience with domestic abuse, he or she can gain the necessary competency by working closely with a therapist who has experience with domestic abuse and who has group leadership expertise. Many therapists who have worked with this model have gained their domestic abuse experience in this manner.

GROUP LEADERSHIP: IMPORTANT CHARACTERISTICS

In addition to education, training, and experience, some specific personal characteristics are part of being an effective group leader. The following material covers the most important ones.

Having a Clear Personal Philosophy
About Domestic Abuse

Therapists need to develop and be clear about their own personal philosophy regarding anger, control, and domestic abuse. This cannot be overemphasized. Abusive men, their partners, or others in the community will challenge the therapists' beliefs on occasion. It is important to be able to respond in a coherent and articulate fashion and offer a meaningful rationale for the treatment model. Some of these challenges might include the following:

- Why does a domestic abuse program have to be so long?
- Why not just hold a short-term anger management class to address these issues?
- Why is couples therapy not always an alternative when battering is present?
- Isn't anger okay to express?
- What is the difference between anger and abuse?
- Is it okay for women to be emotionally and verbally abusive with their partners?
- Is it okay for women to be violent with their partners?
- Aren't women just as controlling, abusive, and violent as men are?
- Is controlling behavior ever okay in any life situations?
- Is abusive and violent behavior ever okay in any life situations?
- What is the difference between male and female violence?
- Why is this program philosophy so focused on men and their behavior?

Therapists must also be aware of covert manipulative and controlling behavior and its impact in a battering situation. Battering is more than physical violence. Many men are able to stop the violence due to their fear of possible consequences. Subtle manipulative and controlling behaviors in the group need to be identified and confronted directly as well. It is also important for therapists to live what is taught to clients in these areas. To have a coherent domestic abuse philosophy, therapists must be able to think clearly about and understand all forms of control, abuse, and violence in their clients' and their own lives.

Acknowledging That Domestic Abuse
Is a Community and Societal Issue

Therapists need to acknowledge that domestic abuse is part of a broader societal issue. One aspect of this is a willingness to actively work together and with other parts of the community to effectively address this issue. Domestic abuse is not just an individual's or a couple's problem; it is also a community and societal issue. Violence is illegal, and this often means that others are involved in identifying the issue and helping to provide remedies. Therapists must be willing to work closely with shelters, legal advocates, survivors' groups, judges, probation officers, places of worship, medical facilities, attorneys, and other social service, chemical dependency, and mental health agencies. Such cooperative efforts often take additional therapist time and energy for the battering to be adequately addressed.

Believing in the Power
of the Group Process

The group milieu offers a unique and powerful opportunity for growth and change. Although group does have the potential to create a negative and destructive atmosphere that encourages entitlement beliefs and controlling attitudes and behaviors, it can also offer a rare chance for men to connect with and learn from one another, perhaps for the first time in their lives.

An ongoing group, especially, offers a sense of hope as new members realize the benefits of applying what is taught in the program through other men's willingness to take risks and try new behaviors. Group therapy helps many batterers deal with the shame they experience by allowing them to observe other men directly talking about and addressing control, abuse, and violence. Addressing these issues with others in group keeps them from feeling isolated and alone. The process of reaching out to others in group who offer feedback and emotional support gives men the opportunity to feel needed and valued, to experience empathy for others, and to raise their self-esteem. Ideally, the group becomes a safe place to practice assertiveness, communication, and conflict resolution skills that can then be transferred to their relationships with partners and others.

To be effective in this or any other group model, therapists must believe in the value of the group process and see it as different from individual, or even couples, therapy. Therapists must have an appreciation for, and trust in, the group's power to change batterers' attitudes and behaviors.

Being Open, Honest, Genuine,
Courageous, and Present

To be effective, therapists must be open and honest about themselves and open to the men with whom they are working. This does not mean revealing all the personal details of their lives, but it does mean sharing enough to give group members a sense of who they are as human beings. Therapists' honest reactions and feedback can express caring and, at the same time, confront the destructive attitudes and behaviors that have brought men into group. This genuineness is a powerful tool in connecting with men and helping them change.

Courage is also required because many people whom a batterer encounters are intimidated by, and unwilling to directly confront, the attitudes and behaviors that are creating so many problems in the batterer's life. It takes enormous courage to state clearly what one observes and experiences when dealing with a batterer. This honesty has the potential to help the batterer begin to trust and respect the therapist and to increase the batterer's belief in the possibility of change.

All of the previous characteristics are part of the therapist being emotionally present in the group process. Being present involves allowing oneself to be emotionally touched by group members' pain, struggles, and triumphs. Group members will gain confidence that they can change what has brought them to the program when they feel that the therapist is present as someone who is there for them.

Handling Personal Attacks, Being Able to Confront Batterers Directly, and Modeling Respectful Behavior

Batterers are easily shamed. Transference, the tendency for clients to attribute feelings and attitudes of significant people in their early lives to those currently important to them, is common. Often, the batterer will view the therapist as the abusive parent he experienced in his family of origin due to the therapist holding him accountable for what he says and does. Therapists should expect emotional overreactions and personal attacks stemming from clients' transference and shame and be willing to address these issues directly, without losing the ability to hold them accountable and to stay focused on the treatment process.

Confrontation and accountability in a batterers' program are critical. Therapists who work with batterers must have moved beyond a need to be "liked" by their clients. Therapists need to be clear, direct, and matter of fact in confronting client issues. It is easy to personalize batterers' anger and hostility and become frustrated, punishing, and shaming or to withdraw and retreat when working with abusive men. Their attitudes and behaviors are often difficult to comprehend. Batterers' actions are frequently alienating and threatening for those who come in contact with them. Therapists do not need to like a batterer initially to work with him. They do, however, need to recognize their own negative self-talk and emotional responses to remain calm and effective in facilitating the treatment process.

It is vital for therapists to work actively to avoid a judgmental and shaming attitude. Clients need to be treated respectfully, especially if one goal of the treatment process is that they will become respectful of their partners and others. When therapists are shaming and punitive, batterers are given yet another model of human interaction that reinforces what they learned during childhood. Therapists need to model respectful and compassionate behavior. They also need to clearly acknowledge to themselves that it is, in fact, a client's right to decide whether he will make the choice to benefit from the treatment process. Therapists cannot control the treatment outcome, no matter what they say or do. The more therapists lapse into their own desire to control the client and his treatment process, the greater the potential for therapists to become abusive or shaming with their clients.

Having an Awareness of Personal Issues
Regarding Anger, Abuse, Power, and Control

Working with batterers has the potential to raise therapists' personal issues related to anger, abuse, power, and control. Ongoing self-awareness of these is crucial, including being aware of their own family-of-origin experiences and how these experiences affect their reactions to working with batterers in the present. Countertransference can easily be triggered in therapists, whereby they attribute to the batterer feelings and attitudes that stem from their own life experiences but that do not really involve their clients. This can be especially significant if a therapist's father or mother was abusive and the therapist has not effectively addressed those issues in his or her own life. Countertransference can also be triggered if therapists have come out of an abusive relationship with a partner in their adult years or have worked in controlling and abusive organizational settings.

Other aspects of this characteristic are somewhat gender related. A male therapist may become aware of shameful feelings about being a man when listening to other men talking about the abuse they have perpetrated against their partners and children. A female therapist might be inclined to overidentify with the batterer's partner, thus becoming hostile and shaming with the man concerning his past and current behavior. A vital part of this characteristic involves being aware of the need to avoid power struggles because batterers are often adept at instigating these, thus stalemating the treatment process.

One important power struggle to avoid is trying to convince the batterer that he needs treatment or attempting to "sell" him on the idea that therapy would be good for him. This is manifested by therapists working too hard in the treatment process when the client is disinterested, indifferent, or actively hostile. What helps is to provide him with a different perspective on what abuse is and how it is affecting his life and let him make the decision about whether he wishes to do anything about it. This again addresses the whole issue of his level of motivation. Therapists must communicate clearly that if a man is not interested in working on changing his abusive and controlling behaviors, he does not need to continue the assessment or the group itself. If this is the case, refer him elsewhere.

Part of the challenge for therapists in this particular situation is to again work at being direct but matter of fact in addressing a client's motivation. A judgmental or punitive response to his unwillingness to look at his control and abuse issues is not helpful. Much of the learning for abusive men stems from hearing the same message about their behavior from a number of people, whether through going to a number of different therapists and programs or through returning to court and spending time in jail.

Having an Understanding of How Batterers Have Become Controlling and Abusive

Therapists need to have a clear understanding of how these men have become who they are. These men were generally controlled, shamed, victimized, and abused in their own families of origin, and they carry that emotional pain into their interactions with the rest of the world. To be truly effective in helping men change their controlling and abusive attitudes and behaviors, therapists must be able to feel some compassion and empathy for the batterer. In addition, therapists must be willing to go beneath their clients' cynicism and hostility to see the potential good that batterers possess within them. To do successful work with batterers, it is critical for the therapists to believe that some possibility of real change in the batterers' lives exists. Without this therapist attitude, growth and change become much more difficult, in any treatment model. Batterers need to be respected and valued as human beings despite their destructive attitudes and behaviors.

One aspect of this characteristic is therapists' ability to recognize and build on clients' strengths and competencies. Often, it may be difficult to identify these strengths. However, one competency can be immediately identified for batterers, that is, their remaining nonabusive at certain times even when they are feeling angry and controlling. For example, they may not react abusively at work because they do not want to get fired. Showing them that they have control is part of the process of teaching them to make better choices about how they express their anger. This helps them to understand that they are not out of control. Pointing out their competency in this specific area allows therapists and their clients to recognize their ability to control themselves and make better choices in other parts of their lives.

Being Willing to Take Care
of Themselves Emotionally

As a part of working with batterers, therapists must acknowledge their own feelings and have the ability to take care of themselves. The impact of working with batterers can be profound, and an ability to recognize and handle client escalations is critical.

It is common, in individual or group sessions, for a therapist to become a secondary victim to a batterer's abusiveness. Therapists may begin to feel intimidated by their clients' escalations, defensiveness, and attempts to control the treatment process. Therapists need to have a level of confidence that allows them to assertively point out and discuss escalations that occur. These escalations in treatment represent the same kinds of interactions that are frightening and difficult for the batterers' partners.

It is also vital to set clear limits concerning escalations that occur during the sessions and be willing to confront batterers even though the therapist is feeling fearful. This intervention includes interrupting a client's escalations and not allowing him to lapse into name-calling, swearing, or using put-downs directed toward the therapist, his partner, or others. It is not helpful for him to continue to practice his abusive ways with the therapist. Making statements such as "You don't need to agree with me, but I still want you to listen" or "I'm not willing to continue talking with you if you don't calm down" communicates clearly that the batterer will not be allowed to control what happens in treatment. If these escalations continue, it is important to stop the session and have him take a time-out or, if necessary, terminate his involvement in the session at that point.

Another aspect of this characteristic is acknowledging personal reactions and feelings and asking for and accepting emotional support from colleagues. This also includes a willingness to offer others this same kind of support. It is critical to take care of yourself and your colleagues when working with the issue of domestic abuse. In programs that are unstructured and chaotic, a high likelihood of counselor burnout exists. Even in structured and well-run programs, secondary victimization does occur due to the anger, hostility, and controlling behavior that these clients sometimes manifest.

Therapists may feel fearful and intimidated when in a batterer's presence, which can lead to not confronting or addressing important treatment issues. Therapists may become overly sensitive to issues related to abuse and violence in the larger culture, which can lead to becoming depressed and despairing in their own lives. Therapists may begin to take work concerns home and become preoccupied with them. As a result, their personal lives may suffer. They may isolate themselves and withdraw from partners and friends, lose their sense of humor, and become too serious and self-absorbed. Finally, therapists may feel intense sadness about the pain their clients feel and inflict on others. They also may experience frustration and disappointment when the violence and abuse recur.

These are all normal and natural reactions to working with the issue of domestic abuse. Therapists must be willing to allow themselves, at times, to drop their professional facade and experience the human pain that surrounds this issue. This means actively connecting with colleagues and seeking out and offering support whenever necessary. Sharing personal reactions with trustworthy colleagues is one of the best ways to avoid the burnout related to working with domestic abuse.

GROUP LEADERSHIP: GENDER ISSUES

Both men and women can be effective therapists and group leaders with men who batter. Both men and women have used this model. The ideal configuration for group is one male and one female therapist to provide men with a different vision of women in general and of a strong female presence in particular. Having both a man and a woman in leadership roles in the group also allows the facilitators to model a healthy and respectful male-female relationship. This means that both therapists need to be aware of the power dynamics in their relationship and that they need to discuss and make clear and conscious decisions about how they will model these roles. This includes thinking about and deciding ahead of time who starts the group, who presents the educational topics, who brings up individual or group issues, who guides task accomplishment, and who confronts destructive and unhealthy attitudes and behaviors in the sessions.

Both male and female therapists have the potential to collude with batterers to help them avoid addressing the issues concerning control, abuse, and violence. Males may relate to the batterers' difficulties and oversympathize with what they say about their partners and their interrelationship struggles. A male therapist may become part of a "good old boys" network and smile or laugh at inappropriate comments or jokes made by men in the group. Conversely, males may be fearful of, or intimidated by, escalations in the group and "back off" when these and other behaviors need to be addressed directly.

Similarly, a female therapist may become apprehensive of, or intimidated by, the batterers' sexism, coarseness, or abrasiveness and assume that this is just part of his being male. Consequently, she may feel uncertain about confronting attitudes and behaviors that are contributing to his abuse of his partner. On the other hand, she may smile at inappropriate comments or jokes due to her discomfort with his reports of the violence he has directed at his partner. Also, she may respond indirectly to attempts by the batterers to connect with her as a woman in an inappropriate way. For instance, when one man asked a female therapist to go out to lunch at an early point in the group, she smiled and, in a casual way, told him that would not be such a good idea rather than directly confronting the behavior and the attitude behind it.

This group model can also be facilitated by two men, two women, or one therapist of either gender. The last option, unfortunately, is often the most common alternative due to cost-related issues. In any case, if two therapists are running the group, they need to communicate effectively inside and outside the group, trust and respect each other, and work together to make the group an effective environment for men to confront their abusive and controlling attitudes and behaviors and to grow as human beings.

THE RESPONSIBILITY OF THE AGENCY OR ORGANIZATION

Last, the agency must have a strong commitment to the domestic abuse program. Part of this involves the realization that working with abusive clients (and battered women) is often more difficult and time-consuming than working with a general mental health client population.

This agency commitment means supporting therapists administratively, emotionally, physically, and legally. Specifics of this support might include decreasing clinical expectations due to the additional crisis and case management time and collateral contact with partners, probation officers, and others. Such support might involve providing ongoing supervision and consultation specifically geared to the emotionally draining aspects of working with this high-risk population, acknowledging that therapists need personal and emotional sharing and support. It might mean hiring and maintaining a team of competent supportive clinicians who can count on one another. It might also require developing safety plans for therapists and the agency to follow when addressing the crises and threats to therapists that can arise.

Therapist safety planning might include an unlisted home phone number and discussing any immediate threats with his or her partner and children. Agency safety planning might mean locked outside doors and the use of door buzzers at night, knowing and having contact with the local police department, scheduling different times for partners' individual appointments and for men's and women's groups, and installing emergency buttons in both individual offices and group rooms in case of a client escalation.

A violent incident, murder, suicide, or personal threat has the potential to create a devastating impact on therapists and the agency for which they work. However, the long-lasting effects can be minimized by identifying and putting into practice concrete strategies to assist and support those who are working with the issue of domestic violence.

CHAPTER II:
THE INTAKE PROCEDURE

Part 1: Conducting the Intake

The assessment is a critical component in the treatment of an abusive man. During this time he begins to learn about abuse and its impact on his own and others' lives. Ideally, this process determines the extent of the problem and what type of intervention is most appropriate. The intake phase in this model is significantly longer and more involved than the process used in many batterers' programs. Intakes generally involve four to six individual sessions of fifty minutes but may, with certain individuals, take even longer.

For group treatment, assessment is an important first step in a man's becoming an active and motivated participant in the domestic abuse group, setting the tone for his entire involvement in treatment. It also allows the therapist to identify and address any and all issues that may be a part of his current and past domestic abuse. The following sections outline the process that is used when a man first comes to the agency. Client handouts for the intake can be found in Part 2 of this chapter.

EDUCATION

At the first meeting, several educational components are discussed. Handouts are given to the man during the first session to take home and read during the week prior to the next meeting. Whether he actually follows through with the reading and the homework helps assess motivation in this and subsequent sessions.

One handout defines what anger is and what it is not. Understanding Your Anger highlights the difference between anger, the emotion that everyone experiences, and the destructive attitudes and behaviors that may arise from it. Types of Abusive Behavior, another handout, defines eight types of abusive behavior that can occur in a relationship and begins the process of identifying what abuse is and discussing its effect on partners and others. A third handout, How Violence May Occur in a Relationship, addresses violence in relationships using a cyclical model originally developed by Lenore Walker in 1979. A fourth handout, Using Time-Outs, discusses the concept of taking "time out," which forms the cornerstone for this domestic abuse program. Men are encouraged at this time to discuss the idea of time-outs with their partners as a first step toward intervening in the explosive and abusive incidents that have been occurring. Many partners are initially uncomfortable with time-outs because they view them as just another way for the man to avoid significant relationship issues. However, an important part of taking a respectful time-out is making a commitment to return after a predetermined time to re-initiate a discussion about the issue that preceded the time-out and then actually following through with this commitment. The therapist also discusses time-outs with the man's partner later in the assessment process.

The program's domestic abuse philosophy is then discussed in detail. Important concepts in this philosophy are that men make choices when they are violent, that abuse and violence are learned behaviors, and that men can unlearn these destructive attitudes and behaviors.

Finally, men are given the handout Domestic Abuse Group Description, which outlines the purpose and the objectives of the group itself. It is also helpful to discuss the group objectives one by one and ask the men whether any of these are appropriate for them. Most men see a majority, or all, of the group goals as relevant to their situation.

This information provides education about domestic abuse and the program that immediately describes to the man the process with which he is becoming involved. The therapist must immediately assess the man's openness to the information being presented. In addition, it is helpful to notice his levels of internal motivation (e.g., feeling genuine sadness, guilt, and remorse about the effects of his abuse on his partner and children) versus his levels of external motivation (e.g., legal involvement; fears about separation/divorce). Initially, most motivation, in this model's experience, primarily involves external factors. Even men who are not court-ordered to treatment are almost always "partner mandated" to do something about the abuse. Thus, the goal is to move his motivational level toward a more internal locus so that he is involved with the program for himself and for his own good rather than simply to get the court off his back or to salvage the relationship.

Handing out written materials can help identify illiteracy issues that may arise because a relatively high level of literacy is necessary to be involved with, and to benefit from, this particular program. If the client is illiterate or has difficulty with reading, writing, or comprehension, he should then be referred to literacy classes if he wishes to continue his involvement with this program. The relationship between illiteracy and low self-esteem should also be addressed at this point. If he is willing to become involved with literacy classes, additional individual assistance can be provided by the group therapists and other group members to help him work on tasks, group homework, and the like.

If a man is unwilling to do remedial work regarding his literacy skills, he should then be referred to another program in which literacy is not as significant a factor in his ability to benefit from and complete the group. We have, however, had a number of men actively pursue literacy classes simultaneous to their involvement in group and complete the program. For these men, their initial problems with illiteracy served as a bridge to connections with other group members, who often became mentors and tutors after the illiteracy issues were raised during the members' first night in group.

THE ESCALATION PREVENTION PLAN

Another important part of the intake is to begin work on the Escalation Prevention Plan (EPP) (see Chapter III for more information about this tool), which is the foundation for addressing controlling and abusive attitudes and behaviors. It begins the process of emotional, behavioral, and cognitive self-monitoring that will help a man better recognize the pressure or tension buildup that occurs prior to his making the choice to be abusive or violent. Generally, in the second session, the EPP is discussed and the man is assisted in coming up with examples from each of the eight stress signal cue categories. In addition, he is encouraged to think about specific ideas for his de-escalation strategies section of the plan, with the time-out skill at the top of the list.

He is then asked to add to his EPP between sessions and return with additional examples of cues for the next meeting. What he does with this homework assignment serves as an indicator of both his understanding and his motivation. It also gives us answers to the following questions:

- Can he understand and does he begin to recognize that a gradual escalation process leads to controlling and abusive anger?
- Does he see that his explosive anger does not just "erupt out of nowhere" and that his violence is not "out of control"?
- Is he willing to begin to acknowledge and identify specific escalation cues and triggers?
- Does he begin to see that he can make conscious alternative choices to becoming abusive and violent?
- Is he willing to invest additional time and effort outside of the therapy sessions?

The primary reason that four to six individual sessions are included in the assessment process is to obtain a clearer picture over a longer period of time about whether the man recognizes that he has a problem with controlling and abusive attitudes and behaviors and whether he has the willingness and motivation to effectively address this problem.

GATHERING INTAKE INFORMATION
AND RELEVANT HISTORY

During his first intake session and throughout the entire assessment process, the standard intake information, which is an important part of any mental health assessment, needs to be gathered. This process may be part of any, or all, of the individual sessions and would include the following information:

1. The presenting problem
   - His and others' versions
2. His current life situation
   - His relationships with his partner and his children
   - His work/school life
   - His current alcohol and drug use
   - Other areas that may cause stress (e.g., finances, physical health)
3. His relevant history/background
   - Descriptions of his relationships with parents and siblings
   - His parents' relationship with each other
   - How anger was experienced and expressed in his family
   - How he and his siblings were disciplined
   - Family "rules" and values
   - Chemical use and mental health problems in his family
   - Significant childhood experiences
   - A history of his relationships with previous partners, his school/work endeavors, his chemical use, and his violence with others (including prior legal involvement related to violence or other criminal activities)
4. A DSM-IV (American Psychiatric Association, 1994) diagnosis, which may be necessary to meet state licensing requirements for an outpatient mental health clinic and which is necessary to satisfy third-party reimbursers' (e.g., insurance or managed care companies) expectations. DSM-IV is the *Diagnostic and Statistical Manual of Mental Disorders* (Fourth Edition), published by the American Psychiatric Association, which lists all diagnoses relevant to mental health treatment. See the following section for more information about specific diagnoses that may be relevant to batterers' mental health issues. In many programs, however, a diagnosis may not be necessary if it is not part of a program's licensing requirements and third-party reimbursement is not the method of payment for program costs.

MENTAL HEALTH DIAGNOSES
AND THE USE OF PSYCHOTROPIC MEDICATIONS

It is this model's belief that other mental health issues should not be overlooked if the domestic abuse is to be adequately addressed. A variety of diagnoses are common among men who have been in the program. Most of the men who have entered the group exhibit significant symptoms related to either depression or anxiety. These symptoms may stem from current circumstances (e.g., being in the midst of a separation or a divorce), but for many men depression or anxiety has often existed since childhood and is masked by chemical abuse or irritability and explosive anger. It is unfortunate that DSM-IV acknowledges the presence of irritability in depression related to children and adolescents but does not discuss it as part of a depressive syndrome for adults. To diagnose mental health problems, the therapist should have training and experience using the DSM-IV, and depending on the clinical setting, a licensed therapist may need to oversee and "sign off" on any diagnoses that are made.

In terms of specific diagnoses, the following are the most common with men in this program: Dysthymia (300.4), Major Depression (296.xx), Depressive Disorder Not Otherwise Specified (311), Generalized Anxiety Disorder (300.02), and Anxiety Disorder Not Otherwise Specified (300.00). In addition, Adjustment Disorders (309.xx) and Personality Disorders, especially Paranoid PD (301.0), Antisocial PD (301.7), Narcissistic PD (301.81), Obsessive-Compulsive PD (301.4), and Personality Disorder NOS (301.9) may be a part of the clinical picture. Substance Abuse Disorders, particularly Alcohol Abuse (305.00), Alcohol Dependence (303.90), and Polysubstance Dependence (304.80) may also be diagnostically relevant. Two V codes that are new to DSM-IV address the battering specifically, Physical Abuse of Child (V61.21) and Physical Abuse of Adult (V61.1), and are also helpful in presenting a more complete diagnostic overview. However, the V codes, in and of themselves, generally will not satisfy most third-party expectations regarding reimbursement for clinical services.

It appears that many of these men have long-standing mood disorders. Often, these problems have simply never been addressed in any effective manner over the course of their lives up to the present. It is critical not to excuse their violent and abusive behavior with a diagnosis of some other emotional disorder or by using psychotropic medications. However, if other mental health problems do exist that could complicate the treatment process and they are not identified and treated, a man is significantly less likely to understand and put into practice the ideas and tools presented in the program.

For this reason, having ready access to consulting psychiatrists who can provide psychotropic medication evaluations whenever appropriate is an important part of this domestic abuse treatment model. This is especially critical if a man is actively suicidal or particularly obsessive in his thought patterns. The medications most often prescribed are antidepressants.

If a man presents with suicidal ideation, he is asked to commit to, sign, and date a No-Suicide Contract, which states the following:

> I, _____ (his name), have reviewed the safety concerns expressed to me by my therapist. As a result of this discussion, and as part of my becoming involved with the domestic abuse program, I agree not to engage in any self-destructive or life-threatening behaviors during the time that I am in therapy. If I am having difficulty with thoughts about harming myself, I agree to call the clinic during business hours. After business hours, I agree to contact one of the crisis phone numbers listed below to get emotional support so that I do not act out my self-destructive thoughts.

This is a contract with himself, his therapist, and other group members and is a means of solidifying his commitment to the process of recovery and growth. This contract is one of the areas he needs to address directly in his Introduction task at the first group session he attends. He also needs to comment on this contract each week when he checks in at the beginning of group. In addition, this contract highlights, and hopefully disarms, one of the weapons in his arsenal of abusive behavior with his partner, as threats of suicide are often used to manipulate and control the partner's behavior in a relationship.

CHEMICAL USE/ABUSE

An important part of the intake, as previously noted, is to discuss a man's current and past alcohol and drug use. The purpose of this is to determine the appropriateness of a chemical dependency evaluation or chemical dependency treatment before or during domestic abuse treatment. This discussion also can help decide whether to ask the man to sign a Sobriety Contract, an agreement not to use mood-altering chemicals for the duration of his treatment.

If chemical use concerns are identified, the man is asked to commit to, sign, and date the following statement:

> I, _____ (his name), agree not to use any mood-altering chemicals (alcohol and/or drugs) during my domestic abuse treatment involvement.

The Sobriety Contract is a commitment to himself, his therapist, and the other group members that he will completely abstain from any chemical use throughout his group program. This becomes a particularly important issue when much of the violence perpetrated by the man has been while he is under the influence of alcohol or drugs, as is often the case (Byles, 1978; Fagan, Stewart, and Hansen's, 1983). Whether he has a Sobriety Contract is another area he needs to address directly in his Introduction task at the first group session he attends. He also needs to comment on whether he is maintaining this contract when he checks in each week at the beginning of group.

This may also become an issue if the man has an extensive history of chemical use or abuse and the therapist is concerned that his continued use of chemicals will interfere with his benefiting fully from the program. An important part of this issue involves assessing whether he has the potential to use chemicals to blunt the emotional pain that might arise during his treatment, as he begins to address his feelings about himself, his control and abuse, and his life in general.

Men often initially excuse their violence by focusing on their alcohol and drug use as the real problem. Some men go through chemical dependency treatment believing that their domestic abuse problem will be solved through their decision to remain sober. Some may even hear that from their chemical dependency counselors. This model's experience is that domestic abuse and violence toward others may increase or decrease after chemical dependency treatment. The man needs to understand that these are separate, freestanding issues, both of which must be effectively addressed. At times, men who have been sober for several years have reported that their abuse and violence became more frequent or severe because the chemicals were no longer there to numb their emotional reactions to life's stresses.

If the client agrees to a Sobriety Contract and violates it during the treatment process, he needs to further address the chemical issues if he is to continue in treatment. Addressing these issues might include going through a chemical dependency evaluation if one was not done during the intake. It might mean completing and discussing the Violation of Sobriety Contract Assessment (see Chapter III) if he is involved with the domestic abuse group. It might involve attending weekly Alcoholics Anonymous or Narcotics Anonymous meetings and bringing proof of attendance. It might also mean participating in regular urinalyses, which can often be arranged through a probation officer, if he is involved with the courts.

PSYCHOLOGICAL AND SCREENING INSTRUMENTS

Psychological testing is not necessary to make a sound clinical decision about whether a man is appropriate for admission into the group program. This is especially true if the therapist has experience and competency in domestic abuse issues. However, the instruments described here can be used to obtain a second opinion to validate the therapist's clinical judgment, if this is desired. If instruments are used, they must be scored and interpreted by a clinician who has training and competency in psychological testing.

Administering the Minnesota Multiphasic Personality Inventory (MMPI-2) (Butcher et al., 1989) can serve as another means of determining a man's level of motivation and whether he could benefit from the group. This psychological test also provides more information about relevant mental health diagnoses by identifying issues related to major mental illness (i.e., thought disorder and psychotic symptomology), severe depression with pronounced suicidal ideation, intense and debilitating anxiety, and extreme levels of anti-social personality features. In addition, the MacAndrew scale can be helpful in detecting the potential for substance abuse issues. Three content scales, Anti-Social Practices (ASP), Anger (ANG), and Cynicism (CYN), may be used in pre- and posttest evaluations of the effectiveness of the program.

In addition to the MMPI-2, the following instruments can be used to assist in gathering more assessment information. The Beck Depression Inventory (Beck et al., 1961) is a helpful tool for addressing the severity of a man's depressive symptoms. The Michigan Alcohol Screening Test (Pokorny, Miller, and Kaplan, 1972) is an instrument commonly used to assess the severity of alcohol and drug abuse. Levels of anger and hostility can be assessed using the Buss-Durkee Hostility Inventory (Buss and Durkee, 1957) or the Novaco Anger Scale (Novaco, 1975). The Shipley Institute of Living Scale (Shipley, 1940) can be used to assess reading skills and intellectual functioning. Finally, in *The Clinical Measurement Package: A Field Manual* (Hudson, 1982), the Generalized Contentment Scale (GCS) measures the level of depression and the Index of Self-Esteem (ISE) measures self-esteem problems.

COURT-ORDERED CLIENTS

If the client is court-ordered, we require, at the first session, that he sign an information release so that we can talk with his probation officer about the arrest report and court order to treatment. This release also allows us to regularly apprise the probation officer of the client's ongoing treatment issues, concerns, and progress. If the client says he does not have a probation officer, it can sometimes be difficult to discover whether he actually does.

However, if he has been in court, the judge involved in his case can still be contacted to discuss his situation. It works best, if he is being referred to specific programs by his probation officer, to arrange to have the client sign a release immediately after court while he is with his probation officer.

If the abusive man has been court-ordered and wishes to become involved with this program, he has no choice about signing this information release. If he is unwilling to do this, he is offered referrals to other programs. Contact with the probation officer is a critical part of helping court-ordered men remain accountable to the court's and the program's expectations. During the initial contact with the probation officer, police reports of the domestic assault, copies of any Orders for Protection, and the court order to treatment are requested.

The probation officer is notified by phone and in writing after the client's first session and when the man actually starts the group. The probation officer is also notified about concerns that may arise at various times during the group, such as a man not working effectively in the program or being close to quitting or being terminated. A final contact occurs when we send a written treatment summary within two weeks after a man has quit, been terminated, or completed the group to discuss his progress, concerns about his involvement, and recommendations for the future.

If the client is extremely resistant about addressing his domestic abuse issues or about becoming involved with the program, contact with the probation officer and having potential legal consequences (usually jail time) suspended if he completes treatment can be used as leverage.

THE ABUSE QUESTIONNAIRES

Near the end of the intake, generally during the fourth or fifth session, we work with the man to complete a history of his abusive behavior toward his partner and others called Abuse Questionnaire-M. The Abuse Questionnaire-M addresses the frequency of verbal and emotional abuse over the previous year and the frequency of physical abuse perpetrated toward all significant partner relationships over the course of his lifetime. It also asks about the most recent and most severe violence in a current relationship and past verbal abuse and violence with other partners, parents, siblings, friends, acquaintances, and strangers.

The questionnaire is adapted from some of the ideas in the Conflict Tactics (CT) Scales developed by Straus, Gelles, and Steinmetz (1980). For the purpose of our assessment, however, we needed a much more comprehensive instrument because we wanted to identify very specific ways that the man has abused his partner emotionally, verbally, physically, and sexually and to have him recall violence perpetrated against others as well. This prepares him to report honestly in the group the extent of his violence and abuse throughout the course of his life, not just with his current partner. As a result, it helps take the focus off her as "the only one I get angry with."

The questionnaire is generally administered near the end of the assessment because a man may be more willing to be honest as a result of developing some trust in his relationship with the therapist. It is also at this point that he may see some potential benefit in becoming involved with the program. Despite this, most men still tend to deny and minimize the extent of the abuse and violence, usually significantly more than their partners do. For example, one client, who reported in the intake three incidents of violence directed toward his partner, eventually acknowledged scores of incidents in the group itself. The group atmosphere and mutual sharing tend to significantly decrease the shame associated with discussing perpetrations of violence.

It is important, after completing Abuse Questionnaire-M, to check in with the client about how he has been affected by talking about his abuse and violence. This part of the intake often triggers shame, remorse, sadness, and other powerful feelings that can be discussed as part of the reason he may want to change how he relates to his loved ones and others. Men also frequently make statements such as "I never knew I was so violent" or "I never thought of myself as that abusive." Such awareness can help them better understand the impact their behavior has had on others.

The final reason that this questionnaire is so important is that it offers a "reality test" for the man who joins the group and begins to deny problems related to being violent or abusive. This tends to occur most frequently when a man is first introducing himself to other members or during the Abuse Inventory task, for which he is asked to recount a history of the violence he has perpetrated against others. On occasion, it is helpful to actually leave the group and return with his chart and intake information to confront him about discrepancies between his current group statements and what he has previously stated in the assessment.

PARTNER CONTACT

It is also expected that the abusive man will sign an information release so that we can talk with his partner, by phone or in a session, about her perception of the history of the abuse and control in their relationship. The outline of the questions we ask makes up Abuse Questionnaire-W, which is tailored for his partner. This is especially important if the client is resistant to addressing his issues concerning domestic abuse, is denying any violence, or is unwilling to acknowledge any concerns related to explosive anger and control.

In addition, this contact provides the opportunity to tell his partner about the group program for women who have been abused, about other therapy and support options at our agency, and about other community resources (e.g., shelters and advocacy programs). It is also a time to do some protection and safety planning with her using a handout titled Safety Plan; to give her information about abuse, violence, control, and the men's program; and to encourage her to call during the treatment process with her observations and concerns about his involvement. This is especially important if violent incidents occur during the course of the man's group involvement, as he may decide not to report these. It is still her decision, even if she calls to report violence, whether she feels safe enough to allow the information she provides to be directly addressed with her partner in the group setting.

It is also required that a man sign a release to allow the program therapist to inform his partner about his progress in treatment. This serves as a way of respecting her need for safety and of indicating his desire to be accountable. Even though he signs a release to allow discussion of his progress and concerns with her, program staff should be clear with her in the initial contact that she is the best judge of whether he is truly making progress and actually benefiting from the program. She is encouraged to look for a consistent pattern of behavior change over time to determine whether he is actually using the de-escalation tools that are recommended. This, in the end, is the most effective way for her to figure out whether he is changing and to assist her in deciding whether she wishes to remain with him. Unfortunately, he may be complying with program expectations and appearing to be benefiting even if he is not actually changing the way he relates to his partner and his children.

As mentioned previously, the man's partner is also encouraged to contact the therapist at any point in his group involvement to express her concerns about his behavior at home. She is continually reassured that any information she provides will not be used without her explicit permission but that her perspective, nonetheless, is always helpful in working with her partner in the group.

GOAL SETTING

Near the end of the intake, usually during the sixth session, the man is asked to set some specific and concrete behavioral goals about what he wishes to change about himself as a result of his involvement in the domestic abuse treatment. His input is helpful at this point as a way of involving him in treatment planning and as another means of assessing his level of motivation. It is particularly important that he includes issues related to explosive anger, control, and abuse in his goals. If he has no goals concerning these areas, his resistance about directly identifying these as treatment issues needs to be explored further prior to his starting the group. For more information about goal setting, see the Individual Member Goals task in Chapter III.

MAKING RECOMMENDATIONS

At this point, the therapist will make recommendations regarding a treatment plan. Group is the preferred and most effective method of treatment for abuse and violence issues. This is generally the recommendation that would be offered. If a man has not been court-ordered to treatment and he wishes to remain in individual therapy or go into couples therapy, this could be considered as an option. However, using this option requires that the violence in the relationship has stopped and that he is actively using the skills he is learning to remain nonviolent and nonthreatening and to decrease his verbal and emotional abuse and other controlling behaviors. While he is in individual or couples therapy, the issue of entering the group would be revisited. For some men, it takes more than the four to six individual sessions that we normally allow to prepare them to actually enter group treatment.

If violence is ongoing during an individual or couples therapy process, the man would need, at that point, to enter the group program or discontinue therapy. Couples and family therapy are only options if strong evidence exists, from him and his partner, that he has the tools and the willingness to use them to remain nonviolent with his partner, no matter what she says or does.

GROUP PREPARATION

Finally, if a decision is made that he will enter the domestic abuse group, the man receives the group member booklet (see Chapter III) in the final individual session and the group goals, rules, and expectations are reviewed. Especially important are issues concerning safety in the group, reporting any violence that occurs, absences, and staying current on expected tasks and weekly payments for the therapy.

Also at this time, the individual tasks that he is expected to do to complete the treatment are discussed one by one. In addition, the man's fear and apprehension about participating in the group, especially if he has had no prior group experience, must be addressed.

Part 2: The Intake Handouts

UNDERSTANDING YOUR ANGER

Your anger can be an ally or an enemy. Anger generally feels painful and uncomfortable when you experience it, but it is an integral part of your humanness and important to your physical and emotional survival. Anger is a fact of life. However, being angry does not mean you need to be controlling, punishing, and abusive. Depending on how you use it, your anger can build self-confidence and self-esteem and enhance relationships, or it can create guilt, shame, and remorse and destroy relationships and intimacy. This handout offers some ideas about what anger is and what it is not and how you can make your anger a more helpful force in your life.

Definitions

Anger

1. A normal and natural *emotion* that arises from how we interpret and label the physical arousal from the "fight or flight" stress response we all experience. This stress response is triggered when we are startled, when we feel fearful or threatened, when we believe that things around us are out of control, or when we feel insecurity, uncertainty, or self-doubt. Anger generally serves as a protection against some sort of emotional or physical pain.
2. Anger is:
   a. Appropriate, whenever it is handled effectively and respectfully
   b. A source of discovery
      • It tells you that "something important is going on" that needs to be attended to and helps clarify who you are.
   c. A warning signal
      • A "core hurt" from the past has been activated by a person or situation in the present.
      • Your wants, needs, rights, and values aren't being addressed.

(HO) ©1999 David J. Decker, MA

- You have compromised yourself in some way.
- An injustice has been done to you or those you care about.

d. An important part of being assertive (e.g., setting personal limits and maintaining healthy boundaries for yourself)

e. A tool to educate others (e.g., about your likes, dislikes, wants, and needs)

f. A useful release of energy
  - It takes enormous effort to suppress your anger and the other feelings it often covers; trying to deny anger completely only creates stress, tension, and anxiety within you.

g. A catalyst
  - It helps motivate you to solve your problems and accomplish what you need to do.

h. A form of protection
  - Anger often surfaces in a destructive fashion for you and those close to you if it is not addressed directly.

i. A gift to others
  - Sharing your anger *and the other feelings it hides* involves taking a risk and allows you to become vulnerable with others, which can open the door to trust and intimacy.

If you allow your anger to build and fester, it can lead to the attitudes that follow.

Cynicism/Hostility/Disgust/Contempt

1. These are *attitudes* that consist of mistrusting the motives of other people and of brooding about and focusing on others' real or perceived injustices toward you. These attitudes lead to viewing the world as an unfair and unsafe place and to continually looking for and expecting others to:
   a. be incompetent and inadequate
   b. be inconsiderate, unfair, and untrustworthy
   c. go out of their way to hurt you
   d. take advantage of you
   e. "cross" you in some way

2. These attitudes can also involve critical, judgmental, and shaming thoughts about yourself, your mistakes, and your problems.

3. These attitudes promote the idea that you are powerless and a victim and that the situation is hopeless.

(HO)   ©1999 David J. Decker, MA

4. Cynicism, hostility, disgust, and contempt are best represented by your negative self-talk or a negative rehearsal in your mind about some future situation. When you regularly engage in negative thoughts, you are constantly fueling your stress response and prolonging and increasing the intensity of your anger.
5. Chronic cynicism, hostility, disgust, and contempt always lead to physical damage and emotional consequences for you and others.
6. If these attitudes become your way of looking at the world, they then contribute directly to the violation of another person's rights or boundaries through the following behaviors.

Aggression/Withdrawal

1. *Aggression* involves *behaviors* acted out with the intent to hurt, punish, intimidate, or control others emotionally, verbally, physically, or sexually as a means of gaining revenge for the real or imagined "wrongs" done to you and getting your way in a particular situation.
2. *Withdrawal* involves *behaviors* designed to disengage emotionally from difficult situations. The can be *punishing withdrawal* that is used to hurt and get back at someone (e.g., sulking and pouting) and/or it can be a *protective withdrawal* when you pull back if you are feeling uncertain or unsafe (e.g., becoming passive and "stuffing" you anger). Or a withdrawal can combine elements of both of these.
3. These behaviors, used on a consistent basis, will always eventually result in disrespect and emotional distance in relationships with others.

Some Distortions of Anger: What Anger Is Not

1. Being aggressive: being pushy, rude, abrasive, bullying, and intrusive and ignoring what others think, feel, and want (e.g., "I don't care what you want"/"To hell with you")
2. Blaming: not taking responsibility for yourself; continually focusing on others as the reason for your difficulties (e.g., "You're the real problem in this relationship")
3. Lecturing: "going on and on" to try to make a point or convince someone that you are right
4. Labeling: Making simplistic and critical judgments about others (e.g., "What an idiot!"/"You're a moron")
5. Preaching: moralizing and making right/wrong assessments about others (e.g., "No one should ever say something like that")

(HO) ©1999 David J. Decker, MA

6. Therapizing: making "grand interpretations" about why others do what they do (e.g., "You're just saying I'm abusive because of what your last boyfriend did to you")
7. Being sarcastic: making devious and hostile jokes at someone else's expense (e.g., "You're really a winner!"/"Right. . . . I'm sure you know what you're talking about")
8. Being vicious: taking advantage of another person's vulnerability (e.g., going for the throat/hitting below the belt)
9. Being punitive: wanting to punish someone by making your reaction so strong that they will not repeat the behavior you dislike
10. Being vindictive: acting vengeful; trying to get even with and get back at others for wrongs they have done to you
11. Being controlling: demanding or expecting that others will do what you want (e.g., saying and believing "It's my way or the highway")
12. Sulking: trying to hurt others with a silence that is hostile, ominous, and threatening (e.g., withdrawing from your partner and refusing to talk for long periods when you are angry)
13. Scapegoating: dumping your anger on others who do not deserve it but who are safer and easier targets than the original person (e.g., yelling at your partner or your children rather than asserting yourself with your boss)
14. Being violent: allowing your internal pain to build to the point at which you make the choice to strike out at others physically or sexually (e.g., grabbing, pushing, restraining, slapping)

When Anger Becomes a Problem
(When It Becomes Cynicism/Hostility/Disgust/Contempt
or Aggression/Withdrawal)

1. The intensity of the angry reaction is too great.
2. It occurs too frequently.
3. It lasts too long.
4. It triggers fear and intimidation in others, creates emotional distance between you and others, and disrupts your relationships with those around you.
5. It interferes with getting your work done or creates problems for you on the job.
6. It restricts your ability to have fun, be spontaneous, play, and relax.
7. It begins to cause physical symptoms, such as headaches and back pain.

(HO)   ©1999 David J. Decker, MA

8. It leads to emotional consequences such as feeling guilty, remorseful, and shameful and experiencing low self-esteem.
9. It leads to throwing, hitting, or breaking things.
10. It leads to emotional, verbal, sexual, or physical abuse of others.
11. It leads to legal consequences related to how you express your anger (e.g., restraining orders, disorderly conduct, or assault charges).

How to Express Your Anger Effectively and Respectfully: The Short Course

1. *Become aware of your anger triggers* and learn to notice when you are escalating.
2. *Admit your anger to yourself* and accept the fact that you are angry.
3. *Take a respectful time-out* to cool down if you need to.
4. *Separate the energy and intensity* of the anger *from the issue* directly related to your anger at the moment. *Identify the other possible sources* of your anger by asking yourself some questions:
   a. Is your anger coming from hurt and pain you experienced in your childhood or other past life experiences that is somehow related to the current situation?
   b. Does your anger involve other current stressors that do not have much to do with the present situation?
   c. What negative, controlling, and vengeful thoughts are you experiencing, and how do they contribute to the buildup of intensity? Are you doubting yourself or feeling incompetent, inadequate, worthless, unimportant, powerless, or unlovable? Does this negative self-talk involve unrealistic expectations of yourself or others?
   d. What other emotions are being hidden by your anger (hurt, sadness, fear, disappointment, etc.) that, if expressed, might make communication more effective if you decide to share your anger with the other person?
   e. Is your anger in this situation "justified"? Is someone or something really "out to get you"?
      • If your answer is yes, how did you decide this to be the case? Even if you have clear and specific evidence that your anger is "justified," this still does not give you permission to become explosive, disrespectful, or abusive.
5. *Calm yourself by using de-escalation strategies* such as deep breathing, relaxation skills, positive self-talk, physical exercise, or talking with a friend.

(HO) ©1999 David J. Decker, MA

6. *Determine what you want to do with your anger.* You may or may not want to share it with the person directly involved.

7. If you choose not to share your anger, *work at "letting go" of it and learning from it.*

8. *Consider the following when expressing your anger directly to the other person involved in the situation:*

   a. Choose how, when, and where you will do this.
      • Pick an appropriate time and place.

   b. Share your anger and your other feelings in an open, assertive, and respectful way.

   c. Use "I" statements and take responsibility for your self-talk, all your feelings, and your expectations.

   d. Actively listen to the other person's point of view and accept that his or her perspective may not be the same as yours and that he or she has a right to see things differently.

   e. Be aware of your expectations and your intentions in sharing your anger.

   f. Avoid the temptation to try to win the argument and force the other person to accept your point of view. This is CONTROL!

   g. Try to view this as an opportunity to better understand each other and to potentially become closer as a result.

9. If necessary, *take the ultimate responsibility for yourself and your anger* and identify what you need to do to care for yourself in similar situations in the future. *Then actually do it!*

10. *When evaluating how you have expressed your anger, ask yourself some questions:*

    a. Was your anger useful or helpful to you in this situation?

    b. Did your anger lead to an effective response or a constructive action?

    c. In retrospect, do you feel proud about how you handled the situation? Do you feel better about yourself as a result of what you did? Do you feel worse?

TYPES OF ABUSIVE BEHAVIOR

Volatile anger and abusive behavior are always destructive in a relationship and always contribute to a loss of trust, respect, and intimacy. They are never helpful in problem solving or conflict resolution. Both men and women can be abusive in relationships. Abusive behavior, as it is defined in this handout, occurs in many relationships at some point. Abuse by either partner is not okay. However, the gender of the person who is abusive can make a significant difference in the ongoing impact of abusive actions, especially when a consistent pattern of abuse exists in the relationship. Although abusive behavior can occur between any two people, in the large majority of cases, men in heterosexual relationships are more able and more likely to use methodical and systematic physical force to maintain control in a relationship. Even when men do experience physical abuse by their partners, they are less likely to feel the intense fear, humiliation, and intimidation or to suffer the severity of physical damage that women do. Because of basic differences in musculature and socialization, women generally cannot compete with men once a physical conflict has begun. Men are, on the whole, more likely to be able to dominate a relationship through the use of physical force than are women.

Moreover, once a man has actually been physically or sexually abusive in a relationship (or if his partner believes that the potential exists for him to do so), other types of abuse have additional impact. For example, emotional and verbal abuse can then become much more frightening and controlling for the female partner. A single act of physical force clearly demonstrates that, if unable to control his partner through verbal and emotional abuse and threats, a man has the potential to up the ante again to physical abuse to maintain his dominance in the relationship. Both the man and his partner know that he has already used violence in the past so it becomes that much easier for him to violate this physical boundary the next time he becomes explosive and threatening. The eight types of abuse commonly seen among men in the program are presented in this handout with examples of each. Read through them and see which of these you have used in relating to your partner.

Male Entitlement

Male entitlement is an attitude that conveys male dominance, a general disrespect for women, and the idea that men are more competent and capable than women. This attitude leads to the belief that "I, as a man, have the right and the responsibility to control how my partner thinks, feels, and acts and to make her into the person I think she should be." This desire to control underlies all abusive behavior and is characterized by the following actions:

(HO)   ©1999 David J. Decker, MA

1. Making generalizations, telling disrespectful jokes, and believing stereotypes about women (e.g., "Women are irrational"; "It's a woman's job to take care of me and the kids")
2. Having the expectation that you will make all the important decisions in the relationship
3. Treating her like a servant (e.g., demanding that she do things for you and expecting her to wait on you; saying to her, "Go get me a drink" or "Get dinner ready")
4. Controlling how household money is handled (e.g., forcing her to account for all the money she spends, withholding money from her, giving her an allowance, acting as if her work around the house and with the children has no economic value to the family and is not as important as your outside job, keeping the checkbook or charge cards in your possession)
5. Believing that you need to be the breadwinner (e.g., discouraging her from going to school or getting employment, sabotaging her job by coming home late when she needs to get to work)
6. Deciding who does what in terms of household chores and parenting
7. Communicating to her or others that she is your property, or that you own her, or that she belongs to you because you are in a relationship or marriage
8. Being possessive and acting extremely jealous (e.g., assuming that she is always "on the make," brooding about or continually bringing up her real or imagined relationships with other men)

Emotional Abuse

Emotional abuse is the use of behavioral or nonverbal methods, such as the following, to hurt, punish, intimidate, or control your partner:

1. Sulking or withdrawing affection from her (e.g., punishing her with silence)
2. Sneering at her and acting disgusted with or contemptuous of her (e.g., dirty looks, rolling your eyes when she is talking)
3. Yelling and screaming at her
4. Staring or glaring at her
5. Following her around the house or apartment to continue an argument whether or not she wishes to do so
6. Standing near or over her and using your size to intimidate her (e.g., "getting in her face")

(HO) ©1999 David J. Decker, MA

7. Monitoring her behavior and doing "detective work" (e.g., following her or having her followed to find out where she is going or who she is spending time with, listening in on her phone conversations or taping her phone calls, calling to see if she is where she says she is going to be)
8. Attempting to control her movements or to isolate her (e.g., trying to keep her away from family and friends by taking her car keys, removing the car battery or disconnecting the distributor cap, preventing her from using the phone, or not giving her phone messages)
9. Interrupting her while she is eating (e.g., finishing a discussion during dinner)
10. Forcing her to stay awake or waking her up (e.g., to resolve an argument)
11. Forcing her to humiliate herself (e.g., making her kneel in front of you)

Verbal Abuse

Verbal abuse is the use of words to hurt, punish, intimidate, or control your partner, including the following behaviors:

1. Criticizing/discounting her thoughts, feelings, opinions, and values (e.g., saying to her "That's a stupid idea" or "You're nuts to feel that way")
2. Mocking her or mimicking what she has said (e.g., in a singsong voice)
3. Lecturing her about what's right or about the way she should be
4. Twisting what she says to make her feel confused, "crazy," and off balance (e.g., manipulating her with lies and contradictions)
5. Making negative/derogatory comments about activities she likes and places she goes
6. Interrupting her
7. Interrogating her (e.g., continually questioning her about where she goes and who she sees)
8. Accusing or blaming her for things that go wrong (e.g., around the house, with finances, with the children, in your relationship)
9. Swearing/cursing at her ("Fuck you"; "Go to hell")
10. Name-calling (e.g., "bitch," "asshole")
11. Insulting, ridiculing, or belittling her or people she cares about (e.g., put-downs about her parenting or calling her friends "losers" or "dykes")
12. Being demanding (e.g., pressuring her verbally to do what you want her to do and be who you want her to be)

(HO) ©1999 David J. Decker, MA

Threats

Nonphysical Threats

Nonphysical threats communicate (either directly or indirectly) an intention to do something, thereby creating emotional distress, fear, and indecision and increasing your ability to control your partner. This includes threatening to do the following:

1. Withdraw affection or refuse to talk to her
2. Expose personal things she has told you to others (e.g., "Wait until I tell your parents what you just said")
3. File assault charges or get a restraining order against her
4. Take or kidnap the children if she leaves
5. Withhold money
6. Throw her out in the street
7. Go out with other women
8. End the relationship, separate, or divorce

Violent Threats

Violent threats communicate (either directly or indirectly) an intention to do physical harm to your partner, your children, other relatives, friends, pets, yourself, or property, including the following actions:

1. Standing in her way or "cornering" her
2. Throwing objects in her direction or at her
3. Hitting walls or slamming your fist on surfaces (e.g., on countertops or tables)
4. Threatening to hurt pets
5. Making vague statements (e.g., "You're really asking for it," "Go ahead, keep it up," or "Remember the last time you got me pissed off")
6. Making physically intimidating gestures such as holding up a clenched fist in front of her face or raising your arm as if to hit her
7. Making statements about pushing, grabbing, or hitting her (e.g., "I'd like to smash your face right now" or "I really feel like letting you have it")
8. Threatening to be harsh or abusive with the children
9. Driving recklessly when you are angry to frighten her or "make a point"

(HO)   ©1999 David J. Decker, MA

10. Threatening her with an object (e.g., a belt or broom)
11. Playing with or discharging a weapon around her
12. Making direct or veiled threats to kill her, the children, her parents, or others
13. Making direct or veiled threats to hurt or kill yourself (e.g., "I can't go on without you")

Battering/Psychological Abuse

This category can include any or all of the previous four categories. Battering and psychological abuse occur as a result of a consistent and ongoing pattern of abusive behavior by one person in an intimate relationship who is more powerful than his or her partner. They are present when the less powerful partner either feels fearful that violence might occur or has experienced at least one incident of property destruction or physical or sexual abuse by the other partner toward her or others. When the potential for violence exists, or when violence has already occurred in a relationship, verbal and emotional abuse and threats take on added impact. At this point, these behaviors are significantly more likely to create an atmosphere of terror, degradation, and humiliation than would occur in a relationship in which threats or violence have been absent. Many relationships involve some of the abuse types previously noted on an occasional or infrequent basis. However, battering and psychological abuse become part of the relationship dynamic when a man systematically and persistently, through the use of violence, threats, and other abusive and controlling attitudes and behaviors, tries to

1. undermine a woman's self-esteem, self-confidence, and motivation;
2. create a devastating and debilitating emotional insecurity in her; and
3. render her less capable of caring for and protecting herself and of functioning independently in the future.

Violence Toward Property or Pets

This type of abuse involves destroying property or hurting pets to intimidate or coerce her into doing what you want her to do, including the following actions (these actions can also be perceived as violent threats to those who are around when they are occurring or who see the damage when they return):

(HO) ©1999 David J. Decker, MA

1. Hitting walls
2. Slamming your fist on surfaces (e.g., desk, countertop, arm of a chair, car dashboard)
3. Throwing or breaking household items
4. Taking, hiding, or destroying her possessions (e.g., favorite pictures, family heirlooms, jewelry)
5. Hitting, kicking, or killing a pet to intimidate or hurt her

Sexual Abuse

Sexual abuse consists of any sexually inappropriate verbal statements, any physical affection or touch forced on another person, or any nonconsensual sexual act, including the following:

1. Telling dirty jokes and making sexually demeaning comments about her or other women around her (e.g., calling her or other women "whores," "sluts," or "frigid")
2. Staring at other women's bodies when you are with her or making sexual comments about other women around her
3. Viewing and treating her or other women like sex objects (e.g., making unwanted or inappropriate sexual comments to her or about her in front of others, expecting or demanding sex from her)
4. Insulting her body (e.g., the size of her breasts/hips) or her love-making ability (e.g., "You make love like a corpse")
5. Insisting that she dress in a certain manner (e.g., in a sexy or prim-and-proper fashion)
6. Touching sexual parts of her body without consent (e.g., grabbing or pinching her breasts or buttocks when she tells you not to do it or when she says that it hurts)
7. Coercing or pressuring her into performing specific sexual behaviors that she does not wish to do (e.g., making her perform oral or anal sex, expecting her to have sex with multiple partners or with your friends)
8. Forcing sex in the following situations:
   • She is sleeping.
   • She is not asked.
   • She is sick or it is damaging to her health.
   • She says "no" or sets a limit (verbally or nonverbally).
   • She is intoxicated and unable to say "no" effectively.
   • She is fearful about the consequences of saying "no."
9. Raping her

(HO)   ©1999 David J. Decker, MA

Physical Abuse

Physical abuse is the use of any physical actions or force to control a person or situation (this includes violence perpetrated against yourself), such as the following:

1. Pinching/scratching/biting her
2. Tripping her
3. Ripping her clothing
4. Pulling her hair
5. Bumping into her as you walk by
6. Grabbing/pushing her
7. Wrestling with or restraining her physically
8. Tying her up
9. Throwing her bodily (e.g., on a couch, on the floor, on a bed)
10. Slapping/punching her
11. Choking/strangling her (e.g., putting your hands near or around her throat and squeezing)
12. Using an object or weapon with her (e.g., a broom, belt, knife, or gun)
13. Hitting, hurting, or killing yourself (e.g., punching yourself in the head, attempting suicide)

HOW VIOLENCE MAY OCCUR IN A RELATIONSHIP

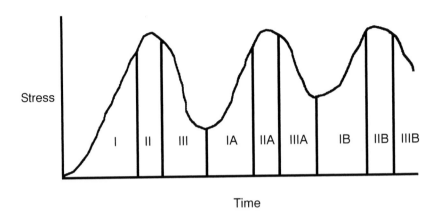

Many couples can clearly recognize and talk about how violence occurs in their relationship over the course of time. Women tend to see this pattern most clearly, but men frequently acknowledge the pattern as well. The following material describes the three phases of violence that both this program and others (Walker, 1979) have identified.

Escalation Phase (I)

This phase is characterized by a period of increased tension that builds over time and may include unresolved arguments in the relationship, job stress, financial pressures, increased chemical use, passive responses to conflicts (in and outside the home), and a buildup of resentments. Generally, the man has little, if any, awareness of the stress that is building and rarely does he talk about the tension and the feelings behind it. Nor does he use other healthy ways to handle the stress in his life. The more powerless he feels inside, the greater his aggression and need for control tend to become. Verbal and emotional abuse, threats, destruction of property, and some less severe physical abuse may occur as the tension mounts and becomes unbearable for him. An escalation can last minutes, hours, days, weeks, or months, but the eventual outcome is violence. The woman is often significantly more aware that tension is building than her partner is.

(HO)   ©1999 David J. Decker, MA

WHAT HAPPENS WITH HIM

- blames her for his increased stress and anger and his controlling and abusive reactions
- makes unreasonable demands/has unrealistic expectations
- becomes more oppressive and controlling
- feels more and more powerless at home and in the rest of his life
- denies and minimizes the stress in his life and the impact of his control/intimidation on others
- often feels jealous/distrustful of his partner
- feels escalated/angry much of the time (but generally denies feelings behind the anger, e.g., hurt, fear, insecurity, inadequacy, disappointment)
- believes it is her responsibility to make him feel better
- feels more and more "out of control"
- becomes more and more isolated
- may increase alcohol/drug use to try to reduce his stress
- views her withdrawal from him as rejection/abandonment, which further escalates him

WHAT HAPPENS WITH HER

- often believes she can (or should be able to) control his moods and outbursts and attempts to do so
- often hides her own anger due to fear of reprisal
- blames abusive incidents on external situations (e.g., work/financial stress) and works to control as many as she can (e.g., children's behavior)
- believes that nothing she does is "good enough" and feels as if she is "walking on eggshells"
- denies and minimizes the abusive incidents and their impact on her and their children (if they have any)
- starts to realize that she is not able to control his outbursts and feels powerless to stop the abuse (may appear, at times, to be "inviting" the abuse due to her desire to "get it over" and decrease the stress level that exists)
- tends to withdraw to protect herself, which only increases his frustration/irritation
- often blames herself for the abuse and becomes more and more isolated from friends and family
- with each incident, her self-esteem and self-confidence is further depleted

Explosion Phase (II)

This second phase involves a seemingly uncontrollable discharge of pent-up and accumulated tension that is actually a conscious choice to strike out at his partner to relieve stress and to control her and the situation. Choices may include time and place, weapon (e.g., open hand versus closed fist), target (e.g., assaulting only certain parts of her body), and duration (i.e., how long the incident lasts). This phase begins and ends with more serious and destructive violence than that which generally occurs during the escalation phase and has the greatest likelihood of attracting outsider (e.g., police, neighbors, relatives) involvement. Eventually, such severe emotional and verbal abuse and threats can become as devastating as the physical abuse, and violence may no longer be necessary to exert control over the woman in the relationship.

(HO)   ©1999 David J. Decker, MA

WHAT HAPPENS WITH HIM	WHAT HAPPENS WITH HER
• starts out to "teach her a lesson" to prove that he is in control of the relationship (wants to punish her for not being who he thinks she should be) • feels "out of control," full of rage, hateful, and vindictive and expresses these emotions by striking out verbally and physically • blames her for his abuse and violence (feels justified) • often surprised and scared about the intensity of his rage and the severity of the abuse • does not understand what happened or how he got so out of control and tends to deny the severity of his abuse and its impact on his partner • may believe that he has resolved the problems in the relationship with his abusive behavior • may experience enormous physiological/emotional release from perpetrating the abuse and often feels and looks calm and relaxed immediately afterward • often cannot remember or describe the incident and his abusive behavior due to his denial and shame • may blame his violence/abuse on his (or her) excessive use of alcohol/drugs • payoffs such as the stress release and control over the situation reinforce the likelihood that the violence will be repeated	• her behavior does not affect outcome, although she may be more seriously injured if she defends herself physically • views escape from the situation as futile • disassociation often occurs (i.e., she may "stand back"/detach emotionally from the abuse and watch it happen to herself) • feels terrified, hurt, humiliated, ashamed, degraded, angry, and resentful • symptoms after acute assault can include shock; disbelief; denial; minimization; anxiety; rationalization; listlessness and lethargy; feelings of hopelessness, helplessness and powerlessness; depression; and rage • often blames herself for his abusive behavior (looks for what she could do differently to experience some sense of control and power in her life) • often more able to remember and describe the violent incident in specific details • may attack the police to assist her partner or request that assault charges not be filed to demonstrate her loyalty to her partner so she can avoid further violence/abuse

Calming Phase (III)

This final phase is often referred to as the "honeymoon stage." However, it is not really a honeymoon at all. In reality, it is often a time when the man deceives himself in an attempt to convince his partner, and his partner deceives herself into believing, that the violence, control, and abuse will stop. This phase can also involve genuine remorse and shame on the part of the man due to his fear that he has gone too far in trying to assume control of the relationship. For the woman, this phase may simply be a signal that the violence is over for now. At this point, the man may also fear that his partner will leave him or involve outsiders (e.g., police, relatives) in their relationship. Because of his fear, he may "bend over backwards" to be kind, attentive, loving, and considerate, and his "model behavior" often involves mak-

(HO)   ©1999 David J. Decker, MA

ing promises about the future, buying gifts, or doing something special for his partner. His partner often desperately wants to believe the promises about how he will change and she begins to feel hope for herself and the relationship, thus solidifying her victimization. Over time, if the man does not actually seek help for himself, the promises become hollow and this phase disappears completely. For some couples, however, this phase does not even exist: the time after the explosion phase is only a short period with the temporary absence of battering and few, if any, attempts at even the kind of deception noted previously.

WHAT HAPPENS WITH HIM

- frightened by his own rage and aggressive behavior and often realizes that he has gone too far
- may express regret about his behavior and feel guilty and shameful about what he has done
- often asks for her forgiveness and vows that the abuse will never happen again (may believe violence will not be necessary because he is now "in control")
- may accept some responsibility for his behavior but his primary motivation is not to learn from or to stop the abusive behavior but rather to appease her, save their relationship, and/or avoid legal consequences
- may promise that he will change (e.g., stop using/abusing alcohol/drugs; work less or more or get a new job; give her more freedom and not act so jealous; spend more time with her and the children; cease doing other things that irritate her; stop going out with other women; stop being abusive/violent)
- may act caring, affectionate, and considerate of her and her needs (e.g., buying her flowers, candy, and other presents; taking her out on "special" dates; offering to do things for her)
- at the same time, stress begins to build once again due to his belief that he has to "bend over backwards" and to convince her to forgive him and stay with him

WHAT HAPPENS WITH HER

- terror and anger motivate her to think about leaving (wants to escape the abuse but feels fearful and guilty about going)
- struggles with her inability to control his abusive behavior but may still feel responsible in some way for his actions
- wants to believe the promises that he will change and may choose to do so, enjoying his caring and attention to her and idealizing him and their relationship, seeing once again the part of him that she loves, thus ensuring her victimization
- may also return/remain out of fear, believing that being around him is safer than not knowing where he is or what he is doing
- feels "stuck," trapped, depressed, anxious, powerless, and hopeless
- if she does not follow through with legal actions and/or decides against leaving or goes back to him, others concerned about her may become frustrated and exasperated with her and give up, once again leaving her isolated and alone

(HO)

WHAT HAPPENS WITH HIM

- may enlist children, extended family, and even friends to plead his case with her and work on her guilt about ending the relationship
- at times, encourages her to see "what she did wrong" to cause or provoke the violence
- eventually, when he also realizes that he will not stop being violent, he may stop apologizing, offering gifts, and making promises to change because he knows he will not follow through

Without consequences (e.g., legal intervention, his partner leaving), professional intervention, and the acquisition of new skills to cope with the emotional and physical stresses and the desire to control experienced in the escalation phase, these phases may continue to repeat themselves in the relationship.

Phase IA (IB, etc.) is similar to Phase I except that the stress from the first violent incident increases the overall tension level in the relationship, which means that the potential for violence to occur sooner becomes greater.

Phase IIA (IIB, etc.) is similar to Phase II, but now the type of violent behavior necessary to bring about the stress release or to control the situation may need to be even more severe or more frequent. Also since violence has already occurred in the relationship, the man's verbal/emotional abuse and threats have an even more intimidating and damaging effect.

Phase IIIA (IIIB, etc.) is similar to Phase III except that the deception phase may become shorter or disappear completely because both partners begin to realize that the violence and abuse will not end unless the man does something significantly different to change his controlling and abusive attitudes and behaviors. His apologies and promises may stop or seem more insincere as his shame about his abusiveness builds and as he increasingly denies and minimizes his responsibility for the abuse and its impact on his partner and his children.

Adapted from L. Walker, *The Battered Woman* (1979), who writes about a "Cycle of Violence" involving the "tension-building phase," the "acute battering incident," and the "calm, loving respite."

(HO)   ©1999 David J. Decker, MA

USING TIME-OUTS

The cornerstone for learning to handle explosive and volatile anger more effectively is the concept of taking a time-out when you feel yourself escalating. The time-out is an important strategy for couples whose relationship includes the potential for abuse and/or disrespect and for individuals who are feeling stressed, anxious, or frustrated in a particular situation.

Basically, using a time-out means taking a break or getting away from a situation in which you are becoming increasingly tense, uncomfortable, or angry. In essence, a time-out in human relationships is no different from a time-out in sports, which is often called because the team is not following the game plan. The time-out gives you the opportunity to step back from a distressing or difficult situation to reassess your "game plan" about who you want to be and how you wish to act at that time.

The goals in taking a time-out are to slow down your internal process, work at letting go of your tension, begin to think more clearly and realistically, and avoid feeling out of control, which can otherwise result in your becoming disrespectful, emotionally or verbally abusive, or violent (e.g., doing and saying things that, from past experience, you know you will regret later).

Steps That Will Help Couples Put the Concept of Time-Out into Practice

Discuss the concept and use of the time-out. Sit down (when you are both calm), even before you first use the time-out to talk about the guidelines you will agree to follow in using it in a respectful manner. Being respectful in this process is absolutely critical. Avoid viewing and using this as just another weapon in your arguments. Rather, start to see the time-out as a tool that can bring about more effective conflict resolution and real intimacy in the relationship.

Decide how to indicate the need for a time-out. Come to some sense of agreement on what you will say or do to communicate that you want a time-out. For example, you could say "I need some time" or "I need some space" or "I need a break," or you could use a nonverbal sign such as the "T" hand signal for a time-out in sports. Remember that directly communicating the need for a time-out is an important way to show your partner respect and to begin to reestablish trust in the relationship.

Write out and use a time-out plan. Determine the rules and guidelines that you will follow to make this a respectful and effective tool in your rela-

(HO) ©1999 David J. Decker, MA

tionship. Note aspects of the time-out such as where you will go, what you will do while you are gone, how long you will be gone, and how you will reenter the situation.

Respectfully communicate your desire for a time-out. During a disagreement, conflict, or argument, assertively and clearly tell your partner that you are beginning to feel tense and that you need some time to cool down so you can think more clearly. Let the other person know that you are not merely attempting to avoid the problem or the issue that has been raised. Avoid such statements as, "I've got to get out of here or I don't know what's going to happen," as these can easily be perceived by the other person as threats. Learn to identify and tune into your "cues" and "triggers" that can help alert you to when you are escalating and a time-out is necessary. It is also important to be specific about approximately how much time you will take before returning to discuss the issue.

Take responsibility for your own time-out. It is not someone else's responsibility to tell you that you need a time-out, nor is it up to others to keep you from being abusive or violent. Remember that the other person may not like or agree with your decision to take the time-out. Keep in mind, however, that taking a time-out when you have the potential to be explosive or abusive is a good way to take care of yourself and to communicate respect and caring to others around you (although others may not recognize this at first).

Get away from the person and/or the situation. Couples will find it most effective to leave the house or apartment completely. At a minimum, go to a previously agreed-upon place in your residence and stay separated. Avoid the temptation to get in the last word or a parting shot. Make an effort to respond respectfully to your partner even if you believe your partner is being hurtful and is trying to provoke you at this point. If at work, leave the situation to go to the bathroom or for a short walk, if possible.

Give yourself enough time. Take at least thirty minutes to one hour to de-escalate, relax, and reassert control over yourself and your emotional reactivity and defensiveness. When you become stressed and angry, the release of adrenaline and other chemicals in your body works to increase your heart rate and raise your blood pressure. Allow yourself time for these changes in your body to return to their normal state. As you practice taking your time-outs, you will get a better sense of how much time you actually need.

Actively work to calm yourself both physically and emotionally. Do this after you have left the situation. Immediately after you separate, go to a "quiet space" in your mind. This involves visualizing a place you have actually been or a place you could imagine yourself being where you can feel calm, peaceful, relaxed, and safe. This "quiet space" might be a beach near the ocean or walking in a beautiful woods. Go there in your mind at this time to de-escalate and center yourself. Avoid continuing to brood about the perceived wrongs your partner has done to you; try to think about and appreciate the other person's perspective and what he or she might be experiencing and feeling. Use positive self-talk to look at the situation in a new light. Slow down your breathing by taking deeper breaths. Go for a walk or a bike ride. Contact a friend who is supportive yet calming (not someone who's simply going to "bash" the other person). Use a combination of physical and cognitive activities to help you de-escalate. It is not recommended that you drive a vehicle during a time-out because you may escalate further as a result of encountering other drivers and because a vehicle can become a lethal weapon (for you and others) when you are feeling tense, angry, and explosive. It is also not recommended that you use alcohol or other mood-altering drugs during a time-out as these can intensify the problem.

Make a commitment to return to discuss the issue and follow through on that commitment. This will help you begin to address relationship issues, talk about your feelings with each other as they come up, and learn to resolve conflict in the relationship together. Otherwise, the time-out strategy becomes just another way to avoid and escape from the issues you and your partner need to discuss. As part of the process of returning, it is also important to ask clearly and directly if your partner is ready to talk once again. If your partner is not ready, then your time-out needs to continue until your partner communicates a desire to reconnect. If you return to the situation and again begin to escalate, take another time-out until you are able to talk about the issue with no risk of being abusive or violent.

Actively work at and practice the use of time-outs. This will help you integrate the skill into your life. However, remember to give yourself time to make this a positive tool in your life. Be patient with yourself as you are learning this new way of coping with your anger and your desire to control. Continue to practice it whenever necessary and make it an integral part of how you want to behave. This can be an enormous step in truly intervening in your controlling and abusive attitudes and behaviors and in promoting trust and intimacy in your relationships with your partner and others.

DOMESTIC ABUSE GROUP DESCRIPTION

Purpose

This is an ongoing weekly treatment group to assist men who have been explosively angry, controlling, and emotionally, verbally, and physically abusive with their wives, girlfriends, children, or others. The group involves both educational and process elements to help men learn to deal more effectively with their controlling attitudes and behaviors, their escalation patterns, and their feelings of anger, frustration, and resentment that have led to abusive behavior in the past.

Objectives

1. End the violence and the threat of violence.
2. Accept responsibility for your past violence and abuse and change your controlling attitudes and behaviors that have led to your being abusive.
3. Better understand your anger and how it affects you and others around you.
4. Identify and express more openly all the feelings that you experience.
5. Learn to deal more effectively with life stressors.
6. Actively use the group and others in your life for support and sharing as a means to lessen your emotional overdependence on your partner.
7. Examine and work on family-of-origin issues that relate to emotional, verbal, or physical abuse you experienced as a child and understand how these issues contribute to your current controlling and abusive attitudes and behaviors.
8. Address cultural issues that contribute to your current controlling and abusive attitudes and behaviors.
9. Explore, examine, and change all the ways you attempt to control others, including emotional/verbal abuse, threatening/intimidating actions, and other forms of manipulative behavior.
10. Learn to experience more control over yourself and your actions and take responsibility for your thoughts, feelings, wants, and behaviors in the present.
11. Learn and actively practice and use new skills, tools, and techniques to feel better about yourself and increase your compassion and empathy for your partner, your children, and others.

(HO)   ©1999 David J. Decker, MA

Length of Group

Men must be willing to make a minimum commitment of twenty group sessions. Most members need thirty to forty sessions to finish the group. The time it actually takes depends on how responsible you are in completing and presenting the individual tasks expected of group members.

Time and Location

_____

Intake Process

Group member assessments (usually four to six individual sessions) must be completed by the time a prospective member starts the group. If concerns about alcohol and/or drug use exist, a chemical health evaluation must be completed as well. Call _____ to set up an intake.

Fees

The cost is $_____ per session. Fees may be covered by insurance.

ESCALATION PREVENTION PLAN

Abusive anger and violence do not just happen. A gradual buildup of emotion and tension occurs over time that you will be better able to recognize if you pay closer attention to your stress level on a regular basis. Increases in tension and stress need an outlet. You may turn your stress inward on your own body, which can lead to physical illness; you might use chemicals more frequently or eat more than usual; you may spend especially long hours trying to be productive in your work setting or at home; you might lack energy, become lethargic, or feel tired much of the time; or you may lash out at someone emotionally, verbally, physically, or sexually.

Anger is a normal and natural emotion (even though it is also painful and uncomfortable) that allows you to set healthy limits and to increase the potential for intimacy, if it is expressed in an assertive and respectful manner. The purpose of this plan is to assist you in realizing when you are feeling tense, escalated, and angry and to help you find positive and constructive ways of expressing your emotions. The cue categories provided in the following material will help you pay closer attention to your stress buildup. The more awareness you have of the specific information about you and your life that fits into these categories, the greater potential you will have to moderate and intervene in the controlling, abusive, violent, and self-destructive behaviors that have been part of your anger in the past. Being aware of your cues and understanding where you are in your escalation process can help you use your Escalation Prevention Plan to find the means to de-escalate and calm yourself before you become abusive and say or do something that you will regret later.

Remember, too, that an "escalation" is not just feeling full of rage or "out of control" or behaving in an abusive manner; it is also the process of experiencing any and all feelings (e.g., anxiety, depression) and signs (e.g., hunger, increased heartbeat) that may eventually lead to controlling and abusive behavior and the potential for violence. The key to using this plan is to slow down your internal emotional arousal and to learn to effectively intervene in your escalation as early as possible. This will also allow you to communicate your anger (and your other feelings behind it) in a more calm, assertive, and respectful manner. Write out as much information as you can about your cues and your plan to take care of yourself (and the others around you) in the spaces provided after each category. *Be as specific as possible.* This task will need to be presented in group after you have filled it out completely.

(HO)   ©1999 David J. Decker, MA

Cues That Indicate When You Are Becoming Escalated, Tense, and Angry

Problem Situations and Issues

What situations and issues in your life trigger your escalation and anger (e.g., others getting angry with you, not getting your way, experiencing conflict with a co-worker, someone disagreeing with or criticizing you, your children misbehaving, being cut off on the highway)?

People/Animals

Who are the specific people or animals from the past or present with whom you are more likely to escalate when you are around them or think about them (e.g., your boss, your parents, your in-laws, your partners, former partners, your children, co-workers, family pets)? This can also include *categories of people* who are frustrating or irritating to you (e.g., slow drivers, inattentive clerks).

Places

Where do you tend to escalate most frequently (e.g., specific rooms in the house or apartment, such as the bedroom or kitchen; in the car; specific locations at work, such as your boss's office or your workstation; at bars; sports settings, such as a racquetball court or a softball diamond)?

(HO) ©1999 David J. Decker, MA

Times

What are some specific times when you are more likely to escalate?

During the day (e.g., at dinner, just before leaving for work, getting your children ready to leave in the morning, on the way to or from work)

During the week (e.g., on weekends, Sunday evenings before returning to work)

During the month (e.g., at the end of the month because you run out of money, when you write out the bills)

During the year (e.g., on specific holidays, vacations, slow times at work, particular seasons)

Self-Talk

Self-talk involves the words, phrases, and sentences that you say to yourself. The following categories illustrate different aspects of self-talk.

Negative thoughts/worries. Give general examples of when you think, brood, or "stew" about situations from the past or in the present until you become tense, angry, and controlling (e.g., thinking that your partner is going out with another man, worrying about the level of conflict in your relationship, "stewing" about not having enough money to pay all your bills, brooding about the mistakes you have made in the past, fretting about how your kids are doing).

(HO)   ©1999 David J. Decker, MA

Negative rehearsal. Give examples of when you visualize, plan for, or anticipate a negative outcome in the future, even before anything actually occurs (e.g., planning a confrontation with your partner that might not even be necessary, getting worked up over a situation that does not even necessarily turn out the way you thought it would, imagining your partner flirting with another man, thinking about yelling at your partner ahead of time).

Specific negative self-talk. What words, labels, and phrases do you think to yourself about yourself and about others that indicate when you are angry, tense, or escalated or that indicate that the potential exists for you to escalate and become controlling?

- *Thoughts about yourself* (e.g., "How can I be so stupid?" "I'm a loser," "I've screwed it up again," "I'll never get it right," "What a dummy")

- *Thoughts about others* (e.g., "Here she goes again," "Why doesn't he get off my back?" "She's really asking for it now," "She's a jerk," "He's an asshole," "I can't stand what she's doing to me")

Trigger Words/Phrases

What are some specific words and phrases that others say to you which are instantly irritating or frustrating and that you say to others which let you know that you are escalated or escalating?

Words/phrases others say to you (e.g., "Grow up," "You'll never amount to anything," "Get a life," "Screw you," "Get with it," "What's wrong with you?" "You're an abuser")

(HO)

Words/phrases you say to others (e.g., "You're crazy"; specific swear words that you say when you are escalating, such as "Get fucked" or "bitch")

Physical Signals

How does your body tell you that you are becoming angry, tense, and escalated? What happens to you physically when you are escalating (e.g., tight jaw, clenched fists, rapid breathing, heart racing, tension in your neck)?

Emotional Cues

What feelings do you experience just before and as you escalate (e.g., anger, frustration)? What feelings are hidden or covered up by your anger and escalation (e.g., hurt, sadness)?

De-Escalation Strategies

These strategies will help you to intervene in your escalation process and to deal respectfully with others when you are tense, stressed, or angry. What will you do to calm yourself and slow down your escalation process? Your strategies should be designed

1. so that you do not become controlling, intimidating, threatening, and emotionally, verbally, sexually, or physically abusive to those around you and
2. so that you can learn to communicate more effectively and respectfully with others

Remember, too, that this de-escalation section of the Escalation Prevention Plan is not just for acute escalations involving the potential for abuse, but also can and should be used for long-term preventive maintenance concerning anger, stress, and control issues in your life.

(HO)   ©1999 David J. Decker, MA

ABUSE QUESTIONNAIRE-M

Name: _____

Date: _____

1. When was the last time you became violent with property or used any kind of physical force with your partner? Describe what happened.

2. How long have you been in the relationship with your current partner?

3. How many separate incidents of being violent with property or using any kind of physical force have occurred throughout the relationship with your current partner?

4. How often have verbal blowups occurred over the course of the relationship with your current partner and/or your children? When did the last blowup occur, and what happened?

5. Have others ever told you they were concerned about how you expressed your anger or that they were afraid of or intimidated by you? If so, who told you this, and what did they say?

(HO) ©1999 David J. Decker, MA

6. On the average, how frequently did you use the following behaviors with your partner during the last year (if separated, during the last year prior to the separation)?

0: never 1: rarely 2: occasionally 3: often 4: very often 5: all the time

—— Make generalizations, support stereotypes, or tell disrespectful jokes about women around her

—— Interrupt her when she is talking

—— Feel tense, stressed, anxious, or angry when you are discussing important issues with her

—— Jump to conclusions or make assumptions about what she is saying rather than gathering more information

—— Try to get her to change her mind, to see things your way, or to convince her that you are right

—— Blame her for your feelings by saying things such as, "You're making me mad," or thinking to yourself "She's the reason I get so pissed" (rather than using "I" language and taking responsibility for what you are feeling)

—— Act critical and judgmental about her thoughts, ideas, opinions, and feelings

—— Blame her when things go wrong (e.g., around the house, in the relationship, with the children, with finances)

—— Blame her for your abuse and violence (e.g., saying "I wouldn't have grabbed you if you wouldn't have . . ." or thinking to yourself "She just keep pushing my buttons")

—— Stomp out in the middle of an argument (*not* taking a respectful time-out)

—— Follow her around and not allow her to stop talking about a conflict

—— Listen in on her phone conversations

—— Look for her/follow her when she leaves the house

—— Sulk or withdraw into silence (How long? _____)

—— Glare/stare at her when you are angry

—— Insult or belittle her (e.g., with put-downs, name-calling)

—— Insult or belittle other people she cares about (e.g., her friends, her parents)

—— Raise your voice, yell, or scream at or around her

—— Swear or curse at or around her

(HO)   ©1999 David J. Decker, MA

7. How many significant relationships with partners have you had over the course of your life? What were their first names and how long did the relationship last? Were you emotionally/verbally abusive, physically abusive, or sexually abusive in these relationships? (Specify)

8. How many times have you behaved in the following ways during the entire course of the relationship with your current partner and with your past partner(s)?

— — Interrupt her while she is eating or sleeping (e.g., waking her up to "finish" an argument)

— — Tell her that you do not want her leaving or spending time with specific people

— — Verbally or emotionally pressure her to have sex or perform sexual acts with which she feels uncomfortable

— — Make threats to go out or be sexual with other women, withhold money from her, leave or get a divorce, or take the children away from her

— — Stand near or over her in an intimidating manner (e.g., "getting in her face")

— — Make verbal or nonverbal threats to hurt her

(Give examples: _____)

— — Make verbal or nonverbal threats to hurt or kill yourself

(Give examples: _____)

— — Stand in her way, block her, or "corner" her to keep her from going somewhere

— — Slam your hand or fist on surfaces or hit a wall or a door

(Give examples: _____)

— — Throw, kick, or destroy household objects and personal property

(Give examples: _____)

(HO)   ©1999 David J. Decker, MA

__ __ Unplug/rip out the phone or tamper with the car to keep her from somewhere

__ __ Hit/kick/throw/hurt family pets or other animals

__ __ Drive recklessly when you are angry and she is in the car with you

__ __ Grab, pat, or pinch her breasts or butt when she does not want you to do this

__ __ Spit at or on her

__ __ Pinch her (nonsexual parts of her body)

__ __ Poke her with your finger "to make a point" (e.g., in her arm or chest)

__ __ Bump into her (e.g., to "give her a message" as you walk by)

__ __ Trip her

__ __ Scratch or bite her

__ __ Rip or tear her clothing

__ __ Throw something at her or in her direction

__ __ Push or shove her

__ __ Grab her (e.g., by the face, by the arm)

__ __ Shake her

__ __ Physically restrain her (e.g., wrapping your arms around her to control her)

__ __ Pull her hair

__ __ Throw her around (e.g., onto the floor, a couch, a bed)

__ __ Kick her

__ __ Sit on top of her

__ __ Slap her with an open hand

(Where? _____)

__ __ Punch her with a closed fist

(Where? _____)

__ __ Physically force her to have sex

__ __ Hit her in the stomach when she is pregnant

__ __ Burn her (e.g., with a cigarette, a lighter, or a match)

(HO)   ©1999 David J. Decker, MA

— — Choke or strangle her (e.g., putting your hands near or on her throat and squeezing)

— — Beat her until she passes out

— — Threaten her with an object or weapon (e.g., broom, hammer, shovel, baseball bat, knife, gun), including "playing with" a weapon or discharging a gun around her

(Give examples: _____)

— — Use any object or weapon on her

(Give examples: _____)

— — Hit or hurt yourself

(Give examples: _____)

— — Attempt to commit suicide

(Give examples: _____)

- Have you used any other physical force with partners that was not described above?

- What kind of physical force or discipline have you used with the children? If you have done this, what was done and to whom, how often was it done, and when was the last time it was done?

9. When did the most violent or worst abusive incident occur with your current and past partner(s) and what happened (i.e., the time when you did the most damage, you felt the most out of control, and/or she [or they] felt the most frightened)?

(HO)   ©1999 David J. Decker, MA

10. Are you now or have you ever been involved with the legal system as a result of your violence with your partners or others (e.g., police calls, restraining orders, assault or disorderly conduct charges, spending time in jail)?

11. Have your partners or children ever needed medical treatment as a result of your violence? If so, when and for what?

12. Have you used physical force with other partners besides those noted on the previous page? If so, give examples of when this occurred and what happened.

13. How often have verbal blowups occurred with strangers, acquaintances, friends, co-workers, parents, siblings, relatives, or others throughout the course of your life? Give examples of when this has occurred and what happened.

14. Have you used physical force in the past with strangers, acquaintances, friends, co-workers, parents, siblings, relatives, or others as a child or as an adult? If so, give examples of when this occurred and what happened.

15. How frequently (give a percentage) has chemical use coincided with when you were violent (with your current partner or others)?

- Do you think your violence is related to your chemical use? In what way?

- Have others expressed concerns about your chemical use at any time? If so, who expressed concerns and what were their concerns?

- Do you have concerns about your own chemical use? If so, what are they?

Parts of this questionnaire are adapted from ideas in the Conflict Tactics (CT) Scales (Straus, Gelles, and Steinmetz, 1980).

(HO)   ©1999 David J. Decker, MA

ABUSE QUESTIONNAIRE-W

Name: _____

Date: _____

1. When was the last time your partner became violent with property or used any kind of physical force with you? Describe what happened.

2. How long have you been in the relationship with your current partner?

3. How many separate incidents of your partner's being violent with property or using any kind of physical force have occurred throughout the relationship?

4. How often have verbal blowups occurred over the course of the relationship between you and your current partner or between your partner and your children? When did the last blowup occur, and what happened?

5. Have you ever felt afraid of or intimidated by your partner? If so, when? Did you communicate this to him in anyway?

6. On the average, how frequently did your partner behave in the following ways toward you during the last year (if separated, during the last year prior to the separation)?

   0: never 1: rarely 2: occasionally 3: often 4: very often 5: all the time

___ Make generalizations, support stereotypes, or tell disrespectful jokes about women around you

___ Interrupt you when you are talking

___ Feel tense, stressed, anxious, or angry when he is discussing important issues with you

___ Jump to conclusions or make assumptions about what you are saying rather than gathering more information

___ Try to get you to change your mind, to see things his way, or to convince you that he is right

___ Blame you for his feelings by saying things such as, "You're making me mad," or "You really piss me off" (rather than using "I" language and taking responsibility for what he is feeling)

___ Act critical and judgmental about your thoughts, ideas, opinions, and feelings

___ Blame you when things go wrong (e.g., around the house, in the relationship, with the children, with finances)

___ Blame you for his abuse and violence (e.g., saying "I wouldn't have grabbed you if you wouldn't have . . ." or "You just keep pushing my buttons")

___ Stomp out in the middle of an argument (*not* taking a respectful time-out)

___ Follow you around and not allow you to stop talking about a conflict

___ Listen in on your phone conversations

___ Look for you/follow you when you leave the house

___ Sulk or withdraw into silence (How long? _____)

___ Glare/stare at you when he is angry

___ Insult or belittle you (e.g., with put-downs, name-calling)

___ Insult or belittle other people you care about (e.g., your friends, your parents)

___ Raise his voice, yell, or scream at or around you

___ Curse at or around you

(HO)   ©1999 David J. Decker, MA

7. How many times did your partner use the following behaviors during the entire course of the relationship?

___ Interrupt you while you are eating or sleeping (e.g., waking you up to finish an argument)

___ Tell you that he does not want you leaving or spending time with specific people

___ Verbally or emotionally pressure you to have sex or perform sexual acts with which you feel uncomfortable

___ Make threats to go out or be sexual with other women, withhold money from you, leave you or get a divorce, or take the children away from you

___ Stand near or over you in an intimidating manner (e.g., "getting in your face")

___ Make verbal or nonverbal threats to hurt you

(Give examples: _____)

___ Make verbal or nonverbal threats to hurt or kill himself

(Give examples: _____)

___ Stand in your way, block you, or "corner" you to keep you from going somewhere

___ Slam his hand or fist on surfaces or hit a wall or a door

(Give examples: _____)

___ Throw, kick, or destroy household objects and personal property

(Give examples: _____)

___ Unplug/rip out the phone or tamper with the car to keep you from going somewhere

___ Hit/kick/throw/hurt family pets or other animals

___ Drive recklessly when he is angry and you are in the car with him

___ Grab, pat, or pinch your breasts or butt when you do not want him to do this

___ Spit at or on you

___ Pinch you (nonsexual parts of your body)

___ Poke you with his finger "to make a point" (e.g., in your arm or chest)

___ Bump into you (e.g., to "give you a message" as he walks by)

___ Trip you

—— Scratch or bite you

—— Rip or tear your clothing

—— Throw something at you or in your direction

—— Push or shove you

—— Grab you (e.g., by the face, by the arm)

—— Shake you

—— Physically restrain you (e.g., wrapping his arms around you to control you)

—— Pull your hair

—— Throw you around (e.g., onto the floor, a couch, or a bed)

—— Kick you

—— Sit on top of you

—— Slap you with an open hand

(Where? _____)

—— Punch you with a closed fist

(Where? _____)

—— Physically force you to have sex

—— Hit you in the stomach when you are pregnant

—— Burn you (e.g., with a cigarette, a lighter, or a match)

—— Choke or strangle you (e.g., putting his hands near or on your throat and squeezing)

—— Beat you until you pass out

—— Threaten you with an object or weapon (e.g., broom, hammer, shovel, baseball bat, knife, gun), including "playing with" a weapon or discharging a gun around you

(Give examples: _____)

—— Use any object or weapon on you

(Give examples: _____)

—— Hit or hurt himself

(Give examples: _____)

—— Attempt to commit suicide

(Give examples: _____)

(HO)   ©1999 David J. Decker, MA

- Has he used any other physical force with you that was not described above?

- What kind of physical force or discipline has he used with the children? If he has done this, what was done and to whom, how often was it done, and when was the last time it was done?

8. When did the most violent or worst abusive incident occur and what happened (i.e., the time when your partner did the most damage to you, you felt he was the most out of control, and/or you felt the most frightened)?

9. Is your partner now or has he ever been involved with legal system as a result of his violence with you or others (e.g., police calls, restraining orders, assault or disorderly conduct charges, spending time in jail)?

©1999 David J. Decker, MA

10. Have you or the children ever needed medical treatment as a result of your violence? If so, when and for what?

11. Has he ever, to your knowledge, used physical force with previous partners? If possible, give examples of when this occurred and what happened.

12. How often has your partner had verbal blowups with strangers, acquaintances, friends, co-workers, parents, siblings, relatives, or others throughout the course of his life? If possible, give examples of when this occurred and what happened.

13. Has he ever, to your knowledge, used physical force in the past with strangers, acquaintances, friends, co-workers, parents, siblings, relatives, or others as a child or as an adult? If possible, give examples of when this occurred and what happened.

14. How frequently (give a percentage) has his chemical use coincided with when he was violent (with you or others)?

- Do you think his violence is related to his chemical use? If so, in what way?

- Have you or others expressed concerns about his chemical use at any time? If so, who expressed concerns, and what were your or their concerns?

- Do you currently have concerns about his chemical use? If so, what are they?

15. Have you ever been violent with your partner? Give examples. How do you discipline your children? Do you have concerns about how you express your anger with him, your children, or others? If so, what are your concerns?

16. How often has your chemical use coincided with his violent episodes? Do you have concerns about your own chemical use?

17. Have previous partners been violent and/or abusive with you? If so, give examples.

Parts of this questionnaire are adapted from ideas in the Conflict Tactics (CT) Scales (Straus, Gelles, and Steinmetz, 1980).

SAFETY PLAN

The goal of this plan is to help you care for yourself and take responsibility for your safety in situations in which domestic violence could potentially occur. We know from research and experience that battering often repeats itself and intensifies, and emotional and verbal abuse frequently escalates to physical and sexual abuse. A safety plan gives you concrete ways to protect yourself (and your children, if you have any): first, it helps you to become aware of signs that usually precede your partner's violent actions, and second, it enables you to become familiar with using personal and community resources available to you. Your need to be aware of your partner's cues does not imply in any way that you are responsible for the abuse or violence he perpetrates. A safety plan should address the following questions and concerns:

1. What warning signals (cues) do you sense or notice in your partner that indicate you might be in danger (e.g., your partner's actions, what your partner says, how your partner appears when he is escalating)?

2. What are some of your own internal warning signs (cues) that indicate you might be afraid, tense, or in danger (e.g., your behaviors, your thoughts, your physical or emotional responses)?

3. What are some of the external circumstances or stressors that could lead to an explosive situation (e.g., his or your chemical use, financial pressures, issues with the children, time of day, location in the house or elsewhere, problems with relatives)?

(HO)   ©1999 David J. Decker, MA

4. How have you protected yourself and your children from being hurt in the past? How effective do you think these efforts have been? How have you survived in this relationship?

5. The following are people and organizations that you can turn to for help (list names and phone numbers):

   a. PERSONAL

      • Friends:
      • Relatives:
      • Neighbors:
      • Counselor/Clergyperson:
      • Support Group Members:

   b. CRISIS LINE(S)

   c. SHELTER(S)/CRISIS CENTER(S)

   d. MEDICAL

      • Hospital/Emergency Room:
      • Health Care Provider:
      • Emergency Services (911):

   e. LEGAL

      • Police (911):
      • Legal Advocates:
      • Order for Protection Information/Phone Number (for your county):
      • Attorney:

6. Other issues to consider:

   a. Hide your safety plan somewhere your partner cannot find it.
   b. Be aware of escape routes from your home or apartment (doors, windows).
   c. Get extra sets of car and house keys and keep them in a safe place (*not* in your purse).
   d. Talk to family, friends, or neighbors ahead of time about coming to stay with them.
   e. Pack a small overnight bag (with clothing, medication, etc.) that can be ready on short notice; include your children's needs, and keep the bag someplace safe (e.g., at work or at a friend's house).
   f. Think about transportation options (e.g., bus schedules/contacting cabs) in case you do not have a car or are unable to use it.
   g. Hide some easily accessible cash for necessary expenses (e.g., for food or a motel).
   h. Keep money on your person at all times for emergency phone calls.
   i. Arrange for a place to stay (e.g., a friend's or relative's house) in advance in case you need to leave quickly.
   j. Try to remove firearms and/or ammunition from the home (store them elsewhere or get rid of them).

CHAPTER III:
THE INDIVIDUAL MEMBER TASKS

Part 1: Facilitating
the Individual Member Tasks

HOW TO HELP GROUP MEMBERS
GET THE MOST OUT OF THE TASKS

This chapter discusses the individual member tasks that each member is expected to complete to fulfill the requirements of the domestic abuse group. Each man, at the end of the individual intake sessions, is given a group booklet that outlines his responsibilities in participating in the group. Ten individual member tasks must be written out and presented in the group by all participants. In addition, two other tasks may be included as part of a man's program if he is violent (see "Task XI: Violent Incident Assessment" in this chapter) or if he uses alcohol or drugs when he has agreed to abstain (see "Task XII: Violation of Sobriety Contract Assessment" in this chapter) during his involvement in treatment. The entire Domestic Abuse Group Member Booklet, which includes these tasks and other information given to prospective members, is included in Part 2 of this chapter.

Tasks are presented in a step-by-step fashion. The Introduction, the Exercise Program, and the Individual Member Goals are written out prior to a man's starting the group and are presented the first night he attends. The Aftercare Plan and Final Feedback task is discussed his final night in group. The remaining tasks are presented in the sequence illustrated in this chapter as they are completed.

When a man has completed a task, it is his responsibility to ask for time to present the task during the ten- to fifteen-minute check-in at the beginning of group. When men take time in group, they generally speak for twenty minutes and then receive five minutes of feedback from other members about what they have presented. The members of the group monitor who takes time and when they take it and announce when the twenty minutes of time and five minutes of feedback are over.

Understandably, some men take longer to write out the tasks and to ask for time to present them than others. This is one way that the group can be adapted to individual men's needs, levels of motivation, and abilities and one reason why some men finish group in the minimum twenty sessions and some men need much more time.

The group facilitator's ongoing responsibility in this process is to listen to what is presented, ask questions to clarify when necessary, and offer comments and feedback about the specificity, completeness, and overall quality of the man's effort as the man is presenting the task. It is also the facilitator's responsibility to decide whether a man has done an adequate job of addressing the issues raised in each task. If a task is done poorly, the facilitator needs to ask the man to rewrite and re-present it. This part of Chapter III provides an overview of the twelve individual member tasks. The actual tasks that men are expected to complete and present in group are included in Part 2 of this chapter.

TASK I: INTRODUCTION

Task Objectives

1. To openly and honestly acknowledge to other men that he has been emotionally, verbally, and physically abusive with his partner and others and to discuss specific examples of this abusive behavior
2. To begin to acknowledge and understand the consequences of his being abusive
3. To openly acknowledge to the group if alcohol and drug use have been a problem for him in his life
4. To openly acknowledge to the group if he is currently experiencing suicidal thoughts
5. To begin to reduce the shame and alienation that is associated with his abuse and violence by starting to talk about it and by realizing that he is not alone in having been abusive
6. To decrease his emotional isolation by developing an emotional support system through beginning to take the risk to share important parts of who he is with other men
7. To begin to share emotions other than anger with men in group
8. To begin to identify and acknowledge positive aspects of his character
9. To begin the process of learning to listen to and hear feedback from other people

Task Description

Most men who come into the group are apprehensive and resistant, to say the least. But because of the preparation that occurs in the intake and because they have gone through a difficult process even to be admitted to the group, men generally do not come into the group with an openly belligerent attitude. In addition, they are often given, in their first group session, strong and positive messages about the helpfulness of the program by the men already in the group, all at different stages in their own treatment process. This is a significant advantage of having an open-ended and ongoing rather than a closed-ended group. An ongoing group also discourages much of the overt acting out that is frequently seen in the early stages of many closed-ended batterers' programs, in which the peer culture is often negative.

The group check-in process is explained by another member and occurs prior to the new member taking time to introduce himself. Part of this check-in involves other men sharing why they are in group and what they are working on in the program. This is a time when testimonials are likely to occur about the benefits of the group and the positive impact it is having on other members' relationships with their partners and on their own self-esteem. This positive peer culture quickly fosters the idea that the group can be a valuable learning experience and defuses the notion that this is simply another place where men can practice their controlling and abusive attitudes and behaviors.

The Introduction task asks men to comment on why they are in group and what they want to learn from their treatment involvement. Men are expected to be specific in their description of the reasons they are there and to relate specific incidents of emotional, verbal, and physical abuse they have perpetrated. This is especially important because it immediately decreases the shame that is generally associated with being a batterer. The new member hears others mention their violence and this opens the door for him to do likewise. If he does not bring up his violence, he needs to be reminded by the therapist that this is the primary reason he has come to the group.

Men are also asked to discuss the consequences associated with their abuse, including whether they have been court-ordered to the program (about 60 percent of the clients over the years have been court-ordered). If court-ordered, they are expected to discuss the incident for which they were arrested and the details of their legal involvement. This helps clearly indicate to the "voluntary" (i.e., non-court-mandated) clients and to the man himself that battering does have legal consequences, which also serve as additional motivators for all group members. Appealing to a man's self-interest (e.g., avoiding jail and other punishment) is critical because most abusers initially have little empathy for their victims and little understanding of the impact their abusive behavior has had on others.

In addition, men are asked whether they have signed a Sobriety Contract. If they have, they are encouraged to discuss how chemical use has been a part of their abusive behavior and their lives. A majority of the members either view themselves as chemically dependent or have agreed to a Sobriety Contract during their involvement in the program. This is another important way that men in the domestic abuse group can relate to one another's experiences because many are also involved with Alcoholics Anonymous or other self-help programs connected to their chemical abuse.

Men are also asked to discuss whether they have signed a No-Suicide Contract. If they have, they are encouraged to address how their suicidal thinking and depressive symptoms are affecting them in the present and whether they have used threats of suicide as part of their controlling and abusive behavior with their partner in the past. At this point, men are encouraged to use other members for emotional support rather than expecting their partners to be there for them.

Another part of the Introduction is the expectation that the man will provide a phone number where he can be reached throughout the course of the group. Most provide both their home and work numbers. We ask men to initiate and make at least one phone call per week for the duration of the group. Most men make two to three calls each week. Whether a man actually does this is monitored during the check-in at the beginning of each group.

The expectation regarding phone calls directly addresses abusive men's tendency to emotionally isolate themselves from everyone except their partners. The goal here is to build an emotional support system so that the man can begin to actively interact with other men and to talk about his past abuse, discuss current escalations, and emotionally connect with other men, often for the first time in his life. In addition, this expectation directly addresses his emotional overdependence on his partner and his frustration over the times when she is unavailable to meet his needs. During the first week in group, the new member can expect that all the other group members will contact him by phone. After the first week, each man needs to initiate and complete at least one phone call to another member in the group. After being in group for a period of time, most men make two to three calls per week and begin to count on and use other members for support in a way they have never previously experienced.

Finally, men are asked to identify one positive aspect of their character. For some men, this is a difficult proposition. Their self-esteem is often low and they frequently tend to feel shame about their abusive behavior and their involvement with the courts and a domestic abuse program. As a result, they have difficulty pinpointing anything positive about who they are. This question does need to be answered, however, and the therapist should encourage an answer despite the discomfort that some men experience in offering one. The reality is that abusive men need to raise their self-esteem. People who truly possess high self-esteem are not disrespectful, abusive, and controlling with others. Abusive men need to begin to recognize positive aspects of their character and to build on their strengths and competencies if the battering behavior and the attitudes behind it are going to change.

The last part of this task for the new member is to listen to questions and feedback from other men. This is his first attempt at truly hearing how others react to what he has said and how he presents himself. Even at this point, other members frequently point out blaming and justifying stances that he has demonstrated in the Introduction process.

When given feedback at this early point, most men try to respond and explain why the feedback does not "fit." This offers an immediate opportunity for the therapist or the other members to remind the man about the importance of intervening in his defensiveness and argumentativeness, taking in the feedback, and thinking about what the feedback may have to teach him. This is the first time in the group when he is directly asked to stop talking and simply listen to what is being said to him.

TASK II: EXERCISE PROGRAM

Task Objectives

1. To commit to, and follow through with, a regular nonviolent, noncompetitive, and aerobic exercise program as a means
   - to manage ongoing day-to-day and longer-term life stresses more effectively and
   - to assist in handling acute escalations when they arise
2. To begin the process of becoming accountable to his group in this and other aspects of the program

Task Description

This task reinforces the idea of broader life change as an integral part of the domestic abuse program, and it should be presented in the first group the man attends. It focuses on the expectation that he set up and follow through with a regular exercise program during his group involvement that is *nonviolent* (no hitting, striking, or kicking motions), *noncompetitive* (no activities that have the potential to increase the man's stress level through competition), and *aerobic* (activities that raise the heart rate to allow for the release of endorphins and to encourage stress reduction). Examples of this type of exercise include walking, jogging, swimming, biking, cross-country skiing, weightlifting, exercycling, and roller blading.

Men are asked to do their exercise regimen three times a week for at least twenty minutes at a time. The expectations of this task do not mean that men cannot also participate in contact (e.g., football, hockey) or competitive (basketball, softball) sports during their time in group. However, these kinds of activities would not suffice for the group's purposes. The exercise program does not allow men to include activities they do at work (e.g., physical labor for a construction worker, walking for a mail carrier) to fulfill the expectations regarding exercise. It is recommended that men exercise by themselves or with male friends rather than planning to exercise with their partner or their children to decrease the potential for escalation during their exercise time.

The benefits of regular aerobic exercise are well known. Research has shown that people who build an ongoing exercise program into their lives increase their self-esteem and can more readily adjust to life stresses and challenges as they arise (Davis, Eshelman, and McKay, 1989; Raglin and Morgan, 1985). For men in the group, this type of exercise serves as "preventive maintenance" when done on a consistent basis by decreasing their daily buildup of tension. Exercise is especially helpful because abusive men are escalated much of the time.

In addition, the Exercise Program task gives men a positive option to assist them in handling an acute escalation. For example, a man may adapt the habit of going for a walk during a time-out after leaving an argument. It also sets up a situation in which men give themselves the "gift" of taking time for themselves over the course of the week. Most men report that engaging in a regimen of structured and regular exercise becomes an important part of their overall recovery process. The Exercise Program also serves as another example of setting a goal and following through. Thus, it stands as another sign of their commitment to themselves, to the program, and to other men in the group.

The accountability regarding the exercise program occurs during check-in when each man relates whether he has accomplished the expected exercise for the week. Occasionally, resistance to committing to an exercise program or an unwillingness to follow through on a weekly basis becomes an issue for men in the group. A problem in this area is often indicative of a broader problem with being an active and involved participant in the program. A failure to follow through in this area could be grounds for termination from the group, although, as yet, no one has ever been terminated for this issue.

TASK III: INDIVIDUAL MEMBER GOALS

Task Objectives

1. To acknowledge and accept the general group goals for all members
2. To identify and present at least three to four specific behavioral goals that he wishes to achieve in his treatment as a means of making a personal commitment to the group process
3. To make a clear and unequivocal commitment to being nonviolent with his partner, his children (if he has any), and others in his life
4. To recognize the potential danger that firearms pose in any domestic abuse situation and to agree to remove firearms from his residence and store them elsewhere for the duration of his group therapy

Task Description

This task, which is also presented by the man in his initial session in group, has two important purposes. The first is to acknowledge and accept the five major group goals for all members, which include working to intervene in current abusive and violent behavior, accepting full responsibility for past abuse, examining and changing controlling attitudes and behaviors, actively using the group for sharing and support, and working at improving his self-esteem and increasing his ability to feel compassion and empathy for his partner and others. The second is to delineate and present to the group at least three to four specific behavioral goals that he wishes to achieve in the treatment process.

Examples of members' goals might include the following:

- To become aware of my negative/vengeful self-talk and to decrease the frequency of those episodes
- To take respectful time-outs when I am escalated
- To identify and express all my feelings respectfully and assertively
- To increase the frequency of episodes of listening to my partner and others
- To increase the frequency of nonabusive parenting responses with my children

- To identify and decrease the frequency of my controlling behaviors with my partner and my children
- To increase my assertive (versus aggressive) communications with my partner
- To develop and use positive conflict resolution skills in my relationship
- To increase my awareness of cues and triggers that indicate that I am escalating
- To develop and maintain an emotional support system of other men

For a member, setting his own goals will help him to make a personal commitment to the group program. In addition, these goals give him some guideposts by which he can assess his progress throughout the group. The goals are especially important in his Midgroup Evaluation and Aftercare Plan and Final Feedback tasks, for which he is asked to comment on how well he has accomplished what he set out to do in the domestic abuse treatment program. After he presents his goals, other group members are asked to offer feedback about the specificity of what he has shared and the goals' relevance to his reasons for being in a domestic abuse program.

Other significant parts of this task include making a clear and unequivocal commitment to being nonviolent and acknowledging to himself and the group the potential danger that exists regarding firearms in a domestic abuse situation. This latter issue is addressed by a man agreeing to, and following through with, removing guns from his residence and storing them elsewhere for the duration of his treatment. The firearms issue can become problematic for hunters or even target shooters, and there are few ways to monitor whether he has removed the guns from his home. However, the importance of doing this must be stressed. If he is not honest about this issue and his dishonesty is discovered, this becomes a therapeutic issue and needs to be addressed in group. The man is asked to sign and date this task, and a copy is made for his chart.

TASK IV: ESCALATION PREVENTION PLAN

Task Objectives

1. To accept that a gradual buildup of external and internal stresses occurs that can result in a desire to control and in abusive behavior and to give up the ideas that violence and abuse just happen and that he is somehow out of control

2. To identify specific external and internal cues and triggers that signal this escalation and the potential for becoming controlling, violent, and abusive
3. To identify a specific de-escalation plan, including concrete ideas and behaviors that will assist him in interrupting his escalation and decreasing his potential to become controlling and abusive
4. To begin to recognize and acknowledge his patterns of controlling attitudes toward others that set the stage for abusive and violent behavior
5. To begin to realize that he is able to make conscious choices about his reactions to what occurs within and outside of him
6. To slow down his thought process in order to become more aware of the negative self-talk and its impact on his moods, escalation, and abusive behavior and to make it "public" to decrease the power it has had in the past
7. To become more cognizant of the emotions that his anger tends to hide from his awareness
8. To decrease the shame he experiences about his escalation and his potential to be controlling and abusive
9. To begin to take clear and full responsibility for his thoughts, feelings, behaviors, and wants

Task Description

The Escalation Prevention Plan (EPP) is part of the early homework in the intake sessions. At that point, it is used to assess a man's level of motivation and to gain a sense of whether he understands how stressors in his life can contribute to an escalation that leads to controlling and abusive behavior. The EPP serves as the foundation for the entire program. Most men come to treatment saying, "I just go off," ". . . and then, I went ballistic," or "I just went nuts," with the belief that their explosive anger and their abusive behavior just happen and are beyond their ability to control.

Overall, these men have little, if any, awareness of their usual level of escalation or of the gradual process that triggers their use of verbal or physical abuse with a partner or others (Edleson and Tolman, 1992). They are men who usually deny or minimize both the trivial and major stresses in their lives, especially those which are not related directly to their partners. They also have limited knowledge about how these stresses affect their moods and emotional well-being. They are often oversensitive and overreactive to people and situations around them rather than looking inward at their self-talk, expectations, assumptions, and perceptions and how these influence their moods and escalations.

The purpose of the EPP is to help them slow their internal processes and self-observe to identify all the external and internal cues and triggers that help signal this gradual buildup of stress within them. This opens up the possibility that they will be more alert to their potential to become controlling and abusive at a particular time. Such self-monitoring is critical in beginning to intervene in their escalations (Kazdin, 1974; Edleson and Tolman, 1992).

The Escalation Prevention Plan is divided into eight discrete categories of cues. Offering separate categories helps men impose some structure on what otherwise is often an overwhelming and confusing barrage of situational, emotional, and cognitive stimuli. These categories include problem situations and issues, people, places, times, self-talk, trigger words and phrases, physical signals, and emotions. The EPP explains what these categories are and gives examples of relevant cues. For each of these categories, men are asked to think of specific examples of situations in their own lives in which they have noticed stress, tension, anxiety, irritation, frustration, anger, and other feelings. It is emphasized that any and all feelings can contribute to an escalation that ends in controlling or abusive behavior. Men are also asked to note cues both inside and outside their primary relationships because they especially tend to minimize the impact of nonrelationship stressors on their potential to escalate.

As men add items to the EPP, cross-references are made among the categories, giving them more specifics for each one. For example, if one of the daily Times cues is "at 7 a.m. when I get my children ready for school," then "getting the kids ready for school" becomes a Situation cue and "the kids" become a People cue. In addition, negative self-talk may be associated with this situation (e.g., "Those damn kids are always running late.").

Some of what is discussed in the EPP (e.g., situations such as "when my partner yells at me" or "when my partner criticizes me") could be considered blaming in another context in the group because the focus is on his partner, not on what he is feeling or thinking. However, cues in the EPP are not considered blaming, nor confronted as such, because they do, in fact, represent an actual situation that triggers the man's escalation, and it is important for him to start to notice cues such as these.

Clearly recognizing negative self-talk in the Self-Talk section of the EPP is especially important for men in group. This is due to the importance of cognitive processes in the potential to dramatically increase the likelihood of controlling and abusive behavior if they go unnoticed and unheeded (Edleson, 1984). Men are strongly encouraged to be completely honest about their self-talk and trigger words and phrases, including identifying and "making public" any of the abusive and disrespectful words that they think or say about others and themselves. Verbalizing the curse and swear words (e.g., "bitch," "cunt," "asshole") in a public arena in a matter-of-fact and detached manner tends to diminish the power that these words would otherwise hold, either when screamed at a partner or when said to himself. Bringing up the "dirty little secrets" and discussing them in group also allows a man to look at whether this is really how he wants to talk about someone he says he loves.

A critical part of beginning to notice stresses, as mentioned previously, is for the man to realize that the escalation process can include any and all signals and feelings that affect his sense of well-being. Thus, an escalation could be triggered by not only feeling angry with a situation or person, but also feeling sad, inadequate, incompetent, or anxious. Because of his lack of social support and his difficulty in addressing most of the feelings he experiences, any emotional response could be a part of, and contribute to, an eventual escalation to control, abuse, and violence. Identifying nonanger emotional reactions in their lives is especially helpful because these men tend to use their anger as an "umbrella" to cover and hide other feelings that they experience (McKay, Rogers, and McKay, 1989).

The final section of the EPP includes de-escalation strategies that outline what the man will do differently to interrupt his escalation process and respond in a more positive, respectful, and nonabusive manner. The cornerstone of this section is the time-out (Bach and Wyden, 1970). When using a time-out, a man makes a commitment to leave a frustrating or difficult situation for a period of time to calm himself physically and emotionally. This is a time to rethink the situation or issue at hand. Men are encouraged to be as creative as possible in devising de-escalation strategies for themselves. It is also recommended that they call other members to discuss what strategies others have used and to think back to previous times in their own lives when they may have had some more positive ways of handling their stress and anger. For a list of some of the ideas that men in group have used, see "Escalation Prevention Plan De-Escalation Strategies" in Part 2 of Chapter IV.

Men are asked to present this task in group after it has been completely written out. They then need to listen to feedback from the other members and the therapists. Feedback generally focuses on the specificity of the cues and the de-escalation strategies (versus being rambling, overgeneral, and tangential). It also targets whether major stress areas (e.g., work) have been short-changed or ignored completely. Finally, feedback addresses whether the EPP is complete and whether the man understands that an escalation process does, in fact, exist. Men are strongly encouraged to continue adding to the EPP throughout their involvement in the group and into the future. This is their "game plan" for reacting differently and becoming less abusive and controlling.

In offering feedback for this task, other men in group often point out patterns of controlling attitudes and behaviors directed toward the member's partner and others that are clear from his cues. At this point, the man is asked to begin to take clear responsibility for his thoughts, feelings, and wants and, due to his increased recognition of cues, to start to react differently and nonabusively in response to these triggers.

It is strongly emphasized that, although these may be the "buttons" his partner and others "push" (this is often used as an excuse to erupt), it is he who is completely in charge of whether an "explosion" occurs. A metaphor used to describe this process is the relationship between a puppet and a puppeteer: the man becomes a "puppet" to his partner and others by giving them control over who he can be and how he acts in a particular situation. In the end, it is he who is responsible for controlling and abusive behavior that arises from the cues he has identified.

The EPP is especially important because it highlights the idea that a man is making choices throughout an escalation, up to and including the point at which he becomes controlling and abusive. Men note numerous times when they are escalated but make a clear decision not to become abusive or violent (e.g., at work or in a public setting). This dramatically illustrates that men are not out of control and can make more positive choices even when they feel controlling or explosive. We ask men to build on this competency and the decision-making process it involves and to extend this process to their relationships with their partner and others. Recognizing the concept of choice in human behavior makes it significantly more difficult to maintain destructive behavior (Ellis, 1970; Novaco, 1975).

TASK V: TIME-OUT PLAN

Task Objectives

1. To realize and acknowledge that he has the ability to make the conscious choice to leave any situation in which he notices himself escalating
2. To begin to differentiate the intensity of his cues and triggers
3. To establish a specific plan to leave a variety of real-life situations in which he is escalating and has the potential to be controlling and abusive
4. To learn to communicate assertively and respectfully when he is leaving a situation and when he is returning

5. To learn to respect his partner's own desire for time-outs and to respect her wishes regarding reconnecting with him and discussing the issue that precipitated the need for a time-out
6. To identify people, activities, and thoughts that are both calming and escalating during the time-out period
7. To begin to take full and complete responsibility for leaving situations in which he experiences himself escalating
8. To make a commitment to himself and his group that he will actively use the time-out procedure to intervene in his escalations and to decrease the potential for abuse and violence in the future

Task Description

The concept of taking a respectful time-out is a cornerstone of effective anger management, whether violence is an issue or not (Bach and Wyden, 1970). A time-out involves getting away from a situation in which a man is becoming tense, uncomfortable, or angry and returning later when he has calmed down to readdress the issue that precipitated the time-out. This becomes especially important when violence has been present in a relationship because the potential consequences of staying in a volatile situation are so much greater.

This concept is presented in the first session of the intake process. At that time, the man is encouraged to discuss the Using Time-Outs handout with his partner, when both of them are calm, as a means of introducing her to this recommended tool for beginning to manage conflict. He is also asked to tell her that she has the right to take a time-out as well, if she is feeling in danger or if she is becoming angry, and he is encouraged to respect her taking her own time-outs.

A man's most frequent complaint about his partner regarding time-outs, and his most frequent excuse for not taking a time-out, is "She won't let me take one." At times, his partner may be very resistant to the idea of his taking a time-out. This is often the case because the man has been unwilling, in the past, to return to the issue later and the conflict remains unaddressed and unresolved. In any case, this strategy is strongly recommended and is also discussed with his partner in a phone contact with her during his intake.

The Time-Out Plan essentially fleshes out this concept and puts it into a concrete and practical form that he can then use in his life, as needed. The first issue addressed in the plan is differentiating the intensity of the cues he has identified previously in his Escalation Prevention Plan. He is asked to identify the cues most important in determining whether he needs to take a time-out and then to divide them into three different levels. An example of a lower-level cue, something he notices early in his escalation, might be hunger, fatigue, or struggling with rush-hour traffic. An example of an upper-level cue, something he notices just before he chooses to lash out physically, might be yelling, cursing, feeling flushed, or "racing thoughts." Cues fit in different levels for different men. Each man needs to determine his own unique escalation pattern.

Part of the reason a man is asked to divide cues in this manner is that it is easier to take a time-out when he is less escalated. Unfortunately, this is often also the time when he believes he is the most in control of himself and does not need to take one. However, the need to catch himself early in the escalation process is strongly emphasized and reinforced throughout his involvement in the group.

This task also asks him to state clearly how he will communicate, to his partner and others, that he wishes to take a time-out. This can be a verbal (e.g., "I need some space," "I need a time-out," "I need to get away for awhile") or nonverbal (e.g., the "T" sign for taking a time-out in sports) signal, but it needs to be specified in a respectful and assertive manner. Frequently, men struggle with the desire to punish their partners in potentially volatile situations and one way to do that is simply to leave without communicating what they are doing or when they will return. This transforms the time-out into just another weapon in his arsenal of abuse.

Another important aspect of this task involves looking at a number of very specific situations in which a time-out might be necessary (e.g., at home, in the car, at outside activities, on the phone) and formulating a specific response for each. Each of these invites him to think about different options and reminds him that he is continually making choices in all situations in his life. The issue of an extended time-out is also discussed, in case the couple needs to separate overnight or for several days due to the potential volatility of a particular situation.

A critical part of this task is reconnecting after a time-out has been taken. Due to their own controlling issues, many men believe that if they are calm and ready to talk again, their partners should be ready also. For this reason, men are asked to address how they plan to reenter the situation and talk to their partners about once again discussing the issue that was left unresolved. Men are encouraged to ask clearly whether their partners are indeed ready to resume the discussion and, if the response is "no," to back off and continue the time-out process until their partners feel comfortable continuing.

Frequently, especially in the initial stages of treatment, men report that they do not stay angry and that they "get over the anger right away." However, their partners are not on the same timetable; men may feel a sense of relief after "dumping" their stress, but their partners must continue to deal with the aftereffects of an abusive incident and fears that more abuse may occur.

Final issues addressed in the Time-Out Plan include identifying positive ways the man will de-escalate when taking his time-out and determining which people, activities, and thoughts he needs to avoid. The positive strategies come directly from his Escalation Prevention Plan de-escalation strategies and often focus on visualizing and going to a "quiet space" in his mind where he can feel calm and safe, taking a walk, calling a friend, using positive self-talk, thinking about the consequences of becoming abusive, and the like. Examples of activities to avoid might be driving, drinking, or calling someone who will blame or "bash" his partner rather than help him look at his own responsibility in the conflict.

At the end of his Time-Out Plan, he is asked to sign and date it to make a concrete commitment to himself and the group that he will actively use this procedure to interrupt his escalation and to decrease his potential to become controlling, abusive, and violent. This reinforces the idea once again that he has the knowledge and ability to make the conscious choice to leave any situation in which he notices himself escalating and to continue to take clear responsibility for whether he becomes abusive. It also takes him away from the notion that he is out of control or that he does not know what he is doing when he escalates to violence.

After the man presents his Time-Out Plan, he is again offered feedback by the other members and the group therapist. This feedback usually addresses a lack of clarity and specifics in answering the questions or the mistaken notion that he needs to get permission from his partner to take a time-out. Although some women are initially unhappy when their partners take time-outs, they, too, generally come to see this as a helpful tool for decreasing his abusive behavior, especially if he begins to demonstrate a pattern of returning to finish discussing the issue that triggered the angry exchange.

TASK VI: ABUSE INVENTORY

Task Objectives

1. To write out and discuss a comprehensive history of specific acts of violence he has perpetrated throughout the course of his life against other people (including his partner), property, animals, and himself
2. To begin to recognize ongoing and lifelong patterns of intimidation, abuse, and violence that have been rewarded at times by others through praise, recognition, and reinforcement and that he has used these to effectively control people and situations on occasion

3. To better understand the impact of his explosive anger and abusive behavior on others around him and to begin to experience a genuine sense of remorse about how he has hurt people in the past and how he continues to hurt people in the present

4. To begin to understand that his partner is not the only person with whom he has been abusive as a means of decreasing his level of blame toward her in the present

5. To clearly identify the specific justifications and excuses he has used to absolve himself of responsibility for his abuse and violence toward others and to begin to take full responsibility for his abusive behavior in the past and present

6. To identify the conscious choices he made in the process of becoming violent to reinforce the notion that he is very much in control of himself and his actions at all times

7. To address chemical use issues and make an assessment about whether they are connected with the violence and abuse he has perpetrated to determine if the two issues are interrelated for him and to discourage his viewing the chemical use as an excuse to be violent in the future

8. To be clear about the very real payoffs and benefits that he experienced as a result of being violent and abusive

9. To identify specific legal and other consequences to realize the impact that the violence and abuse are having on him as a means of appealing to his own self-interest

10. To identify negative self-talk that has contributed to his objectifying his partner and others and to assist him in beginning to develop empathy and compassion for his victims by realizing that the targets of his aggressive behavior are human beings

11. To identify his unrealistic expectations of his partner and of women in general

12. To decrease the shame that he has experienced about past abuse he has perpetrated by talking openly and honestly about it with other men

Task Description

The Abuse Inventory constitutes one of the most important tasks that a man is asked to do in the course of his group involvement. Many men come to the intake reporting few memories of the abuse and violence that they have perpetrated. They also often believe that their "anger problems" are only with their partner, saying, "I don't get mad with anyone besides her" or "Everyone else thinks I'm a great guy." This task strongly challenges both of those contentions.

Many programs ask a man to discuss a "most violent incident" that has occurred with a partner, which, in essence, makes his interaction with her the focus of much of what is addressed regarding his being violent. The Abuse Inventory, on the other hand, asks a man to write out and discuss a comprehensive history of all his acts of violence against other people (including siblings, parents, peers, partners, and children), against property, against animals, and against himself (e.g., hitting himself, attempting to commit suicide). This forces him to look clearly at his lifelong pattern of being violent and abusive toward others and helps remove his focus from thinking that his partner is the problem. What a man generally gains from this task is a realization of his strong desire to control others that has existed since childhood.

This is not the time to talk about violence that is perpetrated against him, for example, by his parents. This can easily place him in the role of victim and perhaps, in his mind, excuse his own later violence. His early victimization, which is generally a real and important issue, is addressed in a later task, Family of Origin and Childhood. The purpose of the Abuse Inventory is to clearly identify his own violence without blaming, minimizing, or justifying it.

This assignment strongly urges men to recall memories that they have sought to repress for years due to their shame about being abusive and their desire to see themselves as different from the abusive person they have been. One way to gather recollections is to contact their families of origin to fill in some of their history. Another way is to talk with current and former partners, if the men are able to do so without escalating to abusive behavior. We are clear with men that another person does not have to participate in helping them remember the violence if that person is uncomfortable doing this. In the end, this is their task to do for themselves.

The purpose of this exhaustive report, which often takes four to five group sessions for the man to complete, is to begin to recognize the lifelong patterns of being controlling, abusive, and violent with others and to decrease the level of blame regarding his partner. The Abuse Inventory clearly and dramatically takes the man's current situation out of the realm of "this only happens with my wife."

The vast majority of men in this program report significant histories of violence, including fights with peers as children and adolescents, fisticuffs in the military, bar brawls, physical altercations in early adulthood, and some road rage incidents. Some group members report long-standing histories of severe and brutal violence toward others. Most men, by the time they reach our program, however, have stopped being violent toward others besides their partners and children. In the course of this inventory, they can often identify an obvious demarcation point at which they made a clear decision to curtail their violence with others. This generally occurred when they became fearful about being physically hurt themselves or when the more public nature of their violence brought about the potential for legal consequences.

For this task, a man is asked to identify and discuss his most violent incident with his current partner, which is defined as the time when he did the most damage to her or the surroundings, the time when he felt the most out of control, or the time when she seemed or was the most fearful. This includes greater detail regarding cues, ways he attempted to control her, and the emotional and physical effects on his partner and children. The incident, however, is only one part of the whole picture. It is hoped that a man will clearly see from the Abuse Inventory that his controlling and abusive attitudes and behaviors have always been with him; they have only been refocused in more recent times on his partner and children, who, at this point in his life, make safer targets. If a member is continuing to be violent with others, this also becomes part of the inventory and can become part of his Escalation Prevention Plan.

An important part of the Abuse Inventory is to recognize how a man's intimidation and violence has been rewarded and reinforced by others. Men often relate stories of peers, fathers, coaches, and others who have communicated respect and other strong positive messages about handling conflicts or problems through intimidation and violence. Some men report becoming friends with others with whom they have been violent. This history also demonstrates in a powerful way how the man has been able to control people and situations and to get what he wants through his abusive behavior. Both of these issues are raised frequently in feedback as he presents his list of incidents.

The man's negative and destructive thought processes are another area that is addressed in this task. Self-talk forms an important thread throughout the course of the group, with the Escalation Prevention Plan and a separate educational unit on this topic (see Self-Talk in Chapter IV). We ask a man to identify specific examples of his negative self-talk prior to, during, and after his violent incidents. As a result of doing this, he begins to see the thought patterns that have carried through from childhood to the present. Examples might include themes of unfairness, getting even, or crossing the line. This self-talk includes swearing, cursing, name-calling, and put-downs, all of which serve to objectify the other person, making it easier to perpetrate violence against them (Edleson, 1984).

In addition, this section involves identifying the specific justifications and excuses that men use to give themselves permission to be violent. Some examples of these might include "She hit me first," "I was out of control,"

"I was drunk," and "She deserved it." Becoming aware of the negative self-talk and "making it public" is one way to decrease the power it has had in the men's lives in the past.

A critical part of stopping the violence is a man's realization that he is making choices (Ellis, 1970; Novaco, 1975). This is highlighted by the Escalation Prevention Plan and the Time-Out Plan, both of which ask a man to identify ways to react differently when he experiences cues and triggers that have led to abuse and violence in the past. Early in the process, most men are very resistant to acknowledging that they have the capacity to make choices and instead view themselves as out of control when they have been violent. This mind-set needs to change if the abusive behavior is to stop.

Part of the Abuse Inventory addresses this mind-set very directly. We ask men to identify at least four examples of the choices they made and when they made them related to the most violent incident with their partners. These choices can include several aspects. First, men can look at choices related to how they were violent, for example, slapping rather than hitting with a fist, hitting the arm rather than hitting the face, and threatening with a weapon but not using it. Men, when questioned about slapping versus punching, often say, "I knew that hitting her with my fist would hurt her more." This is pointed out as a clear choice even in the midst of "not knowing what I was doing" or "seeing red."

Second, men can look at where they were violent. Generally, men are not violent in public, even if they are feeling enraged and rehearsing abusive behavior, due to their concerns about the likelihood of outside intervention. Instead, they will often wait until they get into a car or until they actually reach their home. They may also make an effort to avoid being violent in front of their children, at least for a time.

Third, men can look at when the decision to be violent was made. Men frequently go through a planning or rehearsal process that culminates in violence at some later point. One man reported being served with divorce papers in the morning at work, brooding about this all day, and plotting what he planned to do. He then returned home after work to tie up his wife and kidnap the children.

Finally, men can look at how they stop if an outside party intervenes. One man reported that he was drunk and in a "blackout" and was on top of his wife beating her in an alley outside a bar. However, despite his intoxication and blackout, he stopped abruptly and completely when a friend touched him on the shoulder, although he could have continued to hit her or could have gotten up and begun to fight with his friend.

All of these aspects clearly demonstrate the choice-making process that occurs even in the midst of rage and violence. Men must begin to see and make more positive choices earlier in the escalation if their violence is to stop. A man's willingness and ability to address this issue provides a sense of whether he understands the decision-making process he used and whether he realizes that he was, at no point, out of control.

Chemical use is also discussed, especially as it relates to his previous abuse and violence. The correlation between chemical use and domestic violence is high (Ackerman, 1988). Therefore, it is important to determine whether these issues are interrelated for him. For a man who has a history of abusive behavior while using chemicals, we generally, at a minimum, expect him to sign a Sobriety Contract, whereby he agrees not to use mood-altering chemicals for the duration of his involvement in the group.

This part of the Abuse Inventory encourages him to discuss how the chemicals have been a part of his abuse and to try to assess how large a role they have played. Many men report that chemical use decreases their inhibitions and exacerbates their abusive reactions, which certainly makes sense. Men are, however, encouraged to guard against the notion that chemicals have somehow caused their controlling attitudes, explosive anger, and abusive behavior. At this point, men are generally clear that they have escalated and been abusive, if not violent, on many occasions while they were sober. Chemical use and domestic abuse are viewed as two separate and freestanding issues by this program. Both must be addressed to adequately deal with a man's controlling and abusive attitudes and behaviors (Gelles, 1993). One important aspect of this discussion involves helping a man to no longer see chemical use as an excuse for his violence or as a means to absolve himself of responsibility for abusive behavior.

Another issue raised in this task is the perceived advantages and payoffs in being violent with a partner and others (Edleson and Tolman, 1992). This is also addressed in an educational topic in Unit 1 of Chapter IV ("Perceived Advantages/Disadvantages of Using Violence"). Many men are perplexed by this issue because they have difficulty acknowledging anything positive that is gained by their violence. The issue is reframed, however, to help men understand that their behavior is always purposeful and that they receive some very concrete short-term benefits from being violent. The most obvious benefit is the ability to control a person or situation and gain compliance with what they want. A number of men also talk about gaining friendships with, and respect from, other males as a result of violence earlier in their lives. Thus, a disturbing relationship exists between violence and getting close to others, and this relationship is seen also in the context of violence that occurs between men and their partners, whom they claim to love. Men frequently believe that, at a minimum, their partners will put up with the abuse and violence and that it may be a way they can actually emotionally connect and be close.

The flip side of this issue is the disadvantages and consequences that come about as a result of being violent (Edleson and Tolman, 1992), which are also discussed in an educational topic in Unit 1 of Chapter IV ("Perceived Advantages/Disadvantages of Using Violence"). Men are asked to identify legal consequences such as assault charges, restraining orders, time in jail, and money spent on attorneys. They are also asked to identify other kinds of consequences, such as separation, divorce, loss of trust and intimacy with their partners and children, less time with their children, becoming less productive at work, shame and depression, and suicidal ideation. This is a critical area because it helps men focus on their own self-interest and realize the direct impact that abuse and violence is having on them and their lives. It is particularly helpful in confronting some of the antisocial qualities that many of these men possess, offering them a clear picture of the difficult and lonely road ahead for them if they continue their controlling and abusive behavior patterns.

A final issue addressed in this task is clarifying the "vision" of what they wanted and expected their partners to be and how this vision contributed to their becoming abusive. Men are asked to list the traits and characteristics they were seeking in a mate. What men often discover during this task is that they have been sending their partners confusing and contradictory messages during their time together. These contradictions have frequently made it very difficult for their partners to function. An example would be the expectation that a partner be independent and strong but also do what the man wants her to do. This discussion hopefully helps men gain a clearer picture of the problems created by their desire to mold and shape their partners into who they think their partners should be. Some men with caretaking and overly involved mothers are clearly aware of their desire to make their partners into what they want, simply and pointedly stating, "I wanted her to be my mother."

The Abuse Inventory is a powerful process that raises enormous shame and anxiety in the men prior to and during its presentation to the group. Some men put off this task for a significant period of time or quit the group just before they are scheduled to do it. A primary goal of this task is for men to realize that the targets of their violence have been human beings rather than objects. This hopefully begins a process of assisting them in developing empathy for those they have abused and in feeling a sense of remorse about what they have done. Some men become sad and tearful during this presentation; some do not.

Considerable feedback is focused on how they have objectified those with whom they have been violent, and men are expected to be very specific about the process of being violent with others. Questions from a therapist such as "How did you grab her?"; "Where did you hit her?"; and "How many times did you hit her?" are common and helpful in this assignment. The reactions of children and the effects on children are also highlighted to further clarify the messages they are communicating through their abusive words and actions. It is directly pointed out that such behavior teaches children, among other things, what it is to be a man and a woman, how people resolve conflict, and what constitutes an adult relationship.

This is a time to be clear with men about their accountability for the violence and the emotional and physical havoc that it has wreaked on those around them. Denial, blaming, minimizing, justifying, and explaining away the incidents must be directly confronted, not for the purpose of shaming men but rather to have them accept full responsibility for their violent behavior. This is generally the first and only time men have been asked to do this since the abuse began.

Part of what needs to occur as well is a lessening of the intense shame that most men experience because they have perpetrated violence against those whom they say they love. Simply acknowledging ways they have tried to keep the abuse a secret and finding a place where they can honestly talk about and explore their abusive attitudes and behaviors will help guide them in that direction. As long as the shame is present and continues to feel overwhelming, it is unlikely that the abusive behavior will stop (Stosny, 1995).

Throughout this task, men are given feedback by the therapists and other group members. This frequently provides opportunities for men to handle escalations they experience in the group that arise from the feedback. By the end of this task, however, most men report a significant decrease in shame and an enormous sense of relief that they have finally found somewhere to share the "horror stories" that have been such an important part of their lives. As a result of this difficult process of sharing, most men report feeling more comfortable in the group and are more honest about themselves and others and more open to the treatment process from that point forward.

TASK VII: MIDGROUP EVALUATION

Task Objectives

1. To assess his progress made to date in addressing issues related to the following:
   - Eliminating his violence
   - Decreasing the frequency of emotional and verbal abuse, explosive anger, and threatening and intimidating behavior

- Taking responsibility for past and current abusive behavior
- Recognizing and changing his controlling attitudes and behaviors
- Taking responsibility for his current thoughts, feelings, and behaviors
- Identifying what he is learning in the group
- Identifying how he is improving his self-confidence and self-esteem and increasing his ability to feel empathy and compassion for his partner and others

2. To begin to identify more subtle ways that he has attempted to control other group members, the therapy process, and people outside the group
3. To assess his level of participation in the group in the following areas:
   - Educational discussions
   - Completing and presenting group tasks
   - Sharing information about himself
   - Providing feedback to others
4. To assess his willingness to accept feedback and listen to others
5. To assess his level of emotional connection with other men in the group and his willingness to confront and support others, both inside and outside the group
6. To continue to focus on and use his Escalation Prevention Plan and to identify specific ways to improve it
7. To set specific behavioral goals for his remaining time in the program
8. To emphasize that addressing his controlling attitudes and behaviors and his potential for abuse and violence in the future is an ongoing concern

Task Description

The Midgroup Evaluation is usually done at about the halfway point of a man's involvement in the domestic abuse program. Essentially, this task is an assessment of the man's progress in the group up until that point. He first presents his perspective on the progress he has made, and he is then given feedback about his progress and participation in group by other members and the group therapist. This task, unlike several others, needs to be completed in one group session so that others' feedback can be directly related to things he has said about himself.

Issues that he is expected to address include how long he has been nonviolent, whether he has decreased the frequency of his emotional and verbal abuse, whether he is accepting full responsibility for his past and current abusive behavior, whether he is recognizing and intervening in his controlling attitudes and behaviors, and whether he is working at taking clear responsibility for his current thoughts, feelings, and actions in his relationships with his partner and others. Included as part of these is a discussion about how he is beginning to develop empathy and compassion for his partner and others, as opposed to his previous mindset that others are simply objects to manipulate and control to get what he desires.

Most men have stopped being violent by this point, but all continue to struggle with emotional and verbal abuse, a desire to control, and a tendency to blame. If he does not honestly recognize and acknowledge these as ongoing issues, if he denies current thoughts and behaviors related to abuse, control, and blaming, or if he refuses to acknowledge any personal issues about which he still feels "stuck," concerns would be expressed about both his awareness and his progress. Abusive and controlling men will not be "cured" by a treatment process. Rather, men will need to attend to these areas for the rest of their lives if they are to remain nonabusive.

To address this issue we request that the man specifically note and ask the group for feedback about how he has been controlling in the group itself. This feedback is especially helpful because it takes into account some of the more subtle and manipulative ways that he may be attempting to control his partner and others outside the group. Examples of this might be interrupting; explaining away feedback; presenting a self-pitying, fragile, or victimized stance; remaining quiet or withdrawn; or frequently attempting to get the last word in. A critical skill that is highlighted here is whether he is willing to listen to others and accept their feedback, a willingness that needs to be transferred to his relationship with his partner if their interactions are ever to become more healthy. Being willing to listen in group provides good practice for doing this at other times in his life.

Part of this evaluation also involves noting his level of participation in the group: during educational discussions; in writing out, presenting, and completing expected tasks; in sharing honestly and openly about himself and his issues; and in providing both supportive and constructive critical feedback for others inside and outside group.

Most men tend to be somewhat quiet and passive during their initial time in the group. However, their activity level is expected to increase as they move through the process. Becoming more active tends to decrease their shame, increase their self-confidence and self-esteem, and enhance their ability to learn and put into practice the tools that the group discusses. If this is, in fact, occurring, the man needs to also note specifically what he is doing to make this happen in the group. Part of this process generally involves his connecting emotionally with other men in the group, thereby decreasing his overall isolation, loneliness, alienation, and emotional overdependency on his partner.

This evaluation continues to focus on the Escalation Prevention Plan as the foundation for the change process and asks how he has improved it, what cues and ideas he has added, and how he is using it more effectively in his day-to-day life. He is encouraged to think of creative ways to include the plan more frequently in his everyday activities, for example, by carrying a pocket-size notebook that summarizes its main points and offers the opportunity to easily add to it or by posting the EPP or a visual reminder of it (using words or graphics) on a mirror at home, in a desk drawer at work, or somewhere in his car.

A final part of the Midgroup Evaluation asks the man to set at least three or four specific and measurable goals for the remainder of his involvement in the program. Included in this goal setting is devising a plan to work on reaching them. The goal setting once again solidifies his commitment to the treatment process and gives him some concrete guideposts to keep him on track.

TASK VIII: FAMILY OF ORIGIN AND CHILDHOOD

Task Objectives

1. To examine and understand how he learned to be controlling and abusive by identifying the ways in which significant others in his childhood modeled these attitudes and behaviors while he was growing up
2. To recognize who was controlling and abusive in his childhood and to acknowledge and understand his own victimization in his family and by others (e.g., peers) in his life
3. To allow himself to experience grief, loss, and emotional pain related to his own childhood victimization that he was unable to experience at the time due to the dysfunction in the family
4. To become aware of how his victimization and powerlessness as a child has contributed to his negative self-talk and to his abusive and controlling attitudes and behaviors in the present
5. To clearly identify family roles, rules, values, secrets, and dysfunctional attitudes and behaviors and to discover how these have affected his relationships with his partner, his children (if he has any), and others
6. To understand how his parents' relationship, including their expression of anger and other emotions, their conflict resolution style, and their expression of affection, has affected his adult relationships with women, children, and others

7. To clearly identify where and how he learned his disrespectful, condescending, and entitled attitudes toward women
8. To identify the similarities and differences between how he was parented as a child and how he now parents his own children
9. To identify nurturing and healthy people from his past and to begin to use them more frequently as positive role models in his current life
10. To identify specific similarities, attitudinal and behavioral, to his father and mother and to understand how these similarities have affected his relationships with his partner, his children, and others
11. To clearly articulate what he would like to have said or would like to say to his parents about his childhood and what he learned as he was growing up

Task Description

Significant evidence exists to indicate that batterers' violence, abuse, and other controlling attitudes and behaviors are learned by growing up in families of origin in which violence and abusive behavior were present (Roy, 1977; Rosenbaum and O'Leary, 1981b; Stark and Flitcraft, 1987; Dutton, 1995). The purpose of this task is to help men discover how and where they learned to be abusive. The timing of this task is important. Men are expected to accept responsibility for and to stop perpetrating violence themselves before they focus on their own victimization. It is this program's belief that when men look at their own victimization too early in the treatment process, the potential exists for them to use this as just another excuse for the abuse they perpetrate in the present (Edleson and Tolman, 1992). For example, they might think or say to themselves, "Well, no wonder I'm abusive. My father did the same thing to me" or "Well, my wife doesn't have it all that bad. My dad [or mom] was a lot worse than I am." Men need to examine and work on their own current behavior before they delve into the past. For this reason the task is placed nearer to the end of the program.

It is not the program's intention, through this task, to "bash" or blame a man's parents for his abusive actions. This is not helpful, either to the man himself or to his current victims. Many men come into treatment reporting that they had a great childhood or loving parents. At times, they express strong resistance to looking at these issues honestly. It is necessary to get beyond this image men portray or remember if they are to benefit from the task. The breakdown of this denial is often facilitated by hearing other men talk about how their families affected them. At the same time, it does no good to make a man's parents the scapegoats for his actions in the present. The purpose at this point is to help him examine how he learned to become abusive and controlling and to enable him to more fully understand and appreciate his own victimization and how that has affected his choice to be abusive and controlling in his adult life.

The goal of this process, then, is to enable the man to transfer this understanding to his current victims, his partner and his children, and to develop increased empathy and compassion for them and genuine remorse about his abusive behavior toward others. The development of compassion needs to occur if he is to continue the process he has begun toward becoming nonabusive (Carr, 1981; Stosny, 1995). This task "walks a fine line" between being empathetic and supportive to the man and yet, at the same time, continuing to hold him accountable for his ongoing abusive actions. The reality for abusive men is that many were physically abused themselves or have witnessed physical abuse of their mother by their father and all have experienced significant controlling behavior by one or both parents (Pagelow, 1984; Hotaling and Sugarman, 1986; Dutton, 1995). Men have learned their controlling and abusive attitudes and behaviors from significant others who modeled these attitudes and behaviors during their childhoods. Throughout this task, men are asked to think about and clearly label those around them in childhood who were controlling, abusive, and dependent on alcohol or drugs.

An ongoing theme throughout this task is to ask the man to directly and clearly relate what he has learned in each section of this task to its effect on his relationship with his partner, his children (if he has any), and others in his adult life. This tie-in continually refocuses him on his own unhealthy attitudes and behaviors in his current situation. This is illustrated when he is asked to identify where he learned his disrespectful and condescending attitudes toward women, for example, from his family's roles, values, and rules or directly from his parents' ways of relating to each other. However, the most important question raised during this process is "How does what you learned in the past affect you right now in terms of how you view your partner and other women?"

All the men in the group have transferred significant aspects of their parents' relationships, including decision making, sharing anger and other emotions, conflict resolution, and expressing affection, to their own current relationships. In essence, they have often created a situation in which they replay the same struggles and trauma that were experienced in their parents' relationships.

A similar process occurs with parenting and discipline: they end up viewing and treating their children in the same disrespectful and unhealthy way they were handled by their own parents. We ask men to clearly identify how they resemble their parents and how these similarities have affected their current relationships.

This task often taps into intense anger and sadness about a man's own victimization and the losses he suffered, such as the loss of his ability to be a child or the loss of a loving and nurturing relationship with a parent. This pain that he experiences will hopefully put him in touch with what his partner and children have felt with him. Making the connection between the pain he has experienced and the pain he may be causing potentially enables him to develop empathy and to move outside himself to see his partner's, his children's, and others' perspectives.

Important areas in this task include examining family roles, such as caretaker, lost child, and rebel; addressing family values, such as toughness, fairness, hard work, and never making mistakes; and analyzing family rules, such as how boys/men, girls/women, and children in general were viewed and treated. Such family patterns sent men strong messages about the traditional and stereotypical roles that males and females are supposed to play. These messages have contributed to mens' creation of rigid and unrealistic expectations about how their partners and children should be.

This task may address issues with his mother, even if she was not abusive. If she was warm, nurturing, caretaking, and "always there" for him, this can also skew his beliefs about what he has a right to expect from women and his partner in particular. Examining family values is a crucial part of the process, and men are encouraged to be clear about the contradictions between their family's stated values and what was actually lived and demonstrated by the family members.

This task also looks at the impact of others outside the immediate family. For men who were ridiculed, bullied, or ostracized by peers and other significant adults, these situations only exacerbated their feelings of shame, victimization, and powerlessness, thus contributing to an even stronger desire to control and, if necessary, strike out at others. These experiences also fuel their controlling and abusive attitudes and behaviors in the present.

However, some men have also experienced nurturing and caring role models, including grandparents, teachers, and coaches. These men are asked to begin to incorporate these positive "voices" from the past into their current self-talk to help decrease their potential to become explosive and abusive in their current lives.

A critical part of this task encourages the man to draw a parallel between his feeling of powerlessness as a child growing up in an abusive and dysfunctional family and the powerlessness that he generally reports experiencing just prior to lashing out verbally or physically with his current family. He is encouraged to recognize how his partners and children are generally the victims of his unresolved pain from his family of origin and childhood in which he was, at the time, unable to stand up to, or assert himself with, his abusive parent(s) or others who were demeaning and disrespectful with him.

In the present, however, when he feels powerless and victimized by his partner, he is strong enough, and she is deemed a safe enough target, to impose his will on her through force. She has literally become the scapegoat for his life's pain. Instead of continuing this destructive process, the man is asked to think about what he would want to communicate to his parents about his childhood experiences. He may never follow through with this by talking directly to his parents, but hopefully, he may now realize that this is one option available to him. Some men do in fact follow through with this assignment in the therapy or recovery work that follows completion of the domestic abuse group.

This task frequently takes several sessions to complete, and men are given feedback after each time they present. This task often provides a powerful and poignant description of human cruelty and how it shapes future generations (Miller, 1981, 1983). The power of this task relates to the intimate sharing that occurs among the men in group and to the empathy that men receive from other members and the therapist. It is clearly communicated to men that they did not deserve the abuse or violence they experienced during their childhood.

Some men begin to truly understand and accept this perspective for the first time. The hope and the message given to them is to then go one step further and start to realize, at a deeper level, that their partners and children do not deserve their abusive behavior in the present either (Edleson and Tolman, 1992). This understanding will have to be a part of the healing process if a man is to successfully change other types of control and abuse in addition to the violence. If he really does integrate these ideas, the likelihood that his controlling and abusive attitudes and behaviors will be passed on to his own children and grandchildren is greatly decreased.

TASK IX: AMENDS LETTER

Task Objectives

1. To be specific about how he has been emotionally, verbally, physically, and sexually abusive to his partner in the past and to clearly and unequivocally take full responsibility for his abusive and controlling behavior
2. To make amends to his partner (and others, if he wishes) for the abuse he has perpetrated
3. To experience genuine empathy and compassion for his victim(s) and remorse about his abusive and controlling actions

4. To make a clear commitment to continue to address issues raised during his participation in the program so that he will be nonviolent and decrease his other controlling and abusive behaviors with his partner and others in the future
5. To decrease the shame he has experienced as a result of being abusive and controlling and to begin to forgive himself for the serious mistakes he has made in the past

Task Description

An important part of what needs to occur near the end of the program is for a man to be clear about what he has done that he does not feel good about and to make amends for his controlling and abusive behavior. This is true whether the man is to move on in his life with his partner or to go on by himself. This is the purpose of the Amends Letter.

The letter is written for the man himself as part of his own recovery process, not for his partner, his children, or anyone else. He is not expected to share this with his partner because the sharing, in and of itself, could become controlling and manipulative. However, many men do decide to share the letter at some point with the others to whom they have been abusive. This is a significant and powerful way to decrease the shame a man feels and to enable him to move forward in his life if he is indeed committed to continuing to work on being less abusive and controlling.

At a minimum, the man needs to write a letter to the most recent partner with whom he has been controlling, abusive, and violent. In addition, many men use this exercise to write letters to their children or, in some cases, to others they have victimized.

A man needs to be very specific in describing the emotional, verbal, physical, and sexual abuse toward his partner and others. For example, this might include talking about ". . . times when I tried to humiliate you in front of our friends," ". . . times I called you names and put you down," or ". . . times when I slapped and kicked you." A man also must be clear about the effects and impact of the abuse on his partner and others. He might include statements about ". . . the fear that I created in you," ". . . the terror you must have felt," ". . . the insecurity you experienced around me," or ". . . the losses my abuse has created in your life."

Men are encouraged to make clear and unequivocal statements about their responsibility for the abuse. For example, "You didn't deserve the abuse," "I am completely responsible for my abusive actions," or "I chose to hurt you rather than face my own pain." It is also expected that men will avoid blaming their partner, their family of origin and childhood, their chemical use, their depression, or any other extraneous factors. Men are expected to make clear amends for the physical and psychological damage that they have caused. They might say, for instance, "I am very sorry about the abuse I perpetrated against you . . . ." Finally, men are expected, in this letter, to make a clear commitment to continuing to do the things necessary to remain nonviolent and to decrease the potential for emotional and verbal abuse and other controlling behaviors in the future.

Many men balk at this last expectation, believing that they cannot make a promise not to be violent again, as they have done so many times in the past during the calming phase of the violence cycle. Previously, this promise has only led to more violence and intense feelings of failure and shame. That type of promise, however, is clearly differentiated from the commitment that is needed at this point. A strong commitment to continuing to work on a recovery program concerning power and control and violence issues means making the insights and behavioral changes he has experienced in the program an ongoing part of his life. If he has been sincere and genuine in the treatment process and if he continues, on a daily basis, to implement what he has learned in the group, he can, in fact, remain nonviolent and can significantly decrease other abusive and controlling behaviors.

One might ask, at this point, why men are not expected to be completely nonabusive and noncontrolling. Part of this arises from the program's belief that all human beings, at various times in their lives, become controlling and abusive. Wanting to control is a natural part of the human condition. This desire to control can be an effort to exert power over others but it can also be a way of seeking to gain some safety and predictability in our frequently chaotic human existence.

The goal in the program is to have men learn to recognize their cues and triggers and to use this knowledge to intervene more effectively in their potential to become abusive in the future. None of these men are likely to become peaceful, mellow, and nonabusive at all times. They will always have the potential to become abusive again. The key to changing their lives is to dramatically decrease the frequency of abusive behaviors (including activities such as sulking and manipulation) through understanding and positive action. The end result is that the abuse no longer plays as significant a part in their day-to-day lives, thus leading to healthier interactions and relationships with those around them.

The hope with this letter is that the man will, perhaps for the first time, experience genuine remorse about his past abusive behaviors and real empathy and compassion for the victims of his violence and abuse. This does not always occur, but when it does, the letter can be a powerful and healing catharsis for the man, allowing him to clearly recognize the significant mistakes he has made in the past with the people he claims to love. It also allows him to begin to forgive himself for what he has done. This forgiveness can help open the door to a new nonabusive future for him. He needs to develop compassion for himself, as well as for his victims, if he is to truly integrate the learning available in the group.

A final caution regarding this letter involves the importance of directly confronting subtle forms of control in the letter itself. As previously noted, this letter is written as part of a man's own process of healing and forgiveness. Statements such as "I hope I will have the opportunity to make this up to you," "I really pray that you can forgive me," "I sincerely hope that you can recover from my abusive behavior," or even "I love you very much" remove the focus from him and his responsibility and imply the expectation of something in return from his partner (e.g., her being willing to forgive him). This task is meant as an exercise in taking responsibility for what he has done, making amends, and forgiving himself. Overt or covert expectations of his partner in his letter are just another form of controlling and manipulative behavior.

The following is an example of the Amends Letter that was written by a thirty-eight-year-old man who completed the program:

Dear Susan,

I have reached the time in my abuse recovery program where I am ready to write this letter to you. First of all, I want you to know how sorry I feel about what I have said and done to you during our marriage. I have been abusive to you in countless ways and situations. My behavior has been deplorable. When I think of all my abusive and controlling actions, I feel very sad for you. You did not deserve this from anyone, especially from someone who said he loved you.

You have endured many of the worst moments in my life. I've abused you physically by grabbing you, pushing you, pulling your hair, throwing you, kicking you, hitting you, and slamming your head onto the floor. I've abused you verbally by yelling and screaming at you, swearing at you, calling you names, and interrupting you. I've abused you emotionally by putting you down, making you feel guilty, playing mind games, belittling you, being abusive to you in the presence of our son, and lying to you. I've intimidated and threatened you by glaring at you, throwing and breaking things, and using my size to make you feel afraid of me. I've abused you financially by excluding you from big money decisions, making you ask for money, and hiding money from you. All the while, I have minimized, denied, and even blamed you for my abusive actions. I now realize that this is abuse in and of itself.

Susan, I no longer blame you for my actions. I take full and complete responsibility for all my abusiveness toward you. I was always in control of my behavior. I knew exactly what I was doing. And no matter what the situation was, I did have other ways I could have acted. Unfortunately, I made many bad decisions in my life.

Many of these bad choices were related to both my low self-esteem and my overwhelming desire to be in control of you and everything around me. Nonetheless, I clearly chose to be abusive. And I can see now how my abusive behavior has diminished your trust in our relationship. I feel sad about this. I know that, only after much time of being nonabusive, is there any possibility that we might be able to recapture these lost precious gifts.

I have learned so very much during these past thirty weeks. Among other things, I now know how negative self-talk can be turned into positive self-talk with great results; how being assertive reduces my stress and leads to better communication; how controlling myself and my actions instead of trying to control you is easier and works better; how feeling my emotions instead of stuffing them is not only okay but is positive and healthy; how reducing my shame is so very empowering; how being open and honest may at first be the hard way but it's ultimately a much better path for any relationship. And maybe most important, I've learned that this recovery process from being controlling and abusive takes a lifetime. There is no quick fix. The important thing for me is to take one day at a time and to use the knowledge and skills that I have gained.

Susan, I pledge to you that I will never be violent to you again. Furthermore, I will continue to work to eliminate the other types of control and abuse that I done to you and others. I can't believe that I forced you to become the scapegoat for my life's pain. But I did. And I am deeply sorry about the pain I have created in your life as a result.

John

TASK X: AFTERCARE PLAN AND FINAL FEEDBACK

Task Objectives

1. To assess his overall progress throughout the course of the program in the following areas:
   - Eliminating his acts of physical and sexual violence
   - Decreasing the frequency of emotional and verbal abuse and intimidation

- Taking full responsibility for his past and current abusive behavior
- Recognizing and changing his controlling attitudes and behaviors
- Taking full responsibility for his current thoughts, feelings, and behaviors
- Identifying specifically what he has learned in the group
- Increasing his self-confidence and self-esteem
- Increasing his ability to feel empathy and compassion for his partner, his children, and others

2. To assess his level of participation in the following group activities:
   - Educational discussions
   - Writing out and presenting group tasks
   - Sharing about himself
   - Providing honest and assertive feedback to others
3. To identify his initial and midgroup goals and to discuss his progress in attaining them
4. To assess his willingness to accept feedback and listen to others
5. To clearly identify how and with whom he is still being controlling and abusive in his life
6. To identify specific ways in which he will continue to use his Escalation Prevention Plan in the future to reduce life stress, to intervene in his controlling attitudes, and to decrease his potential to be emotionally, verbally, sexually, and physically abusive with his partner and others
7. To clearly accept that addressing his controlling attitudes and behaviors and his potential for abuse and violence in the future is an ongoing concern
8. To set specific behavioral goals for how he plans to continue the recovery process that he has begun in the group
9. To identify and express his feelings about how the group has been important to his recovery process and to verbalize his emotions about leaving the group
10. To appreciate and celebrate his accomplishments of beginning to address his abusive and controlling attitudes and behaviors and of completing the group

Task Description

Men present this task at the last group session they attend. Essentially, it is a look back at what they have learned and accomplished in the program and a look forward at what they need to continue to do for their change process to proceed. Throughout the program, it is stressed that this group is only the first step, a beginning in an ongoing and lifelong process of monitoring and changing abusive and controlling attitudes and behaviors. Its completion is not an end point. Rather, it is just a start.

For most men, group represents the first time they have ever seriously considered and addressed the factors related to the significant emotional pain and other consequences they have created for others and themselves through the abuse they have perpetrated.

Men who finish the program are referred to as completers, not graduates. Graduation implies that a particular phase is over. In fact, this final group task means that men have come through this initial phase, but it is hoped that all they have learned and the painful memories they have unearthed will remain an ever-present part of who they are. Many men come into treatment not wanting to remember what they have done and the pain they have caused. However, recalling this pain and making it an ongoing part of their lives is one powerful way to avoid repeating it in the future with partners, children, and others. The idea is not to forget and move on but rather to remember and move on so that the mistakes of the past are not repeated.

In this task, a man is asked to assess his overall progress during the course of his entire group involvement. Important issues to address in this evaluation include how long he has been nonviolent; whether he has decreased and is actively working on intervening in his emotional and verbal abuse and his controlling attitudes and behaviors; whether he has taken full responsibility for his past and current abusive behavior; and whether he is working at taking full responsibility for his current thoughts, feelings, and actions.

The relationship between control and abuse is again reinforced in this task through its questions. The importance of continuing to monitor even subtle and covert controlling attitudes and behaviors is highly stressed. Men are asked to identify examples of ongoing control and abuse in their lives. If these behaviors are completely denied, concerns are expressed about the man's willingness to recognize what is actually occurring in his life at the present time. One of the obvious ways that a man may become controlling at this point is to use therapeutic and educational tools to attempt to force his partner to make changes he wishes to see her make.

It is the program's belief that a desire to control and the potential to become abusive will be an important characteristic of these men throughout the rest of their lives. Being aware of their cues and doing something different when they arise is the key to becoming and remaining nonabusive, less controlling, and healthier. This is stressed through focusing again on the Escalation Prevention Plan and by asking how this document and its ideas will continue to be a part of the man's life.

A portion of this evaluation also involves commenting on his participation in the group, both in sharing and being open about himself and in providing honest and assertive feedback to others. Most men improve enormously in their ability to be active participants. Men often come into the group wary and guarded, offering little of themselves to other men. Gradually, however, especially after they have completed the Abuse Inventory, men tend to open up to the process and become more involved, engaging in some risk taking. They also tend to become less rambling and more focused in what they present and in the feedback they offer. As men open themselves more fully to the group, they also report a significant decrease in other mental health symptoms, such as depression and anxiety. Almost all completers, by the end of their time in group, report and present, through their behavior in group, an increase in self-confidence and self-esteem.

One of the ways that changes made by completers are highlighted is through the use of a model developed by Greg Meyer. This model asks men to look back and rate themselves from 1 to 10 on a variety of different measures, at the start of treatment and at their last group meeting, including the following:

- Being violent
- Being verbally and emotionally abusive
- Being blaming
- Being controlling
- Willingness to listen
- Willingness to use his Escalation Prevention Plan
- Willingness to take respectful time-outs
- Level of involvement in the group process
- Risk taking inside and outside the group
- Willingness to connect with other men
- Self-esteem and self-confidence
- Insight into himself and others
- Degree of empathy and compassion for others

This model offers a simple, quick, and concrete way for a man to chart the progress he has made. It also offers the opportunity for other group members to think about how they would rate the completer in the same areas from what they have seen him doing.

This group program is often the first time that most of these men have ever shared themselves so openly with other men. Some men continue their friendships with one another beyond the group. However, even if this is not the case, men have experienced a blueprint for respectful and nurturing friendships with males that they can use from this point on, if they choose to do so. An important part of this final task is feedback from other men and the therapist about how they have seen the completer change, including any concerns and recommendations they may have for him at this point. Some group members express warm and powerful sentiments to the man who is leaving about how he has affected them through his words and behavior inside and outside the group. This provides another example of how men can connect with and affect one another in a positive and significant way.

Completers are asked to address their initial and midgroup goals, which often focus on some of the issues mentioned previously, and to discuss their progress in attaining them. Men are also asked to set specific behavioral goals for the future and to discuss how they will implement them. The men who state that they want a "break" from therapy-related concerns are encouraged to return to the process when they are ready or need to do so. Most men have a clear vision of how they want to continue the process for themselves. Some want to pursue couples or family therapy. If the couple plans to remain together, such therapy is a critical component of the recovery process. However, the man is discouraged from making this issue into another example of his controlling behavior by attempting to pressure his partner into complying. A number of men decide to go on with their own therapy, in an individual or group setting, to continue to work on important individual, family of origin, or relationship issues that have been raised in this group. Others may look for ongoing support in a self-help group, such as AA, Al-Anon, or Adult Children of Alcoholics (ACOA), or in a support group designed specifically for men with power and control issues who have completed a domestic abuse program.

Key for these men is to stay involved in a meaningful way with other people, especially other men. This allows them to move from their previous stance of isolation and overdependence on their female partner. It also provides an ongoing reality check regarding their abusive and controlling attitudes and behaviors.

Finally, some men express an interest in "giving back" to other men what they have received in their group. As will be noted in Chapter IV, opportunities exist for men to return to the program to talk with others in later groups about their change process. Also, men can contribute in a variety of ways to making our country and our world a safer and healthier place for women, children, and men. Men who want to help further this goal are strongly encouraged to seek out and volunteer in organizations that promote respect and nurturance in relationships, in this country and in the world at large.

A final part of this task for the man is to talk about how he is feeling about leaving the group. Certainly some men are glad to be done with the group and its expectations. However, many men describe their experience in the group in strong and poignant terms, referring to it as "the best thing that ever happened to me" and "a turning point in my life." Some men feel genuine and profound sadness at leaving a place where, for the first time in their lives, they felt safe, accepted, and cared for and where they were held accountable, in a respectful way, for their attitudes and actions.

As part of the departure ceremony, the completer receives a single red rose to symbolize the "thorns and beauty" that are both aspects of who he has been and who he will continue to be. The rose also symbolizes our hope that he will continue to open and blossom to the world around him as he has done in the group. At first, when the rose is presented, some men feel embarrassed. One man stated, "I thought when you give a red rose, it means I love you." In that way, our giving of a rose further breaks down the notion that men cannot connect with and deeply care for one another. It also clearly represents the pride and sense of accomplishment that men are encouraged to feel about making the choice to involve themselves with and to complete this domestic abuse program. It hopefully has begun their lifelong process of looking at and changing their controlling and abusive attitudes and behaviors. Because of the significance of the completion ceremony, only one man is allowed to complete on any particular group night.

TASK XI: VIOLENT INCIDENT ASSESSMENT

Task Objectives

1. To take complete responsibility for being honest and specific in reporting his use of physical force with his partner, his children, and others (including violence toward property) throughout the course of his involvement in the group
2. To clearly identify triggers and cues in his escalation process during the hours, days, and weeks prior to his use of violence and to reinforce the notion that these cues exist in a hierarchy
3. To identify the choices he has made in deciding to use violence in this particular situation and in deciding not to utilize his Escalation Prevention Plan
4. To specifically address how his violence is connected to his controlling attitudes and behaviors
5. To realize the impact of his violence on his partner and children as a means of appealing to his self-interest (e.g., not wanting to lose trust and intimacy) and of developing empathy, compassion, and remorse for those affected by his abuse

6. To reinforce the connection between his chemical use and his abusive behavior (if chemical use was involved with the violent incident)
7. To be accountable to the group for his violent behavior as a means of reducing his shame and helping him to remain open to, and involved with, the treatment process
8. To listen to feedback from other members about their reactions and feelings regarding his choosing to be violent once again
9. To identify specific strategies and options that he can use when confronted with similar situations in the future as a means of recommiting himself to his goal of being nonviolent in his interactions with his partner and others

Task Description

Although the primary goal in the program is to completely eliminate violence in group members' family relationships, the reality is that violence does occur at times during group treatment. This task addresses that reality. It is important that men be honest about their choices to use violence during their treatment experience rather than to hide this information from the group. Being dishonest about perpetrating violence only increases their shame and causes them to withdraw further from the group and its ideas. Consequently, they derive less benefit from the treatment process.

Whenever a man uses any physical force, including any physical discipline of his children and throwing, hitting, kicking, or destroying property, it is expected that he will be honest and specific in writing out this Violent Incident Assessment. He is then expected to bring the assessment to share with the group at the next session. If violence is not reported and it is discovered from some other source (and there is permission to use the information), the man faces possible termination from the program.

This task addresses the specifics of the violent incident, including prior life stressors both inside and outside the relationship, immediate events leading up to the violence, and the violence itself. This is another example of focusing on the escalation process and not just the violent incident. Men are often unaware of escalating prior to becoming abusive. This exercise is another method used to reinforce the notion that a gradual buildup of stress can result in explosive anger and violence.

He is asked to specify all the abuse, not just the violence, that he has used during the escalation process and to focus once again on how control and his abusive behavior are inextricably linked. He is also expected to break down the cues he noticed into lower, middle, and upper levels to encourage him to recognize and attend to these early warning signs. This also assists him in coming up with additional cues to add to his Escalation Prevention Plan.

Chemical use, if it was present around the time of the incident, is also addressed in this task. The goal is to further clarify whether a link exists between the man's alcohol or drug use and his abusive behavior. If substance use is a part of his violence, a Sobriety Contract will be required, at a minimum, and other options may also be pursued at that time, including attendance at Alcoholics Anonymous or a chemical dependency evaluation.

A critical part of the Violent Incident Assessment relates to when the choice to be violent was made, how the violence was justified and excused, and why the man decided not to take a time-out and use the Escalation Prevention Plan he had developed. This is another opportunity to reinforce the concept of his making choices and the notion that he has the power to react nonabusively even when he is feeling frustrated, angry, and explosive or wants to control a situation.

A final issue to be addressed involves the emotional and physical effect of his violence on his partner and children. Men often report becoming more aware of their family members' fear and pain as they progress in the group. This question is used to reemphasize the damaging impact of abuse and violence and the fear and loss of trust and intimacy that accompany it.

After they have presented this assessment, men are given feedback about how honestly and realistically they are addressing the situation that has occurred. This is a time when blaming, denial, and minimizing are directly confronted. If these are significant problems in the presentation of the incident, men are asked to go back and redo the assessment in its entirety. After he has written out and presented the Violent Incident Assessment, he must turn in a copy of this to his therapist.

TASK XII:
VIOLATION OF SOBRIETY CONTRACT ASSESSMENT

Task Objectives

1. To take complete responsibility for being honest and specific in reporting any use of chemicals (when a Sobriety Contract is a part of his treatment) throughout the course of his involvement in the group
2. To identify specific stressors and feelings he was experiencing in the hours, days, and weeks prior to his chemical use to understand how stress (and his response to it) and his feelings play a part in his choice to drink and/or use drugs
3. To clearly identify the connection between his self-talk (and the justifications and excuses that were generated by it) and his substance use

4. To acknowledge and be clear that his chemical use was a choice that he made
5. To recommit himself to his Sobriety Contract for the remainder of the group or to address and discuss issues that prevent him from doing this
6. To identify specific cues, strategies, and options that he can use when confronted with similar situations in the future as a means to help him view his Escalation Prevention Plan as a tool that can assist him in remaining sober as well as nonviolent
7. To listen to feedback from others in the group about their reactions and feelings related to his violation of the contract with himself, the other group members, and the program
8. To be accountable to the group regarding his chemical use as a means of reducing his shame and remaining open to the treatment process

Task Description

Domestic abuse and chemical use are highly correlated (Byles, 1978; Fagan, Stewart, and Hansen, 1983). A significant number of men who come into the domestic abuse program identify themselves as chemically dependent, having undergone previous chemical dependency treatments. Still others have histories of problematic chemical use, including "Driving While Intoxicated" charges (DWIs), arrests for other alcohol- or drug-related crimes (e.g., disorderly conduct charges related to drinking), or other significant consequences (e.g., divorces or being fired from a job due to chemical use). In addition, some have been using alcohol or drugs on a consistent basis when abuse or violence has occurred. Finally, there are those who have used chemicals as a primary stress reliever to "numb out" the tension or pain in their lives. Because chemicals have been an important part of their lives, all of these men are at risk of not benefiting fully from the treatment process if they do not make a commitment to sobriety, at least for the duration of their involvement in group.

When concerns regarding chemical use are identified, as in the previous situations, men are asked to commit to, sign, and date a Sobriety Contract, which states:

> I, _____ (his name) agree not to use any mood-altering chemicals (alcohol and/or drugs) during my domestic abuse treatment involvement.

This generally occurs during the intake but may, in fact, happen at any time during his treatment.

The Sobriety Contract is a commitment to himself, to the therapists, and to the other group members that he will completely abstain from any alcohol and drug use throughout his treatment process. When a man chooses to violate this contract and use chemicals (and this is viewed as a clear choice), it is expected that he will be honest and specific in reporting his chemical use at the next session he attends. This is done by writing out the assessment and bringing it to share with the group. If his chemical use is not reported and it is discovered from some other source (provided we have permission to use the information), the man may be terminated from the program.

One of the obvious difficulties in asking a man to remain sober for his treatment is that he may be dishonest about whether he is, in fact, using. Unfortunately, it is relatively easy for a man to lie about his use and get away with it. If information about chemical use is discovered from other sources, the man would face additional consequences if he was not being terminated from the group. He might be asked to get a chemical dependency evaluation or to attend mandatory Alcoholics Anonymous or Narcotics Anonymous meetings, with written verification of attendance. Also, arrangements might be made (often with a probation officer) for random drug testing. In the end, however, it is the man alone who suffers when he is dishonest. It is consistently emphasized that he is undermining his achievements in the program whenever he withholds important and relevant information from the group process.

This task addresses the specifics of the chemical use, including prior life stressors, both inside and outside the relationship, immediate events leading to the use, and a description of with whom, when, where, what, and how much was used. Both feelings and self-talk before, during, and after the chemical use are addressed, as is the choice process and the way in which the man gave himself permission to violate the contract. This is, for the program, simply another aspect of focusing on healthy versus unhealthy choices. Chemical use in this context is not seen as a slip or an out of control reaction to having an illness, but rather as part of a process that the man uses to violate a commitment. In this way, his chemical use is viewed as very similar to the process he goes through when he chooses not to use his Escalation Prevention Plan and escalates to violence. Men are encouraged to think about how they "planned for" their use or "set themselves up" to use rather than accepting the frequently offered notion that "it just happened." Beginning to see how they make decisions in all areas of their lives is a crucial part of what the program teaches.

Chemical use after signing a Sobriety Contract also brings into question the entire commitment the man has made. This is addressed directly by asking men what their use means in relation to their decision to be sober, including whether they still see maintaining sobriety during the group as an important goal. If they are uncertain whether sobriety is important to their treatment involvement, they have the opportunity to discuss what is different at this point in their lives that renders the contract unnecessary.

No man in the history of the program has attempted to argue that his Sobriety Contract no longer serves a meaningful purpose. However, this opportunity clearly states to him that his behavior is purposeful and that his decision to use is meaningful in the context of his domestic abuse treatment and the commitment he made to himself and other members. His decision to use may indicate anger with the treatment process or it may be an example of his difficulty in following through with commitments to his partner and others in his life.

Finally, men are asked to identify cues/triggers and ideas for the de-escalation strategies section of their Escalation Prevention Plan that they can add to assist them in choosing not to use chemicals in the future. This reinforces the notion that the EPP can be used in a variety of circumstances to help the man make healthier decisions.

After men have presented this assessment, they are given feedback about how honestly and realistically they are addressing the chemical use that has occurred. This is another time when blaming, denial, justifying, and minimizing are directly confronted.

Other members are also asked to comment on their reactions to the man's violating his commitment to them and the rest of the group. This breach of trust can become especially important to the other men who are struggling with their own commitment to maintain sobriety. If there are significant problems in the presentation of this assessment, men are asked to redo it completely.

Part 2: The Domestic Abuse Group Member Booklet

HOW TO USE THIS BOOKLET

This booklet includes everything you will need to complete the domestic abuse program. Be sure to read through the entire booklet before you start the group. The first section in the booklet describes the domestic abuse group. The second section discusses the group rules and expectations. The third section explains about how the group works and gives directions on how to actually participate in the group.

Following these introductory sections are the twelve basic tasks (see "Domestic Abuse Group Members' Tasks") that are a major part of your involvement in the program. The tasks ask you some very specific questions. You need to think about these questions, write out the answers outside of group, and ask for time during check-in at the beginning of group to present the task. If you are able to get time on that particular day, you then need to present your task and get feedback. Different tasks will take different amounts of time to complete, depending on the length and difficulty of the task, how open you are to the process, and how clear and complete you are in the presentation of your answers.

Each group member gets time to present tasks on a rotating basis and then must wait until everyone else has taken time before he gets it again. Generally, men take twenty minutes to present their tasks and then get five minutes of feedback from the other members and the group therapist. You can probably count on getting time to present your tasks every two to three groups. Be sure that you are prepared to present when it is your turn. Otherwise, you miss your turn and have to wait until everyone else in the rotation has presented. Your being responsible in the treatment program is critical to your completing the domestic abuse group.

The first three tasks, Introduction, Exercise Program, and Individual Member Goals, must be written out and presented at the first group you attend. The

143

fourth task to be presented is the Escalation Prevention Plan, which generally takes several sessions to complete. The fifth task is the Time-Out Plan, which usually takes one session to complete. The sixth task is the Abuse Inventory, which is one of the longer tasks, requiring several sessions to complete. The seventh task is the Midgroup Evaluation, which occurs at about the halfway point of your involvement and takes one session. The eighth task is the Family of Origin and Childhood task, which is another long task that requires several sessions. The ninth task is the Amends Letter, which should be presented in one session. The tenth task is the Aftercare Plan and Final Feedback, which is presented at the last group you attend.

Two other tasks are also part of the program, but you may or may not need to do them during your involvement in the group. The first is a Violent Incident Assessment. If you use physical force with anyone during the program, including physical discipline of your children, this task needs to be written out and presented at the next group you attend. The second is the Violation of Sobriety Contract Assessment. If you signed a contract during your intake stating that you would not use any alcohol or drugs during your program involvement and you decide to use chemicals anyway, you must write out and present this task at the next group you attend following the violation.

The actual tasks included in this booklet offer a longer explanation of what you need to do for each of them. If you have questions about task requirements, talk to other group members or contact your group therapist as soon as possible.

DOMESTIC ABUSE GROUP DESCRIPTION

Purpose

This is an ongoing weekly treatment group to assist men who have been explosively angry, controlling, and emotionally, verbally, and physically abusive with their wives, girlfriends, children, or others. The group involves both educational and process elements to help men learn to deal more effectively with their controlling attitudes and behaviors, their escalation patterns, and their feelings of anger, frustration, and resentment that have led to abusive behavior in the past.

Objectives

1. End the violence and the threat of violence.
2. Accept responsibility for your past violence and abuse and change your controlling attitudes and behaviors that have led to your being abusive.
3. Better understand your anger and how it affects you and others around you.
4. Identify and express more openly all the feelings that you experience.
5. Learn to deal more effectively with life stressors.
6. Actively use the group and others in your life for support and sharing as a means to lessen your emotional overdependence on your partner.
7. Examine and work on family-of-origin issues that relate to emotional, verbal, or physical abuse you experienced as a child and understand how these issues contribute to your current controlling and abusive attitudes and behaviors.
8. Address cultural issues that contribute to your current controlling and abusive attitudes and behaviors.
9. Explore, examine, and change all the ways you attempt to control others, including emotional/verbal abuse, threatening/intimidating actions, and other forms of manipulative behavior.
10. Learn to experience more control over yourself and your actions and take responsibility for your thoughts, feelings, wants, and behaviors in the present.
11. Learn and actively practice and use new skills, tools, and techniques to feel better about yourself and increase your compassion and empathy for your partner, your children, and others.

(HO)   ©1999 David J. Decker, MA

Length of Group

Men must be willing to make a minimum commitment of twenty group sessions. Most members need thirty to forty sessions to finish the group. The time it actually takes depends on how responsible you are in completing and presenting the individual tasks expected of group members.

Time and Location

_____

Intake Process

Group member assessments (usually four to six individual sessions) must be completed by the time a prospective member starts the group. If concerns about alcohol and/or drug use exist, a chemical health evaluation must be completed as well. Call _____ to set up an intake.

Fees

The cost is $ _____ per session. Fees may be covered by insurance.

(HO)　　　　　　　　　　　　　　©1999 David J. Decker, MA

GROUP RULES AND EXPECTATIONS

Group Rules

Any infraction of the following rules may constitute grounds for immediate termination.

1. No violence or threat of violence to therapist or other group members.
2. No use of any alcohol or drugs at any time on the day of group. (No using chemicals at all for the duration of the group if you have agreed to a Sobriety Contract during your intake.)
3. No more than four (4) misses are allowed within the first twenty group sessions you attend. Two (2) additional misses are allowed within the next ten group sessions and two (2) additional misses are allowed within the ten group sessions that follow those (however, you cannot miss more than two groups in a row at any time). (Absences are not included in the twenty-group minimum expectation.)
4. Confidentiality ("what is said in group stays in group") must be respected and maintained.
5. Violence (which we define as using physical force with anyone, including physical discipline of your children) must be brought up immediately after the violence occurs and discussed in group. (See "Task XI: Violent Incident Assessment" in this group member booklet.)
6. You are expected to make weekly payments for the group sessions at the time of service.
   a. You will be charged for absences since we cannot fill your spot on a one-shot basis.
   b. If you are not responsible regarding payment, this will be addressed in group and you will receive a letter to that effect from the business office. If you do not remedy the situation at that time, you face the possibility of termination from the group.

Group Expectations

1. Be on time: group will begin promptly at the designated time.
2. We want you to call to notify us if you will not be attending group on a particular night so that we can let other members know that we have

heard from you. Remember, too, that even if you do not attend, you will still be charged for the session since a spot has been reserved for you in the group (there are no excused absences).

3. We expect you to complete written assignments (e.g., group tasks) and homework before coming to group. No time will be set aside to do them during group.

4. The quality of your work is as important as your attendance. It is not acceptable to simply "put in time" or "sit through group." We expect you to:
   a. actively participate in group discussions,
   b. talk about yourself and how you are using or not using the program tools, and
   c. offer feedback to others.

5. We expect you to be willing to look at yourself and your own issues rather than focusing on or blaming your partner and others for your violence and abuse and for your current thoughts, feelings, and behaviors.

6. We expect you to avoid arguing and debating about the program's domestic abuse philosophy during your therapy, for example,
   a. doubting the existence of an escalation process and cues that you can identify to begin to intervene in your escalation;
   b. denying your responsibility for your abusive and violent behavior;
   c. claiming that you are unable to make conscious choices about whether you continue to be threatening, intimidating, and abusive; or
   d. disbelieving that you can unlearn your controlling attitudes and bad habits related to the way you think and behave and become nonabusive if you wish to do so.

7. We expect you to avoid touching others in the group without their permission as a means to begin to address issues concerning crossing others' physical boundaries (e.g., reaching over and touching someone spontaneously while in group).

8. We expect you to avoid being abusive and disrespectful toward others in the group (e.g., pointing, name-calling, raising your voice, interrupting). We want you to listen to feedback from others even if you do not like it or do not especially want to hear it.

9. We want you to refer to adult females (eighteen years and older) as "women," not "girls," "gals," or other derogatory names (curse and swear words that describe women, e.g., "bitch"). Hopefully, this will give

(HO) ©1999 David J. Decker, MA

you the opportunity to notice how you view and describe your partner and other women. It is our belief that thinking about women in diminutive terms, in negative terms, or as objects sets the stage for you to become controlling and abusive with them. In this same regard, we also want you to refer to your partner by her first name rather than by calling her "my wife," "the wife," or "my old lady," which can be part of communicating that you own her or that you view her as your property.

HOW TO PARTICIPATE IN GROUP

1. Completing the domestic abuse program involves two major areas:
   a. First, you need to attend at least twenty weekly sessions. Most members take thirty to forty sessions to complete the group. The time it actually takes depends on how responsible you are in writing out and presenting the individual tasks expected of all group members.
   b. Second, you need to completely write out and present to the group each of the tasks that is outlined in this booklet.
2. Each group itself generally proceeds in the following way:
   a. The group opens with a five- to ten-minute check-in, during which members
      • state their names;
      • talk about how they are feeling at that moment;
      • review their week, noting escalations and use of time-outs, positive accomplishments, whether they made their required phone call and did the expected exercise, whether they have followed contracts they have with the group (e.g., Sobriety Contract); and
      • ask to take time during the group session to present tasks that they have ready to share or to address other issues that have arisen during the week.
   b. The next twenty minutes are spent on educational units that address a variety of topics, including such things as anger control, stress management, communication, conflict resolution, assertiveness, parenting, and shame and empowerment.
   c. The next section, which uses most of the time in group, involves members actually taking time to present their completed tasks.
   d. The final five minutes are devoted to a check-out, during which members discuss their feelings and reactions regarding the day's group and also their concerns about significant plans, activities, or potential escalations during the coming week.
3. You can ask for and take time to discuss anything that relates to your thoughts, feelings, or actions and that creates stress and tension in your life. It does not have to relate only to your past or current violence and abuse, although you are encouraged to bring up any escalations that occur during the week and discuss briefly how you handled them.
4. State clearly how much time you want and care for yourself by learning to be assertive and asking for as much time as you really think you will need. Do not "shortchange" yourself! The amount of time that people get will be negotiated by all members of the group, which gives you

and others an opportunity to practice compromise rather than control and intimidation. You can generally count on getting time for yourself every third week.

5. Time is always a major issue in the group. Be conscientious about staying within the time limit that you have set for yourself by
   a. staying focused on the issue and your behavior (versus "rambling" and blaming),
   b. summarizing as soon as possible, and
   c. asking the group directly for what you want (e.g., feedback, support).
      You can also be responsible about the time by requesting that another member watch the time and let you know when your time has elapsed and by assertively asking other members for more time if you really need it.

6. Ask for and expect feedback from others and try to be open to the feedback you receive:
   a. Attempt to listen to and really hear all the feedback a person is offering before responding. Try to avoid explaining away the feedback, arguing, becoming defensive, trying to prove your point, or attempting to get the last word in.
   b. If you have difficulty understanding what the person is saying to you, ask for clarification or try to think of specific ways that the feedback could fit for you. Beware the use of "not understanding" as a defense against truly hearing the feedback.
   c. Whenever possible, share your feelings about the feedback with the group in a respectful and nonblaming manner.
   d. Remember that another person's feedback is their opinion and not the gospel. Listen to the feedback, think about it, take what fits for you, and try to learn from it. Learn to become aware of when your shame and other negative feelings about yourself are activated because this can often interfere with your accurately hearing, understanding, and learning from the feedback.

7. Be direct and honest about offering your feedback to others:
   a. Take the risk to make a specific point or express a specific concern or feeling rather than simply asking questions of the member who is taking time (which can be a way to stay "safe" and avoid honesty and conflict). Remember that you are an expert on control and abuse and generally know what you are talking about when you are offering feedback to others. Part of being in the group is sharing your expertise openly with other members. Men usually learn more from one another than they do from any other part of this process.

(HO)   ©1999 David J. Decker, MA

b. Be specific about the behaviors or attitudes to which you are reacting. Help the person taking time to understand what you are trying to say by giving brief examples from your own life experience. Remember to keep the focus on the person taking time, however.

c. Use "I" statements and take responsibility for your thoughts, feelings, and reactions. Remember that what you see, hear, feel, and believe is not necessarily the absolute truth.

d. Be descriptive rather than judging, accusing, condemning, labeling, or being disrespectful with other members. You are here to listen to and learn from one another's honest reactions; you are not here to shame others in the group.

e. Avoid protecting, caretaking, or "rescuing" others in the group (and watch out for being overly polite). If you hold back your reactions because you fear that the other person will become angry, defensive, and rejecting or because you do not want others to be honest with you, then you and the other members will not benefit fully from the group. You have a great deal to teach and to learn from one another if you allow yourself to be open to the process.

f. In summary, when offering feedback use the following guidelines:
   • Be direct and specific
   • Be brief
   • Avoid asking questions
   • Do not use the feedback time to focus on yourself and your own issues

8. You have the right to take a time-out at any point in the group if you are escalating and the potential exists for you to become disrespectful or abusive to the therapists or other group members. If you decide to take a time-out, it is expected that you will let others know that you are going to do so prior to leaving the group and that you will talk about why you took the time-out when you return.

9. Try to view the group process as a "laboratory," a safe place where you can actually practice skills such as communication, assertiveness, and conflict resolution and where you can begin to develop honesty, openness, and closeness with other people. These same skills and qualities can then be transferred to your relationships with your partner, your family members, and your friends if you choose to do so.

DOMESTIC ABUSE GROUP MEMBERS' TASKS

The following is a list of individual tasks that make up the domestic abuse program. Everything that you need to complete each of these assignments is included in your packet. Each of these tasks must be written out completely outside group prior to asking for time to present them in group itself. At that point, you are expected to ask for time during check-in to present the completed task. The first three assignments should be presented at the first group you attend. After that, you are responsible for writing out the assignments and for being assertive in asking for and taking time to present them in the group in a timely fashion. The Aftercare Plan should be presented at the final group you attend.

Members must finish all of the following tasks to successfully complete the group program. Most members take thirty to forty sessions to do this. However, the time it takes for you to finish the group will depend on how responsible you are in writing out the tasks, how assertive you are in asking for time, and how complete you are in presenting these tasks in group.

Individual Tasks	Group Number and Date When Completed
1. Present Introduction to other group members and give out phone number(s) where you can be reached at your *(first group)*	_____
2. Present Exercise Program at your *(first group)*	_____
3. Present Individual Member Goals at your *(first group)*	_____
4. Present Escalation Prevention Plan and get feedback	_____
5. Present Time-Out Plan and get feedback	_____

(HO)   ©1999 David J. Decker, MA

6 Present Abuse Inventory and get feedback _____

7. Present Midgroup Evaluation and get feedback _____

8. Present Family of Origin and Childhood and get feedback _____

9. Present Amends Letter and get feedback _____

10. Present Aftercare Plan and get feedback/recommendations at your *(final group)* _____

11. Present Violent Incident Assessment(s) when you use physical force with anyone during the course of the group *(ongoing, if necessary)* _____

12. Present Violation of Sobriety Contract Assessment(s) when you choose to use chemicals during the course of the group if you have signed a Sobriety Contract as part of your participation in group *(ongoing, if necessary)* _____

(HO)   ©1999 David J. Decker, MA

TASK I: INTRODUCTION

Write out answers to the following questions (on a separate sheet of paper if necessary) as a means to introduce yourself to the other members of the group *at the first group you attend*. Other members will also briefly introduce themselves to you at this time.

1. What is your name?

2. How did you feel on the way to group tonight and how are you feeling about being here in a domestic abuse group?

3. Why are you here? Be sure to talk about how you have been abusive with your partner and others and mention some of the consequences that you have experienced as a result of being explosive, controlling, and abusive or some of the difficulties your being abusive has created in your life.

4. What do you want to learn or gain from your participation in this group?

5. Are you court-ordered to domestic abuse treatment as a result of prior legal involvement? If so, what happened?

6. Has chemical (alcohol and/or drug) use been a part of your previous abuse and violence? If so, in what way? Did you agree to a Sobriety Contract with your intake therapist during your assessment?

7. Did you sign a No-Suicide Contract with your intake therapist during your assessment? Have you used threats of suicide with your partner in the past? If so, give examples.

8. What is one thing you like about yourself?

9. What is a phone number where you can be reached by other group members?

Part of the expectation for the domestic abuse program is that you *initiate and make at least one phone contact per week* with another group member throughout the course of your time in group. One way to begin to intervene in your emotional overdependence on your partner is to use other members for sharing and support, both when you feel escalated and at other times. In addition, this can be a first step in beginning to trust, get closer to, and form friendships with other men (which can apply to group members and to others in your life). During the first week, all of the men in the group will call you. From then on, you must make at least one call each week. Take time at the end of your first group to write down the other group members' names and phone numbers on a sheet of paper so you will have them available. Listed below are crisis and support resources.

(HO) ©1999 David J. Decker, MA

NAMES OF OTHER GROUP MEMBERS   PHONE NUMBER(S)

_____   _____

_____   _____

_____   _____

_____   _____

_____   _____

_____   _____

_____   _____

_____   _____

_____   _____

_____   _____

IF YOU ARE IN CRISIS AND NEED ADDITIONAL HELP OR SUP-
PORT DURING YOUR INVOLVEMENT IN THE DOMESTIC ABUSE
PROGRAM, YOU CAN CONTACT THESE RESOURCES:

_____

_____

_____

_____

_____

_____

_____

(HO)   ©1999 David J. Decker, MA

TASK II: EXERCISE PROGRAM

At the first group you attend, you are expected to devise and present to your group an exercise program that you agree to follow throughout your involvement with your domestic abuse treatment. The primary reason for this expectation is to give you a means to regularly release some of the physical buildup of stress that you experience (i.e., what you wrote about in the "Physical Cues" section of your Escalation Prevention Plan that you began in your assessment process).

We want your group exercise regimen to be both *nonviolent* (e.g., dissimilar to violent motions such as hitting or kicking) and *noncompetitive* (since competition often creates stress rather than alleviating it). This exercise also needs to be separate and different from exercise that you might normally get at work. Examples of the type of aerobic exercise we expect you to do would include walking, biking, jogging, swimming, skating, calisthenics, cross-country skiing, weight-lifting, roller blading, and using an exercycle, rowing machine, or stairclimber. Our expectation is that you will do the exercise you choose *at least three times a week for at least twenty minutes each time.*

My exercise program to reduce the stress level in my life will be:

_____

_____

I commit to doing this exercise, as a part of my domestic abuse treatment, at least three times a week for at least twenty minutes each time for the duration of my involvement in the group program. I will record the times I exercise in the spaces below.

_____　　　_____

(Signature)　　　　　　　　　　　　　(Date)

(HO)　　　　　　　　　　　　　　　　©1999 David J. Decker, MA

Date and Amount of Time

Week 1: _____ _____ _____

Week 2: _____ _____ _____

Week 3: _____ _____ _____

Week 4: _____ _____ _____

Week 5: _____ _____ _____

Week 6: _____ _____ _____

Week 7: _____ _____ _____

Week 8: _____ _____ _____

Week 9: _____ _____ _____

Week 10: _____ _____ _____

Week 11: _____ _____ _____

Week 12: _____ _____ _____

Week 13: _____ _____ _____

Week 14: _____ _____ _____

Week 15: _____ _____ _____

Week 16: _____   _____   _____

Week 17: _____   _____   _____

Week 18: _____   _____   _____

Week 19: _____   _____   _____

Week 20: _____   _____   _____

Week 21: _____   _____   _____

Week 22: _____   _____   _____

Week 23: _____   _____   _____

Week 24: _____   _____   _____

Week 25: _____   _____   _____

Week 26: _____   _____   _____

Week 27: _____   _____   _____

Week 28: _____   _____   _____

Week 29: _____   _____   _____

Week 30: _____   _____   _____

(HO)

TASK III: INDIVIDUAL MEMBER GOALS

General Goals for All Members:

1. Learn and use new skills to intervene in my emotional and verbal abuse, my threatening and intimidating behavior, and my violence toward my partner, my children, and others.
2. Accept responsibility for the emotional, verbal, sexual, and physical abuse I have perpetrated in the past against my partner, my children, and others.
3. Examine and change my controlling attitudes and behaviors that underlie my abuse.
4. Address family-of-origin and cultural issues and understand how they contribute to my current controlling and abusive attitudes and behaviors.
5. Actively use my group for emotional sharing and support.
6. Work at improving my self-esteem and feeling better about myself and increasing my ability to feel compassion and empathy for my partner and others.

An important and necessary part of any treatment process is to set specific, concrete, and measurable goals for yourself so that you have some sense of the progress you are making in the group. In the space provided below, write out at least three or four goals on which you agree to work during your therapy involvement. These must be presented *during your first group.*

My Own Goals in Therapy

_____

_____

_____

_____

_____

_____

_____

_____

(HO)   ©1999 David J. Decker, MA

I understand and agree to the goals designated by the Domestic Abuse Program, and I have added my own goals as well. I agree to this treatment plan. I understand that I can, with my therapist(s), renegotiate my goals and the treatment plan as I progress in the group. As part of my participation in the domestic abuse group, I commit myself to being nonviolent with my partner, my children, and others in my life. I also agree to remove any firearms from my residence(s) and store them elsewhere for the duration of the group.

_____   _____

(Signature)   (Date)

TASK IV: ESCALATION PREVENTION PLAN

Abusive anger and violence do not just happen. A gradual buildup of emotion and tension occurs over time that you will be better able to recognize if you pay closer attention to your stress level on a regular basis. Increases in tension and stress need an outlet. You may turn your stress inward on your own body, which can lead to physical illness; you might use chemicals more frequently or eat more than usual; you may spend especially long hours trying to be productive in your work setting or at home; you might lack energy, become lethargic, or feel tired much of the time; or you may lash out at someone emotionally, verbally, physically, or sexually.

Anger is a normal and natural emotion (even though it is also painful and uncomfortable) that allows you to set healthy limits and to increase the potential for intimacy, if it is expressed in an assertive and respectful manner. The purpose of this plan is to assist you in realizing when you are feeling tense, escalated, and angry and to help you find positive and constructive ways of expressing your emotions. The cue categories provided in the following material will help you pay closer attention to your own stress buildup. The more awareness you have of the specific information about you and your life that fits into these categories, the greater potential you will have to moderate and intervene in the controlling, abusive, violent, and self-destructive behaviors that have been part of your anger in the past. Being aware of your cues and understanding where you are in your escalation process can help you use your Escalation Prevention Plan to find the means to de-escalate and calm yourself before you become abusive and say or do something that you will regret later.

Remember, too, that an "escalation" is not just feeling full of rage or "out of control" or behaving in an abusive manner; it is also the process of experiencing any and all feelings (e.g., anxiety, depression) and signs (e.g., hunger, increased heartbeat) that may eventually lead to controlling and abusive behavior and the potential for violence. The key to using this plan is to slow down your internal emotional arousal and to learn to effectively intervene in your escalation as early as possible. This will also allow you to communicate your anger (and your other feelings behind it) in a more calm, assertive, and respectful manner. Write out as much information as you can about your cues and your plan to take care of yourself (and the others around you) in the spaces provided after each category. *Be as specific as possible.* This task will need to be presented in group after you have filled it out completely.

(HO)   ©1999 David J. Decker, MA

Cues That Indicate When You Are Becoming
Escalated, Tense, and Angry

Problem Situations and Issues

What situations and issues in your life trigger your escalation and anger (e.g., others getting angry with you, not getting your way, experiencing conflict with a co-worker, someone disagreeing with or criticizing you, your children misbehaving, being cut off on the highway)?

People/Animals

Who are the specific people or animals from the past or present with whom you are more likely to escalate when you are around them or think about them (e.g., your boss, your parents, your in-laws, your partners, former partners, your children, co-workers, family pets)? This can include *categories of people* who are frustrating or irritating to you (e.g., slow drivers, inattentive clerks).

Places

Where do you tend to escalate most frequently (e.g., specific rooms in the house or apartment, such as the bedroom or kitchen; in the car; specific locations at work, such as your boss's office or your workstation; at bars; sports settings, such as a racquetball court or a softball diamond)?

Times

What are some specific times when you are more likely to escalate?

During the day (e.g., at dinner, just before leaving for work, getting your children ready to leave in the morning, on the way to or from work)

During the week (e.g., on weekends, Sunday evenings before returning to work)

During the month (e.g., at the end of the month because you run out of money, when you write out the bills)

During the year (e.g., on specific holidays, vacations, slow times at work, particular seasons)

Self-Talk

Self-talk involves the words, phrases, and sentences that you say to yourself. The following categories illustrate different aspects of self-talk.

Negative thoughts/worries. Give general examples of when you think, brood, or "stew" about situations from the past or in the present until you become tense, angry, and controlling (e.g., thinking that your partner is going out with another man, worrying about the level of conflict in your relationship, "stewing" about not having enough money to pay all your bills, brooding about the mistakes you have made in the past, fretting about how your kids are doing).

(HO)   ©1999 David J. Decker, MA

Negative rehearsal. Give examples of when you visualize, plan for, or anticipate a negative outcome in the future, even before anything actually occurs (e.g., planning a confrontation with your partner that might not even be necessary, getting worked up over a situation that does not even necessarily turn out the way you thought it would, imagining your partner flirting with another man, thinking about yelling at your partner ahead of time).

Specific negative self-talk. What words, labels, and phrases do you think to yourself about yourself and about others that indicate when you are angry, tense, or escalated or that indicate that the potential exists for you to escalate and become controlling?

- *Thoughts about yourself* (e.g., "How can I be so stupid?" "I'm a loser," "I've screwed it up again," "I'll never get it right," "What a dummy")

- *Thoughts about others* (e.g., "Here she goes again," "Why doesn't he get off my back?" "She's really asking for it now," "She's a jerk," "He's an asshole," "I can't stand what she's doing to me")

Trigger Words/Phrases

What are some specific words and phrases that others say to you which are instantly irritating or frustrating and that you say to others which let you know that you are escalated or escalating?

Words/phrases others say to you (e.g., "Grow up," "You'll never amount to anything," "Get a life," "Screw you," "Get with it," "What's wrong with you?" "You're an abuser")

Words/phrases you say to others (e.g., "You're crazy"; specific swear words that you say when you are escalating such as "Get fucked" or "bitch")

Physical Signals

How does your body tell you that you are becoming angry, tense, and escalated? What happens to you physically when you are escalating (e.g., tight jaw, clenched fists, rapid breathing, heart racing, tension in your neck)?

Emotional Cues

What feelings do you experience just before and as you escalate (e.g., anger, frustration)? What feelings are hidden or covered up by your anger and escalation (e.g., hurt, sadness)?

De-Escalation Strategies

These strategies will help you to intervene in your escalation process and to deal respectfully with others when you are tense, stressed, or angry. What will you do to calm yourself and slow down your escalation process? Your strategies should be designed

1. so that you do not become controlling, intimidating, threatening, and emotionally, verbally, sexually, or physically abusive to those around you and
2. so that you can learn to communicate more effectively and respectfully with others

Remember, too, that this de-escalation section of the Escalation Prevention Plan is not just for acute escalations involving the potential for abuse, but also can and should be used for long-term preventive maintenance concerning anger, stress, and control issues in your life.

(HO)   ©1999 David J. Decker, MA

TASK V: TIME-OUT PLAN

After reading through the Using Time-Outs handout, write out your answers to the following questions (using additional sheets if necessary) as a way to begin thinking about and integrating time-outs in your life. Use this plan as a tool to help you actually implement this skill with your partner and others. Take time to present this in group when you are ready.

1. What are the *most important cues* (i.e., stress signals such as problem situations/issues, negative thoughts/rehearsal/self-talk, trigger words/ phrases, emotions, physical reactions) from your EPP that indicate you may be escalating and becoming prone to using controlling behaviors and/or potentially explosive/abusive anger and may need to take a time-out? *Rank them below* (e.g., upper-level cues are those that you experience just before you choose to act out your anger and desire to control in a physical way.

   • LOWER-LEVEL CUES:

   • MIDDLE-LEVEL CUES:

   • UPPER-LEVEL CUES:

2. How will you communicate to your partner, your children, or others that you need a time-out (this can be a *verbal* or *nonverbal* method) when you are beginning to escalate and there is the potential for abusive or explosive anger? Be specific.

   • With your partner

   • With your children

   • With others (give some examples of when this might be necessary)

3. What will you do or say if the other person does not want you to leave to take a time-out? *Be specific.*

4. Be clear in identifying how you will handle time-outs and where you will go at that time, and be sure to include *any of the possible situations below.* Also talk about how you will care for your children (if you have any) when you or your partner takes a time-out.

   • AT YOUR HOME

   • IN THE CAR

   • AT FRIENDS' OR RELATIVES' HOMES (e.g., on holidays, at social gatherings)

   • AT OUTSIDE ACTIVITIES/EVENTS (including public places such as restaurants, stores, malls, sporting events)

   • AT WORK

   • ON THE PHONE

5. How long will your time-out period with your partner last (at a minimum)? Be sure to give yourself enough time.

©1999 David J. Decker, MA

6. Where can you go if you need to take an *extended* time-out (e.g., if you need to be away overnight or for two or three days)?

7. At the end of this time, how will you reenter the situation that you have left. *Be specific* about a plan to come back (i.e., how will you approach/reconnect with/talk to your partner at this point? What will you do if your partner or the other person doesn't want to talk at that time?)

8. During your time-out, what specific *positive* actions will you commit to taking to de-escalate and calm yourself (from the de-escalation strategies portion of your EPP)? Be sure to identify your "quiet space" (the place in your mind you will visualize where you can feel calm, peaceful, and safe).

9. What *people, activities, and thoughts should you try to avoid* during your time-out period (i.e., people, activities, and thoughts that might exacerbate your escalation)?

10. What *excuses* will you use (or have you used in the past) to avoid taking respectful time-outs? What positive statements will actually help you in taking a time-out when you need it. *Be specific.*

I commit myself to further developing and actively using my Time-Out Plan with my partner and others to intervene in my escalation and to decrease my potential for controlling, abusive, and violent behavior in the future.

_____   _____

(Signature)   (Date)

©1999 David J. Decker, MA

TASK VI: ABUSE INVENTORY

An important part of recovery and taking responsibility for your past and current abusive and controlling attitudes and behaviors is to address openly and honestly how you have treated others in the past. The purpose of completing the Abuse Inventory is to examine your entire history of abuse and violence as a means of understanding how and when you became abusive and violent and how your desire to control others in these and additional ways has been reinforced and rewarded.

It is vital that you work hard at remembering incidents from your past, even though your shame and your defenses, such as denial and minimizing, have probably become an important part of "forgetting" what you did to others and how it affected you and them. If you have difficulty remembering, one option is to talk to your partner, family-of-origin members, relatives, or friends who may be able to help you remember incidents from your past that you have tried to forget. Keep in mind, however, that it is still your responsibility to use these people as resources only if you can do so without escalating and becoming abusive regarding their perspectives and memories and only if they feel comfortable with this process and are willing to help you with it.

The following questions must be *written out completely on separate sheets of paper* and presented to the group for feedback when you are ready.

1. List and discuss *all the previous incidents* when you have been violent, from your first recollection as a child to the present. These episodes of violence can be with parents, siblings, friends, peers, strangers, girlfriends, wives, children, animals, or yourself. Describe the incidents *in as much specific detail as possible*. Be sure to include examples of your verbal and emotional abuse, threats toward others, and destruction of property.

2. Describe the *most violent and abusive incident* with your partner (i.e., the time you felt the most out of control, the time your partner felt the most afraid, or the time you did the most damage).
   a. What cues did you experience?
   b. List and describe in detail your emotional, verbal, sexual, and physical abuse toward her and any other ways in which you attempted to control her in that situation.
   c. What was the effect on your partner and your children (if you have any and if they were present or heard the incident)?

(HO)   ©1999 David J. Decker, MA

3. What has your *negative self-talk* been *prior to, during, and after* you have chosen to be violent and abusive? Go back to the incidents described above and think of as many specific examples of your self-talk as you can.

4. How have you given yourself *permission* to be violent and abusive or how you have justified your violence and abuse in the past (i.e., *excuses* you have used to avoid taking responsibility for your controlling and abusive behavior)?

5. Give *at least four specific examples of the choices* you made and when you made them at various points in the most violent incident (MVI) you have discussed above. Use this part of the inventory to break down your MVI into steps and to identify the sequence of choices you made that led you to be violent in the situation you have described. This can also include ways in which you built up to, rehearsed for, or planned for the violence that occurred and/or the specific decisions you made during the process of becoming abusive. This is a concrete way to indicate that you understand the decision-making process you used and that you realize you were not out of control when you were being abusive.

6. What are some of the specific ways that you tried to keep your abuse and violence a *secret* from others outside the relationship? How successful were you in actually keeping the secret?

7. What was your *vision of what you wanted and expected your partner to be* in your relationship with her? Be honest and specific about characteristics and traits that she was supposed to have (in your mind) to make you happy. How was your vision of your partner related to your becoming abusive with her?

8. How much has *chemical use* (alcohol, street drugs, caffeine, nicotine, prescription, and over-the-counter medications) been a part of your past violence and abuse? Do you see your chemical use being related to your abusive behavior? In what ways?

9. What were/are the *advantages* of using physical force and violence with your partner and others (i.e., you would not have been abusive unless being violent offered *payoffs* for you)?

10. What *legal consequences* have you experienced as a result of your violence, threats, and abuse (e.g., police calls, restraining orders, assault or disorderly conduct charges, time spent in jail, probation)?

(HO)   ©1999 David J. Decker, MA

11. What *other kinds of consequences* have you experienced as a result of your violence and abuse? List as many as you can for the following areas:
    a. Relationship
    b. Emotional
    c. Social
    d. Job-related
    e. Financial
    f. Spiritual

TASK VII: MIDGROUP EVALUATION

The following questions should be considered in assessing your progress in the group thus far. Write out your assessment of your progress on separate sheets of paper and be prepared to take time to share your thoughts with the group when you have completed this task. At that point, you will also have the opportunity to receive feedback from other members and your therapists about how they perceive your functioning in the group, your willingness to address your abuse and control issues, and your recovery program in general.

1. How long have you been nonviolent with your partner, your children, and others? How often have you been emotionally and verbally abusive (on an average) with your partner, children, and others since you started the group?
2. How much responsibility have you taken for your abusive and violent behavior and how have you demonstrated this to the group and to your partner? How much are you continuing to blame your partner and others for your thoughts, feelings, and abusive behavior? How are you working at taking full responsibility for yourself?
3. How willing have you been to accept, and how have you begun to change, your controlling attitudes and behaviors? Give specific examples with your partner and others.
4. Identify ways that you have attempted to control others in the group and your treatment process itself (e.g., explaining away feedback, being unwilling to listen, interrupting, withdrawing into silence, trying to get the last word in). *At this point*, ask for feedback from other members about how they have seen you trying to exert control.
5. How actively have you participated in group (e.g., sharing your thoughts and feelings about yourself, offering honest feedback to others, speaking up in the educational discussions)?
6. How *confrontive and supportive* have you been with other group members, both inside and outside the group? Give at least four specific examples of how you have been confrontive and supportive with other members.
7. How else are you different now as compared to when you first came to treatment? Are there any other ways in which you feel better about yourself? How are you working on developing more empathy and compassion for your partner and others (i.e., how are you trying to see things from others' perspectives)? *Be specific.*

(HO)   ©1999 David J. Decker, MA

8. How and with whom are you still being abusive and controlling in your life? Which personal issues are still difficult for you (i.e., where do you feel "stuck")? *Be specific.*
9. What cues have you added to your Escalation Prevention Plan, during your first half of group? In what other ways can you improve your Escalation Prevention Plan, and how can you use it more effectively in your day-to-day life?
10. What are your goals for the rest of the program? *Note at least three or four and be specific.* How do you plan to reach these goals?

TASK VIII: FAMILY OF ORIGIN AND CHILDHOOD

To benefit fully from the recovery process, men who have been abusive should try to understand how what they learned in their families of origin and during their childhood has contributed to their being violent, emotionally and verbally abusive, and threatening, intimidating, and controlling with their partners. Understanding how these attitudes and behaviors developed can help a man decide whether to continue being abusive in the present and whether to pass these attitudes and behaviors on to his own children and future generations.

For this assignment, you are expected to write out the answers to the following questions on separate sheets of paper and share the answers with your group when the task is completed.

1. *List* (names and ages) and *describe in detail* all family members and others who were important to you and your family (e.g., relatives, hired help, exchange students) and with whom you were around during your childhood.
2. Who of the above people (including yourself) took on the following roles in your family network and how were these roles played out?
   a. *Caretaker:* a person who tries to care for others' emotional and physical needs
   b. *High achiever:* a person who continually tries to accomplish great things to make parents and family proud to distract from the family's tension and pain
   c. *Scapegoat:* a persons who acts out the family's pain or who is the target of the parents' or the family's anger
   d. *Lost child:* a person who seems "out of it" or "lost in his or her own world"
   e. *People pleaser:* a person who tries to do everything possible to get others' approval
   f. *Clown:* a person who jokes around or uses humor to decrease the tension in the family
   g. *Rebel:* a person who flaunts parental and other authority and refuses (aggressively or passively) to do what is asked or expected of him or her

   How have the roles you played in your family affected your relationships with your partner, your children (if you have any), and others?

©1999 David J. Decker, MA

3. What *values* were "prized" and important in your family? Check the ones below that fit; add your own if you can think of some. Think and write about how these values relate to you and other family members. Talk about how these values were communicated to you and also consider whether the *stated values* were different from the way others *actually behaved*.

—— Be honest	—— Be self-sufficient
—— Be tough	—— Never make mistakes
—— Do not be emotional	—— Be "right"
—— Be the "best"	—— Work hard
—— Be religious	—— Be loyal
—— Be intelligent	—— Be in control
—— Make a lot of money	—— Be fair
—— Go to school/be educated	—— Do not talk
—— Have material possessions	—— Take responsibility for yourself

How have each of the values that were prized in your family affected your relationships with your partner, your children (if you have any), and others?

4. What were your family's *rules* regarding the following:
   a. How boys and men were viewed and treated
   b. How girls and women were viewed and treated
   c. How children were viewed and treated
   d. How children should be and were disciplined
   e. How language was viewed and what was acceptable (and for whom)
   f. How anger was expressed and conflict resolved

How have the rules you learned in your family affected your relationships with your partner, your children (if you have any), and others?

5. Address the following issues in evaluating your family and childhood. After each answer you give, think about and discuss how these issues have affected your relationship with your partner, your children (if you have any), and others (give some specific examples of the effects for each one).
   a. Describe your parents' relationship with each other (e.g., emotional sharing/ connectedness, expressing caring/affection, spending time together, conflict between them and how it was resolved).
   b. Who had the final say in family decisions and how was it enforced?

(HO)   ©1999 David J. Decker, MA

c. Was anyone in your family "always right" and how did you recognize this? Did your parents or caretakers ever apologize for things they said or did?

d. Who was the primary disciplinarian and how were you disciplined? How did you feel about the discipline you received (e.g., did you believe you deserved what you got)?

e. To whom did you feel closest in the family and why?

f. Who influenced you the most to become the person you have become as an adult? How did that person influence you?

g. Who gave you the feeling that you were not wanted or cared about? What did that person say or do to trigger this feeling in you?

h. What feelings were okay to express and how were they expressed? How were losses handled (e.g., death of a pet/family member, friend, or relative; job loss; having to move)?

i. How were affection and caring expressed among family members?

j. What were and are your family's secrets (i.e., sources of shame)? What were you told or what did you believe you had to hide from others?

k. What are some of the phrases, slogans, or mottoes that your parents or other family members frequently used (e.g., "Buck up"; "You shouldn't feel that way"; "It's a great life if you don't weaken"; "The first hundred years are the hardest"; "Act like a man"; "Only babies cry"; "Go play in the road"; "Don't let the door hit you in the ass on the way out")?

l. How was sex talked about and handled in your family? Where and how did you learn about sex? How were your attitudes toward girls and women affected by sexuality and what and how you learned about it?

m. Describe your relationships with childhood girlfriends. Were you emotionally, verbally, physically, and/or sexually abusive with them? If so, in what ways were you controlling and abusive with them and what happened to the relationships?

n. Were you or other family members involved with illegal or criminal activity (e.g., vandalism, burglary, shoplifting) during your childhood? If so, what happened, and did you or others experience any consequences as a result?

o. How were you treated by peers in your neighborhood and in school, by neighbors, teachers, coaches, and others outside your immediate family? What were your relationships with friends like?

©1999 David J. Decker, MA

p. Who in your life treated you in a respectful and nurturing way and let you know that you were an important person who was cared about (including relatives, friends, neighbors, teachers, coaches, and others)? How did they let you know that they cared about you and thought you were special?

q. Did you talk with anyone about the dysfunction, neglect, or abuse in your family of origin and what was his or her response? Did anyone inside or outside your family try to protect you from the abuse or tell you that you did not deserve to be abused or neglected?

6. Who among your family members (*including yourself*) had/has the following characteristics:
   a. Controlling (How were others controlled?)
   b. Emotionally and verbally abusive, threatening, and/or intimidating (Give examples.)
   c. Abusing or dependent on alcohol or drugs (What chemicals were used, how were they used, and what would happen when they were used?)
   d. Physically abusive (Give examples.)
   e. Sexually abusive (Give examples.)

7. How have you been like your father? How have you been like your mother? How have the similarities to your parents affected your relationships with your partner, your children (if you have any), and others?

8. How does what you thought and felt as a child in your family relate to your self-talk and feelings in the present when you choose to lash out emotionally, verbally, or physically with your partner or others?

9. What do you want (or wish you had had the chance) to say to your father and your mother about your childhood experiences?

©1999 David J. Decker, MA

TASK IX: AMENDS LETTER

Another important part of the recovery process concerning the issues related to violence is writing a letter to the victim(s) of your abuse. The purposes of this letter are

1. to take responsibility for what you have done and
2. to make amends to the victim(s) for the violence, the emotional and verbal abuse, and the other controlling attitudes and behaviors that have previously been a major part of your relationship with them.

This letter enables you to think and write about how you truly feel regarding what you have done to your partner, your children (if you have any), and others in your life whom you have hurt with your controlling and abusive attitudes and behaviors. You should not use this letter to ask for or get anything from your partner in return for your taking responsibility and making amends. Be aware of subtle controlling attitudes and behaviors such as asking for forgiveness or communicating that you hope she will stay with you.

This letter does not need to be sent or communicated to your victim(s) if you do not wish to do so, although actually doing this can be a helpful part of rebuilding trust in your relationship, if both of you want this to happen. This letter-writing process can also be a positive and powerful step in reducing the shame you have felt about your abusiveness and in forgiving yourself for the serious mistakes that you have made in the past.

When you are ready, it is expected that you will write this Amends Letter to your primary victim (generally your partner) and present it in group to get feedback from other members. You are also encouraged to write and read letters to your other victim(s) if you wish to do so.

                                        ©1999 David J. Decker, MA

TASK X: AFTERCARE PLAN AND FINAL FEEDBACK

A critical part of your final group session involves assessing your progress throughout the course of your involvement in the group and looking to the future. This includes summarizing how you perceive your progress in the program and listening to positive comments and concerns that other members have for you at this time. It also involves identifying specific and concrete ways that you plan to use to continue the recovery process you have begun in this domestic abuse group. Your group therapists will also provide you with feedback about what they have seen you accomplish, with recommendations for what you can do to continue this process after you leave group.

Keep in mind that completing this group is simply the first step in a lifelong process of monitoring your attitudes and behaviors so that you can continue to effectively intervene in your escalation to controlling and abusive behavior. Below are questions to think about and address in assessing your progress in group and in setting up an aftercare plan to help you continue the progress you have already made. Write out your answers to these questions on a separate sheet of paper and be prepared to share them with other members *at the last group you attend.* This is also an opportunity to get feedback about how other members perceive your recovery program progress, both inside and outside the group.

1. How long have you remained nonviolent with your partner, your children, and others? How often have you been emotionally and verbally abusive (on an average) with your partner, your children, and others since your midgroup evaluation?
2. What were your initial and midgroup goals and how well do you think you have accomplished them? Make specific comments about your progress on them.
3. What did you learn about control and abuse in the group and how has the group been helpful and important in addressing these issues in your life and in your recovery process?
4. In what ways are you different and how have you grown as compared to when you first came to therapy? How have you increased your ability to feel empathy and compassion for your partner, your children, and others? *Be specific.*
5. How much responsibility have you taken for your violence and your other abusive and controlling attitudes and behaviors? How much are you continuing to blame your partner and others for your thoughts, feelings, and actions in the present? *Give examples.*

(HO)   ©1999 David J. Decker, MA

6. How and with whom are you still being controlling and abusive in your life? *Be specific.*
7. How do you plan to continue to use your Escalation Prevention Plan after you have completed this group? *Be specific.*
8. What are your future goals and plans for your recovery? *Specifically, how will you implement them and continue to care for yourself (i.e., what do you need and want to continue to work on and how are you going to do it)?*
9. How are you feeling about the group ending for you tonight?

(HO)

TASK XI: VIOLENT INCIDENT ASSESSMENT

It is expected that you will maintain nonviolence toward others during your time in the domestic abuse group. However, it is also required that if you do make the choice to be violent (i.e., *using physical force with anyone,* including physical discipline of your children), the situation must be written out on separate sheets of paper and reported in group. If violence occurs, use the questions outlined below as a guide to think about and discuss the incident in group *immediately after it has occurred.* If it is discovered later that you have chosen to be dishonest and have not revealed violence you have perpetrated, you may be terminated from the program.

Date of Incident: ——————— Assessment Date: ———————

Write out answers to the following questions on separate sheets of paper, and provide a copy of this to your therapists. Take time to discuss the incident in group and get feedback from others.

1. Describe the immediate events leading up to the violent incident and the violent incident itself.
2. What *specific life stressors* (both within and outside your relationship) were you experiencing in the days and weeks prior to your being violent?
3. Identify the *specific types of violence and abuse* (including threats, intimidation, and other controlling behaviors) that you used.
4. List the *lower-level* (i.e., at the beginning of your escalation), *middle-level*, and *upper-level* (i.e., just before you were violent) cues that you noticed during this escalation. Be sure to include your negative self-talk.
5. *When* did you make the choice to be violent? How did you justify becoming violent or give yourself permission to use physical force?
6. How and what were you trying to control through the use of violence in this situation?
7. Did you use any alcohol and/or drugs before, during, or after the violent incident? If so, how much did you use and how was your chemical use related to your violence in this situation?
8. What was the *effect of your violence on your partner and your children* (i.e., how did they react/what feelings did you notice them experiencing)?

©1999 David J. Decker, MA

9. How and why did you decide not to take a time-out or to use the Escalation Prevention Plan you have developed?
10. What *new cues* have you added to your Escalation Prevention Plan as a result of this violent incident?
11. What will you commit to do the next time this situation occurs so that you do not become controlling, abusive, and violent? *Be specific.*

©1999 David J. Decker, MA

TASK XII: VIOLATION OF SOBRIETY CONTRACT ASSESSMENT

If you signed a contract during your intake agreeing not to use any mood-altering chemicals, it is expected that you will remain completely abstinent from alcohol and drugs during the entire time you are involved with the domestic abuse program. If, however, you do choose to violate this contract with yourself, the program, and your group, it is expected that, at a minimum, you will discuss your use with the group and receive feedback about the choice you made and the process you used in deciding to break your contract and use chemicals.

Write out the answers to the questions below on separate sheets of paper and be prepared to present these to the group, to get feedback from other members, and to provide a copy of your answers to your group therapists. Violating a Sobriety Contract must be reported at the group *immediately following the time when you have used any alcohol or drugs*. If a report is not made and the chemical use is discovered in some other fashion, this may be grounds for termination from the domestic abuse program.

Date of Incident: —————   Assessment Date: —————

1. Describe the specific events leading up to your chemical use and describe with whom, when, where, what, and how much you used.
2. What *specific life stressors* were you experiencing in the days and weeks prior to making your decision to break your Sobriety Contract?
3. What were your feelings before, during, and after your chemical use?
4. What self-talk (i.e., thoughts) allowed you to give yourself permission to break your contract with yourself, the other group members, and your therapists and to make the choice to use chemicals?
5. What were the *specific choices* you made that led to your using alcohol or drugs and breaking your Sobriety Contract? Be sure to think about a negative rehearsal process that may have led up to the decision (i.e., how you planned ahead or "set yourself up" to use).
6. Is your most recent use an indication that you do not believe it is really necessary for you to continue to agree to a Sobriety Contract during your domestic abuse treatment? If this is the case, what is different since you originally agreed to the contract?

(HO)   ©1999 David J. Decker, MA

7. What *new cues* can you add to your Escalation Prevention Plan and how can you more effectively use your plan to assist you in choosing not to use chemicals in the future? Identify what else you can do to avoid using them. *Be specific.*

READING LIST FOR DOMESTIC ABUSE
GROUP MEMBERS

Alberti, Robert E. and Michael Emmons (1970). *Your perfect right.* San Luis Obispo, CA: IMPACT.

Burns, David (1980). *Feeling good: The new mood therapy.* New York: Avon Books.

Davis, Martha, Elizabeth Eshelman, and Matthew McKay (1982). *The relaxation and stress reduction workbook.* Oakland, CA: New Harbinger Publications.

Dinkmeyer, Don and Gary McKay (1982). *The parents' guide: A systematic training for effective parenting of teens.* Circle Pines, MN: American Guidance Service.

Dinkmeyer, Don and Gary McKay (1989). *The parents' handbook: Systematic training for effective parenting (STEP).* Circle Pines, MN: American Guidance Service.

Engels, Beverly (1990). *The emotionally abused woman: Overcoming destructive patterns and reclaiming yourself.* New York: Ballantine.

Evans, Patricia (1992). *The verbally abusive relationship: How to recognize it and how to respond.* Holbrook, MA: Bob Adams, Inc.

Fasteau, Marc Feigen (1975). *The male machine.* New York: Dell.

Forward, Susan (with Craig Buck) (1989). *Toxic parents.* New York: Bantam.

Fossum, Merle and Marilyn Mason (1986). *Facing shame: Families in recovery.* New York: W.W. Norton and Company.

Gardner, Richard (1991). *The parents' book about divorce* (Revised edition). New York: Bantam.

Goldberg, Herb (1976). *The hazards of being male: Surviving the myth of masculine privilege.* New York: Signet.

Goldberg, Herb (1979). *The new male: From macho to sensitive but still all male.* New York: Signet.

Goldberg, Herb (1983). *The new male-female relationship.* New York: Signet.

Jones, Ann and Susan Schecter (1992). *When love goes wrong: What you can do when you can't do anything right.* New York: HarperCollins.

Kaufman, Gershen (1980). *Shame: The power of caring.* Cambridge, MA: Schenkman Publishing Company.

Kaufman, Gershen (1983). *The dynamics of power: Building a competent self.* Cambridge, MA: Schenkman Publishing Company.

Kivel, Paul (1992). *Men's work: How to stop the violence that tears our lives apart.* Center City, MN: Hazelden.

Lerner, Harriet (1985). *The dance of anger.* New York: Harper & Row.

Lerner, Harriet (1989). *The dance of intimacy.* New York: Harper & Row.

McKay, Matthew, Martha Davis, and Patrick Fanning (1981). *Thoughts and feelings: The art of cognitive stress intervention.* Richmond, CA: New Harbinger Publications.

McKay, Matthew and Patrick Fanning (1983). *Messages: The communication skills book.* Oakland, CA: New Harbinger Publications.

McKay, Matthew and Patrick Fanning (1987). *Self-esteem.* Oakland, CA: New Harbinger Publications.

McKay, Matthew, Peter Rogers and Judith McKay (1989). *When anger hurts: Quieting the storm within.* Oakland, CA: New Harbinger Publications.

Miedzian, Myriam (1991). *Boys will be boys: Breaking the link between masculinity and violence.* New York: Doubleday.

O'Hanlon, Bill and Pat Hudson (1995). *Love is a verb: How to stop analyzing your relationship and start making it great.* New York: Norton.

Pittman, Frank (1993). *Man enough: Fathers, sons, and the search for masculinity.* New York: Berkley Publishing Group.

Real, Terrence (1997). *I don't want to talk about it: Overcoming the secret legacy of male depression.* New York: Fireside.

Sonkin, Daniel and Michael Durphy (1982). *Learning to live without violence: A handbook for men.* San Francisco: Volcano Press.

Switzer, M'liss and Katherine Hale (1984). *Called to account.* Self-published.

Tannen, Deborah (1990). *You just don't understand: Women and men in conversation.* New York: Ballantine Books.

Tavris, Carol (1982). *Anger: The misunderstood emotion.* New York: Simon & Schuster.

Weisinger, Hendrie (1985). *Dr. Weisinger's anger work-out book.* New York: Quill.

Williams, Redford and Virginia Williams (1993). *Anger kills: Seventeen strategies for controlling the hostility that can harm your health.* New York: HarperCollins.

CHAPTER IV:
THE EDUCATIONAL UNITS

Part 1: How to Use
the Educational Units

USING THE EDUCATIONAL UNITS IN GROUP

Education is an important part of the change process for men, according to this model. Abusive men need to learn new attitudes and skills and actually apply them with their partners and children if their abusive behavior is to stop. Education offers a means to give them some different ways of looking at themselves and the world around them. The educational units are generally presented after the ten- to fifteen-minute group check-in and are composed of several handouts covering a variety of topics.

Since the group is ongoing, the topics in Units 1 to 10 are covered in a cyclical way as the weeks pass. This may mean that members who are in the group beyond thirty-five to forty weeks will hear the presentations twice. However, when this has occurred in the past, men have reported that hearing the information the second time has been especially helpful since they are listening from a different perspective than the first time around. Units 11 and 12 are covered every six months to ensure that all members are exposed to these topics during the time they are in group. Efforts are made in all the units to directly relate the specific topic to anger, abuse, and control.

The educational section of the group lasts approximately twenty minutes. It is the group leader's responsibility to present information and handouts to men in the group, lead brainstorming sessions, and facilitate role-playing. Group leaders must be familiar with the material, and they are encouraged to use the handouts and other materials in Part 2 of this chapter as outlines for what they actually say in group.

The rest of Chapter IV describes each of the educational units step by step, explaining in greater detail how to use the educational material. All of the handouts discussed in Part 1 can be found in Part 2 of this chapter.

UNIT 1: ABUSE AND ITS EFFECTS

A critical part of our domestic abuse program is to help men learn about abuse and violence. Most men enter the program with little or no understanding of what constitutes abuse and how it affects the man himself and those with whom he is abusive. Several educational components that are covered in the intake are also addressed in the group itself to reinforce learning in this area.

The handout Types of Abusive Behavior defines abuse, giving specific examples from the experience of this model. It also addresses the difference between male and female violence and encourages men to take the first step toward eliminating violence in their relationships, even if their partners have also been violent and abusive with them. During this discussion, men are asked to identify specific ways they have been abusive with their partners, their children, and others.

How Violence May Occur in a Relationship is a handout that offers a three-phase process, adapted from Lenore Walker's *The Battered Woman* (1979), to help explain how violence happens over the course of a relationships. Men are generally able to recognize that the patterns discussed in the handout exist in their relationship. Some men are even able to recognize the specific time line that they have followed. For example, one man reported that he had violent incidents "just like clockwork" every six months. This helps men begin to see clearly that an escalation process exists, that violence does not just happen, and that they are not out of control. Men are asked to comment on how this model fits their relationships with their partners and then to identify which phase they are in at the present time.

Now is the time to introduce the notion of the hierarchy of cues that men experience, encouraging them to become more aware of the lower-, middle-, and upper-level cues that signal an escalation. Recognition of the lower-level cues (e.g., feeling tired/hungry, early stressors related to particular situations, and negative rehearsal in their lives) is particularly important because taking a time-out is easier early in their escalation process.

The handout on Myths About Domestic Abuse asks men to brainstorm societal myths about abusers, victims, and domestic abuse in general. This helps to pinpoint some of the cultural misinformation that exists regarding abuse and also the many ways that men rationalize their own violence and abuse.

The handout Perceived Advantages/Disadvantages of Using Violence is another opportunity for men to brainstorm in group. Men are asked to think about the advantages and disadvantages in being violent with their partners and others. The advantages section highlights the importance of realizing the payoffs associated with being violent and stresses the idea that abusive behavior is both purposeful and intentional. Initially, men are often reticent or completely unwilling to acknowledge that they gain advantages from being violent. Eventually however, most men are able to come up with a variety of ideas that make sense to them, most of which focus on controlling their partners and the situations around them. One advantage that men occasionally cite, which is a "true positive," is that their violence has brought them to treatment and given them the opportunity to address and change their controlling and abusive behaviors.

The disadvantages tend to be easier for men to identify. This is especially true if they have been involved with the legal system or their partners have begun to set limits with them, including filing for a restraining order or separating from them. Identifying the disadvantages is one way to appeal to a man's self-interest to end the violence and abusive behavior. It helps him to think about the consequences that have arisen as a result of his abusive behavior. Actively identifying and considering the consequences when they start to escalate is often one of the ideas that men propose for the de-escalation strategies section of their EPP, allowing them to intervene in the escalation by choosing to take a time-out.

The handouts Effects of Violence and Abuse on Women, and Violence, Abuse, and Their Effects on Children provide specific ways to introduce the idea that men's violence and abuse is having traumatic and devastating effects on the people they claim to love. The discussion related to these handouts begins with an exercise designed to give men a sense of the tension and "edginess" that exists for others in an abusive household. Men are asked to closely gather around a therapist who then begins to blow up a balloon. As the balloon grows larger and larger, men begin to feel uncomfortable, wincing, flinching, and backing away due to their fear that it may pop. A discussion follows about how these are the same types of reactions that women and children experience living with an abusive man because they never know when he may "pop" and become explosive, intimidating, or abusive with them. This is a powerful and graphic way to illustrate the fear others may feel around them.

This discussion hopefully encourages men to develop some empathy and compassion for the other people in their lives. It often serves to help them better understand some of their partners' or children's behavior (e.g., dishonesty, acting out) that may have previously triggered their frustration and aggravation and actually led to violent episodes. It also helps them begin to see the need for therapeutic intervention for their children, either to deal with current symptoms or to help the children intervene in their own abusive attitudes and behaviors. Men are encouraged to have their children assessed by a therapist regarding the impact of the violence, particularly if the children are having problems at home or at school.

Finally, these handouts may give men some insight into messages about control and abuse that they have learned in their own families of origin, which they will directly address in the group task Family of Origin and Childhood (see Chapter III). These sections are presented in lecture format, and men are encouraged to comment on what aspects fit their current families and their families of origin.

Excuses/Justifications for Becoming Violent offers men another opportunity to look at how they have given themselves permission to be violent and abusive with partners, children, and others. Ideas in this handout are brainstormed in the group, and men are encouraged to accept more clear responsibility for their thoughts that lead to the abuse and for the abuse itself.

The handout The Place of Generalized Violence in Our Lives enables men to examine their potential for violence in other areas of their daily lives. Most of the men in our groups have a significant history of violence with other people, male and female, in addition to their current partners. Often men have histories of violence in their childhood, in sports, in the military, at bars or parties, and with past partners. This recounting of the entire history of violence occurs in the group task Abuse Inventory (see Chapter III). For many men, their violence toward other males does not cease until they become fearful that they might be hurt or until they face potential legal consequences related to these altercations. Many men continue to escalate in other situations with nonfamily members, even if these may not currently involve violence. Thus, the issue of generalized violence is a topic that can, and does, relate directly to abuse in the home.

This discussion is introduced by handing out and discussing newspaper and other articles that feature violence on the highway (including shootings and assaults on local freeways), in the workplace, and in other settings. Some examples of these articles follow:

- "Driver Shot for Not Yielding to Pushy Motorist": a newspaper account of a man who was shot by another motorist when he failed to clear a lane on a St. Paul highway in 1990.
- "Violence on the Job": a newspaper article published in 1993 that discusses the increase in threats, harassment, and violence in the workplace in recent years.
- "Man Is Charged with Felony Assault": a newspaper story that discusses the brutal assault of a man who attempted to intervene in a battering incident that was occurring on a downtown St. Paul sidewalk in 1992.
- "You Can Help Create a Violence-Free Minnesota": a handout developed by 180 Degrees, Inc., that identifies some specific strategies that parents, teachers, children, and organizations can use to decrease the level of violence in their community.

Offering such examples helps men to think about the possibility of being hurt themselves or of severely hurting others and facing legal consequences as a result. For this discussion, men are asked to brainstorm solutions to a variety of hypothetical situations. They are also asked to address the thought process that directs the decision about how they will respond in the examples presented. Men are asked to slow their escalation process and to think about their options rather than simply reacting spontaneously with violence or abusive behavior. They are also asked to think about how their escalations in other situations, acted upon or not, affect their potential to escalate with their partners and children at home. This discussion addresses the impact of their decisions on their relationships with their family members, who often feel fearful just being present when an escalation is occurring.

Videos can also be a helpful adjunct in this discussion on abuse and its effects. Short segments of videotape can be used to illustrate examples of the different types of abusive behavior, the three phases in the cycle of violence, and the effects of abuse on women and children. Men are asked to comment on what they have seen and how it relates to their own personal experiences. Actually seeing the abuse acted out can be a powerful learning tool that often evokes intense emotions.

Some excellent films and videotapes are produced by organizations working with domestic abuse, and these can be used as resources. In addition, other video productions can be helpful in demonstrating the dynamics of domestic abuse. One is *The Burning Bed* (1985), the story of Francine Hughes, a woman who killed her husband after years of being battered by him. Another is *Shattered Dreams* (1990), the story of Charlotte Fedders, the wife of a top Reagan official who abused her throughout their marriage. *What's Love Got to Do with It?* (1993) is the story of Ike and Tina Turner, whose relationship included brutal violence. *Sleeping with the Enemy* (1991) is the story of a woman who flees an abusive relationship and is stalked by her husband. A final example is *The Great Santini* (1980), the story of a Marine fighter pilot who is abusive with his wife and children. These and other videos offer powerful enactments of abuse in relationships and are helpful in generating thought and discussion about abuse and control.

UNIT 2: STRESS AND STRESS MANAGEMENT

Stress does not cause battering. However, an important part of a man learning about his escalation process involves identifying what stress is and how it affects him and his reactions to his partner and children (Straus, 1980).

Such is the purpose of this unit, which relates directly to the cycle of violence that is discussed in the intake, the educational unit about abuse and its effects, and each member's Escalation Prevention Plan (see Chapter III).

Most batterers have little awareness of the stressors in their lives and the toll these stressors take on them emotionally and physically (Selye, 1978; Davis, Eshelman, and McKay, 1989). Many men have shut themselves off completely from their reactions to what goes on around them. They often convince themselves that they are able to handle whatever happens in their lives, with the glaring exception of what happens in their families. They are often totally focused on the idea that their partners are the sole reason for their explosive and abusive behavior and their problems in living. The goal of this section is to help men understand what stress is and its relationship to their becoming angry, controlling, and abusive. Such an understanding can also alert them to new cues and triggers, particularly those which do not relate directly to their partners, which they can then add to their Escalation Prevention Plans.

This unit begins with a therapist-led discussion based on the handout What Is Stress? It presents basic information about the nature of stress, how it can be triggered, the various symptoms and compulsive and unhealthy behaviors (e.g., being abusive, drinking too much) that it generates, and some discussion of the physiological process that occurs. An important part of this talk is to emphasize that stress, in and of itself, is not bad or an evil to be avoided. Rather, the focus is on the idea that human beings can never completely rid themselves of stress; people have an optimum level that helps them function more effectively in their lives.

The key to handling stress better begins with recognizing that it exists. The next step is understanding that perceptions and self-talk about a stressor often have more influence on the effects of stress than the stressor itself. The cognitive labeling process that occurs concerning a stressor is critical in determining whether the arousal becomes anger or some other emotional reaction (Schacter and Singer, 1962; Schacter, 1971). This concept flies in the face of the blaming and powerless attitude that abusers have. It also asks them once again to take responsibility for the stress they create in their lives with their partners, their children, and others. This issue of taking responsibility for themselves is a constant thread throughout the educational portion of the program.

The handout Changes and Stress is used to highlight the potential for any occurrence of change to trigger stress reactions and helps men clearly identify specific changes that they have experienced in the past year. This handout also helps men understand that stress can be triggered by major or trivial events, positive or negative experiences, external situations, or their own internal attitudes, expectations, and self-talk.

The idea here is to get men to slow down their internal processes enough to see that, over the course of a few hours, a day, a week, or a month, they may be gradually building to a point at which they might decide to explode with their partners or others. With the explosion, their partners then become a convenient "dumping ground" for accumulated stresses from the course of their lives, of which that they are often unaware. Men are asked to go through this handout in group and identify changes they have experienced in the past year. Most men are surprised at the number of important changes that have been occurring in their lives.

Symptoms That Stress Can Trigger is a handout that helps men understand the physical, emotional, mental, relationship, and spiritual symptoms that can occur as a result of a lack of awareness or poor handling of life stressors. In group, men are asked to name symptoms that they have experienced. Most men clearly identify a large number of symptoms from the handout's list. This helps them continue to become more knowledgeable about their own internal processes and the impact that stress is having on them.

The next handout, Stress Management Techniques, is discussed in group and offers some specific ideas on how to address and handle the stress in their lives more effectively. These ideas can be directly applied to the de-escalation strategies portion of their Escalation Prevention Plan. This handout encourages men to identify specific ways to take better care of themselves physically, emotionally, cognitively, and spiritually.

A part of this unit involves actually beginning to develop and practice some specific relaxation skills that are outlined in the handout Progressive Muscle Relaxation. The most frequent exercise we use in group involves a progressive muscle relaxation exercise (Jacobson, 1938; Wolpe, 1973; Bernstein and Borkevec, 1973) that is led in group by a therapist. This is often particularly helpful because abusive men tend to be almost continually in a state of tension, frustration, and escalation. This exercise serves as an active way for men to relax and de-escalate and helps them clearly see the difference between their states of tension and relaxation. Men are instructed to sit or lie in a comfortable position, preferably with eyes closed, as the therapist reads a relaxation script. Other forms of relaxation that have been used in the group include visualization and meditation accompanied by calming music.

Finally, each year, in the middle of November, the upcoming holidays and the additional stressors they may bring are discussed. We use the handout Stress and the Holidays as a guide for this discussion. Most men identify the holidays as one of their "Times" cues on the Escalation Prevention Plan, and many men also report the occurrence of violent incidents during past holidays. This handout identifies expectations, pressures, and feelings that may trigger an increase in the potential for escalations and violence with partners, children, and others. It also offers some practical ideas about how to deal more effectively with attitudes and situations that may arise.

Some men are physically separated from their partners and families during the holidays, often for the first time, and the emotional pain they experience regarding this change is enormous. At a minimum, all men in the group are emotionally estranged from their partners at this point. Thus, it is important to help them notice and intervene in the unrealistic beliefs they hold about what the holidays should be for them and their families. This is a time when, because of the loneliness and resentment they feel, their desire to control their partners often becomes even more pronounced. Part of this group discussion involves challenging men to devise a more positive plan for how they will handle the holidays. They are asked to discuss their plan in group, which often includes ideas such as spending less time with extended family and friends, developing their own family traditions, or volunteering their time to help others. However, what is most important about this discussion is for them to make some conscious decisions about the holidays so that they do not add to the hostility and resentment they already feel for their partners.

UNIT 3: ANGER

Anger does not cause battering. However, anger and how it is expressed are an important part of a domestic abuse group because batterers tend to be more angry and hostile than men who are not violent in their relationships with partners (Maiuro et al., 1988). Men often view their anger as the "problem" and want to eliminate it from their lives. They are given the clear message by this model that this will not happen.

Many men also equate their anger with hostility, threats, intimidation, abuse, and violence. Most learned this equation from their families of origin and from the cultural messages men receive about what it is to be a real man. This unit seeks to break the rigid link between anger and abuse and to help men understand that their anger and frustration are a natural and normal part of life. The critical issues become how effectively they learn to handle the anger they experience and how actively they are willing to work to decrease the levels of hostility, cynicism, aggression, and withdrawal in their day-to-day lives.

Many abusers feel intense shame regarding their anger because they have viewed it, up until now, as such a destructive force in their lives. Unfortunately, past attempts to overlook irritation and frustration in a passive manner have eventually led to a passive-aggressive or aggressive display of these emotions with their partners and others. Many want to completely rid themselves of this emotion, an unrealistic and unreachable goal, in the treatment process and in life.

As such, men are constantly reminded that it is their abusive and controlling attitudes and behaviors, not the feeling of anger, that they need to alter. Anger, for many men, including abusers, tends to be a cover for other feelings such as hurt, fear, sadness, and disappointment that they often convert immediately into anger and abusive behavior (Ganley, 1981; Sonkin and Durphy, 1982; McKay, Rogers, and McKay, 1989). These "gentler" feelings tend to increase their vulnerability, which opens up the possibility, in their minds, of being hurt even further. Part of the therapist's task in this unit is to help men begin to understand that healthy communication and intimacy cannot exist in a relationship without this vulnerability.

This unit begins with Understanding Your Anger, a handout that helps men clearly differentiate between anger, cynicism/hostility/disgust/contempt, and aggression/withdrawal. Anger is defined as a normal and natural emotion that can serve as a warning signal that a physiological stress arousal is occurring and that some internal or external factor may be the cause. Cynicism, hostility, disgust, and contempt are defined as attitudes consisting of negative self-talk and subsequent feelings of powerlessness that contribute to violating others' boundaries (Williams and Williams, 1993). Aggression and withdrawal are framed as behaviors that are acted out with the intent to hurt, punish, intimidate, and control others and/or to protect oneself when feeling uncertain, and that always result in disrespect and emotional distance.

This handout also addresses some common distortions of anger, such as words that are often equated with anger but, in reality, fit more accurately in the realms of cynicism, hostility, aggression, and withdrawal. Also discussed is when anger becomes a problem, which addresses an abusive man's tendency to be, in fact, escalated for much of the time and the negative emotional and physical consequences this creates in his life. The final topic discussed is about how to handle anger effectively, providing specific ideas and strategies that are expanded on throughout the man's involvement in the group.

After the initial discussion on understanding their anger, men are given the handout Anger Analysis to take home and write out for the next group. This helps men think and talk about their anger, for example, what they learned about experiencing and expressing anger from family, friends, school, work, the media, and other influences; how they act when they are angry and what they think about expressing their anger at this point; and what about their anger and its expression that they need to change.

An important part of this homework assignment is to draw their anger, using pictures, symbols, words, and colors. This graphic representation is shared with other members of the group at the next session. The anger drawings are often vivid and powerful depictions of explosive and destructive forces, such as tornados, volcanos, earthquakes, monsters, and demons. Men are asked to actively use these drawings in their programs by visualizing the drawing when they are angry and then visualizing a "healing image" (e.g., a huge pail of water dousing the heat and destructive potential of a volcano). These visualizations can then become a part of their de-escalation strategies section in the Escalation Prevention Plan.

At this point, we discuss the handout Using Time-Outs. This reiterates the importance of using time-outs as an initial strategy to defuse volatile anger and to reduce the potential for abuse. Time-outs are the cornerstone for learning to handle explosive anger (Bach and Wyden, 1970; Sonkin and Durphy, 1982), and men are first introduced to the time-out concept during the intake process. One of the tasks expected of all group members is the development of a Time-Out Plan (see Chapter III).

This discussion provides, in an educational context, a review of the specific ideas that are important in using the time-out as a way to intervene in the potential to become explosive, abusive, and controlling. Part of this section also involves brainstorming in group some reasons and excuses men may use to avoid taking respectful time-outs with their partners. "Making these public" hopefully helps defuse some of the power these excuses have had in interfering with men's efforts to de-escalate in the past. Some examples of the excuses we have heard from men include the following:

- My wife won't let me take a time-out.
- She'll get more angry if I take a time-out.
- My partner doesn't want me to take time-outs.
- I'm right./She's wrong.
- Why should I? I'm not mad.
- She's the one who needs a time-out./She started it./She has the problem.
- I'm not escalated enough to take a time-out./I can handle this.
- It won't help./It doesn't do any good.
- It didn't work the last time.
- She needs to understand my point of view.
- I have to get the last word in this argument.
- Taking a time-out is running away.
- Taking a time-out means you're a wimp/coward.
- Taking a time-out means I've failed.
- It's manipulative to take a time-out.
- I didn't think about it./I just snapped.

- I'm too "crazy"/out-of-control to take a time-out.
- I forgot about it./It doesn't occur to me.
- I'm "on a roll."/I'm winning this argument.
- This issue has to be resolved right now./This issue can't wait.
- We have to get to the bottom of this.
- It's too late at night to take a time-out.
- It's too cold (too hot) to take a time-out.
- It isn't convenient.
- I don't have any place to go.
- I don't want to.
- I don't have to.
- There isn't enough time to take a time-out./It takes too much time.
- A time-out won't change how I feel.
- I shouldn't have to always be the one who leaves.

We encourage men to be aware of their individual excuses and to work actively at not letting these interfere with their using this skill to help them handle their anger more effectively. They are also expected to write out their individual excuses for their own Time-Out Plan.

Another handout that forms the basis for a brainstorming session in the group is Escalation Prevention Plan De-Escalation Strategies. Men are asked to name examples of de-escalation or calming strategies that they have used or plan to begin using. This exercise helps men to think about specific ideas that can be added to their EPP.

The final section in this unit involves additional homework, the Anger Journal (Sonkin and Durphy, 1982; Purdy and Nickle, 1981), which asks men to identify and discuss some specific situations in which they have become angry and escalated and to think about their self-talk, cues, and "hidden" emotions. It also focuses on how well they handled the situation and what they could do to improve their skills for similar situations in the future. This handout is given to men in group, and they are asked to fill it out over the course of the week and bring it back to share in the following group.

UNIT 4: SELF-TALK

Negative self-talk does not cause battering. However, the concept of self-talk is another critical component in addressing violence and explosive and abusive anger because irrational and arousing self-talk generally precedes the abuse itself (Ganley, 1981; Edleson, 1984). Addressing self-talk is also an important part of intervening in the significant depression, anxiety, and low self-esteem with which many abusers struggle. To notice and change their negative self-talk, men must look inside and slow their internal thought processes enough to be more aware of them, often for the first time in their lives.

Self-talk is addressed directly in the Escalation Prevention Plan, and often, when men first attempt to identify these cognitions in the intake, they report being completely unaware of any negative thoughts. This is especially true regarding negative thoughts about themselves, although they may be very aware of critical and punishing cognitions about others. The self-talk concept and cognitive restructuring are addressed in a variety of educational contexts as the men progress through the group and are considered a vital part of changing their abusive and controlling attitudes and behaviors (Ellis, 1970; Beck, 1976; Meichenbaum, 1977).

The first and most important section of this unit involves the lengthy handout Self-Talk, which discusses how self-talk arises, the three general types of negative self-talk (corresponding to the categories of self-talk cues on the Escalation Prevention Plan), how thought distortions and core beliefs from childhood and the dominant culture underlie negative self-talk (offering specific examples of each), and a schematic representation of the negative self-talk process in action. This handout also presents the idea of "victim thinking." This type of thinking involves the mistaken notion that we are merely passive observers of events in our lives and are powerless to intervene directly in how we react to what happens around us. Men are asked to rethink this victimized, childlike stance that is common with abusers and begin, instead, to take more responsibility for their thoughts, feelings, and actions.

Frequently, abusive men are oversensitive and take things personally when there is no need to do so. The self-talk concept offers a powerful way to change these "knee-jerk" reactions. This handout also offers some specific strategies for directly intervening in the negative self-talk process. The therapist discusses this handout in group and then asks men to take it home and read through it, paying particular attention to their individual thought distortions and core beliefs that lead to their self-talk.

Another handout, Positive Self-Talk and Anger, is also discussed in group. This links self-talk to the escalation process and offers some very specific positive self-talk that can be used in potentially explosive situations with partners, children, and others. Specific examples are helpful because abusive men frequently have great difficulty generating their own positive self-talk. However, given some guidance, they can start to integrate some of these examples into their day-to-day functioning almost immediately.

A second part of this handout builds on the idea of a positive rehearsal (versus a negative and powerless one) in preparing for and handling difficult situations (Novaco, 1975). Again, specific examples are offered for phases throughout the course of the entire escalation process.

A final handout in this unit, the Self-Talk Log, gives specific examples of the entire self-talk process that are discussed in group. It is also assigned as homework for the next week. Men are asked to identify some difficult situations and the negative self-talk they generate. It also asks members to think about specific positive self-talk that they could use in those same situations to reframe what is happening and to look at it in a different light.

This practice in identifying self-talk is vital and must be ongoing if men are to change their abusive and controlling attitudes and behaviors. Their negative self-talk is a way that they generally dehumanize and objectify their partners, their children, and others, which leads directly to abusive behavior. If their self-talk does not change, their abuse and violence will continue.

UNIT 5: SHAME AND EMPOWERMENT

Shame does not cause battering. However, shame, an overwhelming feeling of inadequacy, defectiveness, and worthlessness, appears to underlie all forms of dysfunctional behavior, including abuse and the desire to control (Kaufman, 1980; Miller, 1981, 1983; Stosny, 1995; Dutton, 1995). Shame is a system of living based on old, automatic habits, control, perfectionism, and reactivity that leads to cynicism, negativity, and stagnation. Toxic shame is created when human beings are deeply wounded by the very people who are supposed to care for them when they are children (generally parents or caretakers). These wounds also make them significantly more vulnerable to additional feelings of shame engendered by interactions with others and the surrounding culture. Such people are also more likely to experience shame as a result of their own unhealthy thought and behavior patterns.

The unit on shame is often an eye-opener for many abusers, who have had few words and no overriding concepts to explain the gnawing sense that they have never been "quite good enough" and have never really "measured up" over the course of their lives. This concept naturally has strong roots embedded in the family of origin, and this shame unit serves as an educational counterpart to the Family of Origin and Childhood task that members are expected to complete in the task portion of the program (see Chapter III). Unfortunately, their partners often become the targets for their unresolved shame.

Men are also presented with an alternative vision, empowerment (Kaufman, 1983; Stosny, 1995), which is framed as a system of living based on respect (for yourself and others), the importance of making conscious life choices, and the notions of accountability and proactivity, which lead directly to a sense of optimism, higher self-esteem, and personal growth. It is critical to present this material so that shame is not used as just another excuse for their violence and abuse in the present. The therapist needs to clearly and repeatedly explain that being neglected and abused as a child does not excuse a man from responsibility for his current behavior. However, these concepts do offer many men a better understanding of their life process, by showing that what happened in their past continues to affect them currently. This discussion also offers some concrete guideposts to achieving more respectful and responsible living.

The handout Shame and Empowerment offers an overview of some important ideas related to these concepts. The defining characteristics of shame and empowerment are presented. The information for this discussion is generally presented in lecture form and men are asked to think about ways that these ideas fit for them.

Shame is a handout given to group members that describes the concept of shame and discusses the sources of shame and the rules of shame-based systems. Some sources of shame that are discussed include how men were shamed and abused in their lives and how men maintain in the present the legacy of shame from their family of origin and other sources. This maintained shame is particularly important because it directly addresses the abuse and violence they are currently perpetrating and how these behaviors are contributing to the shame they carry from the past. The discussion of the rules of shame-based systems focuses on some critical cornerstones related to men's abusive behavior, including control, perfectionism, blame, and denial.

Another handout, Signals That Shame May Be Present, highlights nonverbal or physical signs and cognitive, emotional, and behavioral signs that shame is at work, including all types of abuse, compulsive and addictive behaviors, and a variety of cognitive, emotional, and behavioral responses such as depression, anxiety, power struggles, and dishonesty. Men are asked to go through the list and check off signals that fit for them at this point in their lives.

The handout of Potential Effects in Coming from a Shame-Based Family addresses how men have believed the lies that they were told as a child and how they have learned unhealthy and dysfunctional coping methods, including control and abuse, as a result. Men are asked to look through this handout and identify ways they have taken on their family's shame. The handout reinforces the idea that men have learned to be abusive and controlling and helps them think about how they will answer the questions posed in the Family of Origin and Childhood task in the treatment portion of the program, which directly addresses how they developed their own shame.

Another important step in addressing this issue involves asking men to draw their shame, using pictures, symbols, words, and colors. They are then asked to bring the drawing back to group to share with the other men. Completion of this assignment shows whether they truly understand the concept of shame. It also gives them the opportunity to articulate how they experience their shame and how it feels to them.

Sharing their drawings in group is often a powerful and moving experience, as men offer pictures of a small child huddled in a basement corner or a child wearing a dunce cap with numerous sets of eyes staring at him. The therapist needs to look for, point out, and talk about themes related to being exposed, feeling trapped and stuck, being small, helpless, and powerless, and feeling hollow and empty. Men are then asked to discuss what their drawings mean to them. Interpretations should be avoided, but do discuss any apparent themes that may relate to the concept of shame as it has been presented. Men are also encouraged, as with the previous anger drawing, to think about a healing image to counteract the effects represented in the shame drawing.

Next, the discussion focuses on Empowerment, a handout that clearly distinguishes between the shame-based and empowerment-based ways that abusive men view themselves and the world around them and that highlights the differences between the two concepts.

The handout Cycles of Shame and Empowerment, a pictorial representation of these two very different processes, reinforces the importance of self-talk and delineates two separate and distinct cycles that can begin with the same difficult situation or irresponsible and compulsive behavior. This handout illustrates clearly the different directions that men may take following the same event, depending on their internal thought processes and their interpretations of what is happening.

The keys to empowerment are framed as positive self-talk and conscious living and decision making and are juxtaposed with the automatic and habitual negative self-talk and the notions that men are helpless victims or out of control. A specific example of these cycles in action is offered, and men are asked to come up with their own real-life examples of these processes. These cycles are applied specifically to their decisions to become abusive and to their previous difficulty with stopping their violent and controlling behavior. The therapist talks about the cycles and then asks men to pick a difficult situation in their own lives and follow it in both directions.

An important part of the cycle of shame involves the psychological defenses, which, when used without conscious thought, keep others away and contribute to tension building. This sets the stage for the activation of more shame through a triggering event or irresponsible behavior, often an abusive or violent incident. Defenses is a handout that is assigned as homework to assist men in understanding more about the psychological defenses they employ. It also assists them in identifying specific defenses that are an important part of how they currently function. Men are asked to specify four or five of the defenses they use most frequently and to talk with the group about how they have used these with their partner, their children, or others.

The final section includes the handout Moving Toward Empowerment and a discussion presented by the therapist. This section addresses a variety of attitudes, skills, and strategies that can lead to empowerment and growth and away from shame, attempts to control, and the perpetration of abuse. A vital step that is recommended early on is to stop using the behaviors that maintain and perpetuate shame in the present. The most obvious example for these men is their controlling, abusive, and violent behavior. If their own abuse and violence continue, they cannot expect to make any real progress in addressing the origin of their shame or their other self-defeating and self-destructive attitudes and behaviors.

Violence is a primary issue and an enormous generator of shame, whether in a man's past or present. Men cannot move on to a healthier place if their perpetration of violence and abuse does not stop. This is the reason that men are expected to take responsibility for their abusive behavior starting with their first intake session. This is also the reason that men immediately begin working on a plan to intervene in their escalations and their current potential for violence. Finally, this is the reason that the Family of Origin and Childhood task occurs later in the group process. Men will have great difficulty effectively addressing their own victimization if they are continuing to actively practice behaviors that only generate more shame for them in the present.

UNIT 6: CULTURE OF ORIGIN

The purpose of this section is to put men's violence against women and children into the larger context of historical and societal messages about what it means to be a man. It also addresses how violence, abuse, and control are too often viewed as positive and realistic options for males in a variety of situations (Bandura, 1973). This is not done to excuse the violence they have perpetrated against their partners. Rather, it is a means of showing men how the legacy of the past and current societal messages have conditioned them to expect to have control and power over their partners and others. It also helps them recognize that alternatives to this macho, controlling, and entitled attitude do exist.

Throughout history, men have received strong and consistent messages regarding their right and their obligation to control partners, other women, and children (Dobash and Dobash, 1979; Gelles, 1980). The first law of marriage formulated by Romulus in ancient Rome "obliged the married women, as having no other refuge, to conform themselves entirely to the temper of their husbands and the husbands to rule their wives as necessary and inseparable possession" (Dobash and Dobash, 1979, p. 35). Many batterers choose quotes selectively from the Bible to reinforce their rights as husbands. The following is an example I have heard: "Let a woman learn in silence with all submissiveness. I permit no woman to teach or to have authority over men; she is to keep silent" (I Timothy 2:11-12).

More modern times are not much better. English common law made a husband and a wife one legal entity. As that legal entity, the husband answered for the wife's legal difficulties and also had the right, and even the obligation, to chastise his wife, his children, and his servants (Dobash and Dobash, 1979). In the United States, Alabama and Massachusetts were the first states to rescind the ancient privilege of wife battering in 1871 when the courts ruled that, although the husband was still obliged to "teach his wife her duty and subjection," he could no longer claim "the privilege, ancient though it be, to beat her with a stick, to pull her hair, choke her, spit in her face, kick her about the floor, or to inflict upon her other like indignities." It took Mississippi fifty more years before it, too, repudiated battering (Dobash and Dobash, 1979, p. 63).

Batterers, and all males, also receive strong and consistent societal messages today about violence and its place in our lives as a problem-solving and conflict resolution tool. Children's cartoons show numerous acts of violence, all having little effect on the victim, with the battered character "bouncing back" the next moment to continue the adventure. Video games such as Mortal Kombat offer graphic and explicit violence to young people. Most professional sports include frequent examples of violence, not only in the context of the game, but also in the fisticuffs and brawling that have become a regular and disheartening part of not only hockey but also football, baseball, basketball, and many other sporting contests. In addition, more and more professional athletes, including baseball star Darryl Strawberry, golfer John Daly, and football quarterback Warren Moon, are being charged with domestic assault.

Advertising such as the "Swedish Bikini Team" from Stroh's beer commercials trumpets messages that sexually objectify and demean women and glorify male dominance and the need to be successful and "on top." Movies such as *Natural Born Killers* (1994) and *9½ Weeks* (1986) and now even television programming have violence and sexual exploitation as common themes. Musical lyrics, such as the Guns N' Roses verse: "I used to love her but I had to kill her . . . and now we're happier this way," encourage violence and rape. Comedians such as Eddie Murphy and Andrew Dice Clay refer to women in their routines as "bitches," "pussies," and "whores" to be abused and discarded at will. The pornography industry flourishes. This is the context in which battering occurs in this country.

The focus in this unit is on the omnipresent cultural messages that clearly communicate that men have the right to control others and to use violence and abuse whenever necessary to get what they want and to do what needs to be done.

At the beginning of this unit, articles, editorials, and commentaries from newspapers, magazines, and other sources that highlight the ideas noted previously are passed around and discussed. Some address male socialization regarding friendships, intimacy, expression of emotion, and the male role and how it affects men's health and life expectancy. Others address cultural icons, such as O. J. Simpson, a former football player, and Mickey Rourke, an actor, and their battering behavior and the excuses and rationalizations they offer for their violence. Still others present perspectives on the fear, intimidation, and degradation that women experience as a result of society's acceptance and promotion of violence toward them. There are numerous examples of these sorts of articles, and they can provide an excellent vehicle for discussing the historical and cultural context of battering. The following are examples of these materials:

- "Male Stereotype Teaches Suppression of Emotions," from *In Touch*, a publication of the Mental Health Association, discusses how the male stereotype manifests itself and how these rigid sex roles cripple both sexes.
- "America's Slide into the Sewer," an editorial written by George Will that appeared in a 1990 *Newsweek*, juxtaposes testimony in the trial of young men accused of gang rape and other sadistic violence against a female jogger in New York with the lyrics sung by several rap groups that demean, objectify, and brutalize women.
- "Remorse? Not in the NFL," an editorial by Bruce Newman in *Sports Illustrated*, chronicles the story of a professional football player, Freeman McNeil. McNeil lost his "game concentration" after accidentally "shredding" the knee of a linebacker he blocked because he allowed

himself to feel compassion for the other man. He was then "bully-ragged," first by his coach, and then by himself, because he had "let the team down."

- "Women's Lives Now More Restricted by Fear Than by Discrimination," a 1991 editorial by Ellen Goodman in *The Boston Globe,* discusses the constriction in daily life that occurs for women in this culture due to the danger that they feel and that, in reality, exists in their contacts with men.
- "The Masculine Gender Role and Its Implications for the Life Expectancy of Older Men," a *Journal of the American Geriatrics Society* article written by Dr. Kenneth Solomon, addresses issues related to the stress involved with the traditional male role and how this stress affects men's physical and emotional well-being.
- "Simpson Charged with Beating Wife During New Year's Fight," a short article that appeared in the back pages of the sports section of *The Memphis Star-Tribune* in 1989, chronicles the brutal assault that O. J. perpetrated against his wife and the rationalizations that both he and his attorney used to justify and minimize the incident.
- "Men Have Buddies, But No Real Friends," an editorial by Richard Cohen that appeared in *The Washington Post,* discusses the differences between male and female friendships and the isolation and loneliness that men frequently experience due to fears about becoming close to other men.

Men's programs are encouraged to find similar articles in their own communities and in the current events of our country. Examples such as these are everywhere.

This exercise hopefully broadens men's appreciation for the cultural climate in which battering occurs and helps sensitize them to women's fear and "one-down" position. This is the point at which men are asked whether, if given the chance, they would want to be a woman in our country. Despite many abusers' beliefs that men are discriminated against at this time and that domestic abuse laws, in particular, highlight this discrimination, no man in the groups has ever stated that he would become a woman if this opportunity arose. This question alone often serves as a powerful illustration of the positions that men and women occupy in our society.

The handout Male Socialization is then used as a way to discuss how men learn what it means to be a man in our culture. To begin, men are asked to brainstorm stereotypical and traditional notions regarding the roles of men and women in our society.

The following are traits often identified for men:

strong	confident	in charge
powerful	domineering	breadwinner
tough	unemotional	macho
successful	controlling	aggressive
assertive	decisive	knowledgeable
athletic	handsome	wealthy
adventurer	well-built	detached
stud	ambitious	driven
fixer	logical	"human doing"
silent	rational	boss
responsible	fearless	winner
soldier	hero	protector
"don't ask for help"	rescuer	"more is better"
"don't cry"	"never say die"	doer

The following are traits often identified for women:

warm	loving	nurturing
caretaker	emotional	soft
passive	homemaker	submissive
gentle	sentimental	domestic
sweet	supportive	attentive
romantic	sexy	beautiful
attractive	good body	passionate
affectionate	caring	sharing
cooperative	expressive	helpful

Men are asked to personalize this male stereotype further by thinking about males they know who come closest to living up to this image. This exercise often causes them to realize that, generally, such men are not safe to be around, either physically or emotionally. The destructive impact of this traditional role on men's physical and emotional health and on their relationships with those close to them is also discussed. A case is then made for combining the best traits from both the male and female characteristics to form a person who can be strong, assertive, and confident and, at the same time, gentle, caring, and nurturing. Men are asked to think about other men they have known who combine the positive aspects of being male and female and who assume more androgynous roles in their lives. Feelings of safety and acceptance around these men tend to be significantly higher. Finally, men brainstorm the advantages and disadvantages of being a nontraditional male, helping group members see clearly that assuming this role does have its difficulties but that the advantages have the potential to far outweigh the disadvantages.

Another topic addressed in this section focuses on controlling attitudes and behaviors, which serve as the foundation and underpinning for abusive behavior but which can also take on more subtle, yet destructive, forms. Exerting control is often an attempt to bring safety and predictability into our lives. Unfortunately, most attempts to control bring just the opposite. It is stressed that, in general, the more human beings attempt to control people and situations around them, the more out of control they end up *feeling* (which does not mean that they *are,* in fact, out of control). Control is a handout adapted from the ideas and work of Michael Obsatz, PhD, a college professor, trainer, and couple family therapist, that addresses different aspects of control, including overcontrol of others (which is most clearly associated with batterers), overcontrol of self, lack of self-control, and the healthy alternative, self-control.

The tendency to want to control others around them is an important part of who these men have been and will continue to be. It is emphasized that control is not something they will be able to totally eliminate from their personalities. Rather, men are encouraged to become more aware of this part of themselves and to intervene in these attitudes, when they arise, before they have manifested themselves in unhealthy and destructive ways. Men are asked to brainstorm ways that they and traditional males have attempted to overtly control the women in their lives (e.g., violence, being demanding, using economic power). They are also asked to begin to identify the more subtle forms of control that they use with their partners and others (e.g., "acting like a victim," "playing the martyr").

Finally, the handout Types of Abusive Behavior is revisited, with the focus primarily on the categories "Male Entitlement" and "Battering/Psychological Abuse." Male entitlement is defined as having an attitude that conveys male dominance, a general disrespect for women, and the belief that men are more competent and capable than women. This attitude leads to the belief, similar to that which has existed in our culture's historical roots, that a man has the right and responsibility to control his partner and to make her into the sort of person he believes she should be. This desire to control underlies all abusive behavior.

Male entitlement is rampant in our culture and permeates all our societal institutions. Violence against partners cannot exist without a sense of male entitlement being present. We ask men to look through the examples, identify attitudes they have held and behaviors they have used with their partners, and come up with other examples that are not listed. Obvious manifestations of this attitude include such things as a man expecting that he will have the final say on all important decisions in the relationship, that he will control the finances, and that his partner is his property or that he owns her once they are in a committed relationship.

Battering/psychological abuse is present in an intimate relationship when a consistent and ongoing pattern of controlling and abusive behavior is wielded by one person over another. It occurs when a less powerful partner believes that violence might be perpetrated against her or when at least one incident of property destruction or physical or sexual abuse toward her or others has occurred. This pattern adds a "terroristic" element to the relationship climate, creating a sense of fear and degradation that is always present. This is frequently recognized and discussed by men when they complete the Abuse Inventory task. In discussing the Abuse Inventory some men have described their violent incidents as similar to a hostage situation in which their partners become their captives as they act out through an unrelenting and terrifying series of abusive and controlling words and actions.

Once a partner believes that violence may occur or once incidents of violence have actually occurred, male entitlement behaviors, emotional and verbal abuse, and threats take on added impact. Men are significantly more able to create an atmosphere of humiliation, fear, and intimidation. Psychological abuse solidifies the "power and control" position that the batterer desires to achieve with his partner and results in undermining her self-esteem, creating intense emotional insecurity in her, rendering her less capable of caring for and protecting herself, and decreasing her potential to function independently in the future. This concept is discussed at some length to assist group members in understanding more fully how their behavior affects their partners once violence (or the potential for it to occur) exists in their relationships.

UNIT 7: ASSERTIVENESS

A lack of assertiveness does not cause battering. However, assertiveness is included in the educational program because so many abusive men have great difficulty being consistently assertive in their dealings with other people (Rosenbaum and O'Leary, 1981a; Pagelow, 1984; Sonkin, Martin, and Walker, 1985; Hotaling and Sugarman, 1986; Maiuro, Cahn, and Vitaliano, 1986). Abusive men tend to vacillate between being passive and withdrawing or becoming aggressive, explosive, and controlling with their partners and others. Their passivity in interactions often builds stress and tension that then may contribute to (but does not cause) their escalation and blowups with their partner and children, who are deemed safer targets than, for instance, an employer.

Assertiveness, as an educational topic, however, merits some cautionary statements. Unfortunately, this particular topic is one that abusive men may use to enhance the power and control stance they frequently use in intimate relationships. Assertiveness skills can easily become just another weapon in their war to achieve dominance. They might say, "I'm only being assertive," when, in fact, they may be presenting themselves in an aggressive and intimidating manner (especially nonverbally). They may also have the unrealistic expectation that their partners or others will do what they want if they are assertive "in the proper way." It is particularly important to stress the importance of being assertive and respectful with everyone in their lives, as they tend to become overly focused, once they begin to practice assertiveness skills, on becoming more assertive only with their partners. It must be strongly emphasized that assertiveness should not be used as just another tool to manipulate and control their partners.

Despite all of these potential problems, however, learning to be assertive in more life situations is still an important skill for abusive men to develop. If they are able to do this, they are less likely to experience the tension that tends to arise from handling day-to-day interactions in passive or ineffectual ways (Alberti and Emmons, 1970).

This unit starts with handouts that are discussed in group with all members. The first handout, Styles of Relating to Others, clearly defines and gives examples of passive, aggressive, passive-aggressive, and assertive communication styles, noting the goal for each. It also clearly states that the goal of assertion is not "winning" or "getting your way" but rather communicating your thoughts, feelings, and wants directly as a way of caring for yourself and setting the stage for increased intimacy. The second handout, Aggressive Behavior, highlights a variety of specific types of disrespectful and abusive actions and serves as a poignant reminder of the reasons that men are involved with the domestic abuse group. Finally, Verbal and Nonverbal Elements of Assertive, Passive, and Aggressive Behavior offers more specifics about different aspects of those styles of relating. It is important to give special emphasis to the nonverbal aspects because these are often overlooked or minimized by abusive men who deny the actual power and impact they have (e.g., glaring and staring to intimidate).

The next section of this unit involves the handout Assertiveness Synonyms, which is a brainstorming exercise held during the group session. For this exercise, men are asked to come up with different ways of describing the four styles of relating to others. The purpose is to ensure that men understand the concepts that have been presented and are able to clearly differentiate between assertive behavior and the other types of communication. Commonly, men in the group have great difficulty seeing the difference between being assertive and being aggressive, and consequently, changing their behavior becomes problematic.

The Assertiveness Grid handout is given as homework after the previous handout has been discussed. It serves as a concrete means of asking men to examine their relationships with others. This grid notes some specific behaviors and people and asks the men to identify whether they are generally passive, aggressive, passive-aggressive, or assertive with those people in those situations. This activity helps men see the patterns in their willingness to assert themselves with others in their lives. It also gives them an idea of what they should focus on if they wish to start changing some of these patterns. A particularly interesting pattern to note is whether they see themselves dealing differently with males and females.

Next, the handout The Process of Becoming More Assertive is presented and discussed. This handout provides a step-by-step method for identifying and changing the situations in which men have not been assertive in the past. It also assists them in preparing for, and following through with, some specific tasks to help them actually implement their new assertive behavior in their daily lives.

The handout Assertiveness Scenarios is a homework assignment that gives men the opportunity to clearly identify assertive, passive, aggressive, and passive-aggressive approaches to some common problematic situations. After filling this out, men are given the chance to actually role-play the different behavioral responses in the group. This allows the therapist to see whether men are, in a practical way, integrating these ideas into their behavioral repertoire.

The final handout and homework assignment in this section, the Assertiveness Journal, asks men to review situations that have occurred over the course of the week and to note how they handled the situation, what their self-talk and feelings were, and how they might have handled the situation more effectively. Men are asked to describe a situation relating both to their partner and to someone outside the family. This, again, gives the therapist a better idea of whether the men understand and are integrating these concepts into their lives.

UNIT 8: COMMUNICATION
AND CONFLICT RESOLUTION

Often, when a man first appears for treatment concerning battering issues, he will argue forcefully and eloquently that he and his partner "just cannot communicate." Their communication patterns frequently are unhealthy, but communication problems do not cause battering. Nonetheless, learning effective communication and conflict resolution strategies is an important part of what an abusive man must gain from domestic abuse treatment (Bandura, 1973; Rosenbaum and Maiuro, 1989; Edleson and Tolman, 1992).

Words often become just another weapon for abusive men in the ongoing struggles with their partners. Batterers at times report that it is their partners who are "good with words" and often complain about their partners' finesse in verbally abusing them. However, many abusive men are also adept at using words and the communication process as just another means to control and intimidate their partners. Women often report that it is the name-calling, put-downs, and verbal harassment that is most damaging to their self-esteem and their ability to make positive and healthy decisions for themselves.

This unit focuses on the communication process and how to make it more effective for both partners. In group, communication is compared to a game of tennis. However, the object is not to put the ball away and win the point but rather to keep the ball going back and forth over the net. The other integral parts of this unit are acknowledging and addressing conflicts directly when they arise and handling these conflicts effectively and respectfully.

The handout Feelings and the related lecture serve as an important introduction to the issue of communicating more effectively. Often, abusive men view their feelings and their emotional reactions as the "problem," especially when it comes to experiencing and expressing their anger. This discussion attempts to normalize feelings as part of being human and links emotions to the self-talk that fuels them.

This handout again challenges men to slow their internal processes to become more aware of how their emotional responses arise. It emphasizes the importance of accepting feelings and working with them rather than trying to ignore or deny them. It also stresses that a man's feelings are his responsibility and that his overreactions may stem from previous life experiences and may have little, if anything, to do with his present partner or children. This handout raises the issue of making choices about how feelings are expressed and encourages respectful versus abusive communication. Finally, it addresses the whole issue of why feelings are shared, asking men to question their unrealistic and controlling expectation that when they share their feelings "correctly," other people will then respond as the men think they should.

Feeling Words, another handout, is a helpful supplement to the previous discussion. Many abusive men enter the intake process with little or no awareness of any emotions that they experience besides anger, and they often label any emotion they feel as anger (Edleson and Tolman, 1992). Their anger serves as a cover-up for all sorts of other feelings (McKay, Rogers, and McKay, 1989), such as disappointment, fear, sadness, and hurt, which, if shared, would leave them considerably more vulnerable than their explosive outbursts do. They often have few words to even describe these other emotional experiences.

This handout offers general categories of emotions and specific feeling words within each category. Since anger has often been the only recognizable emotion in the past, this handout opens up new possibilities regarding communication and the expression of feelings. It can be very helpful for abusive men to learn new labels and descriptors to help broaden their feeling words vocabulary.

The next handout, Elements of Effective Communication, discusses specific components of the communication process and forms the basis for a lecture on this area. This handout begins with the concept of active listening and paraphrasing to directly address an abusive man's tendency to interrupt and race ahead to his own conclusions rather than tuning into his partner's perspective and trying to understand her point of view. Other highlights of this section include the following:

- Using "I" language and assuming clear responsibility for his thoughts, feelings, and wants
- Being aware of nonverbal signals that he is sending to and receiving from his partner
- Accepting feedback from others as a way to learn more about himself (as he is asked to do in the group)
- Offering descriptive and specific feedback to others that avoids evaluation and judgment (as he is asked to do in group)
- Staying tuned to the "emotional climate" and the communication process in addition to the content of the communication
- Working hard to make communication a cooperative effort rather than a competitive or destructive one

Hitting Below the Belt: Undermining Effective Conflict Resolution is a handout that outlines a number of different conflict strategies that tend to decrease trust, respect, and intimacy. Abusive men generally recognize numerous examples that they have used in their own relationships. This is assigned as homework, and men are asked to identify four or five primary strategies that they have used most frequently with their partners. In group, men are expected to talk about how they have used them.

Conflict Resolution is a handout that forms the basis for a lecture on an alternative and more positive way to experience and work through conflict in a relationship. Conflict is presented as a given in intimate human relationships. Procedure setting in conflict situations is encouraged so that guidelines exist to promote respect even in the midst of disagreement. It is also recommended that men focus on specific behaviors, situations, and concerns that are problematic rather than generalizing and globalizing issues that they wish to raise.

The model proposed here asks men to change their goal in conflict situations from *agreement*, which is part of their need to control, to *understanding*, which has the potential to bring those in conflict closer to each other. This section builds on and reinforces other educational presentations on self-talk, the time-out concept, and communication. It is stressed that in conflict resolution, the bottom line is what the man is willing to give or do himself rather than the idea that it is his right to force his partner to do something different. This model also focuses on the notion that it is all right to "agree to disagree" about most issues and encourages ongoing evaluations of the decisions that are reached in the conflict resolution process (and celebrations when the process actually works).

UNIT 9: SELF-ESTEEM
AND HEALTHY RELATIONSHIPS

Batterers have few, if any, models of healthy attitudes and behaviors toward themselves, toward other people, and in their relationships. Their families were often shaming, controlling, and abusive. Their friends and acquaintances frequently offer a similar vision to theirs about what it means to be a man and the nature of a relationship. Their own previous relationships with women were generally unhealthy and dysfunctional, and their own abusive and controlling patterns are likely to continue if they do not begin to look at themselves and relationships differently. These are men with low self-esteem (Pagelow, 1984; Goldstein and Rosenbaum, 1985). People who are abusive, controlling, and shaming with others do not feel good about themselves (Stosny, 1995).

This section offers an alternative view composed of positive and healthy ways of being human, developing and maintaining self-esteem, and integrating respect, nurturing, and equality into their relationships with partners. It expands on the information discussed in "Unit 6: Culture of Origin" and reinforces the idea that men must leave behind the macho, power-based image if they want to feel better about themselves and be able to develop intimacy with their partner, their children, and others.

Signs of High Self-Esteem is a handout that forms the basis for a therapist-led discussion about self-esteem and highlights characteristics that indicate when self-esteem is present. It focuses on the importance of self-acceptance; taking responsibility for themselves; self-understanding and insight; truly living by their espoused values; treating others in a warm, humane, and respectful way; realistically perceiving the outside world; and actively reaching out to the community and society around them. This discussion provides a different perspective on what these men have previously experienced and reinforces much of the other learning that is offered throughout their group involvement.

Men are cautioned not to measure themselves against this model in a perfectionistic way and thus use it as another means to shame or demean themselves. Rather, men are encouraged to use it to identify some specific attitudes and behaviors that they may wish to work on and change.

Types of Intimacy and Key Ingredients in Having and Maintaining a Healthy Relationship are handouts that extend and build on the previous individual focus to help men become respectful and caring partners in a relationship. These address specific aspects of being a nurturing and nonabusive partner, including maintaining a spirit of trust and cooperation; valuing differences; being aware of, and intervening in, controlling attitudes and behaviors; seeking equality in decision making and task accomplishment; moderating the expression of anger; learning to compromise and "agree to disagree"; working together as a team in parenting; and spending time apart as well as together.

The development of intimacy is a difficult assignment for batterers. Most have few, if any, intimate experiences with others from their childhood to the present. As such, part of this discussion could focus on the fears they feel about allowing themselves to be vulnerable in the ways that are recommended.

UNIT 10: PARENTING

Although not all men in this program have been physically abusive with their children, the majority have been controlling and emotionally and verbally abusive with them. One of the reasons that women frequently decide to leave an abusive relationship is fear for their children. Often they are concerned that their children will learn unhealthy attitudes and behaviors regarding male and female roles. This unit seeks to offer men some different ways to view and approach their children.

Getting men to use an alternative parenting style is often difficult because, by the time the men enter group, their children have often already begun to act out in a variety of ways. At this point, men frequently see their children as out of control, and they revert easily to the abusive and controlling parenting habits they experienced as children themselves.

One of the expectations in the program is that the men will not use physical discipline (e.g., spanking, hitting, ear pulling) with their children during their time in the group. If physical discipline is used, men must fill out and share a Violent Incident Assessment (see Chapter III), which outlines why they chose not to use their Escalation Prevention Plan to de-escalate and what they can do differently the next time.

This is not to say that men should never use physical restraint or control with their children. For example, standing back and calmly talking to a two-year-old who is playing with an electrical outlet is not responsible parenting either. However, if the physical restraint goes beyond moving the child from the dangerous situation to inflicting physical pain (e.g., squeezing arms or shoulders to hurt the child) or erupting explosively to intimidate, concerns would be expressed.

The goal of this unit is to assist men in becoming nonviolent and nonabusive parents with their children. This unit is not designed to be an exhaustive course on all aspects of parenting. Rather, the program simply hopes to introduce some basic concepts about nurturing and respectful parenting and then to encourage men to look other places for more comprehensive groups or classes on parenting principles. A parenting class is often one of the final recommendations when men with children complete the program. A critical step for abusive men is intervening in their belief that their children are acting in a malicious way and "are out to get them." When they are willing to step back from this negative mind-set, they are less likely to continually react in a frightening and intimidating manner when things do not go as they would like.

The basic model that this unit uses is adapted from *STEP: Systematic Training in Effective Parenting*, by Don Dinkmeyer and Gary McKay (1989), which builds on principles from Rudolph Dreikurs' work (1964). It encourages democratic, nurturing, and respectful interactions with children, as opposed to using authoritarian, shaming, and abusive methods. This book is strongly recommended to group members. A number of important concepts from the book are focused on and discussed in group through the use of handouts. These concepts include the following:

- The Goals of Misbehavior
- The Goals of Positive Behavior
- Differences Between the "Good" Parent and the Responsible Parent

- Differences Between Praise and Encouragement
- The Major Differences Between Punishment and Logical Consequences

In addition, a variety of articles from newspapers, magazines, and other sources are used to address and discuss other important parenting issues, such as building children's self-esteem, how to handle "back talk," the pros and cons of spanking, and how to handle children's anger. The following are some examples:

- "Don't Expect Too Much from Your Children," an article written by Ronald Pitzer as part of the "Young Families" series through the Minnesota Extension Service at the University of Minnesota, describes a number of unrealistic and unreasonable expectations that can damage a child's self-esteem and the parent's relationship with the child.
- "Spank or Not Spank? Some Opinions," from a newspaper advice column called "Tender Years," written by Pat Gardner, addresses issues related to using physical punishment with children and the potential effects on them and on their relationships with their parents.
- "How to Raise a Violent Boy," an article written by Peg Meier in *The Memphis Star-Tribune,* clearly outlines what *not* to do if your intention is to see your son become a nurturing and respectful person.
- "Plain Talk About Dealing with the Angry Child," an article from the National Institute of Mental Health (Hilda Fried, Editor), discusses some concrete responses in handling children's aggressive and angry outbursts.
- "Teach Responsibility with Consequences, Not Punishment," another article written by Ronald Pitzer at the University of Minnesota, focuses on the difference between using natural and logical consequences, which teach responsibility and increase self-confidence, and using punishment, which may teach short-term compliance but takes a toll on a child's self-esteem in the process.
- "Children Learn What They Live," a poem by Dorothy Law Nolte, discusses how children model themselves after what they are taught by their parents.

The handout How to Be a More Effective Parent is discussed in group. It offers some basic suggestions about respectful and effective parenting, focusing on the following:

- Moderating men's anger and emotional reactivity
- Asking men to try to understand their child's goals and the motivation behind his/her misbehavior

- Recommending that men learn more about their child's capabilities at particular developmental stages
- Encouraging men to take more time to look for opportunities to connect in a positive emotional way with their children
- Offering choices and alternatives instead of demands and directives to their children
- Using logical and natural consequences to promote cooperation and responsibility

These concepts are often strange, even foreign, to group members, who generally employ with their children the same shaming and autocratic approach directed at them when they were children. It is also recommended that they attend, alone or with a partner, a parenting class to learn more about the concepts presented here and to begin applying these concepts to some practical situations that they confront with their children in their day-to-day lives.

UNIT 11: WOMEN'S PERSPECTIVE ON ABUSE AND VIOLENCE

An important part of what batterers often fail to comprehend is the destructive and devastating impact of their abuse on their partners. Examining this impact is a theme throughout the program, and the development of empathy for their partners and others are critical elements in the change process. One way that this is communicated to men is through having a women therapist who works with battered women come to the domestic abuse group and talk about the healing process for women. She also discusses the effects, from a woman's point of view, of the abuse and violence they have perpetrated against their partners.

The therapist who comes to group generally talks about the women's program, highlighting similarities and differences between the two groups. She often discusses the difference between male and female abuse, as this is frequently an issue that arises during the time she is present. Men are offered the opportunity to ask questions during this presentation about topics of interest to them. These questions often revolve around why their partners are so angry with them, when the woman will "get over this," and how women heal from the abuse. In this session, men frequently look for hope regarding the future of their relationships and are once again reminded that the only possible way to rebuild trust and intimacy in the relationship is to provide their partners with a consistent pattern of behavior change over time that allows them to feel truly safe and to heal from the impact of past abuse.

Prior to this unit, men are prepared to deal with issues such as the possibility of an escalation occurring and what to do in that situation. This is another opportunity for men to practice taking a time-out if the need arises, although no one has ever done so during this presentation. Despite the tension created when men are told that a woman therapist will be joining the group for this period of time, group members have consistently found this exposure to the women's perspective helpful and enlightening. This discussion also decreases the fear men often verbalize during the group that their partners are being brainwashed in the women's program to despise and reject them and men in general.

A woman therapist comes to the group approximately every six months, and thus, this unit does not necessarily follow the sequential order of Unit 1 through Unit 10.

UNIT 12: THE ONGOING RECOVERY PROCESS

Part of what is emphasized with men from the very beginning of their treatment is that becoming and remaining nonabusive requires energy and effort long after they have completed this domestic abuse program. Their completion of group is not considered an end point. The importance of continuing to take care of themselves is regularly stressed. This means attending to their controlling attitudes and potential for abuse and using the tools and skills they have learned and hopefully put into practice during their group experience.

Many men start the process with the unrealistic and unreachable goals of "never getting angry" and "being cured" by the end of the program. Part of what they must be taught is that they will continue to get angry and that there is no "cure" that permanently ends the potential for becoming abusive again. In reality, this potential to become controlling and abusive will always remain with them. The only effective way to remain nonabusive is to stay aware of the cues and triggers that signal their stress, irritation, frustration, and anger and to intervene in the escalation process and their desire to control before they make the choice to become abusive.

The best way to reinforce this philosophy is to bring men back who have completed the group at an earlier time to discuss their ongoing recovery process. Because this program has been functioning for more than twelve years, because a number of our completers continue in therapy, and because a number of these men want to "give back" to the program as a means of enhancing their own recovery (Adams, 1989), numerous men have been willing to volunteer their time and become involved in this way.

We generally ask teams of two men to come to talk in group, with one man who is still involved with his original partner and one who is not. This states clearly that with hard work, the possibility exists that they can build a healthy and nonabusive relationship. It also communicates the understanding that, even if they do not continue in their current relationship, they can still grow and feel good about themselves and be nonabusive with a new partner. The men who visit talk about their past abuse, their experience in the domestic abuse treatment program, and what they have done to continue their progress in addressing their controlling and abusive attitudes and behaviors.

The hopeful aspect of this unit cannot be underestimated. Men in group are frequently estranged in the process of divorce, and, at a minimum, are separated from their partners and their children. A sense of despair and hopelessness is often rampant. These men who return, in telling their stories and talking about what they have done to continue their recovery process, communicate that hard work and commitment make change possible, allowing men's lives to become more fulfilling and satisfying, with or without their current partner.

This is a powerful message to men who are often focused on the bleakness of their current situations. The men who return also offer clear testimony that the anger and the desire to control remain within them, long after the group is over. Even more important, they communicate the idea that ongoing choices can be made to deal more effectively with both the anger and the control if the group members decide to do so.

Former members come to the group approximately every six months, and thus, this unit does not necessarily follow the sequential order of Unit 1 through Unit 10.

Part 2:
The Educational Handouts

Unit 1: Abuse and Its Effects

TYPES OF ABUSIVE BEHAVIOR

Volatile anger and abusive behavior are always destructive in a relationship and always contribute to a loss of trust, respect, and intimacy. They are never helpful in problem solving or conflict resolution. Both men and women can be abusive in relationships. Abusive behavior, as it is defined in this handout, occurs in many relationships at some point. Abuse by either partner is not okay. However, the gender of the person who is abusive can make a significant difference in the ongoing impact of abusive actions, especially when a consistent pattern of abuse exists in the relationship. Although abusive behavior can occur between any two people, in the large majority of cases, men in heterosexual relationships are more able and more likely to use methodical and systematic physical force to maintain control in a relationship. Even when men do experience physical abuse by their partners, they are less likely to feel the intense fear, humiliation, and intimidation or to suffer the severity of physical damage that women do. Because of basic differences in musculature and socialization, women generally cannot compete with men once a physical conflict has begun. Men are, on the whole, more likely to be able to dominate a relationship through the use of physical force than are women.

Moreover, once a man has actually been physically or sexually abusive in a relationship (or if his partner believes that the potential exists for him to do so), other types of abuse have additional impact. For example, emotional and verbal abuse can then become much more frightening and controlling for the female partner. A single act of physical force clearly demonstrates that, if unable to control his partner through verbal and emotional abuse and threats, a man has the potential to up the ante again to physical abuse to maintain his

(HO) ©1999 David J. Decker, MA

225

dominance in the relationship. Both the man and his partner know that he has already used violence in the past so it becomes that much easier for him to violate this physical boundary the next time he becomes explosive and threatening. The eight types of abuse commonly seen among men in the program are presented in this handout with examples of each. Read through them and see which of these you have used in relating to your partner.

Male Entitlement

Male entitlement is an attitude that conveys male dominance, a general disrespect for women, and the idea that men are more competent and capable than women. This attitude leads to the belief that "I, as a man, have the right and the responsibility to control how my partner thinks, feels, and acts and to make her into the person I think she should be." This desire to control underlies all abusive behavior and is characterized by the following actions:

1. Making generalizations, telling disrespectful jokes, and believing stereotypes about women (e.g., "Women are irrational"; "It's a woman's job to take care of me and the kids")
2. Having the expectation that you will make all the important decisions in the relationship
3. Treating her like a servant (e.g., demanding that she do things for you and expecting her to wait on you; saying to her, "Go get me a drink" or "Get dinner ready")
4. Controlling how household money is handled (e.g., forcing her to account for all the money she spends, withholding money from her, giving her an allowance, acting as if her work around the house and with the children has no economic value to the family and is not as important as your outside job, keeping the checkbook or charge cards in your possession)
5. Believing that you need to be the breadwinner (e.g., discouraging her from going to school or getting employment, sabotaging her job by coming home late when she needs to get to work)
6. Deciding who does what in terms of household chores and parenting
7. Communicating to her or others that she is your property, that you own her, or that she belongs to you because you are in a relationship or marriage
8. Being possessive and acting extremely jealous (e.g., assuming that she is always "on the make," brooding about or continually bringing up her real or imagined relationships with other men)

(HO)   ©1999 David J. Decker, MA

Emotional Abuse

Emotional abuse is the use of behavioral or nonverbal methods, such as the following, to hurt, punish, intimidate, or control your partner:

1. Sulking or withdrawing affection from her (e.g., punishing her with silence)
2. Sneering at her and acting disgusted with or contemptuous of her (e.g., dirty looks, rolling your eyes when she is talking)
3. Yelling and screaming at her
4. Staring or glaring at her
5. Following her around the house or apartment to continue an argument whether or not she wishes to do so
6. Standing near or over her and using your size to intimidate her (e.g., "getting in her face")
7. Monitoring her behavior and doing "detective work" (e.g., following her or having her followed to find out where she is going or who she is spending time with, listening in on her phone conversations or taping her phone calls, calling to see if she is where she says she is going to be)
8. Attempting to control her movements or to isolate her (e.g., trying to keep her away from family and friends by taking her car keys, removing the car battery or disconnecting the distributor cap, preventing her from using the phone, or not giving her phone messages)
9. Interrupting her while she is eating (e.g., finishing a discussion during dinner)
10. Forcing her to stay awake or waking her up (e.g., to resolve an argument)
11. Forcing her to humiliate herself (e.g., making her kneel in front of you)

Verbal Abuse

Verbal abuse is the use of words to hurt, punish, intimidate, or control your partner, including the following behaviors:

1. Criticizing/discounting her thoughts, feelings, opinions, and values (e.g., saying to her "That's a stupid idea" or "You're nuts to feel that way")
2. Mocking her or mimicking what she has said (e.g., in a singsong voice)
3. Lecturing her about what's right or about the way she should be
4. Twisting what she says to make her feel confused, "crazy," and off balance (e.g., manipulating her with lies and contradictions)

(HO)   ©1999 David J. Decker, MA

5. Making negative/derogatory comments about activities she likes and places she goes
6. Interrupting her
7. Interrogating her (e.g., continually questioning her about where she goes and who she sees)
8. Accusing or blaming her for things that go wrong (e.g., around the house, with finances, with the children, in your relationship)
9. Swearing/cursing at her ("Fuck you"; "Go to hell")
10. Name-calling (e.g., "bitch," "asshole")
11. Insulting, ridiculing, or belittling her or people she cares about (e.g., put-downs about her parenting or calling her friends "losers" or "dykes")
12. Being demanding (e.g., pressuring her verbally to do what you want her to do and be who you want her to be)

Threats

Nonphysical Threats

Nonphysical threats communicate (either directly or indirectly) an intention to do something, thereby creating emotional distress, fear, and indecision and increasing your ability to control your partner. This includes threatening to do the following:

1. Withdraw affection or refuse to talk to her
2. Expose personal things she has told you to others (e.g., "Wait until I tell your parents what you just said")
3. File assault charges or get a restraining order against her
4. Take or kidnap the children if she leaves
5. Withhold money
6. Throw her out in the street
7. Go out with other women
8. End the relationship, separate, or divorce

Violent Threats

Violent threats communicate (either directly or indirectly) an intention to do physical harm to your partner, your children, other relatives, friends, pets, yourself, or property, including the following actions:

(HO)   ©1999 David J. Decker, MA

1. Standing in her way or "cornering" her
2. Throwing objects in her direction or at her
3. Hitting walls or slamming your fist on surfaces (e.g., on countertops or tables)
4. Threatening to hurt pets
5. Making vague statements (e.g., "You're really asking for it," "Go ahead, keep it up," or "Remember the last time you got me pissed off")
6. Making physically intimidating gestures such as holding up a clenched fist in front of her face or raising your arm as if to hit her
7. Making statements about pushing, grabbing, or hitting her (e.g., "I'd like to smash your face right now" or "I really feel like letting you have it")
8. Threatening to be harsh or abusive with the children
9. Driving recklessly when you are angry to frighten her or "make a point"
10. Threatening her with an object (e.g., a belt or broom)
11. Playing with or discharging a weapon around her
12. Making direct or veiled threats to kill her, the children, her parents, or others
13. Making direct or veiled threats to hurt or kill yourself (e.g., "I can't go on without you")

Battering/Psychological Abuse

This category can include any or all of the previous four categories. Battering and psychological abuse occur as a result of a consistent and ongoing pattern of abusive behavior by one person in an intimate relationship who is more powerful than his or her partner. They are present when the less powerful partner either feels fearful that violence might occur or has experienced at least one incident of property destruction or physical or sexual abuse by the other partner toward her or others. When the potential for violence exists, or when violence has already occurred in a relationship, verbal and emotional abuse and threats take on added impact. At this point, these behaviors are significantly more likely to create an atmosphere of terror, degradation, and humiliation than would occur in a relationship in which threats or violence have been absent. Many relationships involve some of the abuse types previously noted on an occasional or infrequent basis. However, battering and psychological abuse become part of the relationship dynamic when a man systematically and persistently, through the use of violence, threats, and other abusive and controlling attitudes and behaviors, tries to:

(HO)   ©1999 David J. Decker, MA

1. undermine a woman's self-esteem, self-confidence, and motivation;
2. create a devastating and debilitating emotional insecurity in her; and
3. render her less capable of caring for and protecting herself and of functioning independently in the future.

Violence Toward Property or Pets

This type of abuse involves destroying property or hurting pets to intimidate or coerce her into doing what you want her to do, including the following actions (these actions can also be perceived as violent threats to those who are around when they are occurring or who see the damage when they return):

1. Hitting walls
2. Slamming your fist on surfaces (e.g., desk, countertop, arm of a chair, car dashboard)
3. Throwing or breaking household items
4. Taking, hiding, or destroying her possessions (e.g., favorite pictures, family heirlooms, jewelry)
5. Hitting, kicking, or killing a pet to intimidate or hurt her

Sexual Abuse

Sexual abuse consists of any sexually inappropriate verbal statements, any physical affection or touch forced on another person, or any nonconsensual sexual act, including the following:

1. Telling dirty jokes and making sexually demeaning comments about her or other women around her (e.g., calling her or other women "whores," "sluts," or "frigid")
2. Staring at other women's bodies when you are with her or making sexual comments about other women around her
3. Viewing and treating her or other women like sex objects (e.g., making unwanted or inappropriate sexual comments to her or about her in front of others, expecting or demanding sex from her)
4. Insulting her body (e.g., the size of her breasts/hips) or her love-making ability (e.g., "You make love like a corpse")
5. Insisting that she dress in a certain manner (e.g., in a sexy or prim-and-proper fashion)

(HO) ©1999 David J. Decker, MA

6. Touching sexual parts of her body without consent (e.g., grabbing or pinching her breasts or buttocks when she tells you not to do it or when she says that it hurts)
7. Coercing or pressuring her into performing specific sexual behaviors that she does not wish to do (e.g., making her perform oral or anal sex, expecting her to have sex with multiple partners or with your friends)
8. Forcing sex in the following situations:
   • She is sleeping.
   • She is not asked.
   • She is sick or it is damaging to her health.
   • She says "no" or sets a limit (verbally or nonverbally).
   • She is intoxicated and unable to say "no" effectively.
   • She is fearful about the consequences of saying "no."
9. Raping her

Physical Abuse

Physical abuse is the use of any physical actions or force to control a person or situation (this includes violence perpetrated against yourself), such as the following:

1. Pinching/scratching/biting her
2. Tripping her
3. Ripping her clothing
4. Pulling her hair
5. Bumping into her as you walk by
6. Grabbing/pushing her
7. Wrestling with or restraining her physically
8. Tying her up
9. Throwing her bodily (e.g., on a couch, on the floor, on a bed)
10. Slapping/punching her
11. Choking/strangling her (e.g., putting your hands near or around her throat and squeezing)
12. Using an object or weapon with her (e.g., a broom, belt, knife, or gun)
13. Hitting, hurting, or killing yourself (e.g., punching yourself in the head, attempting suicide)

(HO)

HOW VIOLENCE MAY OCCUR IN A RELATIONSHIP

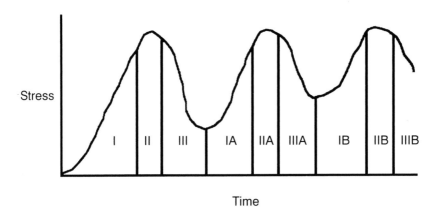

Many couples can clearly recognize and talk about how violence occurs in their relationship over the course of time. Women tend to see this pattern most clearly, but men frequently acknowledge the pattern as well. The following material describes the three phases of violence that both this program and others (Walker, 1979) have identified.

Escalation Phase (I)

This phase is characterized by a period of increased tension that builds over time and may include unresolved arguments in the relationship, job stress, financial pressures, increased chemical use, passive responses to conflicts (in and outside the home), and a buildup of resentments. Generally, the man has little, if any, awareness of the stress that is building and rarely does he talk about the tension and the feelings behind it. Nor does he use other healthy ways to handle the stress in his life. The more powerless he feels inside, the greater his aggression and need for control tend to become. Verbal and emotional abuse, threats, destruction of property, and some less severe physical abuse may occur as the tension mounts and becomes unbearable for him. An escalation can last minutes, hours, days, weeks, or months, but the eventual outcome is violence. The woman is often significantly more aware that tension is building than her partner is.

(HO)   ©1999 David J. Decker, MA

WHAT HAPPENS WITH HIM

- blames her for his increased stress and anger and his controlling and abusive reactions
- makes unreasonable demands/has unrealistic expectations
- becomes more oppressive and controlling
- feels more and more powerless at home and in the rest of his life
- denies and minimizes the stress in his life and the impact of his control/intimidation on others
- often feels jealous/distrustful of his partner
- feels escalated/angry much of the time (but generally denies feelings behind the anger, e.g., hurt, fear, insecurity, inadequacy, disappointment)
- believes it is her responsibility to make him feel better
- feels more and more "out of control"
- becomes more and more isolated
- may increase alcohol/drug use to try to reduce his stress
- views her withdrawal from him as rejection/abandonment, which further escalates him

WHAT HAPPENS WITH HER

- often believes she can (or should be able to) control his moods and outbursts and attempts to do so
- often hides her own anger due to fear of reprisal
- blames abusive incidents on external situations (e.g., work/financial stress) and works to control as many as she can (e.g., children's behavior)
- believes that nothing she does is "good enough" and feels as if she is "walking on eggshells"
- denies and minimizes the abusive incidents and their impact on her and their children (if they have any)
- starts to realize that she is not able to control his outbursts and feels powerless to stop the abuse (may appear, at times, to be "inviting" the abuse due to her desire to "get it over" and decrease the stress level that exists)
- tends to withdraw to protect herself, which only increases his frustration/irritation
- often blames herself for the abuse and becomes more and more isolated from friends and family
- with each incident, her self-esteem and self-confidence is further depleted

Explosion Phase (II)

This second phase involves a seemingly uncontrollable discharge of pent-up and accumulated tension that is actually a conscious choice to strike out at his partner to relieve stress and to control her and the situation. Choices may include time and place, weapon (e.g., open hand versus closed fist), target (e.g., assaulting only certain parts of her body), and duration (i.e., how long the incident lasts). This phase begins and ends with more serious and destructive violence than that which generally occurs during the escalation phase and has the greatest likelihood of attracting outsider (e.g., police, neighbors, relatives) involvement. Eventually, such severe emotional and verbal abuse and threats can become as devastating as the physical abuse, and violence may no longer be necessary to exert control over the woman in the relationship.

(HO)   ©1999 David J. Decker, MA

WHAT HAPPENS WITH HIM	WHAT HAPPENS WITH HER
• starts out to "teach her a lesson" to prove that he is in control of the relationship (wants to punish her for not being who he thinks she should be)	• her behavior does not affect outcome, although she may be more seriously injured if she defends herself physically
• feels "out of control," full of rage, hateful, and vindictive and expresses these emotions by striking out verbally and physically	• views escape from the situation as futile
• blames her for his abuse and violence (feels justified)	• disassociation often occurs (i.e., she may "stand back"/detach emotionally from the abuse and watch it happen to herself)
• often surprised and scared about the intensity of his rage and the severity of the abuse	• feels terrified, hurt, humiliated, ashamed, degraded, angry, and resentful
• does not understand what happened or how he got so out of control and tends to deny the severity of his abuse and its impact on his partner	• symptoms after acute assault can include shock; disbelief; denial; minimization; anxiety; rationalization; listlessness and lethargy; feelings of hopelessness, helplessness and powerlessness; depression; and rage
• may believe that he has resolved the problems in the relationship with his abusive behavior	• often blames herself for his abusive behavior (looks for what she could do differently to experience some sense of control and power in her life)
• may experience enormous physiological/ emotional release from perpetrating the abuse and often feels and looks calm and relaxed immediately afterward	• often more able to remember and describe the violent incident in specific details
• often cannot remember or describe the incident and his abusive behavior due to his denial and shame	• may attack the police to assist her partner or request that assault charges not be filed to demonstrate her loyalty to her partner so she can avoid further violence/abuse
• may blame his violence/abuse on his (or her) excessive use of alcohol/drugs	
• payoffs such as the stress release and control over the situation reinforce the likelihood that the violence will be repeated	

Calming Phase (III)

This final phase is often referred to as the "honeymoon stage." However, it is not really a honeymoon at all. In reality, it is often a time when the man deceives himself in an attempt to convince his partner, and his partner deceives herself into believing, that the violence, control, and abuse will stop. This phase can also involve genuine remorse and shame on the part of the man due to his fear that he has gone too far in trying to assume control of the relationship. For the woman, this phase may simply be a signal that the violence is over for now. At this point, the man may also fear that his partner will leave him or involve outsiders (e.g., police, relatives) in their relationship. Because of his fear, he may "bend over backwards" to be kind, attentive, loving, and considerate, and his "model behavior" often involves mak-

©1999 David J. Decker, MA

ing promises about the future, buying gifts, or doing something special for his partner. His partner often desperately wants to believe the promises about how he will change and she begins to feel hope for herself and the relationship, thus solidifying her victimization. Over time, if the man does not actually seek help for himself, the promises become hollow and this phase disappears completely. For some couples, however, this phase does not even exist: the time after the explosion phase is only a short period with the temporary absence of battering and few, if any, attempts at even the kind of deception noted previously.

WHAT HAPPENS WITH HIM

- frightened by his own rage and aggressive behavior and often realizes that he has gone too far
- may express regret about his behavior and feel guilty and shameful about what he has done
- often asks for her forgiveness and vows that the abuse will never happen again (may believe violence will not be necessary because he is now "in control")
- may accept some responsibility for his behavior but his primary motivation is not to learn from or to stop the abusive behavior but rather to appease her, save their relationship, and/or avoid legal consequences
- may promise that he will change (e.g., stop using/abusing alcohol/drugs; work less or more or get a new job; give her more freedom and not act so jealous; spend more time with her and the children; cease doing other things that irritate her; stop going out with other women; stop being abusive/violent)
- may act caring, affectionate, and considerate of her and her needs (e.g., buying her flowers, candy, and other presents; taking her out on "special" dates; offering to do things for her)
- at the same time, stress begins to build once again due to his belief that he has to "bend over backwards" and to convince her to forgive him and stay with him

WHAT HAPPENS WITH HER

- terror and anger motivate her to think about leaving (wants to escape the abuse but feels fearful and guilty about going)
- struggles with her inability to control his abusive behavior but may still feel responsible in some way for his actions
- wants to believe the promises that he will change and may choose to do so, enjoying his caring and attention to her and idealizing him and their relationship, seeing once again the part of him that she loves, thus ensuring her victimization
- may also return/remain out of fear, believing that being around him is safer than not knowing where he is or what he is doing
- feels "stuck," trapped, depressed, anxious, powerless, and hopeless
- if she does not follow through with legal actions and/or decides against leaving or goes back to him, others concerned about her may become frustrated and exasperated with her and give up, once again leaving her isolated and alone

(HO)

WHAT HAPPENS WITH HIM

- may enlist children, extended family, and even friends to plead his case with her and work on her guilt about ending the relationship
- at times, encourages her to see "what she did wrong" to cause or provoke the violence
- eventually, when he also realizes that he will not stop being violent, he may stop apologizing, offering gifts, and making promises to change because he knows he will not follow through

Without consequences (e.g., legal intervention, his partner leaving), professional intervention, and the acquisition of new skills to cope with the emotional and physical stresses and the desire to control experienced in the escalation phase, these phases may continue to repeat themselves in the relationship.

Phase IA (IB, etc.) is similar to Phase I except that the stress from the first violent incident increases the overall tension level in the relationship, which means that the potential for violence to occur sooner becomes greater.

Phase IIA (IIB, etc.) is similar to Phase II, but now the type of violent behavior necessary to bring about the stress release or to control the situation may need to be even more severe or more frequent. Also since violence has already occurred in the relationship, the man's verbal/emotional abuse and threats have an even more intimidating and damaging effect.

Phase IIIA (IIIB, etc.) is similar to Phase III except that the deception phase may become shorter or disappear completely because both partners begin to realize that the violence and abuse will not end unless the man does something significantly different to change his controlling and abusive attitudes and behaviors. His apologies and promises may stop or seem more insincere as his shame about his abusiveness builds and as he increasingly denies and minimizes his responsibility for the abuse and its impact on his partner and his children.

Adapted from L. Walker, *The Battered Woman* (1979), who writes about a "Cycle of Violence" involving the "tension-building phase," the "acute battering incident," and the "calm, loving respite."

(HO)   ©1999 David J. Decker, MA

MYTHS ABOUT DOMESTIC ABUSE

There is an enormous amount of misinformation about domestic abuse in our culture. This handout presents some of the common myths and the realities behind them. It can be used as a guide for the group leader when brainstorming myths with the men in group and then given to men as a handout.

Domestic Abuse Is Only Abuse
When It Happens "All the Time"

The reality: Even one violent act or threat of violence can create an atmosphere of fear, humiliation, degradation, and terror for the victim.

Domestic Abuse "Is Not That Big a Problem"
or "Does Not Really Exist"

The reality: It is estimated that 2 to 4 million women are battered each year by their husbands, ex-husbands, and male lovers, and according to FBI statistics, 1,400 to 1,500 women are murdered by their partners each year.

Domestic Abuse Is "Normal" Behavior
in a Relationship

The reality: Most relationships do not have a pattern of coercive, abusive, or violent behavior between partners.

Only Physical Abuse Really Matters

The reality: Victims frequently report that emotional and verbal abuse leave devastating scars that sometimes take longer to heal than the physical wounds.

Domestic Violence Is a Private Family Matter

The reality: Domestic violence is assault, a crime punishable by law.

(HO) ©1999 David J. Decker, MA

Alcohol and Drug Use "Cause" Abuse and Violence

The reality: Although the correlation between chemical abuse and domestic abuse is often high, these are, in fact, two distinct and freestanding issues that must be addressed separately: many alcoholics do not batter; some batterers do not drink.

Strong Religious Beliefs Can Prevent or "Cure" Domestic Abuse

The reality: Batterers often buttress their "right" to discipline (i.e., abuse) their partners and children with rigid and narrow religious beliefs and Biblical quotations.

Male and Female Partners Are Equally Violent and Their Violence Is the Same

The reality: Of reported victims of domestic assault, 95 percent are women, and studies that report finding equal male and female violence rates in the home often did not explore whether women's violence was in self-defense (as it often is), nor did they acknowledge or address the strength and power differential when men and women become violent with each other.

Domestic Abuse Occurs Primarily Among the Low-Income, Unsuccessful, Uneducated, Young, or Minorities

The reality: Abuse occurs in all social, racial, economic, educational, age, occupational, sexual orientation, personality, and religious groups, although lower socioeconomic abusers and minorities may be more likely to attract the attention of legal authorities in our culture.

Women Provoke or Deserve the Abuse

The reality: Women may become explosive and hurtful and say or do abusive things to their partners, but this still does not give men the right to batter them, nor does it justify a violent response; in fact, most women do whatever they can to avoid being abused.

(HO)   ©1999 David J. Decker, MA

Women Can Leave Anytime They Want To

The reality: Women do not leave abusive relationships for a number of very valid reasons, including fear of retaliation (men may threaten to stalk, harass, hurt, or even kill them, the children, or other loved ones), economic dependency, lack of awareness of alternatives and community resources, socially learned and prescribed caretaking roles, family and cultural pressures, and emotional dependency and love for their partners when they are not abusive; in addition, the violence and abuse often escalates when women attempt to leave.

Abused Women Are Emotionally Unstable or Mentally Ill

The reality: Battered women often present with severe depression, anxiety and panic attacks, and low self-esteem; however, these symptoms frequently relate directly to the abuse that is occurring in their lives and often subside when the women begin to feel safe and empowered, through their contact with advocates, support groups, and therapy, to make changes necessary to protect themselves and their children.

Abuse Ends When a Woman Leaves the Relationship

The reality: The most dangerous time for a woman is when she leaves the relationship; The likelihood of her being battered or murdered actually increases.

Many Abused Women Actually Like the Conflict and the Abuse

The reality: No one "likes" being verbally or physically abused or violated in other ways, although the batterer may believe that they, as a couple, have been brought closer together if his partner acquiesces to his affectionate or sexual advances in the honeymoon phase because she fears his explosive reaction if she refuses.

(HO) ©1999 David J. Decker, MA

Abused Women Will Always Seek Out
Abusive Relationships

The reality: The idea that a woman involves herself in a series of abusive relationships did not hold true in Lenore Walker's survey of battered women (Walker, 1979); even when a woman does involve herself with another batterer, it is not always easy to tell that he will become abusive when they first begin to date. Men often do not become violent until a commitment is made (i.e., cohabitation or marriage).

Women in Abusive Relationships
Were Abused As Children

The reality: Although some women in battering relationships experienced or observed violence and abuse in their families of origin, the percentage is significantly lower than for their male partners who are abusing them.

The Police and the Legal System
Can Protect an Abused Woman

The reality: Often police and the courts fail to take strong action against a batterer and, even when there is an Order for Protection (OFP), it may not be taken seriously or enforced as it needs to be; many women are assaulted and hurt with OFPs in place.

Women Can Change Their Abusers with Love

The reality: Many women, especially young women, believe this romantic notion that they can somehow transform their partners into nonabusers if they only "try hard enough." In fact, men are responsible for their abusive and violent behavior, and once violence has occurred in a relationship, it is highly likely that it will occur again over time, becoming more frequent and more severe. Only men themselves can make the decision and take the steps necessary to intervene in and change their controlling and abusive attitudes and actions.

(HO)   ©1999 David J. Decker, MA

Abusers Are Mentally Ill, Crazy, or Out of Control

The reality: The vast majority of batterers do not have either "thought disorders" or "impulse control disorders." In fact, men have learned to use violence to control people and situations around them, and they make clear choices about where, how, and when they become abusive with their partners and others.

Abusers Are Easy to Identify

The reality: Although batterers may have a history of generalized violence, often, at a certain point in their lives, they become person specific, focusing the abuse on their partners and, at times, their children. Frequently, when they first meet a prospective partner, they are loving, charming, and attentive, and, even later in the relationship, they are not abusive at all times.

Abusers Will Stop Being Abusive on Their Own

The reality: Occasionally men are able to stop being violent on their own due to fear about legal and relationship consequences. However, effectively addressing the controlling attitudes and the emotional and verbal abuse that arises from these attitudes can best be accomplished in a treatment setting where abuse and control are the focus of the intervention.

Abusers Can Never Change

The reality: Because abuse is a learned behavior, it can be unlearned; most batterers witnessed or experienced control and abuse in their families of origin and can stop the violence and decrease the verbal and emotional abuse through legal and relationship consequences and/or by attending a treatment program that specifically addresses these issues.

Abusers Are Mean and Cruel at All Times

The reality: Abusers go through a "cycle of violence" and can be, at times (especially during the calming phase), loving, nurturing, playful, attentive, sensitive to their partners' needs, exciting, and affectionate. Some batterers abuse their children; some do not.

(HO)

Children Are Not Affected by the Abuse

The reality: Even if they do not see or experience it themselves, children may still hear the violence occurring and/or feel the inherent tension that exists in a household in which abuse occurs. Children can be affected behaviorally, cognitively, emotionally, physically, or socially by living in an abusive home.

Children Are "Better Off" If Their Parents Remain Married

The reality: Divorce can certainly have traumatic effects on children. However, growing up in a controlling and abusive household creates enormous problems of its own, including teaching boys to be aggressive, controlling, and violent and showing girls that it is their role to allow men to victimize them.

Domestic Abuse Is a Couple's or an Individual's Problem

The reality: Domestic abuse is also a societal issue due to the messages men receive about what it means to be a man and the messages we all receive from the media and other cultural institutions regarding male and female roles and expectations.

Domestic Abuse Occurs Only in Heterosexual Relationships

The reality: Although there is currently little research on the prevalence of partner abuse in gay and lesbian relationships, it is estimated that the problem exists at similar rates to those identified in heterosexual relationships.

Mental Health and Health Care Providers Are Helpless in Domestic Abuse Situations

The reality: Although domestic abuse can be frightening and frustrating for professionals who come in contact with it, they can still offer accurate information about what abuse is and its effects on the couple and family relationships. They also can provide validation and emotional support and referrals to appropriate community resources for help.

(HO)   ©1999 David J. Decker, MA

PERCEIVED ADVANTAGES/DISADVANTAGES OF USING VIOLENCE

There are always advantages and disadvantages in using violence and physical force in a relationship. Most abusive men initially deny that there are any payoffs to being violent. However, all behavior is purposeful, and the reality is that violence often helps them to get their way and to feel better about themselves on a short-term basis. Many men dispute this idea initially, but eventually, they see the purpose behind their choices to use violence. If men are unable to recognize the payoffs, it is more likely that the violence will recur in their relationships in the future.

Knowing and articulating the disadvantages is also helpful because thinking about them can help men make the decision to de-escalate when they are feeling explosive, volatile, and controlling. Thinking about consequences is a good de-escalation strategy for a man's Escalation Prevention Plan.

The following are some of the common advantages and disadvantages that men have frequently discussed in group. This handout can be used as a group leader's guide when brainstorming in group and given to men after the brainstorming session.

Perceived Advantages of Using Violence: Short-Term Payoffs

1. You feel powerful, strong, and in charge of your life and your relationship with her.
2. It covers up your emotional dependence on her and makes you appear independent.
3. It serves as a cover for, and a defense against, your insecurities, uncertainties, and feelings, such as hurt, sadness, disappointment, and fear.
4. It allows you to keep her distant/away from you (i.e., you can avoid intimacy with her).
5. It brings on the honeymoon phase, which allows you to feel "close" to her and/or to be sexual.
6. You seem warm/loving/caring when you are not being abusive.
7. It proves that you are right (i.e., "might makes right").
8. It makes her into an object and inferior to you.
9. It gets her attention and respect.
10. Your intensity/overreaction demonstrates that you really care about her and that the issue is important to you (i.e., "I wouldn't have gotten that angry if I didn't care about her and what she does").

(HO) ©1999 David J. Decker, MA

11. It makes it easier to be violent the next time because you have already crossed the line previously.
12. It allows you to control her (i.e., to get what you want when you want it):
    - It changes her behavior (e.g., shuts her up/gets her to stop nagging/calms her down/stops her abuse toward you).
    - It forces her to do what you want her to do and you are able to get your way (e.g., to have sex).
    - It creates an ongoing atmosphere of fear/intimidation and opens up the possibility that emotional/verbal abuse and threats will be enough to control her in the future (i.e., you may not need to use violence again).
    - It effectively stops discussions you do not wish to have.
    - It allows you to get in the last word in interactions.
    - It forces her to live up to your expectations.
    - It makes her listen to you (i.e., it enhances communication for you).
    - It "motivates" her to make changes that you want to see her make.
13. It gets her to focus on caretaking and trying to change you rather than on developing herself and her capabilities.
14. It gives you temporary relief from life stress (i.e., it can serve as a physical and emotional release).
15. It provides an emotional high/rush.
16. It creates intensity and excitement to dispel the boredom you may feel.
17. It changes the topic of conversation from whatever was being discussed to the violence (i.e., it helps you avoid responsibility for your part in the relationship and other important issues and keeps you from having to compromise about any of these).
18. It allows you to physically and emotionally "connect" with her (i.e., "touching" her violently is better than not "connecting" with her at all).
19. It allows you to stay dominant in the relationship and feel one up on women in general (i.e., it reinforces male dominance over women and the idea that men are better and more capable than women).
20. It proves you are a real man (i.e., it validates your masculinity).
21. It serves as training for "warrior status" (e.g., to be a soldier/to "fight for your country").
22. It allows you to get revenge for ways she has hurt and wronged you.
23. It is a way to protect yourself.

(HO)   ©1999 David J. Decker, MA

24. It serves as a means to get psychological help for yourself (i.e., it can get you into a therapy process that can help you to better understand yourself and others and to change your abusive and controlling attitudes and behaviors).

Disadvantages of Using Violence:
Short-Term and Long-Term Consequences

1. You feel out-of-control and crazy or sick.
2. You feel guilty and shameful that you are violent with someone you love, which can have emotional consequences for you (e.g., depression, anxiety, insecurity, inadequacy, low self-esteem).
3. She may be emotionally and physically hurt (e.g., she may experience depression, anxiety, or panic attacks or suffer from broken bones, bruises, or physical illness, or even die).
4. She may end up hurting or killing you.
5. You may end up killing yourself (e.g., in a car accident, suicide).
6. You go against your values and beliefs (e.g., that a man should never hit a woman).
7. You lose respect for yourself and you lose your identity (i.e., you no longer are the person you believed and wanted yourself to be).
8. The violence establishes unhealthy and dysfunctional patterns of responding to important issues in the relationship.
9. Important relationship issues never get addressed and resolved (i.e., the abuse and violence always become the issue).
10. Your partner loses her identity (i.e., she changes the aspects about her that made her special and unique when you first met and were attracted to her).
11. You may have to leave your home and your children (e.g., Order for Protection, separation, divorce).
12. You may experience financial losses (e.g., medical costs, loss of time from work, attorneys' fees, court fines, therapy costs).
13. You may experience legal consequences (e.g., assault charges, time in jail, Orders for Protection, separation, divorce, losing legal custody of your children).
14. Your relationship can suffer irreversible damage (i.e., you experience a loss of trust, caring, and intimacy with your partner).
15. You may become alienated from your extended family and your friends (e.g., you may lose your social network and become isolated and estranged because others dislike you and stay away).

(HO)

16. You may lose the relationship entirely (e.g., she leaves permanently and gets a divorce).
17. Violence has a devastating emotional effect on the children (e.g., it teaches the children to be violent themselves or to accept violence from others; they may become depressed or anxious; their school performance may suffer).
18. You or your partner may use chemicals, overspending, food, or other compulsive behaviors and activities to medicate your pain and your feelings about the abuse and the relationship problems that arise as a result of it.
19. You experience a false sense of connectedness in the calming phase of the cycle of violence (i.e., the honeymoon may convince you that nothing is really wrong and that everything will work out without any real changes on your part).
20. You lose time with, and free access to, your children (e.g., when separation or divorce occurs and your contact is limited).
21. Stress and tension are always present in the relationship and ruin the potential for fun, spontaneity, good times, and personal growth.

EFFECTS OF VIOLENCE AND ABUSE ON WOMEN

The following effects do not always occur with all women who have had violence perpetrated against them in a relationship. And they certainly can arise from other sources as well. However, all of these effects have the *potential* to occur if violence and abuse are present in a relationship.

1. Fear often focused on the following:
   - Speaking up or asserting herself
   - Being abused, hurt, and/or killed
   - Her partner hurting or killing himself or others she loves
   - Losing her economic security (e.g., losing her home, lifestyle)
   - Being abandoned
   - Leaving the relationship and what her life would then be like
   - What others think of her (e.g., about her staying with someone who abuses her)
   - The children being abused and learning to be abusive themselves
   - Losing her ability to work or losing her job
   - Going crazy
2. Depression/low self-esteem/insecurity/self-doubt/negativity/inadequacy/lack of self-confidence/feelings of worthlessness
3. Anxiety/panic attacks (experiencing an overwhelming sense of apprehension and dread)
4. Shame (regarding the way she is treated by a partner who says he loves her, which can lead to many of the other effects listed here)
5. Frustration/anger/irritability/being edgy/defensiveness/rebelliousness (about being told who to be, what to feel, what to think, and what to do)
6. Appearing hysterical/out of control/irrational (e.g., frequent crying spells, yelling and screaming)
7. Being abusive and disrespectful herself (toward her partner, her children, or others)
8. Dependency and feeling stuck/trapped/powerless/helpless/hopeless
9. Disinterest in intimacy and sex (abuse always creates emotional distance and estrangement in a relationship)
10. Isolation/loneliness/feeling disconnected (withdrawal from friends and family, often encouraged by her partner)
11. Compulsive behaviors (e.g., eating too much and gaining weight, abusing alcohol or drugs to dull the emotional pain, spending money to try to feel better about herself)

(HO)   ©1999 David J. Decker, MA

12. Dishonesty/lying (i.e., to avoid her partner's explosive and violent reactions)
13. Having affairs (i.e., looking elsewhere to find more respectful and meaningful companionship)
14. Passivity/indecisiveness/indifference (having difficulty making decisions or offering opinions that may differ from her partner's beliefs)
15. Having difficulty with being spontaneous/playful and having fun (abuse always stifles spontaneity and joy)
16. Loss of trust and respect for her partner (abuse always destroys trust)
17. Loss of respect for herself (she often asks herself such questions as "Why do I stay in an abusive relationship?" and "What's wrong with me that I put up with this kind of treatment?")
18. Guilt, often caused by the following:
    • Feeling responsible for her partner and his problems, including the abuse and violence
    • Her inability to "change" him through what she does
    • The negative effect the abuse and violence are having on the children
19. Feeling controlled and continually monitored (i.e., unable to be her own person)
20. Disappointment (over the loss of dreams and hopes for the relationship with her partner and for her own life)
21. Being passive-aggressive/sarcastic/manipulative/sneaky (because it is not safe to ask for what she wants directly)
22. A desire to escape, leave the relationship, move as far away as possible, and get away from it all
23. Fatigue/lethargy/lack of energy and enthusiasm
24. Trying to hurt or kill herself or her partner

©1999 David J. Decker, MA

VIOLENCE, ABUSE,
AND THEIR EFFECTS ON CHILDREN

Children are *always* affected by violence and abuse in the home. Even if they do not observe or experience it personally, they still feel the tension and stress in the household, and this influences who they are and how they relate to the world around them.

Myths About Children and Abuse

1. If the children do not see or experience the abuse themselves, they have no feelings about it and are not affected by it.
2. Parents should "protect" their children by not talking honestly and openly about the abuse (e.g., why it happens, how it affects others, what it means).
3. Children are resilient and will recover on their own from the effects of being raised in an abusive home (i.e., they do not need any help from "outsiders").

The Reality

1. Children are left confused, frightened, angry, and in emotional turmoil by abuse in the home.
2. Despite the fact that children are astute observers of goings-on in the family, they are generally poor interpreters of what has happened and have great difficulty making sense of the situation.

Factors Determining the Extent
of the Emotional Damage

1. The frequency, severity, and duration of the abuse
2. Whether abuse is directed toward the child (although even simply observing abuse in the home can have profound and damaging effects)
3. How the child interprets the experience
4. What kinds of survival skills the child has developed
5. How much family or outside emotional support is available to the child (e.g., relatives, teachers, counselors, friends)

What Children Learn from Violence
in the Home

1. Experiencing and expressing anger is the same as being abusive and violent.

(HO) ©1999 David J. Decker, MA

2. It is okay to hurt and hit others to control people and situations and to feel powerful and in charge.
3. Men and boys are moody, uncaring, cruel, controlling, intimidating, and aggressive.
4. Women and girls are weak, powerless, passive, ineffectual, and "good targets."
5. Somehow, they, as children, are responsible for the abuse (i.e., it is their fault that violence is occurring).
6. A child's job is to protect or comfort his or her mother or siblings (which can lead to unhealthy caretaking behaviors as the child grows older).
7. Being indirect and manipulative, rather than being direct and assertive, is a better (and safer) way to get what you want in life.
8. Being passive, submissive, and withdrawn is the best way to "get by" in life.
9. No other families are like theirs, and they should be ashamed of their family and themselves.
10. They need to put a great deal of energy into keeping the family secret from others outside the family because their family is flawed and different.
11. They are powerless and incompetent, which leads to low self-esteem, a lack of self-confidence, a sense of inadequacy, and an unwillingness to take healthy risks because they are unable to affect or stop the abuse that is going on around them.
12. Other people cannot be trusted.
13. The world is a hostile and frightening place.
14. Someone needs to be blamed and punished when they have strong feelings something or when someone makes a mistake around them.

Reactions That May Occur with Children

1. Behavioral reactions:
   - Acting out (e.g., temper tantrums, running away)
   - Withdrawing (e.g., continually watching TV or playing computer games)
   - Overachieving or underachieving
   - Refusing to attend school
   - Unhealthy caretaking of others (e.g., filling adult nurturing roles)
   - Being aggressive or passive
   - Having rigid defenses (e.g., being blaming, argumentative)
   - Sleeping difficulties (e.g., bed-wetting, nightmares)

- Continually seeking attention
- Being unwilling to accept parental limits and discipline

2. Emotional reactions
   - Guilt (e.g., seeing themselves as responsible for the violence)
   - Shame (e.g., believing that abuse does not happen in anyone else's home)
   - Fear (about expressing feelings, about Dad's escalations, about what will happen to their mother, their siblings, and themselves)
   - Anger (about Dad being abusive and Mom "putting up with it")
   - Confusion (feeling love and hate for both parents)
   - Helplessness/powerlessness/depression (about not being able to do anything to stop the abuse)
   - Burdened/overwhelmed (especially when taking on inappropriate roles in the family)
   - Grief and loss (about the loss of a carefree childhood and what they want their family to be)
   - Anxiety/nervousness/hypervigilance (e.g., continually being on edge and jumpy)

3. Physical reactions
   - Often having physical complaints (e.g., headaches, stomachaches)
   - Being restless/jittery/hyperactive
   - Being tired/lethargic (may appear lazy to others)
   - Neglecting personal hygiene (e.g., grooming, bathing, brushing teeth)
   - Often being ill with colds and the flu
   - Lack of reaction to physical pain
   - Regression in developmental tasks (e.g., soiling pants or using baby talk when older)

4. Social reactions
   - Being isolated (e.g., having few friends)
   - Having relationships that start with great intensity and end abruptly
   - Having difficulty trusting and being close to others
   - Having poor communication and conflict resolution skills
   - Being unwilling to share (e.g., toys/games) or compromise
   - Being overinvolved with friends (e.g., staying away from home as much as possible)
   - Being a "bully" or a "doormat"

EXCUSES/JUSTIFICATIONS
FOR BECOMING VIOLENT

Myriad reasons are given to explain why men become violent with their partners and others. Use the list below as a group leader's guide to brainstorm in group excuses that men have used with their partners, children, and others. After the brainstorming, this can be given as a handout to the men in group.

Justifying Physical Abuse and Violence

1. It's the way I was raised (It's the only way I know; My father was abusive; It's because of my family of origin; It's the way I was treated; That's what my father [or mother] did to me; What I do isn't as bad as what my father did).
2. She pissed me off (She pushed my buttons; She knows how to get me going; She made me do it; It's her fault; She had an attitude; She pushed me too hard; She pushed me too far; She tripped my trigger; She made me mad).
3. It's just human nature (That's the way men are; It's biological/genetic; A real man doesn't back down; It's just the way I am).
4. She deserved it (She started it; She grabbed/pushed/hit/slapped me first; She hurt me; She was abusive/threatening/violent to me; I was the victim; She provoked me; She's an abuser; She should be in an abuse group; She was hysterical/out of control/"out of it,"; It takes two to tango/It takes two to fight/It takes two to argue; She's the problem; I only have problems with her; It was self-defense).
5. I was drunk (I was high; I blacked out; I was in a "dry drunk" blackout).
6. I was out of control (I didn't know what I was doing; I was just seeing red; It shows how angry I was; I didn't mean to be violent; It's not my fault; I was in the wrong place at the wrong time).
7. I needed to get control (It works; A man has a right to be in control; A man has a right to discipline his wife; A man has the right to wear the pants in the family; A man is the head of the household; I make the money and pay the bills; I'm in charge; I'm supposed to run the show; The Bible says it's okay; It's my house; I'll do whatever I want; It's a private family matter; I'm the boss; I wanted to bring her down a notch; It's the way things are supposed to be).

8. She wouldn't listen (She wouldn't shut up; She's always nagging; She wasn't hearing/understanding me; She wouldn't leave me alone; She wasn't being fair; She called my bluff; It stopped the argument; It made her listen).
9. I have a right to get even/get revenge/get her back for what she said/did."
10. This will teach her a lesson (This will make her a better person; She'll learn from this; This will help her; This will protect her from herself).
11. It was instinct (It was a reaction/reflex).
12. Women are inferior (Women should be subservient/submissive; She's my wife; She belongs to me; She's my property; She's mine; She didn't do what she was supposed to do; She's supposed to follow my lead).
13. I had a bad day (I was stressed-out; I had an attitude; I was "wigged-out" on my medications; I was depressed; I didn't get enough sleep; Little things just built up; I couldn't take it anymore; I was overwhelmed).
14. I had no choice (She crossed the line; She pushed me into a corner; She backed me against the wall; The issue was too important; I had to act that way).
15. I was right (It was OK to be violent; It was the right thing to do; I didn't do anything wrong; She was wrong).
16. It wasn't that big a deal (It wasn't that bad; At least I didn't hurt her; She bruises easily).
17. It won't hurt our relationship (She'll get over it; She'll still love me; We'll get through this).
18. I was jealous (She was staring at another guy; She's a flirt; She's always looking at other men; She's a whore; She went out on me; She's a slut; She had an affair).
19. It wouldn't have happened if I didn't love her so much (What I did proves how much I care; I wouldn't have hit her if she wasn't important to me).
20. She was off her pedestal (A gentleman should never hit a lady, but because of the way she acted, she's not a "lady" anymore).
21. I know how to handle these sorts of situations (Violence is okay in certain situations; I can get away with it; I'm big/tough enough to throw my weight around; I know karate).

Justifying Child Abuse

1. Spare the rod, spoil the child.
2. A father has the right to discipline his children however he sees fit.

(HO)

3. A man has the right to control his children.
4. A father has the responsibility to teach his children what's right.
5. The kids should never talk back to me.
6. There's nothing wrong with a little spanking.
7. I got hit and turned out fine.
8. Kids need to know who's the boss.
9. It's my job as their parent.

Justifying Sexual Abuse of a Partner

1. She wanted it.
2. She said no but she meant "yes."
3. I deserve to get "it" whenever I want "it."
4. Boys will be boys.
5. It's my right as her husband/boyfriend.
6. I need it.
7. She's cold/frigid.
8. She owes it to me.

THE PLACE OF GENERALIZED VIOLENCE
IN OUR LIVES

The following can be used as the basis for a discussion and handout about how to respond to potentially violent situations that the men may encounter in their lives.

We live in a violent society. There are numerous times in our lives when violence may become an option. Often, we have been given strong messages from our families and the culture about what a "real man" would do when confronted with a situation in which violence might be an option. Think about the following questions and how you might respond.

Hitting or Destroying Property and Objects
or Using Physical Force with Family Pets

1. Does hitting a wall actually discharge your frustration and anger and really take care of it?
2. Could throwing something start or continue your escalation process to using violence with people?
3. How does exploding with property affect your self-esteem and how do you feel about yourself afterward?
   - Do you end up feeling embarrassed, "stupid," or "silly?"
   - Could you end up hurting yourself physically in some way?
4. How do family members react when you hit or throw something?
   - Could they perceive it as a threat and could they end up feeling intimidated by what you have done?
5. How often in the past has violence toward property or pets been part of an escalation that led to actual violence directed toward other people?

Defending Property

1. What would you do if you and your son (or daughter) saw someone shoplifting in a store?
2. What would you do if you saw someone snatch a woman's purse and the culprit was running down the street in your direction? What if he was running in another direction?
3. What would you do if you saw a man leaving your home after burglarizing it (none of your family was home at the time). What if you knew that your family was at home?
4. What if you saw two men leaving your home?

(HO)   ©1999 David J. Decker, MA

5. What would you do if someone walked up to you and demanded your wallet? What if there were three men? How would you know if he/they had weapons? What if he/they actually had weapons?

Verbal Abuse

1. What would you do if someone was verbally harassing you at a party or in a bar? What if there were three or four people harassing you?
2. What would you do if someone on the highway was angry with you and drove next to you gesturing and screaming or motioning for you to pull over to the side of the highway so the two of you could "talk"?
3. What would you do if a neighbor became angry and verbally abusive with you because you had parked your car in front of his house?
4. What would you do it someone was verbally abusing you and your partner (or your children) on the street? What if there were three or four people doing this? How would you determine if they had weapons? What if they actually did have weapons?

Physical Violence

1. What would you do if you saw a fifteen-year-old beating up a ten-year-old at a park? What if there were four adolescents beating up another adolescent? If you intervened physically, how much force would you use? How would you determine whether the older youths had weapons?
2. What would you do if you saw an eight-year-old being slapped across the top of the head and pushed around by a man? What if the man said he was the boy's father?
3. What would you do if you saw a man hitting a woman on the street? What if he told you she was his wife?
4. What would you do if someone was physically intimidating you on the street (e.g., grabbing and pushing you)? What would you do if your partner or children were there? What if there were three or four people doing this to you? What if they had weapons?

Commentary

Each Man Must Make His Own Decision About the Kind and Level of Violence He Would Use in These Scenarios

1. There is no right answer for all situations.
2. Reflect on how you have responded to situations such as these in the past.

©1999 David J. Decker, MA

3. Were you happy with/did you feel good about how you responded in the past?
4. How could you react differently and more effectively in the future if you are not satisfied with your past reactions?
5. It is absolutely critical to think about and plan for how you might react, how you could behave, and how much violence you might choose to use (if any) should you be confronted with situations such as those mentioned previously.
6. Keep in mind that *you are still making a choice* to react in a certain way no matter what you end up doing.
7. Think about these and other situations and devise a plan ahead of time about how you want to handle scenarios in which violence might be one option.

Brainstorm with the Group:
What Are the Alternatives to Being Violent?

1. Try to reframe the situation in a more positive light.
   • What does the other person's violence say about him or her?
   • Do you want to simply react to that person and become their "puppet"?
2. Get away from the situation in any way that you can (e.g., running away).
3. Refuse to become violent under any circumstances (a pacifist)
4. Get to a phone and call the police; tell them what is occurring, and give a good description of the perpetrators.

If You Choose to Be Violent, Ask Yourself
the Following Questions:

1. Would you use the least amount of physical force necessary (e.g., restraining someone) or would you "go bonkers" and "beat the hell out of them"?
2. What would you do if they escalated their use of force in response to what you were doing (e.g., if they fought back or tried to get away)?
3. How do you think the legal system would deal with an adult male who beat up an adolescent or brutally beat and/or permanently injured someone who was stealing property?
4. What is the likelihood that you or someone you care about might be hurt, injured, or killed?

(HO) ©1999 David J. Decker, MA

Unit 2: Stress
and Stress Management

WHAT IS STRESS?

Stress in Human Beings Arises from Your "Animal Instincts," the "Fight or Flight" Response of Your Prehistoric Ancestors That Helped Humankind Survive As a Species

1. Originally, the physical stress arousal served as a mobilization of human beings' bodily defenses in response to an actual threat to well-being (e.g., hearing a dangerous animal nearby).
2. Adrenaline and other hormones are released through a biochemical reaction in our bodies. This process:
   a. increases your heart rate and blood pressure so that blood can carry nutrients and oxygen to your tissues and cells with greater speed and waste products can be more efficiently eliminated.
   b. speeds up your breathing to provide more oxygen to the blood and to remove carbon dioxide from the blood.
   c. elevates your blood sugar level and releases more fat into the blood-stream to create additional energy.
   d. dilates your pupils to enable you to see better.
   e. tenses your large muscles for the movement necessary to flee or attack.
   f. slows your digestion so blood is available for your muscles and your brain.
   g. secretes chemicals to make it easier for your blood to clot in case of an injury.
   h. increases perspiration to keep your body cool.
3. All of these changes prepare your body for an emergency, whether it is real or imagined.
4. This physiological arousal is directly related to the physical cues you have been asked to identify in your Escalation Prevention Plan.

(HO)   ©1999 David J. Decker, MA

5. Unfortunately, this physical process still occurs in human beings today even when it does not serve a useful function (e.g., when your boss tells you to do something you don't really want to do, you can't run away from your job or hit him or her).
6. If the adrenaline and other hormones being released are not dealt with effectively and you do not learn ways to dissipate this physical arousal, you force your body to stay "on alert" and "on guard" for long periods of time (this is directly related to maintaining a higher level of escalation and agitation in your day-to-day life).
7. This constant arousal (state of escalation) can trigger reactions that are painful and uncomfortable for you and others (like explosive and abusive anger) and that are even harmful to your physical health (e.g., helping to create symptoms like headaches and ulcers).

Defining Stress

1. Stress was originally an engineering term used to describe how material weakens and breaks when enough pressure is applied.
2. Stress can be defined as the rate of "wear and tear" (physically and emotionally) experienced in the living of your life. Anytime change occurs around you, the potential for stress to arise is present.

Possible Sources of Stress

1. The environment
   a. Demands to adjust and adapt to external situations and the other people in your life
      • Job pressures
      • Time pressures
      • Weather and noise
      • Criticism directed at you
      • Balancing family and work expectations
      • Experiencing conflict with family members and others
2. Your body
   a. Not taking care of yourself physically
      • not getting enough sleep
      • working, eating, or drinking too much
   b. Experiencing physical symptoms as a result of illness or injury

3. Your internal state of mind and your thought process
   a. Continual worrying and brooding
   b. Viewing yourself or others in negative or demeaning terms
   c. Having unrealistic or perfectionistic expectations for yourself and others
   d. Constantly rehashing pain, hurt, and resentment from the past

Relate these sources of stress to the cues you have identified in your Escalation Prevention Plan.

Stress Triggers

1. Major life events or changes which can be:
   a. Positive
      - Getting a promotion
      - Having a baby
      - Getting married
      - Moving to a new home
      - An outstanding personal achievement
   b. Or negative
      - A death in the family
      - Getting a divorce
      - Being fired from a job
      - Going to jail
      - Losing your home to foreclosure
2. Trivial day-to-day situations
   a. Getting a bill in the mail
   b. An argument with your partner
   c. A driver cutting you off on the freeway
   d. Having your boss criticize your work
   e. Losing your keys
   f. Burning your dinner

The Reality Is That We Cannot Escape Stress in Our Lives nor Would We Really Want to Do So

1. Stress is part of the human condition. Your stress response has helped the human race survive.
2. Everyone has an *optimum level* of stress that can help motivate you to be productive and to accomplish what you want or need to do.
   a. Hans Selye, the father of modern thought about stress, coined the term, "eustress," to describe this positive stress (Selye, 1978)

(HO)   ©1999 David J. Decker, MA

3. Absolutely no stress in your life would mean experiencing your life in a vegetative state with no reaction or response to anything that happens around you.
4. In the end, stress is not an "evil" to be avoided but rather a part of life that you need to learn to master and handle more effectively.
5. However, too much stress (or handling your life stress ineffectively) has the potential to produce emotional and physical symptoms that can be crippling and, at times, even life-threatening.
    a. Selye referred to this negative type of stress as "distress" (Selye, 1978).

The Damaging Consequences That Stress Can Create Fall into Several Categories

1. Physical symptoms
   * fatigue
   * headaches
   * dizziness
2. Social symptoms
   * anxiety
   * irritability
   * depression
3. Mental symptoms
   * confusion
   * difficulty concentrating
   * forgetfulness
4. Relationship symptoms
   * withdrawing from and avoiding others
   * impatience
   * envy/jealousy
5. Spiritual symptoms
   * loss of purpose/direction
   * pessimism
   * feeling completely alone

Look at and review "Symptoms That Stress Can Trigger" (p. 270) for a more complete list.

(HO)   ©1999 David J. Decker, MA

In Reality, However, Stress Is Not Caused and Made Worse Simply by External Situations and Other People

1. The original research on stress focused only on the impact of major life events:
   a. In the 1960s, researchers hypothesized that the more significant life events you experienced, the higher the probability that you would become physically or emotionally ill. Numbers of points were assigned for specific situations such as the death of a spouse, a divorce, or a jail term. It was believed that if you totaled up 300 points within a twelve- to eighteen-month time frame, you would have a nearly 80 percent chance of becoming ill within the following two years (Rahe and Holmes, 1966; Holmes and Rahe, 1967)

2. More recent research, however, broadens the picture considerably to look not only at specific life stressors but also at how you perceive those stressors and the role you allow them to play in your life.
   a. In one study, researchers looked at a large group of middle- and upper-level managers for five years, finding that life stress can be neutralized by a psychological quality that they called "hardiness," which consists of:
      - a notion of *challenge,* the belief that change is normal, exciting, and an incentive to grow rather than a threat or an unending series of "hassles"
      - a feeling of *commitment* toward your activities, which includes a sense of purpose and belonging and a belief that what you are doing is good and meaningful
      - a sense of *control* over your actions and events and a belief that you can handle problems that arise

      The researchers found that, after two years, the executives who seemed to have a high level of hardiness were approximately half as likely to develop illnesses as were the others, regardless of how many major life events they experienced. The "hardy" managers seemed to welcome stress and thrived on it while the less "hardy" managers felt powerless and victimized by it and became physically ill as a result (Kobasa, Maddi, and Kahn, 1982).

(HO) ©1999 David J. Decker, MA

***Thus, How You Perceive Life Stressors and How You Assess
Your Ability to Handle Them Are the Critical Factors
in Determining Whether You Will Experience
Harmful Consequences from Life Stress***

1. It is not just experiencing major life events that determines your arousal level and potential damage to your physical and emotional self, but also, and more importantly, how you view what happens around you.
2. The intense and destructive reactions to stress that occur within you are generated by your own individual beliefs, perceptions, expectations, and thoughts, and your own unique reactions to the situations and people in your life.
3. No situation or person, in and of itself, has the power to create crippling stress in you. Rather, it is how you label and define the experience that creates the damaging impact of stress.
4. The reality is that you have considerable control over your reactions to stressful situations and people in your life through the way that you look at yourself and the world around you and how you think about stress.
   a. You have the power to make events more or less stressful depending on how you view them and what you say to yourself about them.
   b. Your self-talk (the words, phrases, and sentences you are continually thinking) is the critical mediating variable that determines whether you experience your stress in a damaging way or learn to handle it effectively
      • (e.g., is your self-talk *negative?)* "Damn it, now there's something else I have to deal with!" and "I'll never be able to get through this mess."
      • (or *positive?)* "I don't like that what's happening here, but I'll find a way to take care of it" and "I know this will work out okay for me."
5. If you consistently label your physical stress arousal as anger, and allow negative thoughts to build and fuel an attitude of cynicism, hostility, contempt, and disgust (for yourself or others), you will tend to keep yourself in an agitated and escalated state for more of the time. Doing this can lead directly to controlling and abusive behavior and significant physical and emotional consequences for you and others.

(HO)   ©1999 David J. Decker, MA

CHANGES AND STRESS

Stress is all around you; it cannot be avoided. It can arise from positive or negative experiences, from major or trivial events, from things happening around you, or from your own internal attitudes and expectations. Essentially, stress can be defined as the rate of "wear and tear" you experience as a result of how you perceive and react to changes in your life. You can never eliminate stress, but you can play an important role in how you are affected by the stressors you experience. The first step is to learn to notice the potential stressors you face and to become more aware of how you view and handle them. The way to manage your stress and feel better in your daily life is to slow down, recognize the changes that have the potential to trigger stress, and learn to intervene effectively in the process as early as possible. This is part of what you are asked to do in your Escalation Prevention Plan. Many of your plan's cues or triggers could be defined as stressors.

The following list identifies some changes in your life that can trigger stress or that can indicate to you that stress may be present in your life. Check off the changes you have experienced in the past year and think about how they have affected, or may currently be affecting, your physical and emotional health.

Changes on the Job

- _____ Dissatisfaction with work
- _____ Being demoted, laid off, or fired
- _____ Changing shifts or work hours
- _____ Looking for work
- _____ Going on or returning from vacation
- _____ Starting or losing your own business
- _____ Accomplishing a significant personal goal
- _____ Being promoted or getting a new job
- _____ Conflict with co-workers or supervisors
- _____ Making a career change (e.g., starting a new type of work)
- _____ Company readjustment (e.g., layoffs, a merger, or reorganization)
- _____ Retirement

Changes in Sleeping Habits

- _____ Sleeping more or fewer hours at night
- _____ Waking up more frequently at night
- _____ Taking more naps during the day

(HO) ©1999 David J. Decker, MA

Changes in Eating Habits

____ Eating more or less food than usual
____ Eating with different people or in different surroundings
____ Eating at different times during the day
____ Eating alone more frequently

Changes in Health

____ Illness
____ Pregnancy
____ Being in the hospital
____ Injury
____ Going to the doctor
____ Having surgery

Changes in Personal Habits

____ Dressing differently
____ Changing the way you act around others (e.g., your manners)
____ Changes in grooming or hygiene

Changes in Social and Recreational Activities

____ Altering the amount of time you spend doing certain activities
____ Doing activities with different people
____ Starting new activities or no longer doing ones you have done in the past

Changes in Financial Affairs

____ Having more or less money than you usually do
____ Being "hounded" by creditors
____ Taking on a new mortgage or loan
____ Foreclosure on a mortgage
____ Declaring bankruptcy

Changes in the Weather

____ More or less daylight or sunlight
____ More or fewer rainy, snowy, or cloudy days than usual
____ Warmer or colder temperatures

(HO)　　　　　　　　　　©1999 David J. Decker, MA

Changes in Residence or Living Conditions

____ Building or buying a new home
____ Remodeling your home or apartment
____ Getting a new roommate or losing an old one
____ Adding children to your living space or having children move away
____ Going from renting to owning or vice versa
____ Moving
____ Moving in with a partner or having a partner move out
____ Deterioration of your home or your neighborhood (e.g., more crime)

Changes in Schooling or Education

____ Making a decision to return to school
____ Beginning or ending school enrollment
____ Doing better or worse than expected in school
____ Changing to a different school or a different type of education

Changes Related to Legal Issues

____ Committing and/or being apprehended for minor violations (e.g., shoplifting, speeding, DWI)
____ Committing and/or being apprehended for major violations (e.g., burglary, robbery, assault)
____ Being part of a legal proceeding (e.g., OFP or divorce hearing, trial deposition for a criminal offense
____ Detention in, or release from, jail, prison, or some other institution
____ Being court-ordered to and attending chemical dependency treatment or other therapy
____ Being sued or filing a lawsuit
____ Being the victim of a crime

Changes in Your Mood or Emotional State

____ Feeling more or less irritable, bitter, angry, resentful, frustrated, rageful, fearful, anxious, or depressed than usual
____ Changes in your involvement in therapy

Changes in Sex Life

—— Changing sexual partners
—— More or fewer sexual partners than usual
—— Going from one sexual partner to many or vice versa
—— More or less sex than usual
—— Onset or cessation of sexual difficulties or dysfunction

Changes in Relationships with Friends

—— Making new friends
—— Feuding with friends
—— Friends moving away
—— Drifting away from or cutting off old friends
—— Friends starting a relationship with a new partner
—— Your moving away from friends
—— Having a friend die

Changes in Family Relationships

—— More or fewer family visits or gatherings
—— Conflict and/or feuds with family members, in-laws, or other relatives.
—— Family members in poor physical (e.g., illness) or mental (e.g., depression) health
—— Family members leaving home (e.g., partner separating or divorcing, children moving out
—— Children acting out at home or elsewhere
—— Getting or giving up pets or having them die
—— Births
—— Adoptions
—— Deaths

Changes in the Partner/Spouse Relationship

—— More or fewer arguments or disagreements
—— Beginning to go out with someone
—— Trying to get pregnant or becoming pregnant
—— Partner or self developing new interests, activities, and/or friends
—— Partner or self having an affair
—— Divorce

(HO)   ©1999 David J. Decker, MA

____ Partner or self losing or leaving job or retiring from workplace
____ Partner becoming ill or injured or dying
____ Reconciliation with partner
____ Moving in together or moving apart into separate residences
____ Getting married
____ The birth of children
____ More or fewer activities together
____ Partner or self beginning or ceasing work or schooling outside the home
____ Separation
____ Partner or self having minor or major physical or emotional illness
____ Partner or self having legal problems
____ Changes in relationship roles (e.g., taking on more child-rearing or housekeeping responsibilities

©1999 David J. Decker, MA

SYMPTOMS THAT STRESS CAN TRIGGER

Stress has the potential to create a variety of symptoms in us. Look over the following symptoms and identify which ones you have experienced in the past year. Also, think about whether a connection exists between the symptoms you have experienced and how much stress (and how you handled it) was in your life during that time.

Physical

——— Frequent illness (colds, flu, often feeling under the weather)
——— Headaches (tension and migraine)
——— Fatigue (feeling tired most of the time, having little energy to do things)
——— Digestive problems (indigestion, bloating, stomachaches, nausea)
——— Ulcers
——— Skin problems (rashes, acne)
——— Chest pain
——— High blood pressure
——— Teeth grinding (including sore jaw)
——— Appetite changes
——— Blurred vision
——— Dizziness
——— Pain in lower back, neck, and shoulders
——— Intestinal problems (constipation, diarrhea, colitis)
——— Allergies (developing new ones, having old ones intensify)
——— Heart problems (heart pounding or racing, heart attack)
——— Stroke
——— Frequent accidents (being accident prone)
——— Sinus problems (congestion)
——— Sleeping problems (insomnia, sleeping too much, interrupted sleep, waking up frequently, needing frequent naps)
——— Eating problems (eating too little or too much, losing or gaining weight, eating compulsively, eating at unusual times)
——— Muscular problems (trembling, shakiness, twitches, tics, sore aching muscles, muscle tension
——— Circulatory problems (hands and feet colder than usual)

(HO)   ©1999 David J. Decker, MA

—— Restlessness (finger drumming, foot tapping, pacing)
—— Decreased sexual drive
—— Procrastination
—— Increased smoking
—— Alcohol and drug abuse (using more chemicals than usual, using chemicals to escape from worries and to feel okay about yourself)

Emotional

—— Anxiety (feeling worried, fearful, and apprehensive)
—— Depression (feeling discouraged, negative, pessimistic, and miserable)
—— Excessive anger/irritability
—— Frustration
—— Lack of joy
—— Moodiness
—— Sadness/crying spells
—— Unhappiness
—— Loneliness

Mental

—— Confusion
—— Lethargy
—— Negative attitude/thoughts
—— Difficulty concentrating
—— Poor memory/forgetfulness
—— Dulled senses
—— Boredom
—— Worrying/brooding/obsessing
—— Difficulty thinking clearly

Social

—— Avoiding and withdrawing from people
—— Mistrust
—— Increased conflict
—— Disrespectful and abusive behavior toward others
—— Blaming
—— Intolerance
—— Impatience

(HO)   ©1999 David J. Decker, MA

—— Decreased interest in affection/touching
—— Resentment
—— Envy/jealousy
—— Loss of intimacy/emotional distance from others
—— Increase in use of profanity, put-downs, name-calling, or sarcasm
—— Feeling abandoned/rejected

Spiritual

—— Apathy
—— Sense of powerlessness and helplessness
—— Loss of purpose/direction
—— Loss of faith
—— Cynicism
—— Emptiness
—— Doubt
—— Loss of meaning
—— Pessimism
—— Feeling completely alone/isolated
—— Feelings of hopelessness

STRESS MANAGEMENT TECHNIQUES

Effective stress management begins with taking one small step at a time toward changing some of the unhealthy habits and patterns that you have developed over a lifetime. The following are some ideas that can be helpful in learning to handle the stress in your life more effectively. Try some of them out, and include the ones that work for you on your Escalation Prevention Plan.

Get Enough Sleep and Rest

1. Go to bed early enough to get seven to eight hours of sleep so you awaken refreshed.
2. Take daytime naps occasionally if you need to do so.

Pay Attention to Your Nutritional Needs

1. Be aware of what, how much, how, and when you are eating.
2. Decrease rich, salty, oily, and fatty foods.
3. Avoid tobacco, caffeine, excessive alcohol consumption, and drugs.

Engage in Regular Noncompetitive Aerobic Exercise

1. Participate in exercise such as walking, jogging, swimming, bicycling, exercycling, calisthenics, or cross-country skiing at least three times a week to release natural relaxing agents (i.e., endorphins) that can help you handle the stress buildup in your life.
2. Avoid creating more stress through excessive competition and the need to be the best when you are involved with sports activities.

Balance Work and Play in Your Life

1. Participate in interesting recreational activities.
2. Pursue creative outlets and develop attention-absorbing hobbies.
3. Take vacations to truly get away from all the work in your life.
4. Schedule fun and time with your friends and family into your life.

(HO)   ©1999 David J. Decker, MA

Learn to Slow Down and Truly Relax

1. Give yourself permission to "escape" at times.
2. Develop and use a variety of creative techniques to "get away from it all" in a healthy way.
   - Progressive muscle relaxation
   - Whirlpool or sauna
   - Deep breathing
   - Listen to calming and peaceful music
   - Take a hot bath/shower
   - Massage
   - Meditation
   - Visualization (e.g., "quiet space"
3. Avoid using alcohol, drugs, or television as a primary means of relaxation.

Organize Your Life

1. Stay aware of your priorities.
2. Set realistic goals and then go for them!
3. Keep your own calendar and do not overschedule yourself.
4. "Divide and conquer" when you have a lot to do (i.e., break up large and overwhelming tasks and take on one thing at a time).
5. Watch out for procrastination:
   - Set reasonable time frames for getting things accomplished and then do them!
6. Get up earlier to make your mornings less hurried.
7. Take advantage of off hours for shopping and errands.

Develop Your Social Skills and a Support System

1. Learn about and work to actively use
   - open and honest communication (including being a good listener),
   - assertiveness skills (e.g., start to "stand up for yourself," say "no" clearly and set limits at times, and ask directly for help and emotional support), and
   - effective conflict resolution strategies when disagreements do arise.
2. Be a problem solver (i.e., clearly identify the problem, look at your options, choose a plan to address it, take action, and evaluate how well the problem has been resolved).
3. Develop and maintain close emotional ties with other people and share your troubles with those you can trust to be helpful and supportive.
   - Make an effort to have friends and confidants.

(HO) ©1999 David J. Decker, MA

4. Look for and find a sense of community (e.g., through family and friends, recreation and hobbies, your place of worship, neighborhood gatherings, community and professional organizations, or self-help groups).
5. Reach out to other people and take the time to connect, even with strangers (e.g., interact with store clerks, your postal carrier, and others).

Use Your Cognitive Abilities to Anticipate and Manage Potential Stressors

1. Become aware of the stressors in your life (your cues and triggers on the EPP).
2. Start to anticipate and prepare more effectively for upcoming events and situations (i.e., create a positive rather than a negative rehearsal).
3. Use more positive, affirming, and validating self-talk to intervene in your negative, critical, blaming, and self-defeating thoughts.
4. In your mind, start to reframe difficult times into positive challenges.

Be Gentle with Yourself

1. Like yourself for who you are (i.e., know and accept your strengths, shortcomings, thoughts, feelings, wants, needs, and values).
2. Take healthy responsibility for yourself and your behavior.
3. Focus on the positive aspects of your life (do not blame others!) and allow yourself to experience a sense of gratitude.
4. Give yourself ongoing credit for what you are accomplishing in your daily living.
5. Be aware of your unrealistic and perfectionistic expectations of yourself and let go of them at times.
6. Learn to ask of and receive from those around you (allow people to be there for you emotionally and in more practical ways).
7. Forgive yourself for things you have done and learn from these mistakes.
8. Develop and use an affirming sense of humor about yourself and others.
9. Make warm and nurturing physical contact with others a priority.
10. Develop a healthy sense of spirituality and use it each day.

(HO) ©1999 David J. Decker, MA

Be Gentle with Others

1. Accept and like others for who they are.
2. Accept what others are willing to give you (versus expecting them to give you exactly what you want).
3. Be open to others' perspectives and ideas and understand that they may be different from yours and that this is okay.
4. Identify and work actively at intervening in your controlling attitudes and behaviors.
5. Tell others directly how much you value them as a part of your life.
6. Avoid long-standing grudges and feuds by learning to forgive others for things that have happened in the past.
7. Make amends and apologize for things you regret saying or doing.

Keep Things in Perspective

1. Learn to acknowledge and accept what you cannot change about other people and the situations that are happening around you. Think about and use "The Serenity Prayer" from Alcoholics Anonymous:

   God grant me the serenity to accept the things I cannot change, the courage to change the things I can, and the wisdom to know the difference.

2. Learn to back off and let go when appropriate.
3. Work to assess the real importance of situations occurring around you. Ask yourself: Will I even remember the situation I am so stressed about right now in a year?
4. Avoid worrying/stewing about situations and issues. Instead, *do something* that will help you take care of yourself and the issue.
5. Actively seek to discover what your struggles in life can teach you. Start to view your difficulties and emotional pain as lessons to help you learn more about yourself.

(HO)   ©1999 David J. Decker, MA

PROGRESSIVE MUSCLE RELAXATION

Progressive muscle relaxation is a good method of learning to relax and is especially helpful for people who are generally "on the go" because it offers an active means of calming yourself down. The basic idea behind progressive muscle relaxation is that you tense and then release specific muscle groups, giving you the opportunity to really notice the difference between when you are stressed and when you are relaxed.

To begin, sit or lie in a comfortable position, preferably with your eyes closed. Tune into your breathing as you tense and release the muscles, taking full, deep breaths and noticing the sense of calm that accompanies breathing deeply. Imagine the stresses and tensions of your day dissolving and flowing from your body into the floor or chair. Allow yourself to let go of all your tightness and enjoy the heaviness (or lightness) of relaxation spreading throughout your body. Notice the profound difference between the tension and relaxation at each point in the process.

You may notice distracting or bothersome thoughts trying to intrude on your attempts to calm yourself. Do not fight these thoughts (e.g., saying to yourself, "Damn it, why can't I stop thinking about that?"). Rather, refocus on a calming word or phrase (a mantra), such as peace, relax, or calm, that you can repeat to yourself or try counting from one to ten and then ten to one over and over again. Another technique to calm your mind is to imagine a quiet, safe, and peaceful place (e.g., a favorite getaway, such as a lake or the seashore) and then picture yourself there during your relaxing process. It is impossible to hold two thoughts in your mind simultaneously, so gradually you will learn to tune out worries and concerns from the day during this relaxation exercise.

Go through the following list, tensing and releasing each of the muscle groups mentioned.

CAUTION: Do not tighten any of the muscles to the point at which they cramp or cause you discomfort. Be gentle with yourself and pamper yourself in the process of becoming more relaxed.

(HO) ©1999 David J. Decker, MA

PART OF BODY	TENSING METHOD
HANDS	Clench your fists as tightly as you can. Relax.
FOREARMS	Extend your arms out against an invisible wall and push against it as hard as you can. Relax.
UPPER ARM	Bend your elbows, pushing them down against the floor, and tense your biceps. Relax.
FOREHEAD	Wrinkle your forehead and lift your eyebrows as high as you possibly can (try to make your eyebrows touch your hairline). Relax.
CENTRAL FACE	Frown, squint your eyes, wrinkle your nose, and pure your lips. Relax.
LOWER FACE AND JAW	Clench your jaw and bite your teeth together hard. Draw the corners of your mouth back and grimace. Relax. Alternate method: Open your mouth as wide as possible, as if you are silently screaming. Relax.
NECK AND THROAT	Press your head as far back as it can comfortably go. Relax. Alternate method: Press your chin against your chest. Relax.
UPPER BACK	Push your shoulder blades together, as if your were trying to get them to touch behind your back. Relax.
SHOULDERS	Shrug your shoulders up to your ears. Relax.
LOWER BACK	Arch your back off the floor. Relax.

PART OF BODY	TENSING METHOD
ABDOMEN	Tighten and pull your stomach muscles in. Relax. Alternate method: Breathe deeply, allowing the abdomen to inflate. Relax.
BUTTOCKS AND HIPS	Pull in your buttocks, tightening them as much as you can. Relax.
UPPER LEGS	Tense your muscles in your upper legs by flexing your thigh muscles and pressing your heels down onto the floor. Relax.
LOWER LEGS AND CALVES	Pull your toes upward toward your head. Relax.
FEET	Curl your toes downward as tightly as possible. Relax.

STRESS AND THE HOLIDAYS

Holidays tend to bring out the best and the worst in us and others. The holiday season may trigger thoughts of happiness, fun-filled gatherings, and close and supportive times with family and friends. On the other hand, however, we could also end up focusing on crowded shopping malls, over-spending and regretting it in January, or the tension and emotional distress that we feel with those close to us.

If the holiday season is going to be a positive, or at least survivable, experience, we need to look closely at the additional stressors faced during this time of year and to come up with some ideas about how we can deal with them effectively. The following are some holiday stressors and suggestions about how to respond differently. Think about and put together a more positive plan for yourself this holiday season.

Holiday Stressors

1. Unrealistic expectations
    a. Of yourself (e.g., having too much to do and too little time to do it, wanting to provide others with the perfect holiday)
    b. Of your partner (e.g., that she will be loving, attentive, and nur-turing and that she will enjoy you, your children, your relatives, and herself during the season)
    c. Of other family members (e.g., that your kids will love you and their presents; that parents, siblings, and in-laws will get along)
    d. That the holidays will fit the stereotype promoted by the media and the "holiday hype" of a calm, peaceful, and loving time
    e. That others will treat you in a particular way (rude/disrespectful or loving/nurturing)
    f. That this year will be worse (or better) than years past
2. Shopping/spending money
    a. Trying to decide who to buy for and how much to spend
    b. Wanting to find the perfect gift for family members and friends
    c. Spending too much and becoming depressed and resentful about it
    d. Worrying about how much your partner is spending and its effect on the family budget

3. Your own and others energy expenditure
   a. Constant "busyness" (including looking everywhere for the perfect gifts, sending out greeting cards and letters [and how honest you want to be in them], and attending family and other functions)
4. Conflict with your partner about who you will spend time with and when this will happen
   a. Rushing around to all the relatives' homes and feeling harried and hassled as a result
   b. Spending time with people you do not like or who do not like you
5. Attending work-related and friends' parties and gatherings
   a. Deciding which parties to attend and how long you will stay
   b. Eating (including lots of fats and sugars), drinking, and smoking excessively
6. Grief and loss issues
   a. Holidays may trigger thoughts about deaths (or other significant losses or events) that have occurred around past holidays
   b. Being separated or divorced and missing your children, your partner, or the family life you used to have or enjoy
   c. Thinking back and remembering the good (or bad) times you had around the holidays as a child
   d. Reflecting back on all the mistakes you made and problems that occurred in the past year and feeling pressure to "change everything" and "be completely different" in the new year
      • Be especially careful not to set unrealistic New Year's resolutions for yourself.
7. The weather
   a. How much snow falls and how cold it is, making it more difficult to get around and do what you want to do
   b. The lack of daylight, making this a dark, dreary, and depressing time of year for some

Ideas for Coping with Holiday Stress

1. Recognize and plan for potential holiday stress (with a positive versus a negative rehearsal)
   a. Think clearly, ahead of time, about how to relax and de-escalate, if necessary, at family gatherings (e.g., using time-outs, going out for a walk, calling friends).

(HO) ©1999 David J. Decker, MA

b. Have realistic expectations of others and the holiday season to avoid setting yourself up for letdowns and disappointments

c. "Share the load," delegate, and ask for assistance when planning and putting on family and other get-togethers and accomplishing other holiday tasks:
   • Have "potluck"-style dinners where everyone brings something to share.
   • Ask for help in writing and addressing cards and baking cookies.

d. Be prepared for large crowds, heavy traffic, long lines, and harried clerks and plan to take more time than you might normally need:
   • Bring along a good book or cards to write when you think you may have to wait

e. Allow yourself to slow down and take time for yourself to do things to help you cope and feel good about yourself:
   • Follow your exercise program, spend special or quiet "connecting time" with your partner or close friends, just sit, rest, and "take a break" occasionally.

f. Allow yourself to experience and express the emotions that arise about present and past holidays:
   • Especially reactions to the anniversaries of losses.

g. Do not expect to be happy and upbeat all the time.

h. Take time to think about yourself to feel whatever you happen to be feeling and to share your emotional responses with your partner or friends whenever possible.

i. Allow yourself to grieve losses you are experiencing currently (e.g., being separated from your wife and children or having your children away on their own for the first time).

j. Get enough sleep and use moderation in eating and drinking:
   • Set limits for yourself about what you will eat and drink at parties.
   • Provide and drink nonalcoholic beverages at get-togethers.
   • Plan parties that include activities not related to eating or drinking (e.g., caroling, sledding).

k. Be prepared for snowy and cold weather and plan shopping trips and travel schedules accordingly (i.e., take more time when necessary).

2. Focus on maintaining a positive attitude

a. Notice and change thoughts and self-talk that is hostile, blaming, judgmental, and self-defeating.

(HO)   ©1999 David J. Decker, MA

b. Look for ways to make your holiday season a positive experience even if your circumstances are not what you would like.

c. Recognize what you are getting done and give yourself credit as you are doing it.

d. Try to see the humor in what happens around you and work at laughing at things rather than blowing up or getting anxious or depressed.

e. Think about the real meaning of the holidays for you and about your spirituality:

   • Make conscious decisions about what you want the holidays to be for you and your loved ones even in the face of the "holiday hype" or your own trauma from the past around the holidays.

   • Make this holiday what you want it to be, including changing parts that do not work for you and developing your own special holiday traditions and rituals.

f. Spend more time with positive people who are nurturing and caring and less time with others who are negative, shaming, and unhealthy:

   • If your family of origin is unavailable, either emotionally or physically, make your close friends into "family" and celebrate with them.

g. Allow others to have a positive influence on you, even if holidays in the past have been difficult.

h. Volunteer some time over the holidays with others who are less fortunate than you to appreciate what you do have (e.g., serving meals at a homeless shelter).

i. Cultivate a sense of gratitude:

   • Focus on appreciating the positive parts of who you are and what you have rather than concentrating on what is not there.

3. Be assertive, say "no," and set healthy limits

a. Talk about and make conscious decisions about how you will spend time throughout the holidays with family and others

   • Be assertive with extended family when you need to.

   • Compromise (e.g., drop by for a short visit).

   • Turn down invitations if you're feeling overwhelmed.

b. Prepare yourself to be assertive with others in difficult situations that may occur throughout the holiday season (e.g., figuring out how you will stand up for yourself in response to a shaming relative).

©1999 David J. Decker, MA

c. Think about your gift list (to whom and why you give) and come up with options if the list is becoming overwhelming (e.g., drawing names, setting spending limits).

d. Do not put pressure on yourself to find the perfect gift for everyone (it rarely happens).

e. Be creative with gift giving, even when finances are not difficult:
   • Present personalized gift certificates for specially-prepared lunches or dinners, provide interesting and fun activities such as taking someone to the zoo or on a day trip to a new place, and offer helpful services such as home repair, housecleaning, and snow shoveling to those who need them.
   • Exchange homemade gifts rather than buying presents.

f. Talk to your children directly and honestly about finances if money is tight this year to help them address their unrealistic expectations.

Unit 3: Anger

UNDERSTANDING YOUR ANGER

Your anger can be an ally or an enemy. Anger generally feels painful and uncomfortable when you experience it, but it is an integral part of your humanness and important to your physical and emotional survival. Anger is a fact of life. However, being angry does not mean you need to be controlling, punishing, and abusive. Depending on how you use it, your anger can build self-confidence and self-esteem and enhance relationships, or it can create guilt, shame, and remorse and destroy relationships and intimacy. This handout offers some ideas about what anger is and what it is not and how you can make your anger a more helpful force in your life.

Definitions

Anger

1. A normal and natural *emotion* that arises from how we interpret and label the physical arousal from the "fight or flight" stress response we all experience. This stress response is triggered when we are startled, when we feel fearful or threatened, when we believe that things around us are out of control, or when we feel insecurity, uncertainty, or self-doubt. Anger generally serves as a protection against some sort of emotional or physical pain.
2. Anger is:
   a. Appropriate, whenever it is handled effectively and respectfully
   b. A source of discovery
      - It tells you that "something important is going on" that needs to be attended to and helps clarify who you are.
   c. A warning signal
      - A "core hurt" from the past has been activated by a person or situation in the present.

(HO)

- Your wants, needs, rights, and values aren't being addressed.
- You have compromised yourself in some way.
- An injustice has been done to you or those you care about.

  d. An important part of being assertive (e.g., setting personal limits and maintaining healthy boundaries for yourself)
  e. A tool to educate others (e.g., about your likes, dislikes, wants, and needs)
  f. A useful release of energy
  - It takes enormous effort to suppress your anger and the other feelings it often covers; trying to deny anger completely only creates stress, tension, and anxiety within you.
  g. A catalyst
  - It helps motivate you to solve your problems and accomplish what you need to do.
  h. A form of protection
  - Anger often surfaces in a destructive fashion for you and those close to you if it is not addressed directly.
  i. A gift to others
  - Sharing your anger *and the other feelings it hides* involves taking a risk and allows you to become vulnerable with others, which can open the door to trust and intimacy.

If you allow your anger to build and fester, it can lead to the attitudes that follow.

Cynicism/Hostility/Disgust/Contempt

1. These are *attitudes* that consist of mistrusting the motives of other people and of brooding about and focusing on others' real or perceived injustices toward you. These attitudes lead to viewing the world as an unfair and unsafe place and to continually looking for and expecting others to:
   a. be incompetent and inadequate
   b. be inconsiderate, unfair, and untrustworthy
   c. go out of their way to hurt you
   d. take advantage of you
   e. "cross" you in some way
2. These attitudes can also involve critical, judgmental, and shaming thoughts about yourself, your mistakes, and your problems.
3. These attitudes promote the idea that you are powerless and a victim and that the situation is hopeless.

(HO)   ©1999 David J. Decker, MA

4. Cynicism, hostility, disgust, and contempt are best represented by your negative self-talk or a negative rehearsal in your mind about some future situation. When you regularly engage in negative thoughts, you are constantly fueling your stress response and prolonging and increasing the intensity of your anger.
5. Chronic cynicism, hostility, disgust, and contempt always lead to physical damage and emotional consequences for you and others.
6. If these attitudes become your way of looking at the world, they then contribute directly to the violation of another person's rights or boundaries through the following behaviors.

Aggression/Withdrawal

1. *Aggression* involves *behaviors* acted out with the intent to hurt, punish, intimidate, or control others emotionally, verbally, physically, or sexually as a means of gaining revenge for the real or imagined "wrongs" done to you and getting your way in a particular situation.
2. *Withdrawal* involves *behaviors* designed to disengage emotionally from difficult situations. The can be *punishing withdrawal* that is used to hurt and get back at someone (e.g., sulking and pouting) and/or it can be a *protective withdrawal* when you pull back if you are feeling uncertain or unsafe (e.g., becoming passive and "stuffing" you anger). Or a withdrawal can combine elements of both of these.
3. These behaviors, used on a consistent basis, will always eventually result in disrespect and emotional distance in relationships with others.

Some Distortions of Anger:
What Anger Is Not

1. Being aggressive: being pushy, rude, abrasive, bullying, and intrusive and ignoring what others think, feel, and want (e.g., "I don't care what you want"/"To hell with you")
2. Blaming: not taking responsibility for yourself; continually focusing on others as the reason for your difficulties (e.g., "You're the real problem in this relationship")
3. Lecturing: "going on and on" to try to make a point or convince someone that you are right
4. Labeling: Making simplistic and critical judgments about others (e.g., "What an idiot!"/"You're a moron")
5. Preaching: moralizing and making right/wrong assessments about others (e.g., "No one should ever say something like that")

6. Therapizing: making "grand interpretations" about why others do what they do (e.g., "You're just saying I'm abusive because of what your last boyfriend did to you")
7. Being sarcastic: making devious and hostile jokes at someone else's expense (e.g., "You're really a winner!"/"Right. . . . I'm sure you know what you're talking about")
8. Being vicious: taking advantage of another person's vulnerability (e.g., going for the throat/hitting below the belt)
9. Being punitive: wanting to punish someone by making your reaction so strong that they will not repeat the behavior you dislike
10. Being vindictive: acting vengeful; trying to get even with and get back at others for wrongs they have done to you
11. Being controlling: demanding or expecting that others will do what you want (e.g., saying and believing "It's my way or the highway")
12. Sulking: trying to hurt others with a silence that is hostile, ominous, and threatening (e.g., withdrawing from your partner and refusing to talk for long periods when you are angry)
13. Scapegoating: dumping your anger on others who do not deserve it but who are safer and easier targets than the original person (e.g., yelling at your partner or your children rather than asserting yourself with your boss)
14. Being violent: allowing your internal pain to build to the point at which you make the choice to strike out at others physically or sexually (e.g., grabbing, pushing, restraining, slapping)

When Anger Becomes a Problem
(When It Becomes Cynicism/Hostility/Disgust/Contempt or Aggression/Withdrawal)

1. The intensity of the angry reaction is too great.
2. It occurs too frequently.
3. It lasts too long.
4. It triggers fear and intimidation in others, creates emotional distance between you and others, and disrupts your relationships with those around you.
5. It interferes with getting your work done or creates problems for you on the job.
6. It restricts your ability to have fun, be spontaneous, play, and relax.
7. It begins to cause physical symptoms, such as headaches and back pain.

(HO)   ©1999 David J. Decker, MA

8. It leads to emotional consequences such as feeling guilty, remorseful, and shameful and experiencing low self-esteem.
9. It leads to throwing, hitting, or breaking things.
10. It leads to emotional, verbal, sexual, or physical abuse of others.
11. It leads to legal consequences related to how you express your anger (e.g., restraining orders, disorderly conduct, or assault charges).

How to Express Your Anger Effectively and Respectfully: The Short Course

1. *Become aware of your anger triggers* and learn to notice when you are escalating.
2. *Admit your anger to yourself* and accept the fact that you are angry.
3. *Take a respectful time-out* to cool down if you need to.
4. *Separate the energy and intensity* of the anger *from the issue* directly related to your anger at the moment. *Identify the other possible sources* of your anger by asking yourself some questions:
   a. Is your anger coming from hurt and pain you experienced in your childhood or other past life experiences that is somehow related to the current situation?
   b. Does your anger involve other current stressors that do not have much to do with the present situation?
   c. What negative, controlling, and vengeful thoughts are you experiencing, and how do they contribute to the buildup of intensity? Are you doubting yourself or feeling incompetent, inadequate, worthless, unimportant, powerless, or unlovable? Does this negative self-talk involve unrealistic expectations of yourself or others?
   d. What other emotions are being hidden by your anger (hurt, sadness, fear, disappointment, etc.) that, if expressed, might make communication more effective if you decide to share your anger with the other person?
   e. Is your anger in this situation "justified"? Is someone or something really "out to get you"?
      • If your answer is yes, how did you decide this to be the case? Even if you have clear and specific evidence that your anger is "justified," this still does not give you permission to become explosive, disrespectful, or abusive.
5. *Calm yourself by using de-escalation strategies* such as deep breathing, relaxation skills, positive self-talk, physical exercise, or talking with a friend.

(HO)   ©1999 David J. Decker, MA

6. *Determine what you want to do with your anger.* You may or may not want to share it with the person directly involved.
7. If you choose not to share your anger, *work at "letting go" of it and learning from it.*
8. *Consider the following when expressing your anger directly to the other person involved in the situation:*
   a. Choose how, when, and where you will do this.
      • Pick an appropriate time and place.
   b. Share your anger and your other feelings in an open, assertive, and respectful way.
   c. Use "I" statements and take responsibility for your self-talk, all your feelings, and your expectations.
   d. Actively listen to the other person's point of view and accept that his or her perspective may not be the same as yours and that he or she has a right to see things differently.
   e. Be aware of your expectations and your intentions in sharing your anger.
   f. Avoid the temptation to try to win the argument and force the other person to accept your point of view. This is CONTROL!
   g. Try to view this as an opportunity to better understand each other and to potentially become closer as a result.
9. If necessary, *take the ultimate responsibility for yourself and your anger* and identify what you need to do to care for yourself in similar situations in the future. *Then actually do it!*
10. *When evaluating how you have expressed your anger, ask yourself some questions:*
   a. Was your anger useful or helpful to you in this situation?
   b. Did your anger lead to an effective response or a constructive action?
   c. In retrospect, do you feel proud about how you handled the situation? Do you feel better about yourself as a result of what you did? Do you feel worse?

ANGER ANALYSIS

Use this exercise to better understand what your anger feels like to you, what you become angry about, how you learned to express your anger from those who influenced you in your life, and how you can begin to change the way you express your anger as you experience it.

1. Draw a picture of what your anger looks like and how it feels to you using pictures, symbols, words, and/or colors (on a separate sheet of paper). Bring this drawing to group and be prepared to share it with others.
2. What are you like when you are angry at this point in your life?
    - What do you think about?
    - What does you anger feel like to you?
    - How do you act?
3. What are you like when you are not feeling angry (i.e., how are you different from how you described yourself when you are angry)?
4. What did you learn (what messages did you get) about being angry and about expressing your anger during your childhood and adulthood from the following influences:
    - Your family (your father, your mother, your siblings, your relatives)
    - Your time at school (administrators, teachers, coaches, classmates)
    - Your time in sports activities on athletic teams (coaches, teammates, opposing players)
    - Your time at work (supervisors, co-workers, employees)
    - Your religious background/training
    - Your time in the military (if applicable)
    - Your friends and peers (outside of school and work)
    - Your past and current partners
    - The media (through television, radio, movies, advertising, books, and magazines). Who were/are your heroes and how did they handle their anger?
5. What sorts of things do you become angry about at this time?
6. What specific thoughts, attitudes, and behaviors would you like to change about how you experience and express your anger?
7. How will you and others know that you have changed how you experience and express your anger? What will be different?

(HO)   ©1999 David J. Decker, MA

USING TIME-OUTS

The cornerstone for learning to handle explosive and volatile anger more effectively is the concept of taking a time-out when you feel yourself escalating. The time-out is an important strategy for couples whose relationship includes the potential for abuse and/or disrespect and for individuals who are feeling stressed, anxious, or frustrated in a particular situation.

Basically, using a time-out means taking a break or getting away from a situation in which you are becoming increasingly tense, uncomfortable, or angry. In essence, a time-out in human relationships is no different from a time-out in sports, which is often called because the team is not following the game plan. The time-out gives you the opportunity to step back from a distressing or difficult situation to reassess your "game plan" about who you want to be and how you wish to act at that time.

The goals in taking a time-out are to slow down your internal process, work at letting go of your tension, begin to think more clearly and realistically, and avoid feeling out of control, which can otherwise result in your becoming disrespectful, emotionally or verbally abusive, or violent (e.g., doing and saying things that, from past experience, you know you will regret later).

Steps That Will Help Couples
Put the Concept of Time-Out into Practice

Discuss the concept and use of the time-out. Sit down (when you are both calm), even before you first use the time-out to talk about the guidelines you will agree to follow in using it in a respectful manner. Being respectful in this process is absolutely critical. Avoid viewing and using this as just another weapon in your arguments. Rather, start to see the time-out as a tool that can bring about more effective conflict resolution and real intimacy in the relationship.

Decide how to indicate the need for a time-out. Come to some sense of agreement on what you will say or do to communicate that you want a time-out. For example, you could say "I need some time" or "I need some space" or "I need a break," or you could use a nonverbal sign such as the "T" hand signal for a time-out in sports. Remember that directly communicating the need for a time-out is an important way to show your partner respect and to begin to reestablish trust in the relationship.

Write out and use a time-out plan. Determine the rules and guidelines that you will follow to make this a respectful and effective tool in your relationship. Note aspects of the time-out such as where you will go, what you will do while you are gone, how long you will be gone, and how you will reenter the situation.

Respectfully communicate your desire for a time-out. During a disagreement, conflict, or argument, assertively and clearly tell your partner that you are beginning to feel tense and that you need some time to cool down so you can think more clearly. Let the other person know that you are not merely attempting to avoid the problem or the issue that has been raised. Avoid such statements as, "I've got to get out of here or I don't know what's going to happen," as these can easily be perceived by the other person as threats. Learn to identify and tune into your "cues" and "triggers" that can help alert you to when you are escalating and a time-out is necessary. It is also important to be specific about approximately how much time you will take before returning to discuss the issue.

Take responsibility for your own time-out. It is not someone else's responsibility to tell you that you need a time-out, nor is it up to others to keep you from being abusive or violent. Remember that the other person may not like or agree with your decision to take the time-out. Keep in mind, however, that taking a time-out when you have the potential to be explosive or abusive is a good way to take care of yourself and to communicate respect and caring to others around you (although others may not recognize this at first).

Get away from the person and/or the situation. Couples will find it most effective to leave the house or apartment completely. At a minimum, go to a previously agreed-upon place in your residence and stay separated. Avoid the temptation to get in the last word or a parting shot. Make an effort to respond respectfully to your partner even if you believe your partner is being hurtful and is trying to provoke you at this point. If at work, leave the situation to go to the bathroom or for a short walk, if possible.

Give yourself enough time. Take at least thirty minutes to one hour to de-escalate, relax, and reassert control over yourself and your emotional reactivity and defensiveness. When you become stressed and angry, the release of adrenaline and other chemicals in your body works to increase your heart rate and raise your blood pressure. Allow yourself time for these changes in your body to return to their normal state. As you practice taking your time-outs, you will get a better sense of how much time you actually need.

Actively work to calm yourself both physically and emotionally. Do this after you have left the situation. Immediately after you separate, go to a "quiet space" in your mind. This involves visualizing a place you have actually been or a place you could imagine yourself being where you can

(HO) ©1999 David J. Decker, MA

feel calm, peaceful, relaxed, and safe. This "quiet space" might be a beach near the ocean or walking in a beautiful woods. Go there in your mind at this time to de-escalate and center yourself. Avoid continuing to brood about the perceived wrongs your partner has done to you; try to think about and appreciate the other person's perspective and what he or she might be experiencing and feeling. Use positive self-talk to look at the situation in a new light. Slow down your breathing by taking deeper breaths. Go for a walk or a bike ride. Contact a friend who is supportive yet calming (not someone who's simply going to "bash" the other person). Use a combination of physical and cognitive activities to help you de-escalate. It is not recommended that you drive a vehicle during a time-out because you may escalate further as a result of encountering other drivers and because a vehicle can become a lethal weapon (for you and others) when you are feeling tense, angry, and explosive. It is also not recommended that you use alcohol or other mood-altering drugs during a time-out as these can intensify the problem.

Make a commitment to return to discuss the issue and follow through on that commitment. This will help you begin to address relationship issues, talk about your feelings with each other as they come up, and learn to resolve conflict in the relationship together. Otherwise, the time-out strategy becomes just another way to avoid and escape from the issues you and your partner need to discuss. As part of the process of returning, it is also important to ask clearly and directly if your partner is ready to talk once again. If your partner is not ready, then your time-out needs to continue until your partner communicates a desire to reconnect. If you return to the situation and again begin to escalate, take another time-out until you are able to talk about the issue with no risk of being abusive or violent.

Actively work at and practice the use of time-outs. This will help you integrate the skill into your life. However, remember to give yourself time to make this a positive tool in your life. Be patient with yourself as you are learning this new way of coping with your anger and your desire to control. Continue to practice it whenever necessary and make it an integral part of how you want to behave. This can be an enormous step in truly intervening in your controlling and abusive attitudes and behaviors and in promoting trust and intimacy in your relationships with your partner and others.

ESCALATION PREVENTION PLAN
DE-ESCALATION STRATEGIES

The following are examples of ideas that men have come up with for the de-escalation strategies portion of the Escalation Prevention Plan. Read through these and try to come up with other strategies that you can use in your own EPP.

- Take a time-out (e.g., leave the situation/room/house).
- Call and talk with a supportive friend/group member/relative (i.e., emotionally connect with others).
- Call a crisis line.
- Notice your cues and where you are in your escalation process, and continue to add cues and de-escalation strategies to your EPP.
- Carry around a notepad to help you notice and remember your cues.
- Work consciously at slowing yourself down.
- Be aware of your self-talk and change the negative to more positive self-talk. Think of specific examples of positive self-talk you can use when you are escalating or escalated.
- Use positive affirmations to begin and end your day (e.g., "I can handle my escalations"; I can be the person I want to be").
- Begin to engage in positive rather than negative rehearsals (i.e., learn to make useful plans to handle difficult situations).
- Go for a walk.
- Go to a favorite relaxing spot (e.g. a nearby park, your backyard). Do nonviolent, noncompetitive, aerobic exercise on a regular basis (e.g., jogging, biking, swimming, calisthenics, weight lifting, skating, roller-blading, cross-country skiing).
- Work at really listening to the other person (i.e., stop talking and simply reacting).
- Share your thoughts and feelings assertively with others when you experience them and set appropriate and respectful limits when necessary.
- Count to ten or one hundred.
- Take deep breaths.
- Have a cool drink of water.
- Splash cool water on your face.
- Eat healthy.
- Get enough sleep.
- Sit down when you are angry; do not stand over others in an intimidating way.
- Take a bath, hot shower, whirlpool, or sauna.

(HO)   ©1999 David J. Decker, MA

- Listen to relaxing music.
- Distract yourself; do something else to change your focus from the escalation situation (e.g., clean your closet, your desk, your shop, your car, or the garage).
- Spend time outdoors (e.g., in the woods or near a lake).
- Use relaxation techniques (e.g., progressive muscle relaxation).
- Use meditation and visualization to calm yourself (imagine that you are at a favorite getaway or a safe and quiet place).
- Begin to look at and take responsibility for your part in the conflicts that arise.
- Try to see your partner's or the other person's perspective in the arguments you have (learn to empathize and "put yourself in the other person's shoes").
- Attend a support group (e.g., AA, Al-Anon, ACOA, a church group, other self-help groups).
- Be spiritual; use prayer.
- Let go of things you cannot control (think about and say the Serenity Prayer from Alcoholics Anonymous to yourself).
- Work on feeling a sense of gratitude for who you are and what you have (e.g., think more about positive moments in your life and recall them at difficult times).
- Focus on a hobby or recreational activity that you enjoy (gardening, reading, refinishing furniture, coin collecting, playing music).
- Keep an anger diary or journal and write about how you are feeling.
- Stroke, walk, or play with your pets.
- Think about past consequences or consequences you may experience in the future if you continue to be disrespectful and abusive (e.g. loss of the relationship with your partner, less time with your children, scaring your children or teaching them to become angry and explosive).
- Whistle/sing/laugh.
- Take some time for yourself (i.e., do not overschedule yourself).
- Carry your EPP with you or post it (or parts of it) in places you see daily (e.g., on the refrigerator, on the nightstand near your bed, in the car, at your place of work).
- Make small signs or pictures and post them at various places to remind you of what you are trying to do (e.g., make up a notice that says "Slow down" or draw a picture of a stop sign).
- Ask yourself this question: "In reality, how important is this issue that I'm so angry about?"

(HO)   ©1999 David J. Decker, MA

Things to Avoid Doing

- Retaliating remarks, parting shots, or getting the last word in.
- Contact with your partner when you need to take a time-out.
- Alcohol and other drugs (including caffeine) that can increase your escalation.
- Driving, which can further escalate you.
- Doing "detective work" with your partner (e.g., following her around when she leaves the house, checking the odometer on the car, listening in on her phone conversations).
- Stress-producing activities (e.g., work/projects that have to be done, competitive sports).

©1999 David J. Decker, MA

ANGER JOURNAL

Use this exercise to become more familiar with your escalation process, to get more information about your triggers and cues, and to develop more effective ways to handle your anger when it arises.

1. Describe the situation in which you became angry (e.g., who was involved and what happened).
2. How angry did you become during the situation (on a scale from 1 to 10)? _____
3. Describe your expectations, assumptions, or negative self-talk about
   * the other person and
   * yourself.
4. What other cues did you experience (e.g., physical/emotional signals, trigger words/phrases)?
5. What were the emotions underneath your anger (what feelings did your anger conceal in this situation)?
6. Describe what you wanted (i.e., what was your goal) from this situation
   * for yourself and
   * for the other person.
7. What was the connection between your negative self-talk and your emotions (anger and the others)?
8. What situations from the past (e.g., from your childhood) were similar to this one in terms of your self-talk and feelings? How were they similar?
9. What positive self-talk did you use (or could you have used) to calm yourself down?
10. What did you like about how you handled this situation?
11. What did you not like about how you handled this situation and what would you do differently in the future?
12. Be sure to ask yourself the following questions whenever you have been angry:
    * Was your anger justified? Was someone or something really "out to get you"?
    * Was your anger useful or helpful? Did it lead to an effective response or a constructive action?
    * Do you feel proud about how you handled the situation?

Unit 4: Self-Talk

SELF-TALK

Almost every moment of your conscious life, you are engaging in self-talk and "automatic thoughts." This is your internal thinking process, and it is basically a continual dialogue with yourself. These are the words, phrases, and statements that you use to describe and interpret your world. Self-talk forms your reality. It runs through your head like a tape recording that you turn on and off. However, most people are not even aware of their self-talk unless, and until, they slow the process down and really make an effort to tune into it.

If your self-talk is accurate and, in touch with reality, you tend to function relatively well and to feel okay about yourself. However, if your self-talk is negative and unrealistic, you will then tend to experience anxiety, tension, and emotional distress. This is often the case if the tape you play is filled with shaming and abusive messages you received as a child from important people, such as your parents, teachers, or peers. Often, we use the very words and phrases that were used in the messages that we got in the past. You end up judging and shaming yourself in the present in the same way you were treated during your childhood. Negative self-talk can be divided into three general types, which also appear on your Escalation Prevention Plan:

1. *Negative thoughts and worries:* These are the general sorts of things that you think, brood, or stew about from the past or in the present until you become tense, anxious, depressed, angry, or shameful. Examples of these might be worrying that your boss does not think that you are doing a good enough job at work, stewing about how much money your partner is spending, or brooding about your children's difficulties at school.

2. *Negative rehearsal:* This is visualizing, planning for, or anticipating a negative outcome in the future even before anything actually occurs. It is almost as if you know or can see in your head that something bad is

©1999 David J. Decker, MA

going to happen. For example, this might include setting up an angry confrontation with a friend even though it might not be necessary, getting a phone message from your partner and thinking that she must be upset with you about something, or planning to really let your partner have it when she is late in picking you up at work.

3. *Specific negative self-talk*: These are the very personal and unique words, phrases, and labels that you tend to think to yourself when you are describing yourself and others in critical, cynical, shaming, and judgmental terms. When you start to objectify yourself, it is easy to become angry, depressed, and anxious. When you start to objectify other people, it is that much easier to become controlling and abusive. For instance, when you make a mistake, you might say to yourself, "God, am I stupid!" or when you are frustrated with your partner, you might think, "She's really a loser."

Victim Thinking

At the heart of all negative self-talk is the basic mistaken assumption that your life circumstances are created by others and by the random events in your life, and often includes the cynical notion that others are incompetent, inconsiderate, and out to get you. This assumption frequently translates into a belief that you have no control over your life or over your reactions and responses in your day-to-day living. In addition, when things do not happen as you anticipate, you then take this as a sign that people really do not care about you and that you are somehow defective and unlovable. Examples of this process would include saying to yourself, for instance, "She really pushes my buttons," "He really messed me over," and "That really brought me down." This kind of thinking is a setup for becoming angry and controlling. It can also contribute to feeling anxious and depressed.

If you think about it, this thought process mirrors your position *as a child*. At that point, you did not have the thinking skills to view things independently. You were totally dependent. You counted on your parents and other important people in your life to care for you and provide a safe place for you to learn to be human. If your parents or others were shaming with you, they did not adequately fulfill these roles and you received inaccurate and painful messages about the world and your place in it. The world often became a terrifying place, and rather than reject the shamers, you accepted and believed their messages about you. If their messages were judgmental, negative, and shaming, you ended up believing the lies that came out of the problems and issues they did not adequately address within themselves.

(HO)   ©1999 David J. Decker, MA

As an adult, however, you have a great many more options in how you view yourself and the world. You can assert more control over your perceptions and reactions. You do not need to live by the childhood script you were given. In reality, little is actually ever done *to you*. In fact, we all have the ability to make choices once we become aware that there are choices to be made. This means being proactive rather than a reactive player in your life.

Now, let us think about an alternative way to view your current situation. First, we will say that events occur around you. You experience those events and you engage in your own particular self-talk as a result of your *thought distortions and core beliefs*. These will be discussed in greater detail further on, but, essentially, thought distortions are bad habits in your thinking style that you use, again and again, to interpret reality in an unrealistic or unhelpful way. Core beliefs are the rules for living that arise from the messages you received from your family or from the culture at large (e.g., movies, religion, advertising) about who you are and what the world around you is supposed to be like. It is only after looking at the event through these filters that you actually experience an emotion or feeling. Most of the time, however, you are not even aware of this internal self-talk process because you do not slow down enough to notice it. Thus, you tend to believe that your feelings really have been caused by someone or something outside yourself. The following is a schematic representation of how negative self-talk works:

THE ANTICIPATED OR ACTIVATING SITUATION OR EVENT
which triggers
▼
YOUR THOUGHT DISTORTIONS (bad habits in your thinking style)
AND YOUR UNREALISTIC CORE BELIEFS
(rigid and shaming "rules for living" from childhood and the culture)
which trigger
▼
YOUR NEGATIVE SELF-TALK
(i.e., blaming, cynical, and critical messages about yourself or others)
which triggers
▼
YOUR EMOTIONS AND FEELINGS
(e.g., anger, shame, disappointment, sadness, hurt)
which trigger
▼
YOUR BEHAVIOR
(e.g., sulking, yelling, swearing, throwing things, pushing,
grabbing, alcohol or drug abuse, compulsive eating)

(HO)

As noted previously, outside events and other people really do not have the power to cause your emotions or make you feel a certain way. That is not to say that they cannot trigger your reactions. In reality, however, the critical variable in determining how you will feel about a situation in your life is your own self-talk. Your self-talk arises from your thought distortions and core beliefs. These are the filters from your past and the culture that determine how you interpret your current life experiences.

To change how you feel, you need to slow down the internal self-talk process. This can help you realize that *you do have choices* about how you perceive or interpret any situation that occurs. All you need to do is put these choices into action. It is important to understand that the goal in identifying your negative self-talk is not to try to eliminate all the negative or uncomfortable emotions in your life. You will never be able to do this. Rather, by being more aware of your self-talk, you can actively question your perceptions and interpretations. This then opens up the possibility of intervening in the self-talk by reframing it in a more positive way, if you wish to do so. And if your self-talk changes, your feelings and actions can change as well.

As mentioned earlier, this approach to life is very different from the one you had as a child when your self-talk first developed. Because you could not reframe the negative messages in your childhood, you did not clearly understand that when someone was being abusive or shaming to you, it was *their* problem, not *yours*. This also meant that you internalized the shaming message and really believed that you were as bad, inadequate, incompetent, or unlovable as you were told. These were especially powerful messages when they were delivered by important people such as your parents, teachers, siblings, and peers.

Much of our negative self-talk, especially when you are experiencing intense emotional reactions, relates to the past. It is literally as if what was said to you in childhood becomes part of a tape recorder in your head. Whenever you run into a difficult situation in the present, you end up pressing the play button on those old tapes, and the same shaming words run rampant through your head, creating all sorts of emotional distress.

However, you do not need to continue living this way. The key to changing how you feel as an adult in the present is to actively monitor, identify, and intervene in your negative self-talk. This means developing and using a new tape with more positive and affirming messages about yourself and others. To do this, you must push the stop button or, at the very least, turn down the volume on the negative tape and begin to create and regularly play a more positive one.

(HO)

This removes your internal process from the hands of your inner child who still struggles with believing the negative and destructive lies that he was told. It allows your more competent adult, who can come to know that these negative messages are not true, to take charge of what is happening within you in the present. Next let us address thought distortions and core beliefs.

Thought Distortions

Thought distortions are your own particular style of making sense out of the world around you. They come directly from watching how those important people in your childhood made sense of their world. They are the bad habits in your thinking patterns that continually keep you in a negative and uncomfortable place in your life by directly generating your negative self-talk. Thought distortions tend to be

- *rigid,* because they encourage only one narrow way of perceiving reality.
- *judgmental,* because they put a value on certain things unnecessarily.
- *inaccurate,* because they involve misperceptions and false assumptions.
- *overgeneral,* because they ignore the complexity of life and the present experience.
- *unbalanced,* because they do not include all the information that could be available.

The following are some examples of thought distortions. Notice which ones you use when you think about yourself and others.

Should/Ought Thinking

This pattern is characterized by the habitual and continual use of should, must, ought, have to, and other such words that change everyday decisions and preferences into harsh and strict rules by which to live. It involves the idea that you are obligated to behave in a certain manner rather than capable of making choices about what you want to do or say in any given situation. Such thinking also implies that no other options are acceptable or available. For example, you might think, "I have to be on time" and "She should know better than to do that."

Generalizing

This pattern involves taking a single negative event or occurrence and converting it into an ongoing and unbending conclusion. One mistake or

©1999 David J. Decker, MA

problem translates into a huge and "never-ending" difficulty rather than being placed in a larger context with other information of which you are also aware. One bit of evidence becomes an absolute. Key words that indicate the presence of such thinking include always, never, every, none, no one, everybody, and the like. For example, after breaking off a relationship, you might say, "She never loved me. . . . Women are all just out to use me" or "No one has ever really cared about me."

Labeling

This pattern involves making simplistic and stereotypical judgments, generally cynical, critical, and shaming, about yourself or others. Since the labels often carry a load of negative emotional baggage, they tend to create intense and uncomfortable feelings (about yourself or other people). These feelings generally keep you stuck in powerless thinking patterns rather than helping you to move beyond the problem at hand. They also objectify human beings and make it easier to become actively abusive. Labeling often occurs because you are not making the distinction between behavior and your own or others' intrinsic worth. Some examples of labels include crazy, dumb, lazy, bossy, ugly, wimp, idiot, stupid, jerk, asshole, and failure.

Blaming

This thinking pattern is characterized by always seeking to find someone who is at fault (either you or others). It can involve viewing yourself as overly responsible and beating yourself up for never getting things right, or it can mean accepting no responsibility at all and seeing other people and circumstances as responsible for your choices and decisions so that you can avoid taking charge of your own life. Examples can include blaming yourself for others not having fun at your party or blaming your partner for not making your life happier.

Either-Or Thinking

This pattern involves a rigid belief that only two choices exist in any given situation: "good or bad"/"right or wrong." There are no "shades of gray," which results in unrealistic and perfectionistic expectations of yourself and others. Unfortunately, neither you nor others can live up to these expectations, which always creates a gloomy shadow over you,

(HO)   ©1999 David J. Decker, MA

others, and the world around you. An example of this would be viewing yourself only as either a success or a failure in your life rather than giving yourself credit for what you do accomplish.

Filtering

This pattern is characterized by constant attention to only the negative and disheartening aspects of whatever situation you face. It includes discounting things that might counteract this negative image and always seeing the glass as "half empty" rather than "half full." It is selectively remembering and experiencing your life, focusing primarily on loss, pain, rejection, despair, unfairness, and injustice, and exaggerating their importance to the exclusion of everything else. An example of this would be stewing over one off-hand comment (that you perceived as negative) made by your partner rather than appreciating the warmth and connection you felt with her throughout the rest of your evening together.

Personalizing

This thinking pattern is characterized by feeling overly involved with everything that happens around you even when, in reality, you have little or nothing to do with what is occurring. It is believing that everything in the world revolves around you and includes taking things personally even when it makes no sense to do so. This belief that you should have control when you do not leads to feelings of inadequacy, powerlessness, and victimization in your relationships and in your life in general. An example of this would be listening to your partner complaining about your kids and thinking to yourself that she believes you are doing a poor job as a parent.

Assuming

This pattern is motivated by the belief that you know exactly what others are thinking or feeling. In fact, however, you have little or no evidence to back up your belief and have made no effort to verify your thoughts. Making these assumptions leads you to believe that everyone thinks and feels exactly the same way you do. It generally produces a cynical and negative conclusion, especially if you are already stuck in a cycle of critical thinking about yourself. An example of this would be seeing a friend at work, saying hello, getting no response, and assuming that the friend was angry with you or stuck up.

(HO)

Predicting the Future

This pattern is characterized by "looking into your crystal ball" and making negative predictions about what will happen in the future and then believing that this is the only possible outcome. Unfortunately, this often leads directly to the negative outcome so your thinking process becomes a self-fulfilling prophecy. An example of this would be struggling with a period of unemployment, beginning to believe that you will never get another job that you really like, undermining yourself in the interview process, and thus not getting a job that you might really enjoy.

Emotional Reasoning

This pattern involves making your feelings the sole criterion that you use to determine the truth and to interpret reality. Your evaluations, decisions, and actions are based on whatever your emotional reaction happens to be, without any objective testing of the facts involved. Your feelings become your life's reality. An example of this would be feeling powerless in an explosive situation with a partner and then truly believing that you can do nothing to stop your escalation so you stay in the situation and continue to escalate instead of walking away. In effect, it is saying to yourself, "I feel powerless so I really am powerless."

Comparing

This pattern is characterized by constantly comparing yourself to others in an ongoing battle to try to prove to yourself that you are good enough. You put yourself in competition with everyone around you much of the time, and, unfortunately, most of the time you come out with "the short end of the stick." This only reinforces your negative appraisal of yourself and your belief that you are inadequate. When you compare, you tend to minimize your own abilities, strengths, and accomplishments; exaggerate others' positives; and minimize others' shortcomings. An example of this would be to look at someone who is attractive and fit and then begin viewing yourself as ugly, slovenly, and fat. On the other hand, this comparing process can also mean that you act grandiose and continually see yourself as better than others, demeaning and devaluing them in your mind. An example of this would be seeing someone driving a car that was older and rustier than yours and concluding that they must be a "loser" when it comes to work and money.

(HO)   ©1999 David J. Decker, MA

Catastrophizing

This pattern involves continually expecting the worst to happen in whatever situation you find yourself. It also involves magnifying relatively trivial events or problems into insurmountable ones. Catastrophizing is "making a mountain out of a molehill." It tends to keep you in an anxious and worried state, wondering "what bad things will happen to me next," and builds on the belief that you will not be able to handle future situations. An example of this might be seeing your partner talking to someone at a party and assuming she is interested in that person and wants to have sex with him.

Notice that similarities and linkages exist between many of the bad thinking habits mentioned in this section. However, the bottom line for all of them is that you disparage and demean yourself or others and fuel your negative self-talk by engaging in these types of distortions.

Unrealistic Core Beliefs

We all have core beliefs that represent the values by which we attempt to live. Unrealistic core beliefs are personal rules for living "written in stone" that many people attempt to impose on themselves, other people, and the world around them. These distorted core beliefs directly generate your negative self-talk. In reality, there is almost always some truth to these beliefs. Similar to the thought distortions, unrealistic core beliefs tend to be rigid, judgmental, inaccurate, overgeneral, and unbalanced.

Unrealistic core beliefs arise from the false perception that life is a certain way and that you know the way it will be. Unrealistic core beliefs can be framed in "positive" ("I must have approval from others") or "negative" ("The world is an unsafe place") language. Either way, however, they fuel negative self-talk because of their inflexibility and their unwillingness to allow for our "humanness" and imperfection. When your overly positive view is proved false or your overly negative view is confirmed, you assume that it is because of your own or others' incompetence, worthlessness, and inadequacy. If you or others violate or confirm one of your unrealistic core beliefs, you tend to automatically lapse into your negative, cynical, punishing, and shaming self-talk.

These more specific beliefs often arise from your thought distortions. They are generally handed down to you in your family of origin and in your childhood through both verbal and behavioral messages and values that you received from those who were important to you. Core beliefs serve as your "Ten (or Twenty or Thirty) Commandments" about how you and others are supposed to live and how life is supposed to be. If they are unrealistic, they often distort the way things really are. Unrealistic core beliefs are the messages from the past through which your reactions to current experiences are filtered. An example of this would be seeing your father acting violently when he was angry and then deciding either that anger is always a bad thing to be avoided at all costs or that violence is a good tool to use when you want to get something done or control someone. Another example is feeling angry and betrayed that your mother did not protect you from your father's abuse and deciding that, as a result, women cannot be trusted.

Unrealistic core beliefs are also communicated from generation to generation via the strong cultural messages we receive regarding gender roles and what it means to be a successful and worthwhile person. One example of this would be seeing how women are portrayed in advertising and deciding that it is a woman's role in life to take care of and please men. Another might be seeing how "real men" are portrayed in the movies and taking on a core belief that a real man should be strong, confident, and in charge at all times.

The following list gives some examples of the unrealistic core beliefs that people may have. Review this list and see how many of these core beliefs tend to influence the way you think and feel about yourself and the people and situations in your life. Following each core belief is the specific negative self-talk that might follow from it. Add your own to this list if you can think of others that fit for you.

1. I have to be strong enough to handle everything by myself (e.g., "If my father dies and I need emotional support, I'm weak-willed").
2. My real value as a person comes from being busy and productive at all times (e.g., "When I take time off or go on vacation, I'm useless").
3. It is my responsibility to take care of others and fix them when they are unhappy or upset (e.g., "If I can't get my partner out of a bad mood, I'm [or she's] not trying hard enough").
4. I have to be competent and successful in everything that I do (e.g., "If I'm not good at something, I'm a loser").
5. Anger is always bad and destructive (e.g., "If I [or others] get pissed off about something, I [or they] will end up out of control").
6. I must have approval from strangers, peers, friends, and family (e.g., "If someone doesn't like me, there must be something wrong with me [or them]").

(HO)   ©1999 David J. Decker, MA

7. Women are not as capable as men (e.g., "If a female co-worker has a better idea than I do, she's a brownnoser [or I'm incompetent]").
8. Other people should always be fair with me (e.g., "If my co-workers don't treat me right, I'm not cared about [or they're jerks for treating me badly]").
9. It is wrong to be concerned about my own needs and wants (e.g., "If I ask my friends for help, I'm being selfish and pushy").
10. I have to always "try my best" to please and satisfy others (e.g., "If others don't appreciate what I'm doing, I must be screwing up and not trying hard enough [or they're inconsiderate slobs who should be noticing me more]").
11. A "real man" should not feel certain emotions (such as sadness, hurt) (e.g., "If I cry when I feel bad, I'm a wimp").
12. Having conflict means that partners do not really love each other (e.g., "If my wife argues with me, she doesn't really care about me [or I must be wrong]").
13. People and things should be the way I want them to be (e.g., "If my partner won't do what I want her to do, she must not really care about me").
14. If people make mistakes, they deserve to be blamed and punished (e.g., "If my girlfriend is late, she's irresponsible, and I have a right to yell and scream at her").
15. People are very fragile and should never be hurt by others (e.g., "If someone does something to upset me, they're mean and an asshole").
16. A partner is supposed to live up to my expectations (e.g., "If my partner doesn't follow through with what she agreed to do, she doesn't really love me [or she's irresponsible]").
17. Good relationships are always based on sacrifice (e.g., "If my girlfriend doesn't give in to me when I need something, she's bad and uncaring").
18. Outside events cause all my unhappiness and bad feelings (e.g., "If I get mad at my wife, it's her fault because she made me feel this way").
19. Marriages are supposed to last forever (e.g., "If I get divorced, I'm [or my partner is] a failure and didn't try hard enough").
20. Men should always be strong, confident, and in charge. (e.g., "If my partner won't do what I want, I must be a weakling").
21. Women should always be polite and passive (e.g., "If my partner speaks up for herself, she's a bitch").

(HO) ©1999 David J. Decker, MA

22. Children should be seen and not heard (e.g., "If my kids sass me, they're brats [or I'm a lousy parent]").
23. People have to make a lot of money to really be happy and lead a good life (e.g., "If I don't have much money, I'm a loser, and I'll never amount to anything").
24. Formal education lets you know how smart people actually are (e.g., "If I didn't finish high school or college, I'm stupid").
25. A woman's real job is to take care of me and the kids (e.g., "If my partner spends time with her friends, she's heartless and selfish").
26. I must have respect from everyone around me (e.g., "If my wife doesn't listen to me as I think she should, I'm disrespected and she's an idiot").
27. Women cannot be trusted (e.g., "If my girlfriend talks to another man, she's a flirt and she is going to leave me").
28. I have nothing to offer anyone (e.g., "If someone doesn't want to be my friend, it proves how awful I really am").

Changing Your Self-Talk

Now that you have a better understanding of what self-talk is, where it comes from, and how it affects you, we need to look at some specific ways to change it. If you do not interrupt your self-talk, you will remain stuck in a morass of negative and uncomfortable feelings and self-defeating and self-destructive behaviors. The key to intervening, as mentioned before, is to slow down your internal process so that you notice your self-talk. Many people do not slow down and look inside. This must happen if any of the following strategies is going to be effective.

Thought Stopping

The first strategy involves what is referred to as "thought stopping," or catching yourself in the midst of your negative self-talk and saying loudly and firmly to yourself (or simply thinking to yourself if you are around others) "Stop" or "Stop it." This interrupts the pattern of negativity and can help remind you of your goal to decrease your negative self-talk. You can also be more gentle with yourself in using this strategy by finding other words to say to yourself to interrupt the flow of negative thoughts, such as "Come on, Dave, you're getting negative again" or "Oh, oh, here I go again." Then, if you find that the negative thought is now gone or less demanding of your attention, give yourself credit, which only adds to the positive momentum that you have started with your thought-stopping efforts.

(HO)   ©1999 David J. Decker, MA

Distracting Yourself

Another strategy is to distract yourself. When you notice your negative self-talk starting, identify something else on which you can focus your attention at the time and try to immerse yourself in it. To do this, either look around at something outside you that may be interesting or go inside and begin to daydream or to visualize something pleasant. If your self-talk becomes negative while you are waiting in a supermarket checkout line, for instance, and you choose to notice something outside yourself, pick up a magazine and read an interesting article or indulge in some people-watching. If you choose to go inward, think about the pleasant vacation you had last summer or imagine a time in your life when you felt positive and confident. Your mind has great difficulty focusing on two things at the same time. When you shift your focus to something new and more positive, you stop the flow of negative self-talk.

Changing Your Negative Rehearsals

Learning to confront and change your negative rehearsals is another important part of changing your negative self-talk. If you think about it, getting yourself involved with a negative rehearsal is a lot like paying interest on a debt you have not even accrued yet. Looking ahead and seeing the worst in a situation that has not even occurred is very similar. It would be like beginning to pay for a car six months before you even took possession and started driving it. You would not do that with a car. Why do it with your life? A negative rehearsal takes you out of the present moment due to the worry and "stewing" you are experiencing and wastes a great deal of your precious time by distracting you from things you could be enjoying in the present.

Now we will turn to an example. Let us say that for the past four Thanksgivings, you have had an awful time with your relatives during family get-togethers. Now it is September or October and you are already dreading the idea of doing the same thing all over again. You anticipate your father being shaming and judgmental; you visualize your uncle drunk and slurring his words; you imagine your mother nervous and agitated; and you can see your partner getting angry about being put in this situation again, which is likely to lead to a fight between the two of you. So, what can you do?

If you are negatively rehearsing, you are brooding about this scene all the way up until you actually leave your house to join the "festivities." And, in doing so, you feel powerless, victimized, and irritable, which may lead to feeling depressed and resentful, which in turn will probably lead to problems for you and others as you approach the holiday. Instead of this scenario, try something different. For example, try sitting down with your partner, discussing your feelings about the holiday, and coming up with some positive ways of confronting and handling this painful situation. This might mean spending less time there, taking time-outs when you are beginning to feel overwhelmed or focusing your attention on each other or on relatives you do enjoy (e.g., playing games with the children). The idea here, though, is to create a positive rehearsal and actually plan, in a constructive way, how you are going to handle the chaos that is bound to exist. This takes you out of your normally powerless position and gives you and your partner options to handle the situation more effectively. Having a positive plan also means that you do not have to worry as much in the month or two prior to the actual event. This idea of turning a negative rehearsal into a positive one can be used in any situation in which you find yourself worrying ahead of time about what might happen.

Challenging the Entire
Negative Self-Talk Process

The final strategy in changing your self-talk assists you in examining and attacking the negative self-talk head on. This involves actively working at clearly identifying and reframing the whole negative self-talk process. The first step is to slow down enough to notice the uncomfortable and distressing feelings that you experience near the end of the self-talk process. Most people assume that these feelings arise directly from the anticipated or activating situation. They do not. The way to uncover the thought process that actually triggers the feelings is to backtrack, first to the self-talk and then to the underlying thought distortions and core beliefs. As you backtrack, you need to work on developing different ways of thinking about yourself and the people and situations involved with your thought process.

For example, you come home at the end of the day and your partner is grumpy and withdrawn. Instead of saying to yourself, "Who does she think she is acting that way around me? She better not keep this up" and "What a jerk!", you might want to work on becoming more tolerant and empathetic. If you were willing to do this, you might instead say to yourself, "She usually doesn't treat this way. Maybe she's having a bad day." This does not mean that you cannot tell her how you feel about her behavior, but more positive self-talk will probably influence how you feel about her and how you relate your feelings to her.

(HO)   ©1999 David J. Decker, MA

The next step involves backtracking to the thought distortions and core beliefs. This would mean noticing when you are personalizing, labeling, or generalizing and catching yourself in that process. It would also mean identifying the core beliefs that are part of the interaction, seeing clearly how they are setting up your self-talk process in the present situation, and thinking about where they originated. In the previous example, the core beliefs in action might be "People and things should be the way I want them to be," "Others should always be fair with me," and "I must have approval and respect from family, friends, and strangers." Having these rigid beliefs in this particular situation means that you are setting yourself up for negative self-talk and then overreacting in what you say and do around your partner. This is a time to question where those beliefs originated. They probably go back to your own family of origin. It is also a time to ask yourself if they really fit in an imperfect world (they do not). At that point, you can make the choice to become more flexible, realizing that "we're all in this together" and, for most of us, doing the best we can.

This last strategy can also be used with negative self-talk about yourself as well, for example, when you make a mistake and are feeling irritated and impatient with yourself (thinking things such as "How can I be so stupid?" or "Why can't I ever get it right?"). Trace these sorts of statements back to similar messages given to you by your father, your mother, or your teachers. Then challenge both the self-talk and the thought distortions and core beliefs. In this situation, your core belief might be "I have to be competent and successful in everything I do." Confront this notion about the way life is supposed to be and try to come up with less shaming and more nurturing things to say about yourself. You might say, "I don't like that I made a mistake, but I can learn from this" or "I need to remember that I don't have to be perfect." Making your self-talk more positive and having more empathy and patience with yourself will help change how you actually feel and act in the situation.

Negative self-talk alienates us from ourselves and others. Positive self-talk celebrates our humanness, uniqueness, and individuality and creates in us more understanding, empathy, and tolerance for who we and for who others are. Working toward the positive makes a lot more sense. Make a commitment to yourself that you will focus on doing just that.

(HO)   ©1999 David J. Decker, MA

POSITIVE SELF-TALK AND ANGER

When people who have the potential to become explosive and abusive change their self-talk (i.e., their internal thought processes), they are significantly more likely to de-escalate and regain their composure and self-control. When you begin to experience your cues (i.e., the signals that you are escalating) and are starting to feel tense and irritable, take a time-out and think about and say some of the following statements to yourself. You are also encouraged to come up with statements of your own that can help you calm yourself down in potentially volatile situations.

- I do not need to prove myself in this situation. I can stay calm no matter what they do or say to me. There is no reason I have to escalate now.
- There is no need to doubt myself. What other people say does not have to matter so much to me. I am the only person who can make me angry or keep me calm.
- It is time to slow things down. I can always take a time-out if I start getting tense.
- I do not have to feel intimidated or victimized in this situation. I can take care of myself by relaxing and focusing on what I need to do right now.
- There is no way I can control other people. However, I do have control over myself, how I express my feelings, and the choices I make about how I act.
- It will not "kill" me to have others criticize or dislike me. I do not have to be perfect. If what they say fits, I will take it in. If not, I will let it go.
- I do not have to "give my power away" to somebody else. I am no one's puppet. I can be who I want to be, no matter what the circumstances.
- I feel badly about screwing things up but it is still okay to make mistakes.
- I cannot force anyone to be who I think he or she should be. People are free to act exactly the way they want.
- Why should I let others control how I feel? I have the right to be in control of myself and my emotions.
- Most of our arguments are not very important. When things become this intense, I know I am just stirring up old feelings from my past.

- I know I do not have to be "on top of things" all the time. It is okay to feel confused.
- If they want to go "bananas," that is up to them. I do not need to react by becoming abusive myself.
- I have the power to "keep my cool" in any situation.
- When an argument starts, I know what I can do to take care of myself.

You also need to begin to think about using positive self-talk before, during, and after a potential escalation. A positive (versus a negative) rehearsal enables you to effectively handle an upcoming situation. Using positive self-talk can assist you even in the midst of a problematic experience. It can also allow you to feel good about getting through a tough time. The following are some specific examples of positive self-talk that you can use in each of these scenarios. Use these or come up with your own when confronted with situations that could trigger an explosive response.

Doing a Positive Rehearsal Prior to a Difficult Situation

- What do I want to do here to address this issue?
- I need to start thinking about being a problem solver.
- I know I will be able to work out a plan to take care of myself in this situation.
- I can handle this.
- If I begin to get upset, I know what to do.
- This will work out all right for me.
- I know how to handle my anger so that I do not become controlling and abusive.
- I do not need to get into a power struggle with her about this.
- I will take some deep breaths to calm myself down.
- I know how to feel at ease, even when I am feeling stressed.
- This could be a challenge for me, but I know what I need to do, and I can do it.
- I can come out of this situation feeling okay.

Handling Your Cues and the Escalation Process During a Difficult Situation

- I will stay "cool" and think about relaxing.
- As long as I stay calm, I am in control of myself.

(HO)   ©1999 David J. Decker, MA

- I will not get "bent out of shape" about this.
- I will stay focused on what I want to accomplish.
- I do not need to prove myself to anyone.
- There is no sense in getting any angrier about this.
- It is just not worth it to give all my power away to her.
- I will not assume the worst or jump to conclusions. I can make something positive out of this.
- For him to be that "pissed off," he must be really unhappy.
- I do not need to doubt myself because of what she is saying.
- It is too bad he or she has to act this way around me.
- Becoming angry will not get me anywhere so I might as well slow things down and relax.
- Even if she keeps this up, I know what to do.
- My chest is starting to tighten up and my mind is racing. I need to slow down.
- Exploding now will not help me or this situation.
- It is just not worth getting so agitated.
- I will look and feel like a fool unless I let this go for now.
- I am feeling pretty bad right now but I do not have to buy into how she sees me.
- It is okay to be irritated about this, but I do not need to explode.
- I really need to take a few deep breaths and slow things down in my head.
- My anger is a signal for me to start using positive self-talk.
- I do not want to get pushed around, but I am not going to go bonkers either.
- He would probably like me to blow, but there is no way I am going to do it.
- I need to remember that I cannot expect people to do what I want them to do.
- There is no way I am going to let her push my buttons this time.
- I am really getting pissed off; I need to take a time-out.
- I can get out of this in a positive way no matter how angry I feel.
- I will just get into trouble if I allow myself to continue to escalate.

Giving Yourself Credit
and Celebrating Afterward

- All right! I got out of there without blowing my stack.
- I could have gotten a lot more pissed off than I did back there.

(HO)   ©1999 David J. Decker, MA

- That was not nearly as hard as I thought it would be.
- I always kept in mind that I would be able to take a time-out if I needed to.
- I am getting better at this all the time.
- I actually went through this without getting all that angry.
- I really like not having to carry bad feelings around with me all day.
- This is getting easier every time I do it.
- I am getting good at taking care of myself in situations like this.
- It is great being the person I want to be around her.
- Taking time-outs really works!
- I knew I could learn to handle my anger.
- It worked! I really am in control of myself, even in situations like that one.

©1999 David J. Decker, MA

SELF-TALK LOG

What was the anticipated/activating situation or event?	What were your feelings about the situation and how did you behave? We notice our feelings and behaviors before we notice our self-talk.	What was your negative self-talk? *Be specific.*
Thinking about trying to put together a kids' playhouse with "some assembly required"	**Feelings:** anxious, fearful, frustrated, angry **Behaviors:** procrastinate putting it together; "snap" at the kids when they ask about when it will get done	I'll never be able to do this; the instructions are always screwed up; I'm such a "klutz"; I'm incompetent; I'm stupid; I shouldn't have bought this for the kids; I'm not much of a man; I'm inadequate.
Seeing your partner talking to another man at a party	**Feelings:** anxious, depressed, jealous, fearful, hurt, angry **Behaviors:** going over to your partner and tell her that the two of you will be leaving *now;* sulking if she doesn't want to leave; getting even angrier as the night goes on and refusing to talk to her in the car on the way home; yelling at her about what a "slut" she is	She doesn't respect me; she's never really loved me; she shouldn't be talking to other guys; she's a slut; she likes that jerk more than she likes me; she's going to leave me; I can't trust her; I'm not lovable; that guy is probably better than I am; I'm not valued; she's going to get it when we leave here.
Getting cut off on the freeway	**Feelings:** fearful, threatened, angry **Behaviors:** chasing after the other driver and honking; flashing your lights; "flipping him off" or tailgating him	I can't let that jerk get away with this; that guy is an asshole and should be taught a lesson; people like that are always "messing" with me; that guy is going to kill somebody and needs to be stopped; he probably thinks I'm a wimp and won't do anything; nobody should be allowed to drive that way; I never drive like that; I'm not important.

©1999 David J. Decker, MA

What were your thought distortions and core beliefs that contributed to your negative self-talk? *Be specific.*	How could you intervene in your negative self-talk by changing it (e.g., reframing it in a more positive way)? *Be specific.*
TD: generalizing, labeling, predicting the future, comparing, catastrophizing **CB:** I have to be strong enough to handle everything myself; I have to be competent and successful in everything I do; real men know how to take care of mechanical things.	I'll be able to figure this out; I can ask for help from my brother if I need to; I can take a time-out if I really start to escalate; it's okay that I don't know how to do everything; I've been able to put things together in the past.
TD: should/ought thinking, labeling, predicting the future, comparing, catastrophizing **CB:** people and things should be the way I want them to be; my wife is supposed to live up to my expectations; no one will ever really love me; women can't be trusted.	I'm just feeling this because of my own self-doubt; this is my issue, not hers; she has a right to talk to other people; her talking to other guys doesn't mean she wants to have sex with them; I want her to have a good time here too; I can take a time-out and think about this more rationally if I need to.
TD: should/ought thinking, personalizing, labeling, comparing, catastrophizing, blaming **CB:** others should always be fair with me; people and things should be the way I want them to be; if people make mistakes they deserve to be blamed and punished; I have to have respect from everyone around me; real men don't let anyone push them around.	I can't control that guy's behavior; I don't like what he just did, but maybe he didn't see me; if I try to get him back for this, I could really get hurt; if I'm concerned about what might happen, I could call the police and report him; even though I felt scared, I'm okay and the car didn't get damaged; maybe there's a good reason he has to rush to get somewhere.

(HO)

Unit 5: Shame and Empowerment

SHAME AND EMPOWERMENT

Understanding the very real differences between shame and empowerment is an important first step in beginning the process of overcoming your shame and moving beyond being a shame-based and unhappy person. A shame-based lifestyle involves old and automatic habits, despair, cynicism, hopelessness, powerlessness, and stagnation. An empowerment-based lifestyle involves conscious choices, accountability, responsibility, optimism, and growth. The following material lists the significant aspects of shame and empowerment and highlights how they differ from each other. As you read through these definitions, try to begin to understand how shame affects the way you look at yourself and the way you live your life.

Defining Shame

Shame is a way of looking at yourself and others and a way of living your life that involves control, perfectionism, blame, reactivity, cynicism, despair, and stagnation. It is developed within you during childhood as a result of being deeply wounded by the very people who were supposed to care for you (generally your parents and others important to your sense of self-worth and survival).

These core hurts create a set of core beliefs about yourself and the world that arise directly from your interactions with and the messages from those who wounded you. The core hurts cause you to experience strong doubts about yourself and you begin to sense that there is something vaguely and indescribably wrong with you. In the end, the emotional pain from these hurts leaves you feeling discouraged, defective, incompetent, inadequate, powerless, unlovable, and completely alone. You end up believing that you are never quite good enough and that you do not measure up to your own or others' standards. The core hurt also tells you that the world is a frightening and dangerous place in which you need to be constantly on guard. In essence, shame is a life script for you by others.

(HO)

These negative attitudes and self-talk create an atmosphere in which you continually judge and condemn yourself and others for mistakes and short-comings. You end up believing that you are a failure as a person and have nothing good or worthwhile to offer others. It also leaves you continually struggling to feel okay about yourself and out of touch with who you really are. You tend to feel alienated and estranged from others around you fearing that they will be able to see through the image you struggle to project to maintain your shaky sense of self.

Living a shame-based lifestyle leads to feeling consistently vulnerable and exposed to others in a painful and humiliating way. It is as if everyone is aware of your intense inner pain and your sense of inadequacy and is attempting to victimize and take advantage of you as a result. Since the world is not a safe place, you need to be constantly alert and wary. Needless to say, this hampers the development of close relationships. You also end up facing daily life with a sense of fear and anxiety, which often interferes with taking risks and tackling life's challenges. In fact, every challenge becomes more proof of your incompetence and inadequacy. Saddest of all, you often see no way to change your perspective of yourself and the world.

The brutal negative self-talk associated with shame leads to harsh and rigid judgments that do not allow for the possibility of improving or redeeming yourself. Some examples include the following:

- I'm a klutz.
- I'm bad.
- I'm worthless.
- I can't do anything right.
- I'm a loser.
- I'm stupid.
- I'm a mistake.
- I'm inadequate.
- I'll never amount to anything.
- I'm incompetent.
- I'm crazy.
- I'm not lovable.
- I'm a totally awful person.
- I'm a failure.
- I'll never get it right.
- There's something horribly wrong with me.
- Nothing in my life will ever get any better.
- I don't even deserve to be here.

(HO)   ©1999 David J. Decker, MA

A Shame-Based Lifestyle Leads To:

- secrets and an ongoing fear that others will discover who you really are;
- an urgent desire to hide, escape, or disappear;
- an interruption of spontaneous behavior, a loss of energy, and a state of paralysis and immobilization;
- an unwillingness to take risks and take on life changes;
- a total inability to connect with others in a meaningful way and a profound sense of loneliness, estrangement, and alienation that comes as a result; and
- an overwhelming sense of despair, cynicism, hopelessness, and stagnation.

Defining Empowerment

Empowerment is a way of looking at yourself and the world and a way of living that involves ongoing awareness, conscious decision-making, respect, accountability, proactivity, optimism, and the ability to change and become the person you want to be. It is actively developed by you in your adult life as you are willing to recognize and intervene in the destructive thought and behavior patterns that you learned at an earlier time. Empowerment is based on a set of positive and more realistic core beliefs and self-talk about you and the world that you develop for yourself (with the help of others) when you change the negative messages, the bad habits, and the life script that were programmed into you during your childhood. In essence, empowerment is a life script written by you for yourself that promotes self-esteem, self-confidence, and the potential for personal growth and intimacy with others.

The awareness that is part of empowerment helps you to differentiate your identity as a person from your mistakes, imperfections, shortcomings, and character defects. This way of looking at life frees you to identify and make conscious decisions to change the attitudes or behaviors that interfere with your living a healthy lifestyle. Empowerment means truly believing that you are a worthwhile, capable, important, and lovable person and being aware of and using you own personal power rather than trying to impose your will on others. It is also believing that the world is generally a safe place where you can connect with other people and count on those you choose to have around you.

These positive attitudes and self-talk allow you to experience painful feelings about your behavior without condemning yourself. This, with a system of accountability and respect for your own and others' rights, can then open up the option of remedying what has happened in a variety of ways, including taking responsibility for what you did or said, making amends, or resolving a conflict or issue in a satisfying way for you and the other person.

The process can then lead to a sense of real resolution, a recognition and deepening of positive core values, growth as an individual and in the context of your relationships with others, and a stronger acceptance of who you are as a whole person (flaws and all). It can also lead to the development of a perspective of yourself as "part of a larger universe," in which you have responsibility to, and empathy and compassion for, both yourself and others.

When you make a mistake and are hurtful to yourself or someone else, the empowerment-based system allows you free and ongoing access to the healthy and necessary knowledge that you have violated a value or a standard important to you (e.g., feeling bad that you have "stepped on" someone else's rights). You are thus able to tune into your responsibility to others and yourself. Responsibility focuses on adequacy, competency, and solutions rather than blame and punishment. The awareness that is part

The positive and affirming self-talk associated with empowerment includes acknowledgement of issues and problems that arise and an understanding that they can be addressed in a responsible and respectful way. You are able to learn and grow from what you have done and what happens around you. The following are some examples:

- I'm having trouble figuring this out but I am still a competent, capable, and worthwhile person.
- I really screwed up, but it's okay to make mistakes and learn from them.
- I don't like what I did, but I can do something about it.
- My behavior was hurtful to her, but I'm still a good person and I can acknowledge what I did and apologize.
- I don't like what's happening here, but I can figure out how to take care of it.
- What she just said really hurt my feelings, but I can get through this because I'm still all right.
- I'm angry about what she just did, but I can talk with her about it and try to understand what was going on for her.
- I'm really feeling overwhelmed by everything that's happening around me, but I have people in my life who can help me get through it.

An Empowerment-Based Lifestyle Leads To:

- a feeling of relief that arises from the idea that you are, at your core, a valuable, competent, worthwhile, and lovable person;
- a sense of being centered and grounded and the ability to be yourself no matter what is going on around you;

(HO)   ©1999 David J. Decker, MA

- spontaneity and freedom of expression that stem from a knowledge and an acceptance of who you really are;
- the ability to tap into your own personal power rather than trying to exert power and control over others;
- a genuine and comforting connectedness with other people and the world in which you live; and
- the strongly held belief that you and others can improve, change, and grow.

SHAME

The first step in beginning the process of overcoming your shame and moving beyond being a shame-based and emotionally stunted person is to understand what shame is, where it comes from, and how it is currently affecting your life.

Shame is a way of looking at yourself and the world and a way of living your life based on control, perfectionism, reactivity, despair, and stagnation. It profoundly affects who you are and how you feel about yourself and others and is closely connected to the negative thought process you have going on in your head. Shame causes you to experience strong doubts about yourself at your very core; triggers a powerful inner sense of worthlessness, hopelessness, cynicism, and powerlessness; creates an intense feeling of being a "failure" as a person; and stops you from being who you really are. Shame first becomes an integral part of who you are and how you function when you are deeply wounded and hurt by important people in your childhood. When these shaming situations occur, you are given the message that you are inadequate, incompetent, defective, and unlovable.

Sources of Shame Over the Course of Your Lifetime

Direct Shame

This type of shame involves trauma caused by an important person in your life (e.g., parents, teachers, coaches, relatives, peers, partners) in the past or present; your thoughts, feelings, or body itself are invaded in such a way that you believe you are dirty, stupid, bad, worthless, unimportant, defective, disrespected, devalued, or unlovable. Direct shame occurs when you are treated like an object rather than a person with human rights and dignity. Direct shame can include both of the following:

1. Active shaming
   a. Emotional abuse (e.g., threatening and intimidating gestures, looks, and actions; having others appear or act disgusted with you)
   b. Verbal abuse (e.g., name-calling and put-downs; having others swear or curse at you; racist, sexist, or homophobic epithets directed at you)
   c. Physical abuse (e.g., discipline that involves pulling hair or ears; being slapped or punched; being hit with objects such as belts, hairbrushes, or sticks)

(HO)   ©1999 David J. Decker, MA

    d. Sexual abuse (e.g., sexualized comments such as statements about boys developing pubic hair or girls developing breasts; sexualized touch such as hugs that last too long or being touched by others in ways that feel uncomfortable to you; sexual assault by nonfamily members; incest by family members)

2. Passive shaming

    a. Having your physical and emotional wants and needs discounted or neglected (e.g., parents showing little or no interest in their children's thoughts, feelings, interests, and activities; parents spending little time with their children)

    b. Being physically or emotionally abandoned or rejected by the people who are supposed to be taking care of you (e.g., parents leaving their children in strange places; parents withholding verbal or physical expressions of love when they are angry with their children)

    c. Being given the message that you do not matter and are of no value (e.g., the absence of nurturing and emotional connections with caretakers)

Entitlement Shame

This type of shame involves families in which a child is treated like a "golden boy" by his overinvolved and doting caretaker(s). These boys are given the message that they can never do anything wrong and have no responsibility when problems do arise. They are overly protected by their caretaker(s) and are never allowed to experience any real or meaningful consequences for their hurtful, destructive, or irresponsible behavior. Thus, they develop a grandiose sense of self-importance, feelings of personal entitlement, and the belief that "the world owes me." They become self-absorbed and self-centered, lack empathy, and have little thought or regard for others. They believe that others merely exist to benefit them so they develop the rigid expectation that others should do things for them and give them whatever they want. This shame, and the feelings of unworthiness and defectiveness that accompany it, is triggered when other people do not treat you as the "golden boy" that you think you are (e.g., your partner not treating you in the same way that your caretaking mother did). This shame has the potential to develop when caretakers

- have no expectations about a child helping around the house and let the child do whatever he feels like doing;

- continually intervene in consequences that a child is about to experience due to his misbehavior outside the home;
- buy or give a child anything that he wants;
- treat the child as if he never makes mistakes; and
- make the child "the center of the universe" so that he has no accountability to anyone else.

Cross-Generational Shame

This type of shame involves trauma or problems that occurred in your family or community even before you were born. This shame builds and generates more shame due to attempts to protect and stay loyal to the family or community by keeping the trauma secret and hidden. This is often justified with such statements as "It's nobody else's business" and "Don't air the family's dirty laundry." The family often feels "cursed" to individual members, and they frequently experience intense anxiety and fear about breaking the powerful taboo related to discussing and making public these issues. Unresolved losses and the grief associated with them are often a major contributor to this type of shame. Examples include the following:

- Poverty that may result from financial mismanagement or bankruptcy but may also relate to simply not having an opportunity to make enough money to have a comfortable lifestyle
- Mental illness (e.g., "the crazy uncle") and alcohol or drug abuse (e.g., "the family drunk")
- Children's accidents or deaths for which the parents believed they were responsible or were being punished by God
- Illegitimate pregnancies or births
- Extramarital affairs
- Family or extended family members' suicides
- Rapes of family members
- Emotional, verbal, physical, and sexual abuse that occurred in previous generations of the family

Cultural Shame

Cultural shame involves the messages that you receive from society at large that communicate clearly that you are somehow failing to live up to society's notions or images of gender roles or of what it means to be a competent, successful, and worthwhile person. These powerful signals con-

(HO)　　　　　　　　　　　　　　　　　©1999 David J. Decker, MA

tinually bombard us through radio, television, the movies, newspapers, and magazines and through societal institutions such as places of worship, your place of employment, the military, and the government. This type of shame can also include being different from the mainstream and dominant culture in a variety of ways (e.g., not being white, not being male, not being a Christian, not being heterosexual, having a disability, getting divorced, being old, being poor, being overweight). The following are some examples of these messages:

- Advertising that tells you what sort of car you should drive, what sort of beer you should drink, what sort of friends and partner you should have, and how you should look
- Television programs and movies that communicate values about relationships and male and female roles
- Religious leaders who describe what type of person you should be and how you should live your life
- Infomercials that tell you how easy it is to make money, how much money you should have, where you should live, how many cars you should own, and what your lifestyle should be like

Maintained Shame

Maintained shame involves passively or actively finding ways to continue your childhood shame in your own individual life or in your relationships with others in the present. This may occur either through your thought patterns or due to your own compulsive, irresponsible, abusive, and self-destructive behaviors that undermine your own and others' dignity, such as the following:

- Having negative, despairing, cynical, hostile, vengeful, and disrespectful thought patterns
- Being emotionally, verbally, physically, or sexually abusive toward others
- Becoming involved with compulsive, addictive, and self-defeating behaviors such as overinvolvement in your work, compulsive gambling or overeating, sexual acting out (promiscuity or continual affairs), or alcohol and drug abuse

Existential Shame

Existential shame is produced by a loss or a lack of significant purpose and meaning (*defined by you in your own terms*) in your life that leads to the belief that you are stuck, adrift, directionless, and going nowhere. It may coincide with cultural shame related to losing a prescribed societal role (e.g., being laid off from your job, having your partner divorce you), but this type of shame also speaks to the need that human beings have for meaning in their lives. This shame can arise from any of the following situations:

- Suffering a debilitating physical or emotional illness, such as cancer or depression
- Remaining in an unsatisfying and unchallenging job solely to maintain a certain income level or a sense of security
- Staying in an unfulfilling relationship that lacks intimacy with no hope for change because you fear taking the risks associated with leaving
- Being a career homemaker and having all your children leave home to begin their own lives
- Retiring from a job that has been important to you and having few other life interests other than your work

The Rules of Shame-Based Systems

The following rules are common to all shame-based systems, whether referring to a family or other types of organizations. These rigid and destructive rules become the credo by which members of the system attempt to live their lives. It is also through these rules that their partners, children, and others who come in contact with them begin to take on the shame themselves. These rules are passed on through what is said and how people act.

Think about the following rules and decide which ones fit for you considering the way you were raised and the way you currently view and treat yourself and others.

Be in Control

If you are a shame-based person, you have been taught that it is absolutely necessary to remain in charge of all your thoughts, feelings, and behaviors. It also means that you need to be in control of the people around you and the situations in which you find yourself. This intense and all-consuming need to be in control is the cornerstone of a shame-based system. This attempt to control may be motivated by a primitive drive for power over others, but it

(HO)   ©1999 David J. Decker, MA

may also be a desire to achieve some sense of safety and predictability in a frightening and threatening reality. *Overt control* manifests itself in such behaviors as using violence, being demanding, or yelling to impose your will on others. *Covert control*, a more indirect way of getting what you want, involves behaviors such as manipulating, being sarcastic, and creating guilt in others.

Be Perfect

If you are a shame-based person, you have been taught that you must always be correct, do what is right, and never make mistakes. Such rules impose a strict requirement to rigidly comply and live up to a perfectionistic image or facade. It is then expected that this facade will be presented to the outside world as an accurate representation of your own and your family's reality. This image includes an intense fear of acknowledging any problems or difficulties because doing so would admit to others that you are flawed and defective. The need to live behind this facade significantly decreases the ability to be fully human, with all your faults and frailties. A strong organizing principle of this rule is living up to all the stereotyped notions, values, and expectations of the dominant and popular culture. Trying to be perfect creates enormous stress and tension in your life. An example of this would be not taking the risk to learn something new because you were not already competent at doing it.

Blame

If you are a shame-based person, you have been taught that if something does not happen as you think it should, you then need to assess blame, pointing the finger either toward yourself or someone else, and harshly punish the offender. Blame tends to be activated in the system when the control and perfection rules break down, as they always do. The shame-based system focuses on *who* did the misdeed rather than on *how* the situation or issue can be handled or remedied. The need to blame means your perspective is continually split into two parts: the judge and the offender. Every problem is then viewed as an opportunity to reject and condemn yourself or someone else for anything that occurs around you. This leads to viewing and judging yourself and others with constant negativity, contempt, disgust, and cynicism. An example would be screaming at a child who spills her milk rather than getting down with her and showing her how to clean it up.

(HO) ©1999 David J. Decker, MA

Compare

If you are a shame-based person, part of the legacy of blame and fault finding is a tendency to continually compare yourself to everyone around you. Other people become your competition, and you end up translating your own and others' differentness into deficiency. As a result, you either feel inferior and shameful, which occurs most frequently, or you feel superior, condescending, and grandiose. This comparing process is taught to you by both your family and the culture at large. This rule demeans you and others who are not able to live up to the shame-based system's ideal of perfectionism. It also contradicts the idea that you and every other individual are unique and special for your humanness alone and have a right to be that way. This sets up a situation in which you begin to view the world in extremes. Because you have to be perfect, there is only one right way to think, feel, and be. Or there is the wrong way. Situations are good or bad and black or white. Everything is viewed in "all or nothing" terms. No middle ground or "shades of gray" exist to allow for differences in who we are as human beings. An example might be talking to someone at a party, discovering that he lives in an exclusive neighborhood, and then berating yourself for where you live.

Deny

If you are a shame-based person, you were taught early to deny the existence and validity of emotions, especially the negative, uncomfortable, and vulnerable ones in yourself and others. Feelings such as fear, disappointment, hurt, anxiety, and sadness pose a threat to the image you are supposed to present to the outside world. You are also taught to deny your wants and needs so you do not dare ask directly for help, support, love, and nurturance. In a shame-based system, asking directly for anything is just another sign of weakness and imperfection. Finally, you are taught to deny responsibility for yourself because acknowledging mistakes and being accountable for how you think, feel, and act only leads to criticism, punishment, humiliation, and more shame. Thus, rigid and prescribed roles consume your humanness, and your interactions with others become hollow and distant, with little or no place for uniqueness and spontaneity. An example would be denying that you are hurt by a friend's actions because you are afraid he would view you as a "wimp."

(HO) ©1999 David J. Decker, MA

Be Unpredictable

If you are a shame-based person, you have been taught not to expect or provide consistency and constancy in relationships with partners, friends, family members, and others. This can lead to a confusing and frightening roller coaster of dramatic mood swings, unexpected disrespectful or abusive behavior, and emotional overreactivity that causes you and others to abandon repeatedly your emotional connections with no discussion or explanation. These interactions breed an intense and justifiable fear that the possibility of being rejected and discarded always exists. They also trigger frantic attempts to find ways to reconnect so you can experience a sense of belonging, which can lead to codependency. You learn that you cannot count on others unless you live in accordance with the rigid and prescribed ways that they and the shame-based system require. For example, living by this rule might mean sulking and withdrawing affection from your partner for several days when she does something you do not like.

Do Not Resolve

If you are a shame-based person, you were taught to avoid completing interpersonal transactions with others and to avoid any meaningful sense of resolution whenever conflicts arise, as they always do. The strongly communicated message is either to avoid disagreement completely or to engage endlessly in arguments that go nowhere. Thus, issues that were perceived as a crisis the day before may not even be considered a problem in the present because they have been dropped or forgotten by one or most of those involved. Unfortunately, however, these situations are generally not truly forgotten but are merely "shoved under the rug" so they live on, especially in those who are victimized in the system. This process builds a reservoir of resentment and mistrust that only creates greater emotional distance. For example, living by this rule might mean becoming verbally abusive with your partner and then telling yourself the issue is taken care of because you feel less tense as a result of dumping your anger on her.

Do Not Talk

If you are a shame-based person, you were taught that you should never identify and talk openly about disrespectful, shaming, abusive, irresponsible, or compulsive behavior that occurs around you. It also means that you

(HO)

should not talk honestly about what you think, feel, or want, especially if your self-disclosure contradicts the rigid rules of the shame-based system. This idea of maintaining the silence, or keeping the secret, is not based on simply choosing the option of privacy. Rather, it is based on the belief that it is unsafe to talk openly about who you are or about your reactions to what is happening around you. It is also based on the idea that it is hopeless to self-disclose because "it won't do any good anyway." The "no talk" rule, and the misplaced loyalty it generates, is probably the single most hindering factor in overcoming the harmful effects of shame. Honest sharing is needed for healing, growth, and recovery to occur. An example of this rule in an alcoholic family is the "elephant in the living room" (i.e., the alcoholic's drinking and behavior), which everyone knows about but which no one will address directly.

Distort

If you are a shame-based person, you were taught to use distortion to disguise or reframe abusive and compulsive behavior into something more acceptable. Thus, the reality of the shaming event is minimized or denied and shifted to justify or excuse the hurtful actions. The goal in doing this is to assist the shaming person to avoid responsibility for what has actually occurred. This distortion process is used to maintain the status quo in the shame-based system and to avoid positive change that might be triggered by understanding the real meaning of the abusive or compulsive behavior. For example, abuse in a family might be excused by saying, "Your father only hits you because he loves you" or "Your mother only yells at you to help you learn right from wrong." These confusing messages contribute to a "crazy-making" atmosphere and interfere with gaining a true understanding of what healthy and nurturing human relationships really are.

SIGNALS THAT SHAME MAY BE PRESENT

A variety of signals indicate the presence of shame in you or other people. Look through the following lists and check off those that apply to you. Noticing when shame is present allows you to identify and intervene in cognitive, emotional, and behavioral patterns that are maintaining and building more shame in your relationships and in your life.

Nonverbal or Physical Signals

—— Averted or downcast eyes (i.e., frequently looking away from others' faces)
—— Lowering your head around others
—— Blushing
—— Slumped shoulders
—— Frozen face (i.e., rigid and tight features or showing no emotion at all)
—— Frequent crying and tearfulness
—— Sneering at others (i.e., looking contemptuous/disgusted)
—— A mocking or mimicking tone of voice
—— Glare-stare (i.e., a fixed and unbending look used to intimidate)
—— Red-faced with neck veins bulging (i.e., communicating hostility/rage)

Cognitive, Emotional, and Behavioral Signals

Being Abusive to Others

—— Emotional abuse (using nonverbal gestures and expressions to hurt, punish, intimidate, and control others; e.g., sulking, withdrawal of affection, yelling)
—— Verbal abuse (using words to hurt, punish, intimidate, and control others; e.g., name-calling, put-downs, swearing, cursing)
—— Physical abuse (using physical force and actions to hurt, punish, intimidate, and control others; e.g., pushing, grabbing, restraining, slapping, punching)
—— Sexual abuse (any inappropriate verbal messages or physical affection that is forced on someone else; e.g., unwanted sexual comments or touching; coercing sexual activity that is uncomfortable for the other person)

(HO)   ©1999 David J. Decker, MA

Compulsive and Addictive Behaviors

These behaviors manifest when you form a primary relationship with a substance or activity that interferes with the rest of your life, such as the following:

____ Chemical abuse (e.g., alcohol and drugs, including nicotine and caffeine)
Compulsive behaviors related to food (overeating, bulimia, anorexia)
____ Workaholism (focusing on work to the detriment of your relationship with your partner or family)
____ Sexual acting out (compulsive masturbation, extramarital affairs, casual sexual encounters with strangers of the same or opposite sex, contact with prostitutes, voyeurism, exhibitionism)
____ Spending and saving compulsions (shopping, gambling, shoplifting, hoarding)

Other Signals

____ Depression (low self-esteem; continual self-doubt; feeling worthless, inadequate, and defective; having thoughts about being helpless, hopeless, and powerless; generally believing that you are a bad person who is doing bad things)
____ Anxiety (feeling nervous, agitated, fearful, timid, insecure, panicky, and apprehensive much of the time)
____ Rage and explosive anger (feeling irritable, hostile, cynical, and vengeful)
____ Intimidating and threatening behavior ("getting in someone's face")
Isolation (avoiding others) and loneliness
____ Controlling attitudes and behaviors that lead to attempts to dominate others
____ "All or nothing"/"right or wrong"/"good or bad" thinking that leaves no room for negotiation and compromise
____ Power struggles and difficulty resolving conflict (arising from defensiveness, argumentativeness, rigidity, and an unwillingness to compromise)
____ Perfectionistic attitudes and behaviors (believing that you or others need to excel at everything you do and viewing yourself and others as failures whenever this standard is not met)

(HO)   ©1999 David J. Decker, MA

—— Self-righteousness, grandiosity, and contempt for others (thinking that you are better than other people and entitled to special treatment), which includes prejudice and bigotry

—— Preoccupation with your image, how you present yourself to others, and appearances

—— Powerful and unrealistic fears about being abandoned by those close to you

—— People-pleasing attitudes and behaviors that lead to an overdependency on others and the belief that you need to protect those around you (having a strong desire to get others' approval, good will, and affection at any cost and focusing primarily on others and their wants and needs rather than on your own)

—— Great difficulty talking honestly about your thoughts and feelings and intense fears about being close and intimate with others (withholding important parts of who you are to avoid rejection)

—— Unwillingness to take responsibility for your thoughts, feelings, wants, needs, and actions

—— Fear about standing up for and asserting yourself with other people

—— Developing and using sneaky and manipulative ways to get what you want and to get others to take care of you (trying to "guilt" or "shame" others into being who you want them to be and doing what you want them to do)

—— Taking on too much responsibility for everything that happens around you and then experiencing despair when situations do not work out as you had hoped

—— Extreme ongoing mood swings, suggesting that indecision about how you feel means that you are unable to provide consistency in your relationships with those around you

(HO)   ©1999 David J. Decker, MA

POTENTIAL EFFECTS OF COMING
FROM A SHAME-BASED FAMILY

If you grew up in a family in which you needed to abide by the rules of a shame-based system, the effects on you and your life can be debilitating and devastating. This does not mean, however, that you cannot change the ways that these messages currently affect you. The following are some of the possible effects that can arise from being raised in a family in which you were shamed and not allowed to be the person you actually are. Read through these and look for the specific ways that you may have been affected by your childhood experience in your family.

- You actively take on shame from your parents and your family of origin and maintain it in your thought and behavior patterns in the present.
- You become a delegate of the family system and find or create other shame-based systems in your own life (to preserve your loyalty to your shaming family).
- Your thoughts, emotions, and wants that were shamed in your family of origin frequently trigger shame and other intense emotional reactions (e.g., explosive anger, rage) for you as an adult in the present.
- You allow the shame to spread and grow so that it takes on a life of its own, and you no longer even need an actual activating situation in the present to experience your shame.
- You hear shaming messages in relationships, at school, at work, and other areas of your life even when others do not intend to be shaming.
- You stunt your emotional development and never quite feel that you have grown up, matured, and become an adult.
- You live in spiritual deprivation (shame and a higher power cannot coexist) and have little or no belief that you are part of and connected to a larger universe.
- You become a partial person by cutting off important parts of who you are as a human being (e.g., your spontaneous, playful, and emotional inner child).
- You allow your negative or shadow side (i.e., what you do not like to admit to yourself or others about who you really are inside) to control you and how you react to others because you are unwilling to acknowledge and address this aspect of your character in a direct and straightforward manner.
- You experience intense fear, anxiety, and dread that you attempt to lessen by trying to control and manipulate others.

(HO)   ©1999 David J. Decker, MA

- You have a distorted sense of appropriate boundaries, with a tendency to violate others' boundaries and to allow others to violate yours.
- You frequently live in loneliness and isolation, no matter how you present yourself to others.
- You experience an intense fear about being abandoned or rejected (e.g., you may often say to yourself, "If others know or find out who I really am, they'll leave").
- You become self-absorbed, self-critical, and self-destructive in an attempt to hide your humanness.
- You attempt to suppress your anger, which is then expressed either by being abusive and punishing, by being passive-aggressive and manipulative, or by being passive and turning it inward on yourself.
- You become ashamed about the shame you experience and angry and contemptuous toward yourself (e.g., this creates self-hatred, the ultimate in self-initiated shame).
- You believe that your thoughts, feelings, fantasies, and behaviors actually prove your defectiveness, worthlessness, and unlovability (i.e., the idea that there is something intrinsically wrong with you), and you are unwilling to share these parts of who you are with others.
- You refuse to take healthy responsibility for yourself, your mistakes, and your problems (e.g., "It's either all my fault or I have no responsibility for anything").
- You attempt to completely avoid legitimate pain and suffering in your life (at any personal and relationship-oriented cost to you) and consequently lapse into self-pity and feelings of victimization, powerlessness, and hopelessness.
- You often believe that you are out of control and that things in your life just happen.
- You never fully accept positives or compliments about yourself from others (i.e., saying to yourself, "If they only knew they wouldn't tell me that") and are unwilling to give yourself credit for what you do accomplish in your life.
- You never allow yourself to feel satisfied, contented, and fulfilled by others' meeting your needs, saying to yourself, "It doesn't count because they don't really know who I am, and if they did, they wouldn't have been willing to help or be there for me."
- You struggle with disbelief and mistrust when you do begin to make healthy and positive changes in your life by saying to yourself that the changes "are not real" or "will not last."

EMPOWERMENT

An important step in moving beyond your shame is to understand what empowerment is and how you can decide to make empowerment an integral part of your life.

Empowerment is a way of looking at yourself and the world and a way of living based on respect (for yourself and others), conscious decision making, accountability, optimism, and proactivity that is closely connected to a more positive and affirming thought process. Empowerment allows you to take healthy responsibility for your thoughts, feelings, and behaviors (including those which hurt others) and promotes self-esteem, self-confidence, self-respect, and the potential for personal growth and intimacy. You are the person who is responsible for empowering yourself in your adult life.

The following chart clearly distinguishes the important differences between shame-based and empowerment-based ways of viewing yourself and the world around you. Look at the lists and see where you fit.

Shame-Based System	**Empowerment-Based System**
• Attacks and condemns you as a person (which leads to negative painful feelings *about the self*)	• Evaluates and assesses your behavior (which may, at times, lead to negative painful feelings *about your actions*)
• Presumes that you are bad/worthless/inadequate/defective/unlovable	• Presumes that you are human, that you have "flaws" and problems, and that you will make mistakes at times
• Presumes that you are not responsible for your feelings and actions through the use of psychological defenses such as blaming, denial, minimizing, and justifying	• Presumes that you are responsible for your thoughts, feelings, and actions *(and your inaction!)*
• Based on a system of perfectionism that breeds isolation, despair, fear, discouragement, and, ultimately, more shame	• Based on a system of accountability that leads to personal growth and a respect for your own and others' rights

©1999 David J. Decker, MA

Shame-Based System	Empowerment-Based System
• An external locus of control leads to continually seeking outside approval and validation and often to feeling powerless, helpless, victimized, and out of control	• An internal locus of control leads to a belief that you are in charge of yourself and have the ability to see options and make conscious and healthy choices in your life
• Attacks uniqueness (you have to be the same as others and do what is expected of you)	• Affirms uniqueness (that you have the right to be different and to be your own person)
• Leads to increasing rigidity, the development of an image or a facade, and an intense desire to control others	• Leads to compassion and empathy for yourself and others, increased flexibility, and a deepening and modification of values learned as a child
• No possibility of repairing the damage done to others, and relationships are always "in jeopardy," leading to a profound sense of terror, loneliness, and alienation	• Leads to amends, remedies, conflict resolution, forgiveness, intimacy, and enhancement of your relationships with others
• Tendency to be reactive toward the world around you	• Tendency to be proactive in the world around you
• The purpose of shame is to avoid change, to judge and punish yourself and others, and to perpetuate the shame cycle.	• The purpose of enpowerment is to produce change and growth in yourself and those around you.
• The shame-based system screams out, "I am bad and rotten and will never be okay."	• The empowerment-based system states clearly and assertively, "I am a worthwhile human being, even when I have problems and make mistakes.

CYCLES OF SHAME AND EMPOWERMENT

Figure 1 clearly illustrates the path that both shame and empowerment follow in playing themselves out in your life. What you say to yourself, your self-talk throughout these processes, determines whether you end up on the cycle of shame or on the cycle of empowerment.

In the *cycle of shame,* either an activating situation occurs around you or you become involved in behaving in a compulsive, abusive, or irresponsible manner. Your immediate reaction and the unhealthy choice that you make at that point is to lapse into a despairing and hopeless thought process. Once you begin to view yourself as bad, defective, inadequate, and unlovable, you end up feeling raw and unabated terror that arises from the belief that you are powerless and immobilized and unable to improve the situation. No one is strong enough to survive this intense fear for very long, and you quickly try to mask your emotional pain with the psychological defenses that you have learned to use.

Unfortunately, this works only temporarily and, in the end, creates more fear that your defensive masks will be ripped away, exposing to the world the sense of worthlessness you feel. As this fear rises, stress, tension, and pressure build in your life and you set yourself up once again to act out in an irresponsible or compulsive manner or you leave yourself more vulnerable to another activating situation from outside. At this point, you once again dip into your shame and negative self-talk. This process, sadly enough, continues in this cyclical fashion until you are trapped in the "empty void" of your consciousness, where there is no light, no energy, and no hope.

The *cycle of empowerment* offers a very different path, however. In this cycle, that same activating situation or compulsive behavior can occur, but you respond very differently. Feeling empowered involves positive self-talk and a deeply felt belief that you have a right to be human and that you do not have to be perfect and "on top of things" at all times. It means that you are still worthwhile even if you make mistakes. This leads to an enormous lessening of tension that is inherent in the situation and to a sense of relief, self-respect, and self-confidence.

You then begin to clearly identify your own and others' unhealthy behaviors and patterns and to see your real choices and alternatives in any given situation. This further gives you the opportunity to care for yourself in a healthy and responsible way by intervening in your dysfunctional patterns, responding more effectively to others' unhealthy actions, and actually making

(HO)   ©1999 David J. Decker, MA

Figure 1. The Cycles of Shame and Empowerment

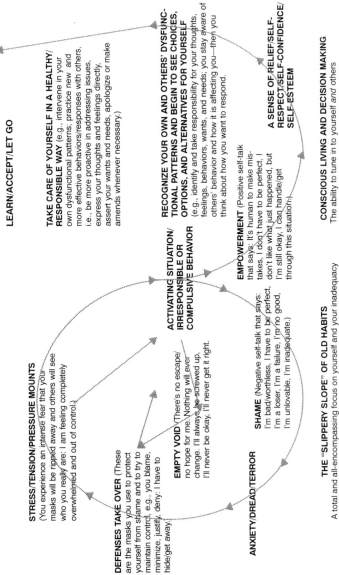

and following through with choices to use new and more effective behaviors and responses. You then consciously move away from the possibility of continually setting yourself up for the same activating situations and unhealthy behaviors that have been problems for you in the past. This process also allows you to learn from the past, to accept yourself and issues that arise in your life in an ongoing way, and to let go of problems and issues when you need to do so. The end result is dramatically different from the cycle of shame, as you open the door to a life of growth, satisfaction, and fulfillment.

The following example illustrates both cycles at work in a real-life situation (thoughts are in italics):

Activating Situation: Yelling and swearing at your children about their toys being strewn all over the house when you return home after a stressful day at work.

Shame. Negative self-talk: *I'm a lousy parent and a jerk!*

Terror. *I'll never learn how to be a good parent and my kids will always be afraid of me and hate me.*

Defenses. *What I did to them wasn't that big a deal. They'll get over it.* (Minimizing) *Anyway, if they weren't such brats, I wouldn't have had to yell.* (Blaming)

Pressure. *I can't stand it when they act so scared and stay away from me. They don't have the right to treat me this way. They'd better come around and be friendly or else!* (Feeling alone, scared, and disconnected)

More Abuse. *Damn you ungrateful kids. You don't get to watch TV tonight because of your lousy moods. I don't have to put up with your bullshit!*

↓

Empty Void. *Now they'll hate me even more. It'll never be any different. There's no hope for me. Nothing will ever get any better. I'll never be a good parent.* (More and more shame; less and less self-esteem, self-confidence, and self-respect; no potential for growth)

Empowerment. Positive self-talk: *I don't like what I just did. I really made a mistake. I'm overreacting and not letting the kids be kids.*

Relief. *I have the confidence and ability to figure out what to do differently.*

Recognition. *What I should do is apologize to the kids and let them know it wasn't their fault. I also need to be more aware of how frustrated I feel when I get home from work, and do something different to relax before I deal with them.* (Seeing different options)

Take Care of Self. *Kids, I'm sorry that I was so mean when I got home today. It didn't have anything to do with you. It was stuff that was bothering me from work. I'm going to start taking a walk after a bad day before I come home.* (Making amends, taking responsibility for himself, and identifying new behaviors to deal with the same situation in the future)

Learn/Let Go. *I need to be more careful in the future about this situation but I feel good about how I handled it with the kids and what I'll do different next time.* (Learning from and giving himself credit and forgiving himself for the mistake he made, which leads to higher self-esteem and more self-respect and greater potential for future change and growth)

(HO)

DEFENSES

Any time shame and emotional pain are triggered within you, you have the potential to tap into your psychological defenses. Everyone uses defenses, at times, to protect themselves from internal and external life stresses and the uncomfortable feelings that these stresses can create. Defenses can temporarily help you to avoid feeling shame and other emotions, such as guilt, anger, sadness, hurt, fear, disappointment, confusion, and anxiety. They can also assist you in coping with changes in your life that are difficult and demanding. They become a problem, however, when they begin to "run the show" in your day-to-day living.

Defenses develop in childhood, generally in your family of origin, to help you cope with painful feelings that were too difficult or overwhelming to experience at that time. Unfortunately, although defenses were necessary to help you survive as a child, we often continue to use them in adulthood without much awareness of their impact on ourselves and others. When, as an adult, you subconsciously use these defenses, you often end up distorting or denying the reality around you and creating distance from others that prevents intimacy and a sense of connectedness. It also sets up a situation in which you are more likely to make the choice to be controlling, abusive, or violent. This keeps you stuck in your shame in the present and leaves you unable to change and grow as a human being.

You will never be able to eliminate all your defenses, nor would this be a good idea. Defenses can still be useful, on occasion, to help you get through tough times. The reality is that defenses can help you or hurt you, depending on how, when, and how often you use them. The challenge is to learn to identify the defenses you use and to become more aware of when you are using them so you can make conscious and healthy decisions about whether you wish or need to use them in a particular situation.

The following list presents common defenses that many people use. Read through the list and try to identify the ones you use most often. In addition, attempt to think of others you may use that are not included.

1. *Denial:* Completely refusing to acknowledge that something exists (e.g., "I don't have any problems" or "What I do to you isn't abusive")
2. *Minimizing:* Making something less than it really is (e.g., "It's really not that big a deal" or "Why do you have to exaggerate everything?")
3. *Blaming:* Placing responsibility on others for your thoughts, feelings, and actions (e.g., "If you wouldn't have said what you did, I wouldn't have called you a jerk")

(HO)　　　　　　　　　　　　　　　　　©1999 David J. Decker, MA

4. *Forgetting:* Not remembering something as a means to avoid taking responsibility for yourself and your behavior (e.g., "I don't recall saying that when we were fighting last night")

5. *Intellectualization/Staying in your head:* Attempting to logically understand and analyze everything that you and others do instead of acknowledging, expressing, and experiencing your emotions as they arise (e.g., "I think you're always acting that way because your parents weren't there for you when you were a kid" rather than telling the other person that you were hurt by what they did)

6. *Justifying:* Offering reasons and making excuses for your behavior (e.g., "I only did that because there's too much pressure on me [because I drank too much]"

7. *People pleasing:* Acting the way you think others want you to act to avoid hurting them, to avoid conflict, or to avoid your own uncomfortable feelings (e.g., always being nice to your relatives so that you do not "make waves" or "rock the boat")

8. *Looking good:* Putting up a front or presenting an image that everything is okay all the time (e.g., playing a happy-go-lucky and upbeat role with everyone)

9. *Compliance:* Acting as if you agree when you really do not; going through the motions to avoid possible confrontation or uncomfortable feelings (e.g., agreeing even when you really do not so you can "get someone off your back")

10. *Stuffing:* Pushing the truth out of your conscious awareness either intentionally or unwittingly (e.g., "I'm not feeling anything right now" when you really are experiencing anger or hurt)

11. *Dishonesty:* Lying to others but knowing the truth yourself (e.g., "I didn't do that" even when you know that you did)

12. *Avoidance:* Changing the subject or being unwilling to respond directly to what someone is saying to you (e.g., trying to distract your partner from talking about your relationship by focusing on your children and their problems)

13. *Escape:* Running away from your thoughts and feelings and the issues you need to address by becoming overinvolved with an activity that absorbs your time and energy (e.g., abusing chemicals, watching TV continually, compulsively eating, working all the time)

14. *Withdrawal:* Turning your attention inside yourself when someone is trying to connect with you (e.g., pouting, sulking, closing down, shutting off)

(HO)

15. *Isolation:* Avoiding contact with other people when you need to reach out to take care of yourself (e.g., not calling friends to talk and get support when you feel angry or depressed)

16. *Humor:* Smiling, laughing, or joking around when you feel uncomfortable or unhappy with something that is happening (e.g., grinning and chuckling when you talk about a painful life experience)

17. *Sarcasm:* Devious, ambiguous, and hostile joking at someone else's expense when that person has said or done something you do not like to avoid confronting their behavior directly (e.g., "You're *really* a winner!" [tone of voice and other nonverbals are important in being sarcastic])

18. *Defiance:* Purposely or unconsciously rebelling against others to avoid taking responsibility for yourself and the decisions you make (e.g., actively or passively resisting others' perceptions, suggestions, or ideas because you do not want anyone telling you what to do)

19. *Intimidation:* Yelling, raging on, bullying, and threatening to keep others from presenting you with their thoughts, feelings, and ideas (e.g., "You'd better shut up or I'll really go off")

20. *Projection:* Attributing to someone else exactly the same thoughts, feelings, wants, and needs that you would have in a situation (e.g., if you feel hurt or angry about something, you assume that everyone else should feel hurt or angry about it as well)

21. *Scapegoating:* Displacing and taking your feelings out on someone else because it is too difficult to confront the original person involved (e.g., dumping anger you feel toward your boss on your partner or children)

22. *Playing the victim:* Not taking responsibility for yourself by falling back on the notion that you are helpless and powerless and that everything has been (or is being) done to you by others or caused by the world around you (e.g., frequently becoming sad/tearful as a way to connect with, gain sympathy from, and control others; being self-pitying; acting out the "poor me" stance)

23. *Being driven:* Continually pushing yourself to stay busy or constantly striving, in a perfectionistic and compulsive way, to be the best at everything you do (e.g., feeling the need to always be productive; to get all As in school, to be a sports superstar, or to continually make more and more money or acquire more and more things)

(HO) ©1999 David J. Decker, MA

MOVING TOWARD EMPOWERMENT

The path to overcoming your shame and becoming empowered involves a lifelong commitment to working at and practicing a variety of skills and strategies that can lead you from abusive and controlling attitudes and behaviors to personal growth and a sense of fulfillment. The following suggestions form a blueprint that you can use to change your shame-based thoughts and actions that contribute to your abuse and control. Remember, however, that the change process is a slow one, and do not expect too much of yourself all at once.

1. Begin to clearly understand what shame is and how it differs from empowerment. Empowerment involves a healthier lifestyle based on acknowledging and accepting your humanness (including your short-comings) and taking full and complete responsibility for yourself and your actions.

2. Stop doing the behaviors that maintain and perpetuate your shame in the present. These can include your emotional, verbal, sexual, and physical abuse of others; your alcohol or drug abuse; your worka-holism; and so forth. *Start making conscious choices and decisions* that allow you to interrupt the self-destructive and self-defeating thought and behavior patterns that trigger and reinforce your shame today (i.e., your maintained shame). If these behaviors continue, you will make little or no real progress in uncovering the shame that originated earlier in your life.

3. Accept that your shame is an important part of who you have been. Search for the thoughts, feelings, wants, and needs that you had to deny as a child and that the shame has been, and is, hiding from your consciousness. Shame is always a "cover-up" that keeps us from our humanity.

4. Begin to understand your attachment to your shame in the present. Identify the payoffs and benefits you have received by maintaining the shame in your current life. These could include not having to take responsibility for yourself, protecting yourself from being hurt in relationships, avoiding intimacy with others, and not having to take risks to change and grow.

5. Identify and talk or write about the original sources of your shame. These are most often found in your family of origin and childhood but may also be found in your adult life. Be clear about some of your significant "governing scenes" (i.e., specific times when you were

shamed, neglected, or abused by others). Translate the shame you felt in those situations into emotional pain. Allow yourself to get in touch with the feelings you had to suppress and deny to get through those experiences.

6. Develop and use an emotional support system to re-build the interpersonal bridge that was destroyed when your trust was violated. With these nurturing people, allow yourself to feel safe enough to express the emotions and the pain from your past. This must occur for you to let go of the burden you have carried alone all these years. This process can happen in support groups, with friends, with a partner, with parents or siblings (if they are helpful), with clergy, or with a therapist. Self-disclosure is a critical part of healing. You need to start talking with others if the shame is to have less power in your day-to-day living.

7. In addition, try to actively work at rewriting the scripts (e.g., through journaling or visualization) of your old governing scenes so that you and the others in these incidents respond in a different fashion. This can help you to experience some healing of the original wounds and some renewed strength and self-confidence in the present. You may also decide to directly confront the people who hurt or shamed you and created the original wounds. This can be done face to face, in a letter, through a role-play, at a gravesite, or in other ways. This confrontation ritual is an important part of recovery. Finally, work at forgiving others who have shamed and harmed you. Forgiving does not mean forgetting. However, it does mean taking back the loving, caring, and compassionate part of yourself and letting go of the compulsion to hurt, punish, and reject others. The desire to get back at others only keeps you stuck and burdened and gives that other person power over you in your current life.

8. Work hard to acknowledge and reclaim the previously disowned parts of who you are. These include the spontaneous, playful, and wounded small child inside you who was not allowed to be a child in your shaming family of origin. It also includes accepting your "shadow side," the negative and hidden aspects of your character, such as your temper and your desire to control or punish others. This process can serve as a means to openly and honestly recognize and accept who you are as a total person with all your flaws and shortcomings. You will not be able to change anything about yourself until you acknowledge and recognize these as part of who you are and who you have been.

Also, if necessary, forgive yourself for not being able to stand up for and care for yourself as a child. Many people experience intense anger toward themselves about this and it adds to their negative and shaming self-talk in the present.

9. Slow down your day-to-day internal process and become more conscious of your patterns of responding to the world around you. This means stopping on a regular basis, in a gentle and nurturing way, to observe your inner workings and your reactions to others.

10. Begin to replace your self-abusive inner dialogue (i.e., your negative, despairing, blaming, cynical, vindictive, and self-defeating self-talk) with more affirming thoughts about yourself and others. Shift from a shame-based to an empowerment-based system by recognizing that some of your attitudes and behaviors may need to change but that you, as a person, are still worthwhile, adequate, competent, valuable, and lovable. You may want to write out affirmations and say them to yourself during the course of the day, for example, "I'm a good and worthwhile person." This is also a time to tap into nurturing voices from the past and present (e.g., teachers, relatives, friends, therapists) and focus on what they might say to you when you are becoming negative or when you say or do things that you regret.

11. Be in tune with and learn to trust the emotions that you experience, and develop your intuition about what feels okay and "not okay" for you in your daily life. If you grew up in a shame-based family, you were not taught to trust this part of who you are.

12. Actively and consciously choose to be vulnerable and to share your feelings in an ongoing and spontaneous way with other people you can trust. Recovering from shame is an interpersonal process, as was developing your shame originally, and cannot be done by you alone or simply through solitary activities such as journaling or prayer. You need other people to listen to you and to be involved with your healing and recovery.

13. Learn to become more assertive with others whenever the need arises:
    a. Identify and assert your thoughts, feelings, wants, and needs without the expectation that others will necessarily do what you think they should do.
    b. Seek approval, attention, support, and assistance directly; take the risk to ask for what you want or need from others; and appreciate what others are willing to give even if it is not exactly what you expect.

(HO) ©1999 David J. Decker, MA

c. Learn and put into practice the difference between your anger strategies (i.e., setting limits and maintaining healthy boundaries) and your abusive behavior (i.e., seeking to hurt, punish, intimidate, or control others).

14. Spend time with people who accept and are supportive of your recovery process and make the conscious assumption that these people can be trusted and do have positive and caring intentions toward you. Let go of the idea that everyone around you is an enemy or adversary. At the same time, spend less time with, or avoid completely, people who continue to be harsh, shaming, disrespectful, and abusive with you.

15. Identify and begin to intervene in your other more subtle controlling, self-destructive, manipulative, and self-defeating behaviors. Take time to identify and assert more conscious control over the psychological defenses (e.g., blaming, justifying, minimizing, denial) that you use to avoid your feelings, self-responsibility, and intimacy with others.

16. Learn to take charge of how you react to and behave in everyday interactions by making conscious choices rather than falling back on the idea that things just happen. Acknowledge to yourself that you are continually making choices. Be proactive rather than reactive by noticing when you feel powerless and victimized and developing the skills to assess the reality with the situation and to tap into your personal power to handle problems and issues that arise. Start to confront your fears and take emotional and behavioral risks in your day-to-day life. Learn to prepare, in a positive way, to handle situations that may be difficult. Start to directly confront those who are shaming and punishing with you in the present and remove yourself from unhealthy situations whenever necessary.

17. Take back your power to be who you really are instead of feeling shameful, hopeless, and powerless. This means acknowledging responsibility for your thoughts, feelings, needs, wants, and actions (*and for your inaction*, which is also a choice you make). Do this both in past situations and in your current life and make amends and apologize to others whenever possible if you feel a need to do so. This can be done in a variety of ways (e.g., face to face; in a letter; through role-play). Begin to view your past and present mistakes as part of your being human and as opportunities to learn and grow rather than as an indictment of who you are as a person. Talk about the secrets in your own life that you thought you needed to keep from others to be okay (e.g., being abusive, getting divorced, being fired, having to file bankruptcy). Do not continue to carry burdens from the past. Be sure

to forgive yourself for how you have hurt others. In addition, forgive yourself for being unable to handle everything that your shame-based part thinks you should have.

18. Consciously monitor your ongoing interactions and thought and behavior patterns. Stay alert for situations, issues, people, and self-talk that trigger feelings from old shaming scenes in the past and create shame within you in the present. This can often occur even when the other person in your current life is not even intending to shame you.

19. Watch out for feeling shameful about continuing to experience your shame at times. Avoid thinking that you should be perfect and able to eliminate all the shame in your life. Instead, use your shame as a warning signal that something important is happening around or within you at a particular time. Look for what you can learn from your shame when it arises.

20. Get in touch with and work to develop your spirituality and use prayer and meditation regularly in your daily life to create a peaceful space within yourself where you can feel centered, grounded, and part of a larger universe.

21. Cultivate ongoing ways to nurture and care for yourself:
    a. Stay busy and involved with activities that are fulfilling and satisfying to you.
    b. Notice and intervene in your internal comparisons of yourself to others.
    c. Separate your worth and adequacy, in a healthy way, from what happens in the outside world.
    d. Focus on your positive experiences and feelings and store them in your consciousness. Take time to think about and express your gratitude about who you are and what you have.
    e. Affirm yourself from within and give yourself credit when you have done something well.
    f. Build tangible rewards into your life on a regular basis.
    g. Reach out to others at times and offer assistance to those less fortunate than you to make the world a better place.
    h. Develop and use a warm and affirming sense of humor with yourself and others, and learn to laugh, in a nonshaming way, at your own and others' foibles and idiosyncrasies.
    i. Be patient, gentle, and forgiving with yourself and others and learn to like and accept yourself and the people you choose to have around you.

(HO)

Unit 6: Culture of Origin

MALE SOCIALIZATION

Frequently, our culture sends very strong messages to men about what it means to be a "real man." Using abuse and violence with intimates and others is often a part of the images men receive from television, movies, advertising, and institutions such as the military and corporate America. Use the following outline as a guide to address the male acculturation process.

1. Brainstorm stereotypical/traditional notions of what it means to be a man in our culture (e.g., traits, roles, adjectives, descriptors).
2. Think about male heroes/images from comic books, television, literature, or movies in your childhood and the present (e.g., Superman, Lone Ranger, Marlboro Man, Sylvester Stallone [*Rambo*], Clint Eastwood [*Dirty Harry*], Steven Seagal and Chuck Norris [karate movies], Bruce Willis [*Die Hard*]).
3. Think about men in your life who come closest to living up to the male stereotype/ideal/image and with whom you have had personal contact or whom you know:
   a. How do/did you like him?
   b. What is/was it like and how do/did you feel being around him?
4. Discuss the destructive impact of traditional male roles for men:
   a. Shorter life span (e.g., heart attacks)
   b. Physical/medical problems related to stress (e.g., ulcers, headaches)
   c. Lack of intimacy/closeness with partner, children, extended family, and others
   d. Obsessive desire to work/produce/make money/accumulate "things" that leaves little time for personal growth or introspection ("human doing" versus "human being")
5. Brainstorm stereotypical/traditional notions of what it means to be a woman in our culture (e.g., traits, roles, adjectives, descriptors).

(HO)   ©1999 David J. Decker, MA

355

6. Identify some men in your life who come closest to combining the positive male and female characteristics and with whom you have had personal contact or whom you know personally:
   a. How do/did you like them?
   b. What is/was it like and how do/did you feel being around them?
7. Think about and discuss the idea of combining the best from both the male and female sides and becoming androgynous rather than remaining stuck in the traditional male norms/roles about who we have to be. What would that be like for you?
8. What are the positives or advantages related to being a nontraditional male? What are the drawbacks or disadvantages?

CONTROL

The desire to control what happens around us in our lives is a natural part of being human, often motivated by a drive for safety and predictability. Control does have healthy aspects, captured best by the description of being in control of oneself (see "Self-Control" in this handout) and examples such as the importance of providing guidance to children as they grow and the need for a supervisor to have some control over his or her employees.

Unfortunately, if you were raised in a shame-based family with rigidly defined roles for you and others, you may have assumed some of the unhealthy aspects related to control. When control becomes an intense and all-consuming desire to force change in a person or situation, it becomes a problem that often leads to manipulative, disrespectful, abusive, and intimidating behavior.

Being controlling generally refers to trying to control others. As men, we are often taught by our family of origin and the larger culture that we are supposed to take charge of what happens around us. However, overcontrol of others is a prison for both the controller and the person being controlled because each person's options and choices are significantly limited. Overcontrol is often, at least in part, about fear: You may be saying to yourself, "What will happen?" or "Things will really fall apart if I don't continue to stay in control." Paradoxically, the more we try to control people and things outside ourselves, the more out of control, powerless, and frustrated we feel in our lives, which often leads to more and stronger attempts to control others. Trying to control other people and their behavior may work in the short term but it just does not work on a longer-term basis. The only person you can control is yourself.

In addition, when we become overcontrolling with ourselves or allow others to completely control us (see the following sections, "Overcontrol of Self" and "Lack of Self-Control"), we end up suffering emotionally as well. Read through the following lists and determine where you fit concerning the issue of control.

Overcontrol of Others

- Having low self-esteem
- Expecting and demanding that others do what you want them to do and be who you want them to be
- Being aggressive and invading others' space and boundaries
- Forcing unwanted advice on others
- Being closed-minded and unwilling to see things from others' perspectives

(HO) ©1999 David J. Decker, MA

- Interrupting and speaking for others
- Attempting to be "one up" and dominant
- Not knowing or caring about how you affect others
- Manipulating and being passive-aggressive to get what you desire
- Playing the victim and acting helpless, hopeless, and powerless to get your way
- Playing the martyr and using guilt and self-righteousness to get what you want
- Using bribes
- Shaming or discounting others
- Threatening and intimidating others
- Using economic control (withholding money, making all the financial decisions)
- Trying to isolate others
- Being critical and judgmental
- Being condescending and "holier-than-thou"
- Using male entitlement (believing that you should make the important decisions in your relationship because you, as a man, are more competent and capable than your partner)
- Using physical and sexual abuse

Overcontrol of Self

- Having low self-esteem
- Feeling tense and anxious much of the time
- Having rigid and inflexible personal boundaries
- Being tight/constrained/careful in how you present yourself and interact with others
- Avoiding spontaneity and playfulness
- Being fearful about making mistakes, being judged or criticized, and appearing stupid
- Being obsessive and compulsive (e.g., regarding neatness, cleanliness)
- Acting overly serious/somber
- Being unwilling to take risks and overconcerned with failure
- Being perfectionistic
- Being untrusting, guarded, and unwilling to self-disclose and to be vulnerable

Lack of Self-Control

- Having low self-esteem
- Feeling worthless and shameful

(HO)   ©1999 David J. Decker, MA

- Lacking self-knowledge (e.g., about your feelings/wants/needs) and self-confidence
- Having difficulty identifying and articulating your values, beliefs, and personal goals
- Feeling adrift and having no life focus
- Being easily influenced and controlled by others
- Having little self-discipline (e.g., little structure/routine)
- Having few clear boundaries (e.g., regarding your body, time, space, and commitments)
- Being passive and unwilling to set limits with others
- Acting helpless and hopeless
- Stuffing anger, resentment, and other feelings until they come out in self-destructive ways
- Being people pleasing
- Allowing others to define and direct you
- Being driven by guilt, shame, and others' expectations of you

Self-Control

- Having high self-esteem
- Knowing yourself and feeling self-confident and self-assured
- Having personal goals and dreams and actively pursuing them
- Knowing and living your beliefs and values
- Being willing to take personal risks
- Maintaining a healthy discipline in your life
- Providing yourself with structure and routine
- Having and maintaining clear boundaries (e.g., about your body, your time, your space, and your commitments)
- Acknowledging and respecting others' boundaries (including listening)
- Feeling empathy and caring for others
- Being accepting of differences in others
- Allowing yourself to experience all your feelings
- Expressing your feelings respectfully and appropriately
- Being assertive with your thoughts, ideas, opinions, wants, and needs
- Offering guidance and wisdom to others *without the expectation* that they will necessarily follow your advice
- Understanding what intimacy is and having intimacy in your relationships
- Being able to trust others and to be vulnerable in appropriate situations

(HO) ©1999 David J. Decker, MA

TYPES OF ABUSIVE BEHAVIOR

Volatile anger and abusive behavior are always destructive in a relationship and always contribute to a loss of trust, respect, and intimacy. They are never helpful in problem solving or conflict resolution. Both men and women can be abusive in relationships. Abusive behavior, as it is defined in this handout, occurs in many relationships at some point. Abuse by either partner is not okay. However, the gender of the person who is abusive can make a significant difference in the ongoing impact of abusive actions, especially when a consistent pattern of abuse exists in the relationship. Although abusive behavior can occur between any two people, in the large majority of cases, men in heterosexual relationships are more able and more likely to use methodical and systematic physical force to maintain control in a relationship. Even when men do experience physical abuse by their partners, they are less likely to feel the intense fear, humiliation, and intimidation or to suffer the severity of physical damage that women do. Because of basic differences in musculature and socialization, women generally cannot compete with men once a physical conflict has begun. Men are, on the whole, more likely to be able to dominate a relationship through the use of physical force than are women.

Moreover, once a man has actually been physically or sexually abusive in a relationship (or if his partner believes that the potential exists for him to do so), other types of abuse have additional impact. For example, emotional and verbal abuse can then become much more frightening and controlling for the female partner. A single act of physical force clearly demonstrates that, if unable to control his partner through verbal and emotional abuse and threats, a man has the potential to up the ante again to physical abuse to maintain his dominance in the relationship. Both the man and his partner know that he has already used violence in the past so it becomes that much easier for him to violate this physical boundary the next time he becomes explosive and threatening. The eight types of abuse commonly seen among men in the program are presented in this handout with examples of each. Read through them and see which of these you have used in relating to your partner.

Male Entitlement

Male entitlement is an attitude that conveys male dominance, a general disrespect for women, and the idea that men are more competent and capable than women. This attitude leads to the belief that "I, as a man, have the right and the responsibility to control how my partner thinks, feels, and acts and to make her into the person I think she should be." This desire to control underlies all abusive behavior and is characterized by the following actions:

(HO)　　　　　　　　　　　　　　　　　©1999 David J. Decker, MA

1. Making generalizations, telling disrespectful jokes, and believing stereo-types about women (e.g., "Women are irrational"; "It's a woman's job to take care of me and the kids")
2. Having the expectation that you will make all the important decisions in the relationship
3. Treating her like a servant (e.g., demanding that she do things for you and expecting her to wait on you; saying to her, "Go get me a drink" or "Get dinner ready")
4. Controlling how household money is handled (e.g., forcing her to account for all the money she spends, withholding money from her, giving her an allowance, acting as if her work around the house and with the children has no economic value to the family and is not as important as your outside job, keeping the checkbook or charge cards in your possession)
5. Believing that you need to be the breadwinner (e.g., discouraging her from going to school or getting employment, sabotaging her job by coming home late when she needs to get to work)
6. Deciding who does what in terms of household chores and parenting
7. Communicating to her or others that she is your property, or that you own her, or that she belongs to you because you are in a relationship or marriage
8. Being possessive and acting extremely jealous (e.g., assuming that she is always "on the make," brooding about or continually bringing up her real or imagined relationships with other men)

Emotional Abuse

Emotional abuse is the use of behavioral or nonverbal methods, such as the following, to hurt, punish, intimidate, or control your partner:

1. Sulking or withdrawing affection from her (e.g., punishing her with silence)
2. Sneering at her and acting disgusted with or contemptuous of her (e.g., dirty looks, rolling your eyes when she is talking)
3. Yelling and screaming at her
4. Staring or glaring at her
5. Following her around the house or apartment to continue an argument whether or not she wishes to do so
6. Standing near or over her and using your size to intimidate her (e.g., "getting in her face")

(HO) ©1999 David J. Decker, MA

7. Monitoring her behavior and doing "detective work" (e.g., following her or having her followed to find out where she is going or who she is spending time with, listening in on her phone conversations or taping her phone calls, calling to see if she is where she says she is going to be)
8. Attempting to control her movements or to isolate her (e.g., trying to keep her away from family and friends by taking her car keys, removing the car battery or disconnecting the distributor cap, preventing her from using the phone, or not giving her phone messages)
9. Interrupting her while she is eating (e.g., finishing a discussion during dinner)
10. Forcing her to stay awake or waking her up (e.g., to resolve an argument)
11. Forcing her to humiliate herself (e.g., making her kneel in front of you)

Verbal Abuse

Verbal abuse is the use of words to hurt, punish, intimidate, or control your partner, including the following behaviors:

1. Criticizing/discounting her thoughts, feelings, opinions, and values (e.g., saying to her "That's a stupid idea" or "You're nuts to feel that way")
2. Mocking her or mimicking what she has said (e.g., in a singsong voice)
3. Lecturing her about what's right or about the way she should be
4. Twisting what she says to make her feel confused, "crazy," and off balance (e.g., manipulating her with lies and contradictions)
5. Making negative/derogatory comments about activities she likes and places she goes
6. Interrupting her
7. Interrogating her (e.g., continually questioning her about where she goes and who she sees)
8. Accusing or blaming her for things that go wrong (e.g., around the house, with finances, with the children, in your relationship)
9. Swearing/cursing at her ("Fuck you"; "Go to hell")
10. Name-calling (e.g., "bitch," "asshole")
11. Insulting, ridiculing, or belittling her or people she cares about (e.g., put-downs about her parenting or calling her friends "losers" or "dykes")
12. Being demanding (e.g., pressuring her verbally to do what you want her to do and be who you want her to be)

(HO)   ©1999 David J. Decker, MA

Threats

Nonphysical Threats

Nonphysical threats communicate (either directly or indirectly) an intention to do something, thereby creating emotional distress, fear, and indecision and increasing your ability to control your partner. This includes threatening to do the following:

1. Withdraw affection or refuse to talk to her
2. Expose personal things she has told you to others (e.g., "Wait until I tell your parents what you just said")
3. File assault charges or get a restraining order against her
4. Take or kidnap the children if she leaves
5. Withhold money
6. Throw her out in the street
7. Go out with other women
8. End the relationship, separate, or divorce

Violent Threats

Violent threats communicate (either directly or indirectly) an intention to do physical harm to your partner, your children, other relatives, friends, pets, yourself, or property, including the following actions:

1. Standing in her way or "cornering" her
2. Throwing objects in her direction or at her
3. Hitting walls or slamming your fist on surfaces (e.g., on countertops or tables)
4. Threatening to hurt pets
5. Making vague statements (e.g., "You're really asking for it," "Go ahead, keep it up," or "Remember the last time you got me pissed off")
6. Making physically intimidating gestures such as holding up a clenched fist in front of her face or raising your arm as if to hit her
7. Making statements about pushing, grabbing, or hitting her (e.g., "I'd like to smash your face right now" or "I really feel like letting you have it")
8. Threatening to be harsh or abusive with the children
9. Driving recklessly when you are angry to frighten her or "make a point"

(HO)   ©1999 David J. Decker, MA

10. Threatening her with an object (e.g., a belt or broom)
11. Playing with or discharging a weapon around her
12. Making direct or veiled threats to kill her, the children, her parents, or others
13. Making direct or veiled threats to hurt or kill yourself (e.g., "I can't go on without you")

Battering/Psychological Abuse

This category can include any or all of the previous four categories. Battering and psychological abuse occur as a result of a consistent and ongoing pattern of abusive behavior by one person in an intimate relationship who is more powerful than his or her partner. They are present when the less powerful partner either feels fearful that violence might occur or has experienced at least one incident of property destruction or physical or sexual abuse by the other partner toward her or others. When the potential for violence exists, or when violence has already occurred in a relationship, verbal and emotional abuse and threats take on added impact. At this point, these behaviors are significantly more likely to create an atmosphere of terror, degradation, and humiliation than would occur in a relationship in which threats or violence have been absent. Many relationships involve some of the abuse types previously noted on an occasional or infrequent basis. However, battering and psychological abuse become part of the relationship dynamic when a man systematically and persistently, through the use of violence, threats, and other abusive and controlling attitudes and behaviors, tries to:

1. undermine a woman's self-esteem, self-confidence, and motivation;
2. create a devastating and debilitating emotional insecurity in her; and
3. render her less capable of caring for and protecting herself and of functioning independently in the future.

Violence Toward Property or Pets

This type of abuse involves destroying property or hurting pets to intimidate or coerce her into doing what you want her to do, including the following actions (these actions can also be perceived as violent threats to those who are around when they are occurring or who see the damage when they return):

(HO)   ©1999 David J. Decker, MA

1. Hitting walls
2. Slamming your fist on surfaces (e.g., desk, countertop, arm of a chair, car dashboard)
3. Throwing or breaking household items
4. Taking, hiding, or destroying her possessions (e.g., favorite pictures, family heirlooms, jewelry)
5. Hitting, kicking, or killing a pet to intimidate or hurt her

Sexual Abuse

Sexual abuse consists of any sexually inappropriate verbal statements, any physical affection or touch forced on another person, or any nonconsensual sexual act, including the following:

1. Telling dirty jokes and making sexually demeaning comments about her or other women around her (e.g., calling her or other women "whores," "sluts," or "frigid")
2. Staring at other women's bodies when you are with her or making sexual comments about other women around her
3. Viewing and treating her or other women like sex objects (e.g., making unwanted or inappropriate sexual comments to her or about her in front of others, expecting or demanding sex from her)
4. Insulting her body (e.g., the size of her breasts/hips) or her love-making ability (e.g., "You make love like a corpse")
5. Insisting that she dress in a certain manner (e.g., in a sexy or prim-and-proper fashion)
6. Touching sexual parts of her body without consent (e.g., grabbing or pinching her breasts or buttocks when she tells you not to do it or when she says that it hurts)
7. Coercing or pressuring her into performing specific sexual behaviors that she does not wish to do (e.g., making her perform oral or anal sex, expecting her to have sex with multiple partners or with your friends)
8. Forcing sex in the following situations:
   • She is sleeping.
   • She is not asked.
   • She is sick or it is damaging to her health.
   • She says "no" or sets a limit (verbally or nonverbally).
   • She is intoxicated and unable to say "no" effectively.
   • She is fearful about the consequences of saying "no."
9. Raping her

(HO) ©1999 David J. Decker, MA

Physical Abuse

Physical abuse is the use of any physical actions or force to control a person or situation (this includes violence perpetrated against yourself), such as the following:

1. Pinching/scratching/biting her
2. Tripping her
3. Ripping her clothing
4. Pulling her hair
5. Bumping into her as you walk by
6. Grabbing/pushing her
7. Wrestling with or restraining her physically
8. Tying her up
9. Throwing her bodily (e.g., on a couch, on the floor, on a bed)
10. Slapping/punching her
11. Choking/strangling her (e.g., putting your hands near or around her throat and squeezing)
12. Using an object or weapon with her (e.g., a broom, belt, knife, or gun)
13. Hitting, hurting, or killing yourself (e.g., punching yourself in the head, attempting suicide)

©1999 David J. Decker, MA

Unit 7: Assertiveness

STYLES OF RELATING TO OTHERS

Learning to be assertive in your day-to-day life is an important part of feeling good about yourself. The first step to becoming more assertive is to clearly understand the difference between being assertive and being aggressive, passive-aggressive, or passive. Read the following definitions and think about how they are different. Also keep in mind that the goal is not necessarily to be assertive in all situations. Sometimes it makes sense to use the other styles. For example, you probably want to be passive when you are stopped by a police officer for speeding. Otherwise, you are likely to create more problems for yourself. You need to develop you own individual style of letting others know who you are and what you want. Use this handout as a way to begin moving in that direction.

Being Aggressive: "I Count; You Don't"

Being aggressive is standing up for yourself and your rights and attaining your goals. But it is doing this at the expense of, and with no consideration for, others' rights, wishes, and feelings. You "run roughshod" over others and no one else matters. In the short term, you may get what you want. But eventually others end up feeling hurt, resentful, and threatened and tend to withdraw from you. Aggression can be emotional, verbal, physical, and/or sexual, and usually involves commands, put-downs, and/or intimidation.

1. The goal of being aggressive is to control and dominate others and to try to appear invulnerable.
2. Examples:
   - You're a jerk!
   - We'll do it my way.
   - If you keep saying that, you're going to get it.
   - I don't care what you want.

(HO) ©1999 David J. Decker, MA

- Don't be so stupid!
- What an idiot!
- Why can't you ever do anything right?

Being Passive-Aggressive:
"I Count; You Don't"

Being passive-aggressive is standing up for yourself and your rights, but it is doing so in a manipulative fashion so that the other person has difficulty knowing what you intend to communicate. It is also an unchanged way to avoid being held accountable for what you are saying or doing. The intention in being passive-aggressive is often to punish others for feelings they have triggered in you by what they have said or done. Being passive-aggressive can involve verbal statements. But it frequently involves behavioral or non-verbal components and is an indirect but powerful way of communicating your thoughts, feelings, and wants without acknowledging them directly.

1. The goal of being passive-aggressive is to get your vengeful message across without taking any responsibility for yourself and your feelings.
2. Examples:
   - Feeling angry that your partner is late for an activity that you enjoy and then looking for an opportunity to get even, by being late for something she enjoys the following week
   - Being sarcastic by saying such things as "I'm sure you *really* know what you're talking about!" or "I guess you must be Ms. Perfect."
   - Feeling hurt that a friend could not get together with you when you wanted to and then not returning his phone calls and not being available to do anything with him for awhile
   - "Forgetting" to do something you agreed to do because you are upset with your partner about another issue
   - Refusing to talk to your partner because you did not like what she did earlier that day
   - Putting off doing something you promised to do because your partner did not do something you wanted her to do

Being Passive: "You Count; I Don't"

Being passive is violating your own rights by being unwilling to express your thoughts, feelings, and wants honestly to other people. It is allowing others to treat you however they wish without taking the risk to

(HO)   ©1999 David J. Decker, MA

challenge them. It is failing to say what you really mean and being fearful about asking for what you really want. It is doing what others want you to do regardless of your own desires. It can also be standing up for yourself, but doing it in such an ineffective way (e.g., with disclaimers such as "I really shouldn't be saying this, but . . .") that others do not take you seriously. When you are consistently passive, you literally train others to take advantage of you. the end result of being passive is submission to everyone around you and both emotional (e.g., depression, anxiety) and physical (e.g., headaches, stomach problems) symptoms.

1. The goal of being passive is to avoid conflict, disagreement, and others' anger and disapproval at any price.
2. Examples:
   - I'll do whatever you'd like.
   - I don't really care whether we go.
   - I'd rather have you decide.
   - Whatever you want is all right with me.
   - It doesn't matter to me.
   - I'm not sure I know what I think about that.
   - Nodding and smiling even when you do not agree with what is being said
   - Becoming quiet and withdrawn because you do not like the way a conversation is going

Being Assertive: "We Both Count" or "I Count and So Do You"

Being assertive is an honest, direct, and respectful expression of your thoughts, feelings, and wants in a manner that takes into account the feelings and rights of others. It means figuring out what your "truth" is and then taking the risk to become vulnerable and share it with others. It is behaving in ways that demonstrate your strength and confidence, standing up for your legitimate personal rights, and giving expression to your own per-spective. It is a means of directly communicating exactly what you want to say in a given situation.

- However, it is doing so *without the expectation that the other person will "back down," agree with you, or do what you want.*

(HO)   ©1999 David J. Decker, MA

The most important part of being assertive is that you have let another person know who you really are and how you experience your world. Being assertive has the potential to build your self-esteem and increases the likelihood that you will experience understanding, trust, emotional connectedness, and intimacy in your relationships with others.

1. The goal of being assertive is clear communication and a desire to allow the other person to know who you really are.
2. Examples:
   - I feel angry about what you just said.
   - I'd like to spend time together tomorrow.
   - I don't like that idea very much.
   - I really appreciate what you just did for me.
   - I'd rather do something else.
   - I felt hurt about what happened last night.
   - I would prefer to go to a different restaurant.
   - I'm not comfortable with you yelling at me.

AGGRESSIVE BEHAVIOR

Aggressive behavior comes in many forms and is always destructive in intimate relationships. Look through the following list and identify some of the ways in which you have been aggressive with your partner and others.

1. Becoming loud/raising the volume to overwhelm and intimidate others
2. Being nasty, cruel, mean-spirited, vindictive, vengeful, for example, using past personal disclosures to hurt someone in a current argument
3. Giving orders and commands, for example:
   - Telling someone what to do
   - Saying "Get with it" to someone
   - Trying to control other people
4. Name-calling, using put-downs, labeling and judging people, for example:
   - You're a jerk.
   - What an idiot.
   - That's a stupid idea.
   - How can you be so dumb?
5. Interrupting others when they are speaking, for example:
   - Trying to talk over others so your point is the only one that is heard
   - Not really listening, but instead thinking only about how you are going to respond to what someone is saying
6. Being rude and abrasive while claiming to say things in the name of "being honest" (i.e., "brutal honesty"), for example:
   - Telling people that they are ugly or that you do not like the way they look
   - Being harsh and then claiming, "I only said that for your own good."
7. Accusing and blaming others, for example:
   - You're the damn problem in this relationship.
   - 'Why don't you get it together so things will be better around here.
8. Speaking for other people (i.e., not taking responsibility for what you are saying), for example:
   - We don't like it when you . . .
   - No one would want to do that.
   - It doesn't make any sense to think that way.

(HO)   ©1999 David J. Decker, MA

9. Completely ignoring what others think, feel, or want, for example:
   - Who cares what you think?
   - It doesn't matter what you want
10. Mind reading (i.e., insisting that you know what other people think or feel no matter what they say), for example:
    - You don't know what you're talking about. You really did that because . . .
    - You're only afraid of me because your last boyfriend hit you.
11. Allowing your own negative attitudes, beliefs, and thoughts to color your perception of others around you and give you a reason to treat them in a condescending manner (including bigotry and prejudice), for example:
    - Women are irrational so they're no good in politics or business.
    - Anyone who has long hair is an irresponsible hippie.
    - Men are smarter than women.
    - Blacks are shiftless welfare cheats.
    - Jews are only out for money.
12. Writing someone off completely with what you say rather than confronting specific behaviors of theirs that you do not like, for example:
    - I hate your guts.
    - You'll never amount to anything.
    - You're worthless.
    - I wish I'd never met you.
    - It's too bad you were even born.
    - You're a loser.
13. Looking down on others or being condescending with or contemptuous of them, for example:
    - You're not even worth my time.
    - .What's the point of even trying to talk with someone like you?
14. Using verbal threats, for example:
    - Keep it up and you're really going to get it.
    - No one else is ever going to have you.
    - Sometimes I just feel like smacking you.
15. Physical Threats
    - Holding up a clenched fist in front of someone's face
    - Standing over someone or "getting in his or her face"
    - Standing in someone's way

(HO)   ©1999 David J. Decker, MA

16. Using physical force, for example:
    - Grabbing
    - Pushing
    - Bumping into someone
    - Restraining
    - Slapping
    - Punching

VERBAL AND NONVERBAL ELEMENTS OF ASSERTIVE, PASSIVE, AND AGGRESSIVE BEHAVIOR

Being assertive involves both verbal and nonverbal components. Use the following chart to help you monitor how you present yourself when you are attempting to be more assertive.

	ASSERTIVE	PASSIVE	AGGRESSIVE
VERBAL	honest statements of wants, thoughts, emotions, and opinions; using objective and descriptive words; direct and clear expressions that communicate what you really mean; "I" messages; not judging or blaming others; being specific, brief, straightforward, and to the point; emotionally expressive; respectful; focusing on the present rather than the past or the future	apologetic words; veiled or hidden meanings; continually hedging and failing to come to the point; at a loss for words; not saying what you really mean to say; being indirect; saying "you know" or "I mean" frequently; being fearful about asking for what you need or want; saying "whatever you'd like"; stumbling over your words; acting ingratiating and overly polite; often saying "I don't know" or "I don't care"; rambling; overexplaining; being vague	using loaded or trigger words; being accusing; using threats; giving orders and commands; using subjective/shaming labels; giving "you" messages that blame and judge others; using put-downs, name-calling, cursing, and swearing; using condescending language; interrupting frequently; being bossy, brusque, irritable, rude, nasty, pushy, controlling, and abusive; using words such as should, have to, always, and never
NON-VERBAL			
Voice	firm; clear; calm; warm; relaxed; well-modulated tone; evenly paced rate of speech	weak, thin, hesitant, soft voice; wavering, whining, "begging," placating tone; unsure, halting, and slow rate of speech	tense, shrill, loud, cold, rapid or slow methodical rate of speech; hostile silence; impatient; "shaking" vocalizations; demanding/superior/condescending tone
Eyes/Face	eyes comfortably open and facial muscles relaxed; looking directly into the other person's eyes; a sense of being alive; aware; attentive	eyes averted/looking away/darting around; sense of pleading/feeling fearful; teary; downcast/sheepish look	face and eyes expressionless or full of rage: cold and steely glaring/staring; furrowed brow; narrowed eyes; looking right through others; frowning; facial muscles tight/hard; red/twitching; clenched jaw

(HO)　　　　　　　　　　　　　　　　　　　©1999 David J. Decker, MA

	ASSERTIVE	PASSIVE	AGGRESSIVE
NON-VERBAL			
Hands/Arms	calm/relaxed motions and movements that do not distract or detract from the message being given	clammy and wet hands; fluttering and distracting motions; fidgeting	abrupt, quick, and jerky motions; finger pointing and fist pounding; arms across chest; hands on hips; over-enthusiastic and intimidating gestures; clenched fists; waving arms
Stance/Posture	erect; well-balanced; relaxed; comfortable; sitting or standing appropriately close	stooping; slouching; bent-over; "hangdog" look; excessive head nodding or other signs of submission, approval, and deference	stiff; rigid; tight; in your face; being intrusive; appearing threatening, intimidating, and overpowering; leaning forward or into others; pacing in an agitated fashion
GENERAL			
	nonverbals congruent with words spoken; self-assured and self-confident manner communicating caring and respect for self and others	nonverbals often incongruent with words spoken; appearing meek, timid, withdrawn, helpless, powerless, inferior, intimidated, anxious, and easy to victimize and take advantage of	continual and exaggerated show of strength to others demonstrating an air of uncaring and disrespectful grandiosity and disdain and a desire to control and dominate

(HO)

ASSERTIVENESS SYNONYMS

Use this as a guide when brainstorming synonyms for the four styles of communication discussed in this unit to ensure that men understand the differences among the styles. This can be used as a handout after the brainstorming session in group.

PASSIVE

polite	wimp
easygoing	resentful
quiet	yes person
"whatever you want"	caretaker
chump	weakling
selfless	"okay"
nice	apathetic
"I don't know/care"	"whatever . . ."
apologetic	martyr
modest	insecure
anxious	indecisive
withdrawn	self-defeating
humble	meek
weak	depressed
self-effacing	resentful
inferior	docile
timid	yielding
diffident	apathetic
agreeable	nonresponsive
fearful about making mistakes	
people pleaser	
inhibited	
low self-esteem	
shy	
victimized	
self-denying	
submissive	
reserved	
helpless	
dishonest	
doormat	
powerless	
self-pitying	

PASSIVE-AGGRESSIVE

indirect	withholding
teasing	two-faced
manipulative	insecure
sarcastic	unknown agenda
underhanded	self-defeating
deceitful	plotting
seductive	smoldering
devious	
sneaky	
cunning	
hostile	
vindictive	
dishonest	
coy	
vengeful	
tricky	
"con"	
sullen	
sulking	
"snake"	
pouting	
often late	
"weasel"	
revenge	
"forgetful"	
punishing	
snickering	
getting even	
low self-esteem	
payback	
cruel	
nasty	
shrewd	
resentful	

(HO)   ©1999 David J. Decker, MA

AGGRESSIVE

controlling/bossy
demanding
disrespectful
unreasonable
intimidating/in your face
harsh/cruel
"my way or the highway"
dogmatic
condescending
emotionally, verbally, sex-
    ually, or physically abusive
angry
badgering
opinionated
domineering
self-righteous
hostile
bullying
overbearing
cocky
blaming
superior
victimizer
dictator/autocrat
uncaring
belittling
tyrant
grandiose
low self-esteem
hard-headed/stubborn
vengeful
shaming
disregarding
getting even
terrorizing
labeling
name-calling
swearing/cursing
threatening
up the ante
punishing

finger pointing
payback
resentful
obnoxious
explosive
arrogant
know-it-all
win/lose attitude
macho
tough guy
should
"you" statements
forceful
harassing
insecure
driven
full of rage
self-defeating

ASSERTIVE

open
direct
honest
flexible
self-aware
cooperative
expressive
self-assured
respectful
"I think/I feel/I want"
understanding
polite
caring
confident
responsible for self
genuine
high self-esteem
appropriate
self-sufficient
nonjudgmental
in touch with feelings
empathetic
effective
healthy
self-enhancing
stands up for self
sensitive
requests from others
congruent
sharing
compromising
unselfish
"I" statements
trust building
thoughtful
communicating
relating
makes conscious choices
understanding
safe
values self and others

connecting
clear
present
strong
calm
self-control
expresses wants/needs

(HO)

ASSERTIVENESS GRID

The following grid can be used to help you look at your patterns of assertiveness with other people in your life. Use symbols (A = assertive; AG = aggressive; P = passive; PA = passive-aggressive) to note how you *generally* act with the different categories of people listed below in the specific situations in which assertiveness is an option. This will give you an idea of where to concentrate if you want to work on becoming more assertive. This grid also can let you know if you behave differently with males (M) and females (F).

ASSERTIVE BEHAVIORS	Partner	Father	Mother	Children		Relatives		Friends		Co-workers Employees		Authorities		Strangers		Groups	
				M	F	M	F	M	F	M	F	M	F	M	F	M	F
Expressing your feelings																	
Asking for what you want/need (e.g., help, support, affection)																	
Offering opinions/suggestions																	
Talking about yourself (e.g., experiences)																	
Reaching out socially																	
Saying positives (about yourself or your relationship)																	
Accepting positives/compliments from others																	
Handling criticism from/confrontation with others																	
Disagreeing																	
Saying no/setting limits																	
Confronting/criticizing others																	
Compromising																	
Looking others in the eye																	
Changing your mind																	

Partner Father Mother Children Relatives Friends Co-workers Employees Authorities Strangers Groups

(HO)   ©1999 David J. Decker, MA

THE PROCESS OF BECOMING MORE ASSERTIVE

Becoming more assertive in your day-to-day life involves a step-by-step process of slowing down enough to notice your reactions and behavior and then, in a planful way, doing something different. The following suggestions will help you to assert yourself more frequently and effectively when you feel the desire to do so.

1. *Identify and understand the basic styles of interpersonal relating:*
   a. Being aggressive
   b. Being passive aggressive
   c. Being passive
   d. Being assertive
2. *Pay attention to and notice your own reactions and behavior* in a variety of situations and keep track of whether you are passive, aggressive, passive-aggressive, or assertive. Use the Assertiveness Grid and the Assertiveness Journal to do this.
3. *Pick out specific situations* in which you want to become more assertive and effective in interacting with others, especially noting situations that cause you to feel angry, anxious, fearful, resentful, or uncomfortable in some way.
4. *Assess your problem scenarios* as specifically as possible. Identify the following:
   a. Who is(are) the person(s) involved?
   b. When and where did it take place (i.e., time and setting)?
   c. What about the situation is bothersome or difficult for you?
   d. How you have generally dealt with the person(s) or situation in the past?
   e. Your thoughts, feelings, wants, needs, and rights in the situation.
5. Identify effective role models in your life who do a good job of being assertive.
   a. Watch how they are assertive
   b. Talk to them about what they are thinking when they decide to speak up
   c. Ask them for advice about your scenario
   d. Imagine how they might handle your problem situation in a more assertive way
6. Come up with your own plan for behaving differently. Identify the following:
   a. All the possible alternative responses in the situation

(HO)   ©1999 David J. Decker, MA

   b. Your fears about what might happen (i.e., possible negative con-
       sequences) if you attempt to be assertive
   c. The specific goal you wish to set for yourself regarding your
       behavior when this problem situation occurs in the future
7. Imagine yourself handling the situation (i.e., think about a positive
   rehearsal or visualize yourself actually behaving differently).
8. Act out your assertive behavior in a role-play
   a. Find someone you can trust (friend, partner, counselor)
   b. Use audio or videotape to record what you are saying, how you
       act, and what you look like if at all possible.
   c. Get feedback from others noting both what you are doing well
       and what you still need to improve
   d. Shape your assertive behavior:
       • Repeat the steps of imagining yourself being assertive, acting out
         your assertive behavior, and getting feedback as many times as
         necessary for you (and those offering your feedback) to feel com-
         fortable with what you want to do
9. Follow through with your plan for acting differently: take the plunge
   and be assertive in the real-life situation (e.g., let us say that the last
   three times you have gotten together with a good friend, he has gotten
   angry about something related to the meal, the service, or the restaurant, and has become verbally abusive with the waiter. This is embar-
   rassing to you, and in addition, you do not believe that others deserve
   this type of treatment).
   a. Arrange a time and place to discuss your issue that is convenient
       for both you and the other person.
       • This step may be eliminated when dealing with spontaneous times
         that you choose to be assertive (e.g., when someone cuts in front
         of you in a line).
   b. Describe the problem situation and the other person's behavior
       clearly, specifically, and objectively and keep this in mind when
       you negotiate for change, expressing your feelings calmly and
       directly using "I" messages:
       • In a detailed manner, using specific references to time, place, and
         frequency (e.g., "I didn't like it last week at our lunch date when
         you got angry and called the waiter an asshole").
       • Try to let go of your tendencies to blame, your desire to hurt or
         punish the other person, and any resentment and self-pity that you

may be carrying around about what has happened in the past between the two of you.

- Make it clear that you attempting to resolve the issue, not bash the other person or prove that he or she is bad or wrong.
- Confine your emotional response to the specific problem behavior, *not* to a condemnation of everything about the person.
    —Avoid judging, blaming, or devaluing the other person
    —Avoid delivering put-downs disguised as "honest" feelings
    —Do not substitute an opinion for a feeling and watch out for statements that confuse your emotions with your thoughts (I feel like . . ." or "I feel that . . ." e.g., "People who 'rant and rave' are acting crazy" or "I feel like you're really acting in an immature way."

c. Express your request regarding the issue in one or two easy-to-understand sentences
- Be specific and firm; ask for changes that are reasonable and clear.
- Do not request more than one or two very specific changes at a time.
- State your want as a desire or preference, *not* a demand or an order (e.g., "When we spend time together, I would really prefer it if you wouldn't get explosive and call people names").

d. Increase the possibility of getting what you want by stating the positive outcome if the other person is willing to take your feelings into account and cooperate with you:
- Make the rewards explicit and desirable (e.g., "If you're willing to do this, I'll feel more comfortable being around you and I'll want to continue to spend time together regularly").

e. If necessary, also be clear about the negative consequences if the other person does not want to listen and does not seem to care about how you are feeling.
- Avoid stating consequences that are no more than idle threats.
- Consequences are not designed to punish the other person.
    —The goal is to take care of yourself in the situation (e.g., "If you're not willing to do this, I am going to get up and leave when you start to curse or put someone down. I'll also feel less comfortable getting together in the same way that we have in the past").

    f. Remember that the other person has the right to refuse your request no matter how clearly, assertively, and respectfully it is stated.
- There is no way you can control how the other person responds to you.
- If the person seems open to your issue, be willing to listen to his or her thoughts, feelings, and perspective and continue to talk about the issue with him or her.
—This may lead to a compromise

    g. Stay focused on your rights and the goals that you have set for yourself so that you can stay on task.
- Do not allow yourself to give in to negative self-talk and feelings of powerlessness, which can lead directly to your withdrawing or becoming hostile and aggressive.
- If the other person becomes hostile or explosive with you, take a time-out and leave the situation.

10. Develop and use assertive body language to accompany your verbal messages.
    a. Your nonverbal messages are a powerful way to communicate and can enhance or detract from your verbal message.
    b. Keep your facial muscles relaxed and try to look into the other person's eyes without appearing as if you are staring or glaring.
    c. Sit or stand appropriately close without appearing menacing or timid.
    d. Make your voice clear, calm, and firm but also try to use a relaxed tone of voice.
- Don't give in to becoming intimidating or "ranting and raving" yourself.
- Don't start "whining" or communicating with an overly apologetic tone of voice.

    e. Make use of appropriate gestures and facial expressions for emphasis without using them to intimidate the other person.
    f. Work hard to present yourself in a self-assured and self-confident manner without appearing cocky or condescending.
- Keep reminding yourself that you have a right to your feelings and perspective and a right to communicate it to others.

11. Allow yourself to *practice* the real-life situation as often as necessary, especially if the other person tries to block your attempts to be assertive.

12. Actively look for *reinforcement* related to your new more assertive behaviors:

a. Be aware of your own positive feelings arising from handling the situation differently (even, and especially, if you do not get what you want).
b. Give yourself ongoing credit for the emotional and behavioral risks you are taking to become more assertive.
c. Take note of others' praise and respect for your efforts to change.
d. Spend less time with or completely avoid the people who do not want to see you change and who try to punish you for your attempts to be more assertive.

ASSERTIVENESS SCENARIOS

Consider the following situations and write out how you would respond to each of them (both in your words and in your actions) if you reacted *passively, passive-aggressively, aggressively,* and *assertively.* Be specific. Be prepared to role-play the ones that would generally be most difficult for you.

1. You are at the doctor's office, thirty minutes have passed, and you have not yet been called for your appointment.
2. You are waiting in the checkout line at a grocery store and someone steps in front of you.
3. You have come home dead tired from work and your partner is restless. She really wants to get out of the house and asks you to go to a movie with her.
4. You are dining at an expensive restaurant and your steak comes to your table well-done rather than medium rare, as you had requested.
5. Your partner is thirty minutes late in picking you up from work.
6. Your boss comes to you at work and asks you to perform a task that you really do not have time to do.
7. A good friend asks you to pick him or her up at the airport but you are already committed to being with someone else at that time.
8. Your friend asks you to help him repair his car but you do not have time to do it when he wants to get it done.
9. You have bought an item at a clothing store (on sale) but decide that you do not want it when you get home.
10. You have always gone to your partner's family's home over the Thanksgiving holiday, but you would really like to spend this time with your own side of the family.
11. You have had some friends over on a Friday night but now it is late and you are tired and want them to leave (they are not tired and do not seem ready to call it a night).
12. A telemarketer calls to sell something that you do not need or want.

(HO)　　　　　　　　　　　　　　　　©1999 David J. Decker, MA

ASSERTIVENESS JOURNAL

Use this assertiveness journal to document how you are using or not using assertiveness skills in your life and to find ways to respond more effectively.

1. Describe what happened in the situation. Who was involved? What did you say and do? What did the other person(s) say and do?
2. Were you: ———Assertive ———Passive
———Aggressive ———Passive-Aggressive
3. Describe your verbal and nonverbal responses and discuss why you view them as assertive, passive, aggressive, or passive-aggressive.
4. What were your feelings about the situation (before, during, and after)?
5. What were your attitudes, expectations, and self-talk about the situation (before, during, and after) and did these interfere with or promote an assertive response?
6. What was the specific goal you wished to achieve in the situation and did you achieve it?
7. What did you like about the way you handled this situation?
8. In what ways could you have handled the situation more effectively? How could your attitudes, expectations, and self-talk before, during, and after have been more positive and empowering?
9. How did (could) you give yourself credit afterward for how you responded?

(HO) ©1999 David J. Decker, MA

Unit 8: Communication and Conflict Resolution

FEELINGS

What Are Feelings?

Feelings are your *spontaneous reactions* to your physical stress responses (e.g., the release of adrenaline) and your self-talk (i.e., thoughts, interpretations, expectations, judgments, and assumptions) that you use to label and make sense of these responses. Often you notice your feelings and little else. Therefore, it is critical to slow down your internal thought process so that you can also tune into your self-talk. Whenever a feeling arises, self-talk is also involved. One does not exist without the other. Your feelings will not control you if you allow yourself to get in touch with your self-talk process. This handout discusses some important ideas related to feelings and how they work.

First and most important, feelings are not good or bad, OK or not OK, right or wrong. *They are just there!* The intensity of feelings varies (e.g., from mild frustration to volatile rage). However, no matter what the intensity, feelings cannot be controlled by ignoring or denying them. When this occurs, they tend to take over and begin to control you and how you react and behave. For example, being passive for a long period of time may lead to blowing up and explosively dumping your anger and other feelings on someone else. It is crucial to take the time to look inside yourself to develop an ongoing awareness of what you are feeling.

Feelings can be expressed verbally, with words, and nonverbally, with gestures, facial expressions, and actions (e.g., slamming a door). Nonverbal messages have a powerful impact on others and often will be noticed and attended to even more than what you say.

1. Feelings serve two major functions:
   * They serve as a signal that "something is going on" within you.

387

- They help to clarify your expectations (your feelings are often triggered by a disparity between what you want and what actually happens).
2. The important tasks with feelings are the following:
    - Recognize the feelings within you as you experience them.
    - Recognize that you have choices about how you share your feelings (you are never out of control and reactions to your feelings do not just happen).
    - Express them assertively and respectfully with others or find other effective ways to handle them when they arise.
3. To notice and tune into your feelings, pay attention to the following:
    - *Physical signals* (e.g., experiencing muscle tension or getting hot when you are angry)
    - *Behavioral signals* (e.g., becoming quiet and withdrawing from a conversation when you are embarrassed)
    - *Indirect signals* (e.g., buying a gift for someone when you feel guilty about something you have said or done to them)

Problems in Expressing Feelings

1. It is frequently difficult to be aware of feelings as they arise or to sort out what you want to do with several that may occur at the same time. We often experience multiple feelings simultaneously. This may mean that you communicate confusing and contradictory information to the other person. At times, our feelings may even be in conflict with one another. For example, you might feel relieved and angry when you find your lost child at the grocery store. Take time to sort out what the different feelings are.
2. Our culture is often very limiting about which feelings are deemed "appropriate" for us to experience. For example, men are frequently given the message "Don't cry," and women are frequently given the message "Don't get angry." Do not allow such cultural messages to limit who you are in your emotional expression.
3. Expressing feelings can be a risky proposition. If you share your feelings, you are allowing yourself to become vulnerable, and your self-disclosure could be used against you, especially in a conflict situation. However, without sharing your feelings, real intimacy is not possible.
4. Disclosing your feelings will not necessarily change a situation or someone's behavior, even when it is done respectfully. Try to stay aware of this expectation that you should get what you want if you tell someone how you feel. Believing that talking about feelings does not do any good anyway is a control issue.

(HO)   ©1999 David J. Decker, MA

5. Watch out for substituting opinions, judgments, and other self-talk for your feelings. For example, "You have no right to say that" is making a judgment; "I don't like what you just said" is expressing a feeling. Also, be aware of "I feel like . . ." or "I feel that . . . ," which are expressions of what you think, not what you are feeling (e.g., "I feel like you were a jerk" versus "I'm angry about what you did").

Sharing Feelings

An important part of sharing feelings and communicating effectively is to recognize clearly that *your feelings are yours and belong to you.* They are your responsibility. Everyone does not react emotionally in the same way that you do in a particular situation. Even though others have the power to trigger feeling responses in you, no one has the power to cause you to feel anything. Often, intense emotional reactions in the present have parallels to situations that occurred in the past and left their mark on you. For example, if you frequently tend to feel rejected and abandoned in the present, this may, in part, relate to similar feelings experienced in the past with people who were significant to you at the time.

Likewise, when others share their feelings with you, remember to realize that their emotional reactions belong to them and are not your fault or yours to fix. Often, just being there to listen to someone else's feelings can be helpful and healing to that person.

Expressing feelings takes practice and a desire to get closer to others. We need to strike a balance between sharing our emotions and feeling safe in our lives. As mentioned previously, some people may take advantage when you talk about how you feel and become vulnerable. If, however, you share too little with the important people in your life, you will begin to fear that they would not accept and love you if they really knew who you were (i.e., shame develops). As a result, emotional distance begins to creep into your relationships.

Clearly stating your feelings to others helps you stay in touch with your own inner experience and enables you to know yourself. This process can also assist others in learning about who you are. Sharing your feelings openly, honestly, and respectfully with others brings zest, vitality, and intimacy to your communication process and your interactions with others. In addition, your feelings can change if you allow yourself to reassess the activating situation and the self-talk you have created about it. Talking with others can help you do just that.

(HO) ©1999 David J. Decker, MA

FEELING WORDS

Everyone has feelings. Unfortunately, many people have tremendous difficulty identifying exactly what they are feeling when they are feeling it. Knowing your emotions and being able to tell others what you are feeling is a critical part of being able to communicate effectively. Below are some specific words that can describe your feeling states. Study the lists and begin to expand your vocabulary when it comes to discussing the emotions you experience.

HAPPY		SAD	SCARED
joyful	exuberant	miserable	fearful
excited	carefree	sorrowful	anxious
delighted	appreciative	hurt	afraid
ecstatic	secure	disappointed	shy
cheerful	worthy	unhappy	terrified
glad	competent	dismal	nervous
gleeful	pleased	disheartened	panicky
optimistic	energized	despairing	insecure
enthusiastic	marvelous	depressed	frightened
elated	fortunate	dismayed	intimidated
content	alive	mournful	worried
satisfied	powerful	lonely	timid
peaceful		distraught	shaken
calm		discouraged	horrified
relaxed		disillusioned	alarmed
confident		tearful	apprehensive
proud		wounded	unsafe
strong		upset	cautious
relieved			guarded
jubilant			uneasy
assured			threatened
grateful			tense
hopeful			petrified
tranquil			vulnerable
playful			frantic
pleased			overwhelmed
good			desperate
fulfilled			uncomfortable

(HO)   ©1999 David J. Decker, MA

FEELING WORDS *(continued)*

CONFUSED	**ASHAMED**	**ANGRY**	**GUILTY**
unsure	embarrassed	furious	regretful
uncertain	shameful	mad	remorseful
indecisive	worthless	frustrated	apologetic
puzzled	inadequate	annoyed	sorry
bewildered	empty	irritated	
perplexed	defeated	resentful	
baffled	helpless	indignant	**OTHERS**
ambivalent	hopeless	disgusted	tired
doubtful	powerless	bitter	bored
undecided	devastated	aggravated	indifferent
unsettled	drained	exasperated	apathetic
curious	exhausted	hostile	mischievous
hesitant	crushed	pissed off	restless
	exposed	irate	disconnected
	immobilized	rageful	awkward
	trapped	infuriated	
	isolated	distressed	
	envious	disgusted	
	humiliated	agitated	
	foolish	hateful	
	inferior	surly	
	stuck	spiteful	
	stagnant	outraged	
	disgraced	defensive	
	alienated	incensed	
	abandoned	peeved	
	degraded	rebellious	
		vengeful	
		perturbed	
		defiant	
		stubborn	
		belligerent	
		obstinate	
		seething	
		contemptuous	
		dismayed	
		displeased	
		offended	
		enraged	
		jealous	

       ©1999 David J. Decker, MA

ELEMENTS OF EFFECTIVE COMMUNICATION

Communicating with others can be a difficult proposition. We all have our own values, beliefs, and life experiences, and these can influence what we hear from others and how we interpret and react to their messages. The following elements, however, can be helpful in "keeping the door open" to partners and others.

Active Listening

1. Active listening is a commitment, a compliment, and a gift to those around you.
2. It clearly demonstrates that you are truly interested in others for who they are, not what you think they should be or want them to be.
3. It means working hard to tune into both the verbal and nonverbal messages and then attempting to truly understand what others want to communicate, which means temporarily suspending your own interpretations and judgments.
4. It means listening with empathy, openness, genuineness, and respect.
5. The experience of being listened to and really heard is often helpful and healing in and of itself.

Reflecting Back

1. Reflecting back is a process that accompanies active listening and involves rephrasing or paraphrasing, in your own words, what the other person has just said, including
   - the *content* of what is said,
   - the *feelings* behind what is being said, and
   - your understanding of that person's *intention* in communicating with you.
2. Reflecting back
   - shows that you are really hearing what is being said,
   - checks out your interpretations and assumptions,
   - clarifies what was communicated, and
   - helps promote further self-disclosure by the other person.
3. A good paraphrase
   - captures the essence of what the other person said,
   - conveys the same meaning (usually with somewhat different words),
   - is clear, concise, and to the point,

(HO)   ©1999 David J. Decker, MA

- communicates to the other person "I am really with you," and
- is tentative (checks out rather than assumes you know the meaning of the message)

4. For example:
   - "In other words, it sounds like . . ."
   - "So you're thinking that . . ."
   - "What I hear you saying is . . ."

Inquiring About the Other Person

1. This means asking *open-ended* questions about, and being truly interested in, the other person's thoughts, opinions, feelings, wants, needs, goals, values, dreams, and aspirations:
   - Open-ended questions actively seek new information and the other person's perspective (e.g., "How do you feel about that?").
   - Closed-ended questions look for "yes," "no," or very short answers (e.g., "You're not angry about that, are you?").

2. Asking open-ended questions helps you gain an understanding of how others view themselves and their world to assist you in realizing that they are separate and different from you.

Accepting Feedback

1. Accepting feedback means being open to, and interested in, others' ideas, suggestions, descriptions, and reactions regarding your behavior and using others as a helpful "reality test."

2. It means using active listening and paraphrasing to understand the feedback.

3. Remember that the other person's feedback is his or her perspective and not the gospel.

4. Try to listen, think about the suggestions/feedback, take what fits for you, and learn from it. Guard against becoming immediately defensive or argumentative.

Allowing Others to Know You (Self-Disclosing and Being Assertive)

1. Self-disclosing means taking the risk to be open by sharing the important parts of who you are as a person, including the following:

- thoughts
- feelings
- wants
- needs
- goals
- values
- opinions
- dreams
- aspirations

2. This means tuning into what you think, feel, and want and sharing it directly and respectfully with others.
3. It means using "I" language and taking responsibility and ownership for what you say.
4. Self-disclosing allows you to be honest about how you see yourself and what you are experiencing.

Offering Feedback

1. Offering feedback means telling other people what you hear them saying and what you see them doing and being honest about how you are reacting to them (in a respectful and nonshaming way).
2. It means using descriptive rather than judgmental terms and specifics rather than generalizations (e.g., avoid "You're a controlling jerk"; instead, use "I get uncomfortable when you lean forward in your chair and raise your voice").
3. Remember that the other person does not have to accept your feedback or do anything with it.
4. Be sure to use "I" language and take responsibility for what you are communicating.

Attending to Important Words in the Communication Process

1. Use "I" to take clear ownership of your thoughts, feelings, wants, and needs
   - Saying "you" can easily become blaming (e.g., "You are the real problem in this relationship").
   - "They," "it," and "that" are often used to avoid taking clear responsibility for what you are saying (e.g., "You know what *they* say"; "*That's* not a very good idea").
2. Clear yes/no answers are critical to effective communication
   - "But" generally allows you to say yes and no in the same sentence (e.g., "I'd really like to do that, but it's just too hard for me").
3. Always/never/no one/everyone and other generalizations are rarely accurate when they are used (e.g., "I can never count on anyone").

(HO)   ©1999 David J. Decker, MA

4. "Should"/"ought to"/"have to" tend to be shaming and judgmental (e.g., "You should have known better").
5. Use "I don't want to . . . , "I'd prefer not to . . . ," or " I won't" rather than "I can't" to take clear responsibility for your choices.

Staying Tuned to Nonverbal Signals

1. Nonverbals are a powerful part of our communication process, including
   - facial expression;
   - voice tone, volume, and inflection;
   - eye contact; and
   - posture.
2. This means being aware of your nonverbal messages and making them as congruent as possible with the words you are saying (e.g., think about how you interpret and respond when someone is smiling and he or she says "I am angry").
3. It also means being aware of others' nonverbal messages and pointing out conflicting messages you receive to find out what the other person actually intended to say.

Staying in the Present

1. This means focusing on what is going on right now versus what has happened in the past.
2. It also means addressing hurts and resentments as they arise in your relationships so that they do not get brought up and interfere with your current communication.

Being Aware of the Emotional Process

1. This means staying tuned to the emotional climate between you and the other person and not just the words and content of your communication.
2. It means attending to *how* you are relating as well as to *what* you are talking about (e.g., noticing when you are escalating or becoming frustrated).

"Agreeing to Disagree" at Times

1. You need to understand and accept that you and others who are close to you come from different backgrounds and have different life experiences.

(HO)   ©1999 David J. Decker, MA

2. This means that you may have very different values, perspectives, and world views.
3. It also means that you need to realize that nothing is wrong or bad about disagreement and conflict. In fact, it is natural and an important part of being close to others.

Making Communication a Cooperative Effort

1. This means beginning to look at your partner and others you choose to have in your life as friends and supporters, not adversaries or enemies.
2. It also means learning to view the communication process with a spirit of caring and love versus one that involves a spirit of control, hostility, and winning at any cost.

Being Complete

1. Work hard to develop and practice all of the previous communication skills.

HITTING BELOW THE BELT:
UNDERMINING EFFECTIVE CONFLICT RESOLUTION

Conflict resolution is an important skill in a relationship because you cannot completely avoid disagreement when you are close to others. Unfortunately, at times, we all lapse into unhealthy and destructive patterns of relating during conflict. Take a look at the following behaviors and note how many you use when you are arguing. Then start thinking about changing them so that your conflict resolution can be growth producing and solution oriented rather than destructive and painful.

Blaming

Blaming is placing all the responsibility for the argument or problem on your partner and refusing to acknowledge any part in the current issue. Important in a blaming attitude is being clear that you will not change and nothing will improve until she changes first (e.g., "I never would have hit you if you hadn't said that to me first" or "You're the one who started this argument").

Ignoring

Ignoring is turning your attention inside and withdrawing when your partner is attempting to work through an issue with you (e.g., pulling back into silence, pretending to fall asleep or read, turning on the TV).

Forgetting

Forgetting is "not remembering" what you have said or done to avoid taking responsibility in a conflict. Often, chemical use or explosive anger are also used as excuses for forgetting (e.g., "I don't recall saying that yesterday" or "I was too drunk (pissed off) to remember what I did").

Exchanging Tit for Tat

Exchanging tit for tat is responding immediately to any issue that your partner raises with an issue of your own that may or may not relate to what she has just brought up (e.g., "If you're so hurt about last night, what about how you treated me last week").

(HO) ©1999 David J. Decker, MA

Being Sarcastic

Being sarcastic consists of devious, ambiguous, and hostile comments made about your partner or her behavior that communicate strong feelings without having to accept any responsibility for what you are saying (e.g., "I'm *really* sure you know what you're talking about," "Get a life," or "Geez, isn't that special").

Being Controlling

Being controlling is attempting to dominate conflict situations so that your partner is unable to effectively present her point of view by refusing to listen and jumping in at every opportunity (e.g., interrupting, talking or yelling over her).

Upping the Ante

Upping the ante is moving as quickly as possible from the issue being discussed to questioning your partner's worth as a person and then questioning whether you should even stay in the relationship. This often involves actively choosing to interpret your partner's shortcomings as concrete evidence of her inadequacy and her lack of real commitment to the relationship (e.g., "You'll always treat me like dirt" and "Being with you just isn't worth the hassle!").

Interrogating

Interrogating is continually asking questions that are meant to keep your partner off balance and on the defensive so that you will not have to speak for yourself and take any personal emotional risks in the argument (e.g., repeatedly asking "How could you say [do] something like that?" or "Where the hell were you?").

Getting Personal

Getting personal involves making negative and disrespectful comments about your partner to trigger defensiveness and to keep the focus away from resolving the issue (e.g., "You're really a loser when it comes to money").

Violating Confidences

Violating confidences is the use of personal and intimate information that your partner has shared with you in the past as ammunition in a current argument (e.g., "Who the hell are you to talk about sex. You let your dad come in and screw you every night when you were a kid").

Taking Things Personally

Taking things personally is going out of your way to interpret your partner's words and actions as being said and done to put you down, pick on you, hurt you, and humiliate you. This means choosing to look at yourself as a victim and at your partner as an enemy rather than a friend (e.g., "You're just telling me that to try to make me feel bad" or "I guess everything's always my fault, isn't it?").

Predicting the Future

Predicting the future is catastrophizing about what lies ahead in your relationship to avoid addressing and working on present issues and to protect you from having to make meaningful changes right now (e.g., "I know you'll never be able to change" or "Nothing will ever get any better in this damn marriage").

Making Judgments

Making judgments involves labeling your partner in a disrespectful and condescending way to make her the reason for all the relationship problems (e.g., "You're crazy [stupid, messed up, a jerk, an idiot]").

Using Poor Timing

Using poor timing is picking inappropriate times to begin a discussion or argument so that there is no possibility of working through the issue. This can include only being willing to talk when you feel like it (e.g., just as your partner is leaving for work, just before you are going over to your in-laws for dinner, late at night when neither of you has any energy, in a public place, or at a social gathering).

(HO)

Playing the Teacher

Playing the teacher is acting like a know-it-all and taking on the role of an instructor whose job is to explain to your partner what she is doing wrong and how she should correct the problem that is occurring between the two of you (e.g., "You just treat me like this because of the way you were raised. You should . . .").

Generalizing

Generalizing is the use of broad and sweeping statements involving words such as always and never that are likely to trigger your partner's defensiveness and quickly move the discussion from the actual issue to your total condemnation of who she is (e.g., "You never want to do what I want" or "You always say things like that to me").

Avoiding Compromise

Avoiding compromise involves an unwillingness to back down from your stance in a conflict and staying focused on the idea that there is only one real winner and one right answer when two people disagree (e.g., "There's no way I'm ever going to do what you want").

Mind Reading

Mind reading is believing that you know the real reason that your partner has said or done something and communicating this belief to her as a way of ending any further discussion about what might be going on between the two of you (e.g., "I know you're just telling me you're sick to get out of going to the party").

Acting Out of Control/Crazy

Acting out of control is allowing yourself to feel so escalated that you can justify being emotionally, verbally, sexually, or physically abusive to your partner to make your point or get your way (e.g., being explosive; cursing; throwing things; forcing sex; grabbing, restraining, or hitting).

Pulling Rank

Pulling rank is attempting to belittle your partner and her perspective by saying that, because of the differences between the two of you, she has no right to express any thoughts about the issue being discussed (e.g., "When you make as much money [have as much education/have as important a job] as I do, then you'll have a right to an opinion around here").

Using Self-Pity

Using self-pity is the lapsing into a one-down, helpless, and victimized position in an attempt to get your partner to feel sympathy for you and to stop the conflict that is occurring (e.g., beginning to cry so that your partner will feel sorry for you and "back off" and comfort you).

Complying

Complying is acting as if you agree with your partner when you really do not and planning, in a passive-aggressive way, to do whatever you feel like doing no matter what has been decided in your discussion (e.g., saying, "Sure, honey, I'll do the bills over the weekend," when you really plan to go golfing).

Distracting

Distracting involves changing the subject or going off on a tangent to avoid responding directly to your partner about whatever you are discussing (e.g., asking "Do you know what happened to my brother yesterday?" after your partner has asked you to commit to doing something around the house).

Overwhelming

Overwhelming is attempting to flood your partner with as many problems, issues, and concerns as possible to avoid focusing on the issue at hand. This often involves resurrecting as many old and unresolved hurts and resentments as you can remember so that the current issue will be completely lost in the process (e.g., asking "What about all those times at the beginning of our relationship when you didn't want to spend time with me?" when your partner has just asked to spend more time together).

(HO)

Exaggerating

Exaggerating makes the issue being discussed so important that it no longer stands by itself, but instead indicates a major problem in the relationship (e.g., "If our relationship was really important to you, you never would have done this to me").

Running Away

Running away is abruptly leaving a conflict in a disrespectful way with no intention of returning to resolve it. This can also involve getting away from the issues or problems by becoming overinvolved with an activity that absorbs all your time and energy (e.g., throwing up your hands and walking out of the room without saying anything, exiting the house and slamming the door behind you; abusing chemicals, watching TV continually, compulsively eating, or being busy all the time).

Keeping a Laundry List

Keeping a laundry list is remembering and bringing up every wrong your partner has ever done so that you can feel self-righteous in the midst of a current argument. This often serves as a way to justify anything that you feel like saying or doing (e.g., "Since you acted like such an jerk with my family last Christmas, I'm not going over to your family's this Christmas").

Intimidating

Intimidating is bullying and threatening to get your partner to back off and resolve the conflict your way (e.g., "If you don't knock it off, I'm out of here" or "If you keep this up, there are really going to be some problems around here").

Minimizing

Minimizing is trying to downplay the importance of your partner's thoughts and feelings about an issue (e.g., "Come on, honey, it's not that big a deal. . . . Why don't you just drop it?").

Justifying

Justifying is offering reasons and excuses for your behavior rather than listening to what your partner thinks and feels about it (e.g., "I just said that because I was tired" or "You let your ex-husband do it to you. Why can't I?").

©1999 David J. Decker, MA

Using Humor

Using humor involves smiling, chuckling, laughing things off, or joking around when your partner has something important that she wants to discuss (e.g., smirking when your partner is angry with you).

Playing Dumb

Playing dumb is acting as if you "don't get it" or just do not understand what your partner is trying to communicate to you so you will not have to address the real issues in the conflict (e.g., "I have no idea what you're talking about" or "You're making no sense at all").

CONFLICT RESOLUTION

Thoughts About Conflict Resolution

Using the following model is no guarantee that you will resolve your conflict. This is especially true if you and the other person do not assume goodwill in your relationship and instead continue to view each other as enemies. Either you or the other person has the right to refuse to become involved in a constructive and positive problem-solving and conflict resolution process. As a result of this stance, you may end up behaving either aggressively or passively with each other. Whatever you or the other person does, however, will give you more information about the health of the relationship and how you may need to care for yourselves as individuals in the context of the future of your relationship. If the other person is completely unwilling to engage in a constructive conflict resolution process, you may need to ask yourself why you are staying in the relationship.

In conflict, each person often has the goal of getting the other person to agree with his or her point of view, as well as the expectation that the other will do what you want him or her to do. This sets up a win-lose situation, essentially making the other person an adversary. When you think about it realistically, who really wants to be a loser? And, even if you win, do you really want to be with a partner who is a loser?

A critical part of conflict resolution is to change your goal from *agreement* to *understanding*. In reality, you do not need to agree. Rather, and hopefully, you will be able to hear and know the other person's position well enough so that you can clearly express it back to him or her, and he or she can do likewise. This is the most effective way to truly understand what each of you is trying to say. Probably the most important part of conflict resolution is having the opportunity to express your feelings and have them heard by the other person. Active listening is critical. Work hard to keep the communication lines open.

Attempt to tune into any *unproductive self-talk and assumptions* that you hold regarding conflict situations and to be aware of how those assumptions are affecting possible outcomes:

- I have to be right.
- Whenever we argue, someone wins and someone loses.
- If someone disagrees with me, they don't really respect me.
- No one has the right to challenge me.
- If my partner criticizes me, she must think I'm a loser.

(HO)   ©1999 David J. Decker, MA

- It's my way or the highway.
- Disagreement means you don't really love each other.
- I'm the man . . . I should have the final say.

Consciously work to substitute *more rational ideas* for your original assumptions:

- It's okay to see things differently on this issue.
- She has a right to her perspective, the same as I do.
- Disagreeing is a natural part of a relationship. It doesn't mean that either of us is bad or wrong.
- There's no way we should expect to agree on everything. We're two different people.
- I know we can get through this. We've gotten through tougher arguments in the past.
- We can both come out of this situation feeling okay about the issue.
- It's really important that we learn to appreciate each other's differences.

Try to be aware of your *bodily reactions* to conflict. If you are feeling tense, take a moment to relax your muscles and breathe deeply and regularly. If you find yourself escalating and you feel the potential to be explosive or abusive, take a time-out and return to the discussion later after you have calmed yourself down. Abusive and disrespectful behavior only hides and obscures the real relationship issues that need to be addressed and resolved.

Procedure setting can be very helpful in keeping your conflict resolution discussions constructive. Think about the following issues for yourself before approaching your partner to negotiate how you will discuss the problem situation:

- What do I want to talk about (address only one issue at a time)?
- Whose issue is it (i.e., is it my issue or a relationship issue)? Remember that if it is bothering you, it is not only her issue.
- Who is involved in this issue? Are there others involved with this conflict?
- Where will we talk?
- When will we talk?
- How much energy is available for the discussion (in myself and the other person)?
- How long will the discussion last?
- How will we agree to stop the discussion (if we are not making the desired progress or if one of us is running out of energy)?

(HO) ©1999 David J. Decker, MA

To effectively resolve conflict, it is absolutely crucial for both of you to have *uninterrupted time* to speak. Continually interrupting or trying to talk over each other will not work. Practice and work hard on your active listening skills.

Try to maintain a *spirit of nurturance and cooperation* even in the midst of conflict and your efforts at resolving it. Make conflict resolution an esteem-building and trust-building process rather than a negative and destructive one.

- Take the initiative to break out of the power struggle mentality.
- Turn conflicts into problem-solving adventures with both of you acting as a team to come up with solutions that work for each of you.
- Before, during, and after the conflict resolution process, take responsibility for things you have said and done that you do not feel good about and make amends and apologize whenever necessary.

If your long-term goal is a caring and respectful relationship, you need to keep this in mind even when you are upset with your partner about a current issue. If you are truly open to your partner's thoughts and feelings and how she perceives the situation, this may result in your feelings changing and your being more willing to see her perspective or to compromise.

Using the following model is a difficult process. You may not achieve immediate success. However, this model can be helpful if your intentions are

- to treat your partner in a more respectful and caring fashion during conflict,
- to reach solutions that are acceptable for both of you, and
- to develop more intimacy in your relationship.

Remember that the bottom line in effective conflict resolution is deciding what you are willing to do or give to make the situation better, not what you can force the other person to do.

Steps to Follow in Resolving Conflict

1. First of all, approach the other person and ask whether he or she is willing to sit down with you and work on an issue that is bothering you. Make this a request, not an order or command. How you actually get started sets the tone for the rest of the process (e.g., "I've got something that's been bothering me that I'd like to talk about. Would you be willing to sit down and discuss this issue with me?").

©1999 David J. Decker, MA

2. Describe the specific behavior/situation that you do not like or the specific concern you are experiencing. Express your thoughts and feelings that go along with the behavior/situation/concern. Try not to blame the other person. Rather, using "I" language, take responsibility for your thoughts and feelings. Your feelings belong to you and the other person does not cause you to think or feel a certain way.
   a. "I'm really feeling uncomfortable with . . ."
   b. "I don't like it when . . ."
   c. "I get upset about . . ."
3. To ensure that the other person understands your concern, ask him or her to paraphrase and reflect back what you have said. If the person has misinterpreted or misunderstood what you said, describe your original thoughts and feelings again. If he or she has clearly understood what you have said, let that person know it and then continue with the process (e.g., "What do you hear me saying about this situation?").
4. Next, allow uninterrupted time for the other person to express his or her thoughts, feelings, and perspective about the situation/behavior/concern you have raised (e.g., "What are you thinking/feeling about the situation?").
5. To ensure that you understand the other person's messages to you, paraphrase back to him or her what you just heard. Give the other person time to let you know if you have understood his or her message accurately.
   a. "This is my understanding of what you're saying. . . . Is that what you're saying?"
   b. "Is there any more? Am I missing anything you wanted me to hear?"

Note: Repeat steps two through five as many times as necessary to make sure that both of you have a clear understanding of each other's position and can accurately paraphrase the other person's feelings and perspective.

6. Next, brainstorm together a variety of alternative ideas to deal with the situation/behavior/concern. This is a time for being creative. Try not to get hooked into a win-lose stance (e.g., "My plan is much better than yours," "That's a stupid idea," "How can you suggest that," or "That's crazy").
   a. "What can we do to resolve this now and in the future?"
   b. "What could we do to make this better?"
   c. "Let's think about all our options in this situation."

7. Then, take some uninterrupted time, after considering all the alternatives, to discuss what you are willing to do and give in this situation. Also, take some time to say what you would like from the other person regarding the problem you have been discussing. Then ask the other person if he or she would be willing to do something different when this issue arises again. Finally, tell the other person what you heard him or her saying and ask that person to do the same for you.

   a. "I'd be willing to . . . ."
   b. "I'd like you to . . ."
   c. "Would you be willing to do anything different if this issue comes up again?"
   d. "I hear you saying that you'd be willing to. . . . What do you hear me saying about what I'm willing to do?"

8. This may or may not lead to a compromise, whereby you each agree to do something to make the situation better. It might lead to agreeing to disagree about the issue, and you may want to bring it up again at some future time. In any case, give yourself and the other person credit for listening and hearing each other and for dealing respectfully with each other about the conflict.

   a. "OK, I'll try what I said and you try what you said."
   b. "It looks like we just disagree on this. I'd like to talk about it again in a couple of weeks. Would you be willing to do that?"
   c. "Thanks for working on this with me. I like the way we did it."

9. If you are unable to accept or feel comfortable with what the two of you have discussed, let the other person know what you plan to do to take care of yourself if and when the issue comes up again. This leaves you with the ultimate responsibility for dealing with the issue and your own thoughts, feelings, and behaviors related to it. Try to make sure that your taking care of yourself is not just a another way to punish the other person for not having things your way (e.g., "I just don't feel good about what we've decided. If this situation comes up again, I'm going to . . .").

10. If you feel comfortable with what has been discussed, try it for a period of time. However, be sure to set up an opportunity in the future to evaluate how you feel about what the two of you have decided. Use this time as a chance to renegotiate the issue if the need arises and the situation continues to be a problem for you. If

you both feel good about how things have changed, take some time to celebrate your effective problem-solving efforts. This celebration of successful conflict resolution often gets forgotten in the busyness of everyday life (e.g., "All right, let's try this for a month and then get back together to talk about how it's going").

Unit 9: Self-Esteem and Healthy Relationships

SIGNS OF HIGH SELF-ESTEEM

Self-esteem involves how you think and feel about yourself: Do you really know who you are? Do you like yourself? Do you feel competent? Do you see yourself as worthwhile and okay? Violence and abuse always affect self-esteem in a negative way and indicate that self-esteem is a problem. People with high self-esteem tend to be respectful and nonabusive with others. The following list presents signs that indicate when self-esteem is present. No one has them all, but they can offer some ideas for you if you want to pinpoint areas to work on in improving your own self-esteem.

Characteristics of People with High Self-Esteem

Self-Accepting and Emotionally Secure

1. Know and accept themselves
   - Recognize their strengths and weaknesses
   - Improve themselves in areas where they see a need to do this
2. Allow themselves to feel the whole range of human emotion (from joy to sadness)
3. Take responsibility for their actions
   - Are self-motivated
   - Set up specific short- and long-term goals
   - Recognize and accept the consequences of their behavior
   - Acknowledge and forgive themselves for current and past mistakes and learn from them
4. Are self-sufficient and independent when appropriate but can also ask for help
5. Are genuine and sincere

(HO)

©1999 David J. Decker, MA

411

6. Are not preoccupied or overly concerned with what others think
7. Have a sense of what feels right and okay for them
8. Are able to receive compliments from others
9. Give themselves credit for who they are and what they accomplish
10. See themselves as likable, capable, and productive

Possess Self-Understanding, Insight,
and a Sense of Humor

1. Can slow down to be introspective and to enjoy the moment
2. Are aware of how and why they have become who they are (i.e., the impact of their family of origin, life experiences, and culture)
3. Take responsibility for their thoughts, feelings, wants, and needs
4. Can recognize and change their shaming and critical self-talk about themselves and work at maintaining a positive view of who they are
5. Are aware of how they affect and impact others
6. Have a warm and nurturing sense of humor

Have a Strong and Unifying Philosophy of Life

1. Know and are able to articulate their values and the way they look at life
2. Are able to make judgments about particular issues and then take action according to the values they hold
3. Have made conscious decisions about important aspects of their lives so that they actually live by the values they espouse

Relate Warmly and Effectively with Others

1. Treat others in a humane, caring, and respectful way
   • Avoid the use of demeaning and derogatory words and threatening, controlling, and intimidating actions
   • Are able to provide support and nurturance to others
2. Work to intervene in their negative, critical, and shaming self-talk about others and strive to view others in a positive light
3. Take emotional risks to interact assertively and genuinely with others
   • Actively talk and connect with others
   • Communicate their thoughts, feelings, wants, and needs clearly, respectfully, and directly
   • Listen and are open to others' ideas, perspectives, suggestions, and feedback

(HO)   ©1999 David J. Decker, MA

- Are willing to disagree, set limits, and say "no" at times
- Are willing and able to work cooperatively with others

4. Have empathy for others and try to understand the different perspectives that people have
5. Recognize and acknowledge conflicts and can resolve them
6. Are aware when they make mistakes with others, acknowledge them directly, make amends or apologize, and learn from the mistakes
7. Are able to compliment and be positive with others
8. Can have deep and intimate involvements with others (with a partner and friends)
   - Take others into their confidence
   - Are less concerned with being loved than with offering love and friendship to others

Realistically Perceive the World Outside Themselves

1. Realize that things can go wrong in life without needing to blame themselves or others
2. Are tolerant of life's ambiguity, uncertainty, and shades of gray
3. Are problem solvers
   - Can define the problem
   - Can generate alternative solutions
   - Can identify and use outside resources when necessary
   - Can anticipate possible consequences (both positive and negative)
   - Can decide what to do and then do it
   - Can evaluate the outcome and celebrate if the problem was resolved
4. Are able to be productive and accomplish what they set out to do

Reach Out Actively to the Outside World

1. Have an interest in new experiences and are willing to explore them
2. Are continually looking to broaden and deepen current skills and interests
3. Approach life with a spirit of zest and excitement
4. Accept and value differences among people and groups
5. Have a sense of the fellowship of the entire human community
6. Have a sense of their own personal and political power, and work, in some way, to improve the world around them and to make a contribution to society

(HO) ©1999 David J. Decker, MA

TYPES OF INTIMACY

Couples can be intimate in the context of a relationship in a variety of ways. No relationship has them all. Look through the list below and pinpoint the types that exist in your relationship with your partner. Then, if you wish, you can use this list as a guide to help you determine other areas where you may wish to develop more intimacy as a couple.

- *Emotional intimacy:* Being aware of, experiencing, and sharing feelings with each other and believing that this emotional sharing is important for your relationship.
- *Communication intimacy:* Being honest, open, and caring in your communication process and being direct and respectful in offering both affirmation/support and criticism.
- *Conflict intimacy:* Being assertive with one another about your anger and directly confronting and struggling with your different perspectives in a respectful and growth-producing manner (e.g., practicing fair fighting).
- *Crisis intimacy:* Being with each other and supporting each other in the times of pain and difficulty in your lives (e.g., the death of a loved one or the loss of a job).
- *Decision-making intimacy:* Truly regarding each other as equals, valuing each other's opinions, and sharing in the decision-making process regarding important issues in your lives and your relationship.
- *Playful intimacy:* Allowing the spontaneous "inner child" within each of you to connect with each other through childlike fun and involvement (e.g., using pet names, baby talk, and playful banter).
- *Affectional intimacy:* Sharing nonsexual physical affection with each other as a means of staying connected (e.g., hugs, holding hands).
- *Sensual/sexual intimacy:* Connecting through noncoercive and mutually satisfying sensual and sexual involvement and experiences.
- *Growth intimacy:* Sharing your partner's vision for herself and attempting to assist her in becoming who she wants to be.
- *Spiritual intimacy:* Identifying and sharing broader concerns such as the purpose and meaning of life and death and your own personal philosophy and religious/spiritual beliefs.
- *Procreative intimacy:* Deciding together to have and raise children, sharing the joys and hardships of parenting, and working as a team in this endeavor.

(HO)   ©1999 David J. Decker, MA

- *Intellectual intimacy:* Sharing the world of ideas with your partner based on mutual respect for each other's intellectual capabilities.
- *Work intimacy:* Supporting your partner in her chosen life work.
- *Social intimacy:* Sharing interaction and fun with friends, both as a couple and as individuals.
- *Recreational intimacy:* Sharing interests and experiences of leisure-time activities (e.g., sports, hobbies, travel).
- *Task intimacy:* Supporting each other in taking care of day-to-day responsibilities (e.g., household/yard tasks).
- *Aesthetic intimacy:* Sharing and appreciating the beauty in the world together (e.g., nature, art, music, dance, theater).
- *Generative intimacy:* Sharing that springs from a belief in common values or from dedication to a common cause that allows for reaching beyond yourselves to contribute to the community at large (e.g., political activism, volunteerism, involvement with your place of worship or neighborhood).

KEY INGREDIENTS IN HAVING
AND MAINTAINING A HEALTHY RELATIONSHIP

A healthy relationship with a partner can be difficult. It requires an investment of time, energy, and emotion and an ongoing commitment to maintain the relationship. The following ideas suggest how to make your relationship more satisfying and fulfilling. Use this handout to identify areas where you can commit to doing some things differently to improve your time with a partner.

Develop Self-Knowledge, Self-Awareness, and Self-Esteem
to Be Ready As an Individual for a Healthy Relationship

1. Know yourself and your strengths and weaknesses.
2. Know and take responsibility for your thoughts, feelings, and behaviors.
3. Recognize that what you saw in your parents' relationships (with each other and with you) has a very real effect on how you relate to a partner in your adult life.

Develop and Maintain a Spirit of Integrity, Trust,
Commitment, and Love

1. Be honest and avoid secrets.
2. Be faithful. Watch out for "affairs" with other people (both emotional and physical), work, television, alcohol, and other substances or activities.
3. Make a conscious decision to trust your partner.
4. Be consistent toward your partner in your attitudes and actions. Remember that love is a verb and it involves what you do and how you treat your partner each day.
5. Follow through with what you say you will do and do not do what you say you won't do.
6. Acknowledge your mistakes and make amends whenever necessary.
7. Understand and accept the natural ebb and flow in your relationship (i.e., every relationship has times when partners do not feel especially close).
8. Focus more on giving love than on getting love.

Maintain Healthy Boundaries to Promote an Atmosphere
of Tolerance, Acceptance, and Mutual Respect

1. Respect, value, and even delight in your partner's differences, changes, and growth.

(HO)   ©1999 David J. Decker, MA

2. Stay aware of, and intervene in, your desire to control your partner and what happens in your life together.
3. Detach in a healthy way from your partner's issues, problems, moods, and feelings.
4. Respect your partner's privacy (e.g., avoid reading journals or listening in on phone conversations without permission).

Develop and Use Communication Skills to Promote an Atmosphere of Closeness and Connection

1. Understand and appreciate the differences in the ways men and women are socialized to communicate.
2. Stay curious about your partner and her perspective.
3. Practice active listening and paraphrasing in your interactions.
4. Allow yourself to experience, identify, and share all your emotions.
5. Express your wants and needs directly and respectfully.
6. Tell your partner regularly what you like, appreciate, and value about her.
7. Be open to your partner's feedback and look for ways to learn about yourself from her.
8. Stay current on your hurts, disappointments, irritations, and resentments inside and outside the relationship.

Develop and Use Conflict Resolution Strategies to Promote an Atmosphere of Safety and Cooperation

1. Moderate the intensity of your anger.
2. Be aware of, and intervene in, negative, vengeful, controlling, or competitive self-talk.
3. Know what abusive behavior is and do not engage in it.
4. Accept that it is okay for you and your partner to see things differently.
5. Learn to accept "nos" and limits your partner has set.
6. Change your goal in conflict resolution from agreement to understanding.
7. Start to view conflicts as problem-solving adventures, whereby you and your partner can work together as a team to arrive at a solution. Stop viewing your partner as the enemy when you disagree.
8. Develop clear and respectful guidelines for resolving conflicts.
9. Learn to negotiate, compromise, and agree to disagree.
10. Learn to forgive and practice this in your relationship.

©1999 David J. Decker, MA

Provide Emotional Support for Each Other to Promote an Atmosphere of Affirmation and Nurturance

1. Be affirming and validating in good and bad times.
2. Know, share, and actively support your partner's vision for herself.
3. Look for ways you can give, in an ongoing fashion, to your partner and the relationship.

Build Fun and Play into Your Relationship

1. Let your spontaneous and fun-loving inner child connect with your partner.
2. Be open to your partner's funny and playful side.
3. Incorporate playful banter, affectionate teasing, and pet names into your time together.

Develop and Share a Vision for Yourselves in the Context of the Relationship

1. Set common mutually agreed-upon goals for yourselves and your relationship.
2. Develop couple and family rituals and traditions.
3. Develop a sense of mission or purpose about something outside your relationship.

Strive for Equality in Family Decision Making and Tasks

1. Make important family decisions together.
2. Discuss and make conscious choices about household chores, finances, and other important life areas.

Build Romance into Your Relationship

1. Look for ways to rekindle your passion for each other (e.g., flowers, candlelight dinners, weekends away).
b. Think back about and keep in mind what attracted you to your partner when you first met.

Develop and Maintain Physical Affection in Your Relationship

1. Share nonsexual and nurturing physical affection (e.g., sitting close to each other, holding hands, cuddling).

(HO)   ©1999 David J. Decker, MA

2. Connect through mutually satisfying and noncoercive sensual and sexual involvement.
3. Be open and talk about what feels good in your physical relationship.

Spend Time Together

1. Look for opportunities to emotionally connect during the day (e.g., phone calls, going out to lunch occasionally).
2. Set aside regular time to do activities as a couple and a family.
3. Relax together at times.

Take Risks in Your Activities Together

1. Be open to your partner's interests and friends.
2. Try new experiences.

Spend Time Apart

1. Take time for yourself and with your own friends.
2. Develop your own hobbies, interests, and activities.

Work Together As a Team in Parenting (If You Have Children)

1. Realize how your parenting is affected by how you were raised in your family of origin.
2. Talk together openly about how you want to parent.
3. Work together in making decisions that affect your children.
4. Attend a parenting class (together or by yourself) to learn more about how to be an effective and respectful parent.

Seek Outside Help and Assistance and Actively Use It When You Need to Do So

1. Talk with friends, relatives, support groups, or therapists when you feel stuck, adrift, or disconnected.
2. Be open to others' suggestions and feedback and make the ideas a part of your relationship when they are useful.

(HO) ©1999 David J. Decker, MA

Unit 10: Parenting

HOW TO BE A MORE EFFECTIVE PARENT

Parenting our children can be one of the most difficult tasks we take on in the course of our lifetimes. It is all too easy simply to fall back on and use child-rearing techniques our own parents used with us, even if what they did was shaming, hurtful, and destructive. The following are some ideas about nonviolent and respectful parenting. Think about and begin to use some of these positive and growth-producing ideas to help your children learn different attitudes and behaviors from the ones with which you have had to struggle.

1. *Convey an attitude of love and respect*, even, and especially, when children are being disrespectful themselves (i.e., do not sink to their level). You are the parent, not their peer, and you need to learn to detach in a healthy way from the intense emotional reactions you may experience as a father. Also, seek to use your reactions to give you some information about the *goals* of your child's misbehavior (adapted from *Children: The Challenge*, by Rudolf Dreikurs and Vicki Soltz, 1964).
   - The child seeking *attention* will trigger feelings of irritation and annoyance in you and a desire to remind and "nag."
   - The child seeking *power* will trigger feelings of anger and of being provoked in you and a desire to fight (e.g., to become aggressive and get into a power struggle) or to give in (e.g., to become passive and avoid the issue).
   - The child seeking *revenge* will trigger intense feelings of hurt and disappointment in you and a desire to get even or retaliate.
   - The child seeking to *show inadequacy* will trigger feelings of despair, hopelessness, and powerlessness in you and a desire to agree with the child that nothing can be done.

Negative attention, from a child's perspective, is always better than no attention at all. Look for positive ways to interact with and attend to your children.

2. *Listen* to and attempt to uncover (in a nonthreatening way) and understand your children's feelings and perspectives. Teach them how to communicate with you and others through your interest in them and your questions. Be sure to physically get down on their level (i.e., sit or kneel) when you are talking about something important with them.

3. *Take time to connect,* have fun, and be with your children in their activities, in your activities, and in family activities.

4. *Look for small ways to encourage* and give your child credit for who they are and what they do (e.g., "I really liked the way you played with your sister before dinner"). There are, in fact, lots of opportunities to do this. *Minimize the importance of their mistakes* (e.g., "Oh oh, the milk spilled. Let's clean it up"). Learn to understand the difference between praise and encouragement as they are outlined here (adapted from *STEP: The Parent's Handbook,* by Don Dinkmeyer and Gary D. McKay, 1989).

   • *Praise* focuses on external circumstances, and "rewards" are offered only for meeting certain standards (e.g., "That's great that you're captain of the soccer team").

   • *Encouragement* focuses on your child's ability to handle life effectively and recognizes effort, improvement, intrinsic worth, and what your child contributes (e.g., "You must have worked really hard to become captain of the team. It seems like you feel pretty good about getting yourself there").

5. *Offer choices and alternatives* regarding behavior that you wish to have your children develop so that they build responsibility and a sense of ownership of their behavior and how it can affect their lives in positive ways (e.g., "Do you want to pick up your toys now or after dinner just before you watch TV?").

6. *Clearly communicate your love and affection* for your child, both *verbally* (e.g., "I love you, Honey") and *nonverbally* (e.g., holding hands, hugs, pats).

7. *Express anger, disappointment, hurt, and other similar feelings in a direct and respectful manner* (e.g., using "I" statements, taking responsibility for your feelings, and moderating the intensity of the emotional response). Then be sure to reconnect at a later time and be clear with the children that you still love them despite your distress over their behavior. Do not punish your children by ignoring, sulking, or refusing to talk. This only teaches them that important relationships are fragile and easily ruptured.

Explosive and abusive anger (expressed directly toward the children or simply around them) is always an extremely frightening and intimidating experience for children, no matter how they seem to react. *Use time-outs* (for yourself and your children) whenever necessary. This is also a way to teach your children about the need for them to be respectful when expressing their anger. When you do "blow it" with your children and become disrespectful, explosive, or intimidating, go back to them, admit your mistake, and apologize for what you regret saying or doing.

8. *Use logical and natural consequences.* These are consequences that follow directly from a child's misbehavior, so they make sense to the child. They also allow for the child's individual choices. *Punishment*, on the other hand, is discipline based on threats, moral judgments, and demands of obedience. An example of natural consequences would be to permit a child not to eat what is fixed for meals but then not allowing snacks between that meal and the next (the child's hunger then becomes a natural consequence) versus punishment, which would be attempting to force the child to eat everything on the plate and making the child sit there until the food is gone (i.e., the "clean plate club" syndrome).

9. *Avoid using physical punishment* (e.g., spanking, hitting, ear or hair pulling). This type of punishment only teaches short-term compliance and fear. It also creates resentment and the belief that it is all right, when the child becomes bigger and stronger, to control others through the use of physical force. Physical restraint is necessary and okay at times as long as the intention is not to intimidate or hurt the child. Be aware of the temptation to squeeze hard enough to inflict pain to get your point across or to get the child's attention. An example of reasonable restraint would be physically stopping a small child from playing with an electric outlet and moving them to another place.

Talk openly with your partner about your parenting styles and decisions and *work together as a team* in your child's best interests (even if you are separated or divorced). Do not put your child in the middle when problems or issues arise between you and your partner.

10. *Take a parenting class* (alone or with your partner) to learn more about being an effective parent. Be open to other strategies, tools, and resources (e.g., books, magazine articles, friends who are also parents) that can help you be the best parent you can be.

(HO)

Unit 11: Women's Perspective on Abuse and Violence

An important part of what abusive men often fail to comprehend is the destructive and devastating impact of their violence, abuse, and control on their partners. Examining this impact is a theme throughout the program, and the development of empathy and compassion for your partner and others is a critical element if you are truly going to change. One way for men to better understand a woman's perspective on domestic abuse is to hear about it firsthand. A woman therapist who works with battered women will come to the group and talk about the healing process for women. She will also discuss the effects of the abuse and violence on your partners and children, from a woman's point of view.

The therapist who comes to group generally talks about the women's program, highlighting similarities and differences between the men's and women's groups. She often discusses the difference between male and female abuse and violence, as this is frequently an issue that arises during the time she is present. You will be offered the opportunity to ask questions during this presentation as well, addressing topics that are of interest to you. These questions may include why your partner is so angry with you, when she will "get over this," and how women heal and recover from domestic abuse. Take some time to think about and write out some questions you may have at this point.

Part of what you need to think about prior to the woman therapist's visit is the possibility of your escalating when she is here and what you plan to do in that situation if this happens. You always have the right and responsibility in group to take a time-out if you need one, and this is another opportunity for you to practice taking a time-out should the need arise. Despite the tension that this discussion sometimes creates, group members in the past have consistently found this exposure to the women's perspective helpful and enlightening.

(HO)

425

Unit 12: The Ongoing Recovery Process

One important realization in this domestic abuse program is that becoming and remaining nonabusive takes energy and effort long after you have completed this group. Your completion of group is not seen as an end point. The necessity of continuing to take care of yourself is vital. This means staying aware of your controlling attitudes and potential for abuse and using the tools and skills you have learned and hopefully put into practice during your group experience.

Many men start this process with the unrealistic and unreachable goals of never getting angry and of being cured by the end of the program. Part of what you must understand is that you will continue to get angry and that no cure will permanently end the potential for becoming abusive and violent again. The reality is that this potential to become controlling and abusive will always be with you. The only effective way to continue to be nonabusive is to stay aware of your cues and triggers that signal the stress, irritation, frustration, and anger in your life and to intervene successfully in the escalation process and your desire to control before you make the choice to become abusive again.

There is no better way to reinforce this philosophy than to bring completers back and have them talk about their ongoing recovery process. Having men return to group to talk about their ongoing progress has been occurring as long as the program has existed. This is primarily because a number of our completers have always wanted to give back to the program as a means of enhancing their own recovery. Thus, numerous men have been willing to volunteer their time and to become involved in this way.

Approximately every six months, a team of two men come to talk to your group. One man is still involved with his original partner and one is not. This helps demonstrate that, with hard work, some possibility exists for you to build a healthy and nonabusive relationship. It also communicates the understanding that even if you do not continue in your current relationship, you can still grow and feel good about yourself and be nonabusive with a new partner. The men who will be visiting the group will talk about the abuse they have perpetrated in the past, their own experience in the domestic abuse treatment program, and what they have done to continue their progress in addressing their controlling and abusive attitudes and behaviors since they completed the group.

The hopeful aspect of this experience cannot be underestimated. At this time, you may be separated, in the process of divorce, or, at the very least, dramatically estranged from your partner and your children. These men who return to group, in telling their stories and talking about what they have done to continue their recovery process, communicate the idea that with hard work and a commitment to continue, change is possible, and your life can become more fulfilling and satisfying, with or without your current partner.

The men who return also offer clear testimony that the anger and the desire to control remain within them, long after the group is over. However, even more important is the idea that choices can be made in an ongoing way to deal more effectively with both your anger and your desire to control if you decide to do so.

In preparation for these former members' visit, think about and write out questions that you would like to ask them about their experience in the domestic abuse group and afterward.

References

Ackerman, R.J. (1988). Complexities of alcohol and abusive families. *Focus on Chemically Dependent Families, 11*(3), 15.

Adams, D. (1989). Feminist-based interventions for battering men. In R.L. Caesar and L.K. Hamberger (Eds.), *Treating men who batter: Theory, practice, and programs* (pp. 3-23). New York: Springer.

Adler, E.S. (1981). The underside of married life: Power, influence, and violence. In L.H. Bowker (Ed.), *Woman and crime in America,* (pp. 300-319). New York: Macmillan.

Alberti, R.E. and Emmons, M. (1970). *Your perfect right.* San Luis Obispo, CA: IMPACT.

American Psychiatric Association (1994). *Diagnostic and statistical manual of mental disorders,* Fourth edition. Washington, DC: American Psychiatric Association.

Bach, G. and Wyden, P. (1970). *The intimate enemy: How to fight fair in love and marriage.* New York: Avon.

Bandura, A. (1973). *Aggression: A social learning analysis.* Englewood Cliffs, NJ: Prentice Hall.

Beck, A.T. (1976). *Cognitive therapy and the emotional disorders.* New York: International Universities Press.

Beck, A.T., Ward, C.H., Mendelson, M., Mock, J., and Erbaugh, J. (1961). An inventory for measuring depression. *Archives of General Psychiatry, 4,* 55-63.

Bernstein, D. and Borkevec, T. (1973). *Progressive relaxation training.* Champaign, IL: Research Press.

Burman, S. and Allen-Meares, P. (1994). Neglected victims of murder: Children's witness to parental homicide. *Social Work, 39,* 28-34.

Buss, A.H. and Durkee, A. (1957). An inventory for assessing different kinds of hostility. *Journal of Clinical and Consulting Psychology, 21,* 343-349.

Butcher, J.N., Dahlstrom, W.G., Graham, J.R., Tellegen, A., and Kaemmer, B. (1989). *Minnesota multiphasic personality inventory (MMPI-2). Manual for administration and scoring.* Minneapolis: University of Minnesota Press.

Byles, J.A. (1978). Violence, alcohol problems, and other problems in disintegrating families. *Journal of Studies on Alcohol, 39,* 551-553.

Carlson, B.E. (1984). Children's observations of interparental violence. In A.R. Roberts (Ed.), *Battered women and their families* (pp. 147-167). New York: Springer.

Carr, E.G. (1981). Contingency management. In A. Goldstein, E. Carr, W. Davidson II, and P. Wehr (Eds.), *In response to aggression* (pp. 1-65). New York: Pergamon Press.

Cautela, J. (1967). Covert sensitization. *Psychological Reports, 20,* 459-468.

Chesney-Lind, M. (1997). *The female offender: Girls, women, and crime.* Thousand Oaks, CA: Sage.

Davis, M., Eshelman, E., and McKay, M. (1989). *The relaxation and stress reduction workbook.* Oakland, CA: New Harbinger Publications.

Dinkmeyer, D. and McKay, G. (1989). *The parents' handbook: Systematic training for effective parenting (STEP).* Circle Pines, MN: American Guidance Service.

Dobash, R.E. and Dobash, R. (1979). *Violence against wives: A case against the patriarchy.* New York: Macmillan/Free Press.

Dreikurs, R. with Soltz, V. (1964). *Children: The challenge.* New York: Hawthorn Books, Inc.

Dutton, D. (1988). *The domestic assault of women: Psychological and criminal justice perspectives.* Boston: Allyn and Bacon.

Dutton, D. with Golant, S. (1995). *The batterer: A psychological profile.* New York: Basic Books.

Edleson, J.L. (1984). Working with men who batter. *Social Work, 29,* 237-242.

Edleson, J.L. and Tolman, R.M. (1992). *Intervention for men who batter: An ecological approach.* Newbury Park, CA: Sage.

Ellis, A. (1970). *The essence of rational psychotherapy: A comprehensive approach to treatment.* New York: Institute for Rational Living.

Ellis, A. (1977). *How to live with—and without—anger.* New York: Reader's Digest Press.

Fagan, J.A., Stewart, D.K., and Hansen, K.V. (1983). Violent men or violent husbands? In D. Finkelhor, R.J. Gelles, G.T. Hotaling, and M.A. Straus (Eds.), *The dark side of families: Current family violence research* (pp. 49-67). Beverly Hills, CA: Sage.

Fantuzzo, J.W., DePaola, L.M., Lambert, L., Martino, T., Anderson, G., and Sutton, S. (1991). Effects of interparental violence on the psychological adjustment and competencies of young children. *Journal of Consulting and Clinical Psychology, 59,* 258-265.

Ganley, A. (1981). *Court mandated counseling for men who batter: A three-day workshop for mental health professionals.* Washington, D.C. Center For Women's Policy Studies.

Geffner, R. and Mantooth, C. (1995). *A psychoeducational approach for ending wife/partner abuse: A program manual for treating individuals and couples.* Tyler, TX: Family Violence and Sexual Assault Institute.

Gelles, R.J. (1980). Violence in the family: A review of research in the seventies. *Journal of Marriage and the Family, 42,* 873-885.

Gelles, R.J. (1993). Alcohol and other drugs are associated with violence: They are not the cause. In R.J. Gelles and D.R. Loseke (Eds.), *Current controversies on family violence* (pp. 182-196). Newbury Park, CA: Sage.

Goldstein, D. and Rosenbaum, A. (1985). An evaluation of the self-esteem of maritally violent men. *Family Relations, 34,* 425-428.

Gondolf, E.W. (1984). *Men who batter: An integrated approach for stopping wife abuse.* Holmes Beach, FL: Learning Publications.

Gondolf, E.W. (1985). Anger and oppression in men who batter: Empiricist and feminist perspectives and their implications for research. *Victimology: An International Journal, 10,* 311-324.

Gondolf, E. and Russell, D. (1986). The case against anger control treatment programs for batterers. *Response to the Victimization of Women and Children, 9,* 2-5.

Hamberger, L.K. (1997). Female offenders in domestic violence: A look at actions in their context. *Journal of Aggression, Maltreatment and Trauma, 1,* 117-129.

Holmes, T. and Rahe, R. (1967). The Social Readjustment Rating Scale. *Journal of Psychosomatic Research, 11,* 213–218.

Hotaling, G. and Sugarman, D. (1986). An analysis of risk markers in husband to wife violence: The current state of knowledge. *Violence and Victims, 1,* 101-124.

Hudson, W.W. (1982). *The clinical measurement package: A field manual.* Homewood, IL: The Dorsey Press.

Jacobson, E. (1938). *Progressive relaxation.* Chicago: University of Chicago Press.

Jaffe, P., Wolfe, D., and Wilson, S. (1990). *Children of battered women.* Newbury Park, CA: Sage.

Jaffe, P., Wolfe, D., Wilson, S., and Zak, L. (1986). Similarities in behavioral and social maladjustment among child victims and witnesses to family violence. *American Journal of Orthopsychiatry, 56,* 142-146.

Kaufman, G. (1980). *Shame: The power of caring.* Cambridge, MA: Schenkman Publishing Company.

Kaufman, G. with Raphael, L. (1983). *The dynamics of power: Building a competent self.* Cambridge, MA: Schenkman Publishing Company.

Kazdin, A.E. (1974). Self-monitoring and behavior change. In M.J. Mahoney and C.E. Thoresen (Eds.), *Self-control: Power to the person* (pp. 218-246). Monterey, CA: Brooks/Cole.

Kobasa, S., Maddi, S., and Kahn, S. (1982). Hardiness and health: A perspective study. *Journal of Personality and Social Psychology, 42,* 168–177.

Maiuro, R., Cahn, T., and Vitaliano, P. (1986). Assertiveness deficits and hostility in domestically violent men. *Violence and Victims, 1,* 279-290.

Maiuro, R., Cahn, T., Vitaliano, P., Wagner, B., and Zegree, J. (1988). Anger, hostility, and depression in domestically violent vs. generally assaultive men and nonviolent control subjects. *Journal of Counseling and Clinical Psychology, 56,* 17-23.

Martin, D. (1985). Domestic violence: A sociological perspective. In D.J. Sonkin, D. Martin, and L. Walker (Eds.), *The male batterer: A treatment approach* (pp. 1-32). New York: Springer.

Mathews, D.J. (1995). *Foundations for violence-free living: A step-by-step guide for facilitating men's domestic abuse groups.* St. Paul, MN: Wilder Foundation.

McKay, M., Rogers, P., and McKay, J. (1989). *When anger hurts: Quieting the storm within.* Oakland, CA: New Harbinger Publications.

Meichenbaum, D. (1977). *Cognitive-behavior modification: An integrative approach.* New York: Plenum Press.

Miller, A. (1981). *The drama of the gifted child.* New York: Basic Books.

Miller, A. (1983). *For your own good: Hidden cruelty in child-rearing and the roots of violence.* New York: Farrar, Straus and Giroux.

Neidig, P. and Friedman, D. (1984). *Spouse abuse: A treatment program for couples.* Champaign, IL: Research Press.

Novaco, R. (1975). *Anger control: The development and evaluation of an experimental treatment.* Lexington, MA: D.C. Heath.

O'Faolain, J. and Martines, L. (1973). *Not in God's image: Women in history from the Greeks to the Victorians.* New York: Harper & Row.

Pagelow, M.D. (1984). *Family violence.* New York: Praeger.

Pence, E. and Paymar, M. (1993). *Education groups for men who batter: The Duluth model.* New York: Springer.

Pokorny, A.D., Miller, B.A., and Kaplan, H.B. (1972). The brief MAST: A shortened version of the Michigan alcoholism screening test. *American Journal of Psychiatry, 129*(3), 342-345.

Purdy, F. and Nickle, N. (1981). Practice principles for working with men who batter. *Social Work with Groups, 4*, 111-122.

Raglin, J. and Morgan, W. (1985). Influence of vigorous exercise on mood state. *Behavior Therapist, 8*, 179-189.

Rahe, R. and Holmes, T. (1966). Life crisis and major health change. *Psychosomatic Medicine, 28,* 774.

Real, T. (1997). *I don't want to talk about it: Overcoming the secret legacy of male depression.* New York: Fireside.

Rose, S. (1977). *Group therapy: A behavioral approach.* Englewood Cliffs, NJ: Prentice Hall.

Rosenbaum, A. and Maiuro, R. (1989). Eclectic approaches in working with men who batter. In P. Caesar and L. Hamberger (Eds.), *Treating men who batter: Theory, practice, and programs* (pp. 165–195). New York: Springer.

Rosenbaum, A. and O'Leary, K. (1981a). Children: The unintended victims of marital violence. *American Journal of Orthopsychiatry, 51*, 692-699.

Rosenbaum, A. and O'Leary, K. (1981b). Marital violence: Characteristics of abusive couples. *Journal of Consulting and Clinical Psychology, 49*, 63-71.

Roy, M. (Ed.) (1977). A current survey of 150 cases. In *Battered women: A psychosociological study of domestic violence* (pp. 25–44). New York: Van Nostrand Reinhold.

Schacter, S. (1971). *Emotion, obesity, and crime.* New York: Academic Press.

Schacter, S. and Singer, J. (1962). Cognitive social and physiological determinants of emotional state. *Psychological Review, 69*, 379-399.

Schecter, S. (1982). *Women and male violence: Visions and struggles of the battered women's movement.* Boston: South End Press.

Selye, H. (1978). *The stress of life.* New York: McGraw-Hill.

Shipley, W.C. (1940). A self-administering scale for measuring intellectual impairment and deterioration. *Journal of Psychology, 9,* 371-377.

Sonkin, D. and Durphy, M. (1982). *Learning to live without violence: A handbook for men.* New York: Berkley Publishing Group.

Sonkin, D., Martin, D., and Walker, L. (1985). *The male batterer: A treatment approach.* New York: Springer.

Stark, E. and Flitcraft, A. (1987). Violence among intimates: An epidemiological review. In V. Van Hasselt, R. Morrison, A. Bellack, and M. Hersen (Eds.), *Handbook of family violence* (pp. 293-318). New York: Plenum Press.

Stosny, S. (1995). *Treating attachment abuse: A compassionate approach.* New York: Springer.

Straus, M. (1978). Wife beating: How common and why? *Victimology* 2(3/4), 443-458.

Straus, M. (1980). Social stress and marital violence in a national sample of American families. In F. Wright, C. Bahn, and R. Reiber (Eds.), *Forensic Psychology and Psychiatry* (pp. 229-250). New York: New York Academy of Sciences.

Straus, M. (1991). *Children as witnesses to marital violence: A risk factor for lifelong problems among a nationally representative sample of American men and women.* Paper presented at the Ross Roundtable on "Children and Violence," Washington, DC.

Straus, M., Gelles, R., and Steinmetz, S. (1980). *Behind closed doors: Violence in the American family.* New York: Anchor Press/Doubleday.

Tolman, R. and Bennett, L.W. (1990). A review of research on men who batter. *Journal of Interpersonal Violence, 5,* 87-118.

Walker, L. (1979). *The battered woman.* New York: Harper & Row.

Westra, B. and Martin, H.P. (1981). Children of battered women. *Maternal Child Nursing Journal, 10,* 41-54.

Williams, R. and Williams, V. (1993). *Anger kills: Seventeen strategies for controlling the hostility that can harm your health.* New York: HarperCollins.

Wolpe, J. (1973). *The practice of behavior therapy.* New York: Pergamon.

Yalom, I. (1975). *The theory and practice of group psychotherapy.* New York: Basic Books.

Index

Payment, 73, 147
Peer culture, 101, 102
Pence, E., 9
Perfectionism, 331, 332, 358
Personal comments, 398, 399
Personalizing, 305
Perspective, 276
Pets, 61-62, 230, 255, 364-365
Phone calls, 102, 362
Physical abuse
  as aggression, 373
  definition, 63, 231, 366
  excuses, 252-253
  first act, 225-226
  of self, 366
  and shame, 326
  while in therapy, 137
Pittman, Frank, 188
Pitzer, Ronald, 220
Play, 414, 418, 422
Playing dumb, 403
Pokorny, A. D., 46
Police protection, 240
Positive attitude, 282, 283
Possessiveness, 58, 226, 361
Power, 7, 31-32. *See also*
  Empowerment
Powerlessness
  and anger, 286
  avoiding, 352, 382
  in difficult situations, 202-203,
    315
  in escalation phase, 232
  and family of origin, 126-127
Preaching, 287
Precautions, for therapist safety, 35
Predictions, 306, 399
Probation officers, 46-47
Procreation, 414
Program philosophy
  causes of male violence, 7
  couples and family therapy, 6, 7
  discussing with perpetrator, 40

Program philosophy *(continued)*
  gender factor, 4, 57
  of group leader, 28
  group versus individual therapy, 5, 7
  self-control, 4, 32
  therapy objective, 129, 145-146
  treatment tasks
    for female victim, 6-7
    for male perpetrator, 4-5, 8-11
Projection, 348
Property
  defending with violence, 255-256
  destruction, 61-62, 137, 230, 255,
    363, 364-365
  hiding partner's, 230
  partner as, 226, 361
Proximity, excessive, 361, 363
Psychological abuse, 61, 212,
  229-230, 364
Pulling rank, 401
Purdy, F., 201
Put-downs, 59

Questionnaires
  for female victims, 86-93
  for male perpetrators, 9-10,
    48, 79-85
  rationale, 47-48
Questions, 228, 362
  open-ended, 393

Rage, 336
Raglin, J., 46
Rahe, R., 263
Rank, pulling, 401
Reading material, 187-188, 208-209,
  220
Real, Terrence, 10, 11, 188
Reckless driving, 60
Recreation, 266, 273, 415
Reflecting back, 392-393
Rehearsals, 202-203, 311-312, 315
Rejection, 333

THE HAWORTH MALTREATMENT AND TRAUMA PRESS
Robert A. Geffner, PhD
Senior Editor

STOPPING THE VIOLENCE: A GROUP MODEL TO CHANGE MEN'S ABU-SIVE ATTITUDES AND BEHAVIORS by David J. Decker. *"A concise and thorough manual to assist clinicians in learning the causes and dynamics of domestic violence." Joanne Kittel, MSW, LICSW, Yachats, Oregon*

STOPPING THE VIOLENCE: A GROUP MODEL TO CHANGE MEN'S ABU-SIVE ATTITUDES AND BEHAVIORS, THE CLIENT WORKBOOK by David J. Decker.

BREAKING THE SILENCE: GROUP THERAPY FOR CHILDHOOD SEXUAL ABUSE, A PRACTIONER'S MANUAL by Judith A. Margolin. "This book is an extremely valuable and well-written resource for all therapists working with adult survivors of child sexual abuse." *Esther Deblinger, PhD, Associate Professor of Clinical Psychiatry, University of Medicine and Dentistry of New Jersey School of Osteopathic Medicine*

"I NEVER TOLD ANYONE THIS BEFORE": MANAGING THE INITIAL DIS-CLOSURE OF SEXUAL ABUSE RE-COLLECTIONS by Janice A. Gasker. "Discusses the elements needed to create a safe, therapeutic environment and offers the practitioner a number of useful strategies for responding appropriately to client disclosure." *Roberta G. Sands, PhD, Associate Professor, University of Pennsylvania School of Social Work*

FROM SURVIVING TO THRIVING: A THERAPIST'S GUIDE TO STAGE II RECOVERY FOR SURVIVORS OF CHILDHOOD ABUSE by Mary Bratton. "A must read for all, including survivors. Bratton takes a life-long debilitating disorder and unravels its intricacies in concise, succinct, and understandable language." *Phillip A. Whitner, PhD, Sr. Staff Counselor, University Counseling Center, The University of Toledo, Ohio*

SIBLING ABUSE TRAUMA: ASSESSMENT AND INTERVENTION STRAT-EGIES FOR CHILDREN, FAMILIES, AND ADULTS by John V. Caffaro and Allison Conn-Caffaro. "One area that has almost consistently been ignored in the research and writing on child maltreatment is the area of sibling abuse. This book is a welcome and required addition to the developing literature on abuse." *Judith L. Alpert, PhD, Professor of Applied Psychology, New York University*

BEARING WITNESS: VIOLENCE AND COLLECTIVE RESPONSIBILITY by Sandra L. Bloom and Michael Reichert. "A totally convincing argument. . . . Demands careful study by all elected representatives, the clergy, the mental health and medical professions, representatives of the media, and all those unwittingly involved in this repressive perpetuation and catastrophic global problem." *Harold I. Eist, MD, Past President, American Psychiatric Association*

TREATING CHILDREN WITH SEXUALLY ABUSIVE BEHAVIOR PROBLEMS: GUIDELINES FOR CHILD AND PARENT INTERVENTION by Jan Ellen Burton, Lucinda A. Rasmussen, Julie Bradshaw, Barbara J. Christopherson, and Steven C. Huke. "An extremely readable book that is well-documented and a mine of valuable 'hands on' information. . . . This is a book that all those who work with sexually abusive children or want to work with them must read." *Sharon K. Araji, PhD, Professor of Sociology, University of Alaska, Anchorage*

THE LEARNING ABOUT MYSELF (LAMS) PROGRAM FOR AT-RISK PARENTS: LEARNING FROM THE PAST—CHANGING THE FUTURE by Verna Rickard. "This program should be a part of the resource materials of every mental health professional trusted with the responsibility of working with 'at-risk' parents." *Terry King, PhD, Clinical Psychologist, Federal Bureau of Prisons, Catlettsburg, Kentucky*

THE LEARNING ABOUT MYSELF (LAMS) PROGRAM FOR AT-RISK PARENTS: HANDBOOK FOR GROUP PARTICIPANTS by Verna Rickard. "Not only is the LAMS program designed to be educational and build skills for future use, it is also fun!" *Martha Morrison Dore, PhD, Associate Professor of Social Work, Columbia University, New York, New York*

BRIDGING WORLDS: UNDERSTANDING AND FACILITATING ADOLESCENT RECOVERY FROM THE TRAUMA OF ABUSE by Joycee Kennedy and Carol McCarthy. "An extraordinary survey of the history of child neglect and abuse in America. . . . A wonderful teaching tool at the university level, but should be required reading in high schools as well." *Florabel Kinsler, PhD, BCD, LCSW, Licensed Clinical Social Worker, Los Angeles, California*

CEDAR HOUSE: A MODEL CHILD ABUSE TREATMENT PROGRAM by Bobbi Kendig with Clara Lowry. "Kendig and Lowry truly . . . realize the saying that we are our brothers' keepers. Their spirit permeates this volume, and that spirit of caring is what always makes the difference for people in painful situations." *Hershel K. Swinger, PhD, Clinical Director, Children's Institute International, Los Angeles, California*

SEXUAL, PHYSICAL, AND EMOTIONAL ABUSE IN OUT-OF-HOME CARE: PREVENTION SKILLS FOR AT-RISK CHILDREN by Toni Cavanagh Johnson and Associates. "Professionals who make dispositional decisions or who are related to out-of-home care for children could benefit from reading and following the curriculum of this book with children in placements." *Issues in Child Abuse Accusations*